Tim Tyler

MEMETICS

Memes and the Science of Cultural Evolution

MOAR

I CAN HAS CHEEZBURGER?

Shut your baby up BEFORE I DO!

THIS IS SPARTA

POPE

BELIEVE

O RLY?

http://memetics.timtyler.org/

Cataloging data

Tyler, Tim.

Memetics.

ISBN 10: 1461035260.

ISBN 13: 978-1461035268.

1. Social evolution. 2. Human evolution. 3. Anthropology.

Publisher

Published by *Mersenne Publishing*: http://publishing.4095.com/

Edition

This is the first edition. Version 1.00. First published in 2011.

Table of contents

This book is dedicated to....

...my darling fiancée, Maja.

1 Introduction - A brief guide to this book

We will start with a brief introduction to the main themes of this book.

1.1 Apes with infected brains

This is a book about a curious and counter-intuitive idea. The idea is that humans are apes with infected brains. That we harbour living things inside our skulls which are even less closely related to us than the bacteria that thrive in our guts are.

These entities are not bacteria, or other microorganisms. They are a *new form of life*, not closely related to the DNA-based life forms that have dominated the planet for billions of years.

It is the presence of these entities that distinguishes modern humans from primitive cave-dwellers. They are what is responsible for out music, literature, science and technology.

It seems likely that these entities have been with us for millions of years - and are a major factor in contributing to making us human in the first place. This means that most accounts of human evolution that fail to take account of these entities are deeply misguided.

Describing humans as "apes with infected brains" is *not* meant to imply that the infectious agents are *necessarily* deleterious - just that they don't necessarily *always* have our best interests at heart. Many visitors are mutualists - useful symbionts. However, others are toxic and harmful - and humans are often in need of strategies for getting their brains disinfected.

Humans have grown dependent on these symbiotic visitors. As with our gut bacteria, most of us are now so dependent on them that we could barely survive without them.

1.2 Brain-zit analogy

At this point an analogy and some diagrams should help to illuminate the situation. Acne is a disease caused partly by bacteria - which infect the sweat glands in human skin. The bacteria help to create a plug which blocks the pore of the gland. They reproduce in the resulting trapped pool of juices, and then explode forth into the world - where *some* of them find their way into other sweat glands - thus completing their reproductive cycle.

The brains of adult humans are typically infected with similar entities. These are contagious *ideas*. The idea spend most of their reproductive cycle in human brains, and then spurt forth - often from the human mouth. Then they find their way through the air, and *sometimes* successfully find their way into another human brain - thus completing *their* reproductive cycle.

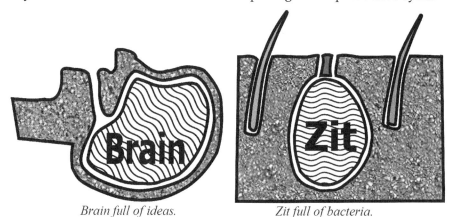

Brain full of ideas.   *Zit full of bacteria.*

In this analogy, certain types of contagious ideas are considered to be similar to the bacteria that cause acne. Like the bacteria, those ideas reproduce themselves using energy derived from their human hosts, and spread from one human to another in a manner *closely* resembling a contagious disease.

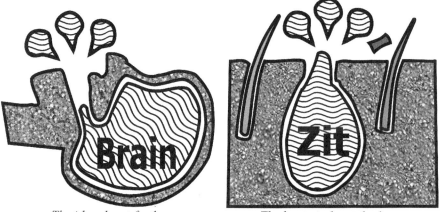

The ideas burst forth.   *The bacteria burst forth.*

Not *all* ideas spread contagiously from one person to the next. Some ideas form inside human minds but never attempt to spread themselves to other humans. However, other ideas have mastered the trick of spreading "horizontally", form one human to the next - and these more powerful ideas are very common.

Also, transmission doesn't *always* occur through the human mouth. Sometimes, the ideas are transmitted using gestures. Sometimes, they are typed into computers. Sometimes, the idea is in the form of a picture - or a movie. The important thing is that they have found a way from one human mind to the next.

1.3 Parasites and mutualists

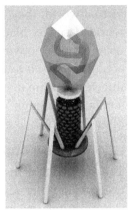

Virus.

On average, these contagious ideas *appear* to be beneficial. In that respect, they are different from typical diseases, which are *normally* harmful to their hosts. Many ideas act more like *gut bacteria* - which are *also* beneficial, on average. There are other cases in nature of beneficial symbiotic relationships with microorganisms. For example, many common plants make use of nitrogen-fixing bacteria living in their root systems - to help them harvest nutrients from the atmosphere. Some plants actively cultivate ants which help the plants to protect themselves against predators. For example, the *Swollen-Thorn Acacias* of Central America have developed special bulbous chambers to act as homes for aggressive species of ants - which then protect the their tree house from predators and parasites.

However, not *all* culturally-transmitted ideas are beneficial to their hosts. Cults, religions, scams, fads and lies are often more like real diseases than they are like a mutually-beneficial symbiosis. *Sometimes*, the host is even sterilised. Sterilisation can actually *benefit* the infectious ideas - since liberating the host's reproductive resources can free up time and energy - which can then be used to propagate the ideas to new hosts.

This picture - of humans as apes with infected brains - is one which relatively few people are familiar with, and which even fewer have fully worked through the implications of.

Many find this kind of perspective to be counter-intuitive. If you open up the skull of a human, no parasites spill out. If you look at it under a microscope, no rapidly-dividing foreign-cells are seen. Some question exactly where these *hypothetical* invaders are - and *indeed* whether they even exist. The short answer is that the parasites live in a virtual world.

1.4 Computer viruses

Fortunately there is *another* type of system which behaves in a similar way. Our personal computers are also frequently infected with parasites. Many computers are susceptible to various strains of computer virus - and yet, if you open up a computer, no viruses come spilling out. As with the parasites that the human mind harbours, this is because they live in a virtual world.

Although computer viruses live in a virtual world, they can *still* cause real-world damage, blackmailing the user, using their network connection by acting as a *spam relay* - and so on. The infected human brain behaves similarly. Though its infections are often unseen, their effects are not.

Computer viruses are also invisible.

1.5 The new organisms

The picture that results from this is dramatic - and for many people it is unfamiliar. After several billion years of evolution a range of new types of self-reproducing creature have arrived on the scene. They have genes that are not made of nucleic acids. In next to no time, they have spread to all areas of the globe. Their effects can be seen everywhere. Suddenly, intelligent design, engineering, simulation, extrapolation, interpolation - and many other novel tools are being used to create the next generation of organisms. This is *a new kind of evolution*, faster than the older kind of evolution by random mutations that preceded it.

This is really the first time in the last three billion years that new, non-nucleic-acid-based self-reproducing entities have succeeded in getting a major foothold in the biosphere. There is currently an explosion of these new creatures. Their rise seems rapid and dramatic, and it shows little sign of levelling off.

1.6 Future prospects

The extraordinary and rapid rise to power of these new self-reproducing creatures raises important questions about what will happen in the future. One possibility is that their meteoric rise *eventually* slow down - and reach some kind of harmonious equilibrium with the older nucleic-acid-based systems that were responsible for their creation. Another is that the new creatures will stage a take over - as they find a way to build bodies and minds for themselves and then proceed unshackle themselves from their more primitive organic precursors.

1.7 Understanding needed

We urgently need to develop a basic scientific understanding of what is happening in this area. Understanding the evolution of culture will throw light on human evolution, so we can better understand human nature. It will allow us to better deal with the modern world and the challenges that we now face - and it will also help us to prepare for the future. This book lays down some of the foundations needed to deal with these issues.

2 Basics - Cultural evolution in a nutshell

In this chapter we will look at the basic idea of cultural evolution.

2.1 The basic idea

The idea that human culture evolves is an old one. In *The Origin of Species*, Charles Darwin (1859) explained his idea of descent with modification in the animal and plant kingdoms by using an analogy with the way languages change and evolve over time. Languages show a branching tree-like structure - with some languages being obvious descendants of other ones. This is very similar to the phylogenetic trees of organic evolution. In the absence of detailed information about how inheritance took place, Darwin typically mixed the concepts of cultural and organic evolution together. In 1871, he wrote:

Charles Darwin.

> *The survival or preservation of certain favoured words in the struggle for existence is natural selection.*

Looking back from our current vantage point, Darwin appears to be well ahead of his time in terms of his understanding of cultural evolution.

There are similarities and differences between cultural and organic evolution. Unfortunately, these days the similarities have become rarely-mentioned - and cultural evolution has become an extremely neglected idea. For example, it is often not mentioned in evolution textbooks at all.

However, it is *fairly* self-evident that some traits of organisms persist down the generations without being coded for in DNA. Speaking a particular language is passed from one generation to the next - but the words of the language are not stored in genes. Surnames are passed down the paternal line. Religion is passed from parent to offspring. Circumcision, body-piercings, hair styles and beards are also passed faithfully down the generations in some cultures. These things are all culturally inherited. Variation of such traits is also common - as are differences in their copying rates and the rate at which they are lost.

2.2 The case for cultural evolution

The *basic* case for cultural evolution is relatively simple - cultural change *is* evolution - according to most modern definitions of the term "evolution". Here is the definition of Strickberger (1996) - in his textbook on evolution:

> *Biological evolution entails inherited changes in populations of organisms, over a period of time, that lead to differences among them.*

Notice that it does *not* say that inheritance must take place via DNA. If circumcised fathers are more likely to circumcise their sons, that is evidently a form of inheritance - but it is not mediated by DNA. The trait is passed on *in some other way*. Strickberger (1996) goes on to put the case for cultural inheritance concisely:

> *In short, humans have two unique hereditary systems. One is the genetic system that transfers biological information from biological parent to offspring in the form of genes and chromosomes. The other is the extragenetic system that transfers cultural information from speaker to listener, from writer to reader, from performer to spectator, and forms our cultural heritage.*

That brings us onto the topic of the two primary inheritance channels of our species:

2.3 Dual inheritance theory

The idea that humans have two main inheritance systems is commonly known as *Dual Inheritance Theory* (DIT). The idea is that humans transmit information down the generations primarily via nucleic acids and human culture - and that other forms of inheritance are *relatively* insignificant. The significant role of cultural transmission implied by *Dual Inheritance Theory* is not yet widely appreciated. However, cultural inheritance is of substantial importance to understanding the evolution of humans, the dynamics of the modern world, and what is likely to happen in the future.

2.4 Shared underlying principles

There have been a number of efforts to identify common principles of cultural and organic evolution. They both exhibit:

- **Heritable information** - which persists for extended periods, allowing transmission down the generations;
- **Imperfect copying** - resulting in variation between the copies;
- **Differential reproductive success** - some copies persist better than others.

These properties (inheritance, variation and selection) are the basic ones required for many definitions of evolution - and therefore cultural evolution is a type of evolution. Cultural evolution also exhibits *cumulative adaptations* - and so it produces *true* constructive evolution - not merely *trivial* or *degenerative* evolution.

Stone wheel.

Wagon wheel.

Car wheel.

The evolution of the wheel - as shown above - illustrates inheritance, variation and cumulative adaptation (seen most clearly in the car wheel).

2.5 Cosmetic differences

However, there are *also* some differences between cultural and organic evolution. Some of the prominent examples:

- **Directed mutations** - in organic evolution, mutations are usually considered to be undirected - and so do not systematically lead towards improvements. However, in cultural evolution mutations are *sometimes* highly directed. They can be made using induction, deduction, and Occam's razor - the full toolbox of intelligent design.
- **Lamarckian inheritance** - among organic organisms, it is rare for modifications of the phenotype to be inherited and transmitted to the next generation. However, in cultural evolution, though *most* inheritance is still pretty *Darwinian*, such things are *fairly* common. For example, if someone sprinkles cinnamon on the muffins - and the guests seem to like it - the next time, the cinnamon might be incorporated into the recipe. The cinnamon gets baked in and *possibly* passed on.

The scale of the differences between organic and cultural evolution causes *some* people to react negatively to comparisons between them. However, the common principles they share are important and deep - and much of value is lost if this common ground is neglected.

2.6 Family trees

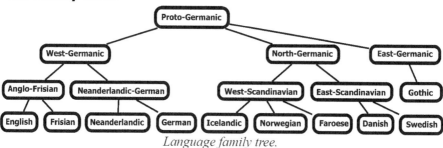

Language family tree.

In organic evolution, lineages can be represented using family trees. The same is possible in cultural evolution. This diagram illustrates the "tree model" of languages, using it to represent the relationships between the Germanic languages. The effects of *horizontal word transfer* between languages complicate these kinds of relationships, but it is *still* possible to construct glossogenetic trees for the world's languages that resemble the phylogenetic trees that can be constructed for organisms. If attention is confined to individual words, then their ancestry and relationships can be traced even more unambiguously.

These relationships between languages were known back in the 1850s - before Darwin wrote *The Origin*. Darwin actually used the descent with modification of languages to explain his theory of organic evolution. Back then, cultural evolution was more widely recognised as being correct than organic evolution.

2.7 Symbiosis

The most powerful, obvious and straightforwards way of modelling culture is as *symbiotic cultural organisms*.

Wrist watch.

Many will be familiar with the idea that wrist watches and wireless headsets can usefully be thought of as signs of the human symbiosis with technology. That is one manifestation of the symbiosis between humans and culture. There is an *existing* framework in biology for modelling symbiosis, and it works well when applied to human culture. Symbiotic relationships are usually classified as follows:

- **Mutualism** - Mutually beneficial relationships;
- **Parasitism** - One-sided relationships;
- **Commensalism** - Neither beneficial nor harmful.

This suggests that some cultural entities may be good ⌐
others could be deleterious. Indeed we see both types of cu.
advertisements are *generally* bad for you, while a knowledge of la.
usually highly beneficial.

2.8 Epidemiology

Cultural phenomena exhibit "horizontal" transmission
between individuals. Ideas spread rather like diseases
do, resulting in *cultural plagues*. Models drawn from
epidemiology treat culture as a symbiotic
phenomenon. Such models are useful when explaining
how news, fads, crazes and fashions spread through
society. Sometimes the cultural infections reach
epidemic proportions. Cultural entities have a certain
level of contagiousness, and if this is below hat is
known as the *epidemic threshold*. This threshold acts as
a kind of *tipping point*. If you are below it, not very

Virus.

much happens - but above it, there is an *explosion* of activity, somewhat like
a fission reaction, resulting in a *cultural epidemic*. Sometimes these
epidemics go global – becoming worldwide *pandemics*.

2.9 Resource limitation

Resource limitation is one of
the key concepts in
evolutionary biology. The idea
went mainstream with
Thomas Malthus and his 1798
work: "An Essay on the
Principle of Population".

Noticeboard illustrates resource limitation.
Messages compete for limited resources, brains.

Malthus's essay went on to
inspire both Darwin and
Wallace to create their theories of evolution. The basic idea is that
populations of organisms have the ability - and inclination - to increase in
size exponentially. So they tend to expand rapidly - up to the limits
permitted by the available food supply. However, resources are typically
much more limited. After a while expanding populations tend to reach a
point where further growth is no longer supported by the available

ces. At that stage, births must be balanced by deaths.

...win (1859) gave *Chapter Three* of "On The Origin of Species" the title ...he Struggle for Existence". The chapter worked through the ...consequences of Malthus's insight. The idea is also highly significant in the realm of human culture. Cultural entities face a struggle for existence too. For them, the primary limited resource is human brains. Most reproduction of cultural entities currently either takes place in human brains - or is triggered by the action of human brains. Those brains have limited storage space for cultural items. So there is competition between the ideas to find their way into human brains.

2.10 Adaptive culture

We can be pretty sure that culture was adaptive among our ancestors since we have adaptations oriented towards spreading culture - our incessant babbling, our ultrasociality and the *huge* libraries of cultural information which we all carry around everywhere on our shoulders. It seems likely that culture is also adaptive today - since culture-free humans are like primitive cave men, and most such creatures would not do very well in the modern world.

To summarise, culture allows individuals to:

· **Reduce costly errors** associated with *trial-and-error* learning;
· **Quickly acquire useful ideas** much more rapidly than *trial-and-error* learning would permit;
· **Acquire better quality ideas** than they would have been likely to produce themselves.

Culture is adaptive because it allows individuals to obtain good- quality ideas quickly, and at low cost. Why transmit these ideas *culturally*, rather than wiring them into the genome, then? The genome is *much* too small to accommodate all the required cultural knowledge. Even if evolution could somehow find a way to wire language, walking, or fire-starting instincts into the genome, the results would not be *much* better than transmitting the knowledge by cultural means. So,

Mastery of fire is culturally transmitted.

this is a challenging task for evolution with a pretty minimal pay-off.

2.11 Internet culture

As time has passed, human culture has expanded and diversified. This has resulted in many more examples of cultural evolution for scientists to study. Where once chain letters, urban legends, languages and scientific theories were used to provide the evidence supporting the idea of cultural evolution, now there is a plethora of new types of digital media on the internet - audio, video, text - all widely available to anyone who cares to look. There is also a *lot* more in the way of tracking and monitoring tools available. If you want to know when a particular computer virus mutated, such details are often archived and can be tracked down. If you want to know whether *The Beatles* were ever more popular than *Jesus*, that too can be investigated.

2.12 Going digital

One issue that seems to hinder understanding of the idea of cultural evolution is low-fidelity transmission. Organic inheritance *mostly* uses digital high-fidelity transmission - but sometimes cultural information is low-fidelity, or is represented in partly-analog systems. When present, high mutation rates can destroy the accumulation of culture, limit the quantity of culture that can exist, and result in fewer cultural adaptations.

Digital media.

Some people have complained that this weakens the analogy between organic inheritance and cultural inheritance.

However, in modern times, we have seen a gradual switch to digital forms of cultural transmission and storage.

This *digital revolution* has resulted in a greater volume of culture, a closer correspondence between cultural and organic inheritance, and *much* more evidence of cultural evolution. The objection that cultural evolution suffers from low-fidelity transmission was a pretty feeble one in the first place. However, it is becoming increasingly irrelevant - as culture is digitised and gains access to high-fidelity storage and transmission media.

2.13 Rise of the idea

The idea that culture evolves dates back to Darwin's era. As time has passed, academic and popular scientific publications supporting cultural evolution have gradually accumulated. Some of the better-known supporters of the idea include Richard Dawkins, Daniel Dennett, Douglas Hofstadter, Susan Blackmore, David Hull, Robert Boyd, Peter Richerson, David Deutsch and Edward Wilson. These days there is a big mountain of evidence supporting the idea. That culture evolves is a *fact*, much as the idea that the organic world evolves is a *fact*. If anything, we have *better* evidence for cultural evolution - since it happens so much more rapidly and so we can see it talking place all the more clearly.

2.14 Significance

Cultural evolution is the single most important idea if you are trying to understand cultural change. In the organic world, evolution forms the central organising principle - the basic concept which practically everything else is explained in terms of. Cultural evolution has a *similar* significance for explaining human culture.

Most of the change in human civilisation is cultural. Organic evolution happens on a *much* slower time scale, and often happens too slowly for us to observe - so cultural evolution explains *most* of the significant recent human changes.

Cultural evolution is *ancient*, going back beyond our split from chimpanzees. It affected the *whole* of the last 7 million years of evolution, with increasing intensity as time passed. It is *not possible* to understand human evolution *without* having an understanding of cultural evolution. Many have attempted to understand human evolution *without* a proper understanding of cultural evolution - but their efforts are uniformly hopeless.

Cultural evolution is the *key* science for understanding change in human civilisation at the present time. Similarly, it is key to understanding where humanity is going in the future. We badly needs to understand the details of how culture changes so that we can act as its steward and steer it in desirable directions. Undesirable culture can result in stagnation, wars, revolutions and genocide.

2.15 Neglect

Though the idea of cultural evolution has been around for a *very* long while, its penetration into the scientific world is poor. Though the basic ideas seem fairly simple and obvious, a series of problems and setbacks have hampered its development. The problems have included mistakes by the founders, resistance from established academics in adjacent fields, and distaste for the whole idea of a Darwinian explanation of human culture. The result is that the field has suffered from slow development, a bad reputation, poor funding and status. Tragically, the idea of cultural evolution has been *widely* neglected.

The neglect of cultural evolution by social scientists has been a pretty major disaster for the scientific enterprise. Evolutionary theory is central to biology, and cultural evolution is central to understanding human culture. *Without* cultural evolution the study of culture remains stuck a pre-Darwinian era – over a century behind the times - in much the same way that the study of organic systems lacked a central organising principle in the days before Darwin. Cultural evolution has the *potential* to unite the social sciences. However, social science has never really got to grips with Darwin. For over a hundred years, most social scientists have refused to face the Darwinian music - preferring instead to put their fingers in their ears and sing their own "la-la" song. This has kept the social sciences firmly stuck in a pre-Darwinian era. As a result the social sciences are highly balkanised - with experts in adjacent fields lacking common principles and a unifying theory. This situation is intolerable. It has *got* to stop.

2.16 Modern ascendance

Though cultural evolution has been neglected, it seems to be fairly clearly in the ascendant in the last couple of decades. The last decade in particular has been an extremely fertile one for the study of cultural evolution, with *hundreds* of publications on the topic, and a *lot* of empirical research being performed. That human culture evolves has always been pretty self-evident, but there has also been a *lot* of work on non-human animals in the last decade. We now know a *lot* more about the topic of cultural evolution now than we have ever done before.

2.17 The role of this book

This book has the modest goal of rectifying the neglect of cultural evolution. The field has struggled for acceptance for over 150 years - but I figure that, now we have the internet, the time is ripe. While the field is a vast and complex one, the *basics* of it are simple enough that it can be explained in a single book. Much of the confusion in the area can be *relatively* easily identified, highlighted and disposed of.

3 Evidence - Support for cultural evolution

What evidence is there that culture has evolved? The evidence that culture evolves broadly parallels the evidence that organic creatures evolved. It is more obvious that culture evolves - since we can more easily see it evolving in real time. As a result of this, cultural evolution (particularly of languages) was discovered before organic evolution. Inheritance, variation and differential reproductive success are all required for adaptive evolution - and there is good evidence that culture exhibits these traits. Culture also exhibits many other characteristic signs of being an evolutionary process. This chapter will review the evidence associated with this idea.

3.1 Evidence of inheritance

Inheritance is ubiquitous in cultural systems. Information is passed from one person to the next - and so finds its way down the generations. To give a few examples:

- **Languages** - Modern languages clearly inherit features from earlier ones. The relationship between languages is sufficiently strong that linguists have constructed family trees - that show the relationships between modern languages with estimates of historical branching points. The first such analysis on record was performed by August Schleicher. He was the first to compare languages to evolving species. He also published an illustration of Indo-European languages as a family tree in 1853 - several years before Darwin's "Origin of Species" was published. Since then the evidence of common descent has become much stronger. Most of world's languages evolved from a common ancestor. The evidence of relatedness underlying the construction of phylogenetic trees is often considered to be one of the best pieces of evidence for organic evolution. In cultural evolution, the situation is similar - the relatedness evidence required for the reconstruction of cultural family trees represents compelling evidence for cultural evolution.
- **Scientific theories** - These provide another clear example of inheritance in cultural evolution. The theories of Newton, Darwin and Einstein have been transmitted down the generations, via a process of iterative copying and repetition.

3.2 Evidence of variation

Variation is a pretty trivial property. If there is copying it is practically bound to be imperfect, with copying errors. So, very briefly:

- **Languages** - These clearly vary. There are around 7,000 languages currently spoken in the world. New words are added continuously - including technical words, jargon, and slang. Other words are fall out of use and are gradually forgotten - or relegated to the history books. Spellings can change - as happened with American English.
- **Scientific theories** - These also clearly vary. If new data does not conform to a scientific theory, one option is patching that theory to handle the exception. Observations of light and the influence of gravitational fields led to revisions of Newton's laws of mechanics. Superconductivity changed theories of electromagnetism. In each case the new theory competed with its predecessors.

In neither case are mutations "random". However: *nowhere in the definition of evolution does it say that mutations must be performed at random.*

3.3 Evidence of differential reproductive success

A lot of culture dies out and goes extinct. However, some cultural elements are extinguished faster than others.

- **Languages** - We can see that there are various languages that have no living native speakers - including Latin and Sanscrit. There are also so-called "extinct languages" which are those which have no native speakers and no spoken descendant. Some languages do better than other ones for various reasons. Sometimes success is accidental - but other times, languages compete with each other for people's attention, and then, sometimes, the best language wins. Ease of learning, spelling, reading, computer entry, existing geographical distribution - all can be factors.
- **Scientific theories** - Old and out-dated science sometimes goes extinct too - though the custodians of the history of science try to keep it alive. First, theories are discredited, refuted and replaced. Then they go into the history books - however, they are still preserved and copied there. Some refuted science is kept around because it marks out sterile regions that have already been explored - or as a reminder of how not to do things. Other refuted science is kept around out of historical interest. However *some* is eventually destined to be forgotten. Probably one of the most dramatic losses of scientific knowledge in recorded history took place when the library of Alexandra burned down.

3.4 Evidence from geographic distribution

Culture is transmitted from person to person. Historically, transmission has been hindered by geographic barriers - resulting in isolated islands developing distinctive cultures. Japan makes a nice example of this.

Darwin used the flora and fauna of isolated island ranges, to illustrate his theory. Cavalli-Sforza and Wang (1986) have similarly studied language differences in the islands of Micronesia. It was found that the chance of languages sharing words varied according to a negative exponential of the distance between those islands. This strongly suggests that these cultural traits migrated between the islands involved; and that the

Islands are natural experiments in evolution.

languages gradually evolved over time. Evolutionary theory also predicts reduced diversity on islands. This too is a phenomenon which has been observed in the cultural realm - for example, see the study of Tasmania by Diamond (1978). Islands also illustrate the founder effect (Baker and Jenkins 1987) - and small islands have limited population sizes which help to illustrate the effects of cultural drift (Laiolo 2007). Just as long-isolated island fauna suffer when they are exposed to creatures from the mainland, so isolated island cultures often suffer when exposed to culture from the mainland. As a result, many islands have both ecological *and* cultural conservation programs.

3.5 Evidence of adaptations

Adaptations are not really part of the definition of evolution. *Devolution* (i.e. the systematic loss of complex adaptations) still counts as evolution - according to most definitions of the term. However, without adaptation, many of the characteristic dynamics of evolution are lost - and an evolutionary perspective on culture would lose much of its interest.

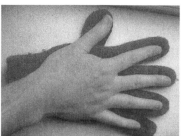 

Fit between organic and cultural.   Fit between cultural and cultural.

However, cultural evolution exhibits cumulative adaptation ubiquitously. The term "*goodness of fit*" refers to the match between an organism and its environment - and *goodness of fit* is seen in many cultural phenomena. As the previous diagram illustrates, cultural entities exhibit adaptive fit both with organic entities (hand and glove) and with other cultural entities (gear and chain drive mechanism). In a similar manner to the way in which a glove "fits" onto a hand, scientific theories accurately describe the world. Recipes result in tasty meals. Computer programs behave as advertised. Languages are effective at communicating with - and so on.

3.6 Evidence from the historical record

Organic evolution is supported by evidence from the fossil record. Cultural evolution is supported by evidence from the historical record. We *know* that cultural change has happened - because we have concrete records of it doing just that. Bibles, nursery rhymes, hymns, dictionaries, laws and science have all *clearly* evolved over time. Their evolution is documented in the history books, and supported by abundant evidence.

3.7 Evidence from controlled experiments

In the organic realm, scientists can observe evolution in the laboratory, if they are sufficiently patient. There is now a relatively young tradition of doing similar experiments in cultural evolution. For example, Kirby, Cornish, and Smith (2008) have looked at cumulative cultural evolution of language in the lab. Alex Mesoudi (2007d) started to investigate experimental techniques for studying cultural evolution. Mesoudi looked at transmission by using set-ups resembling *Chinese Whispers*. He looked at the persistence of culture in the face of gradual replacement of group members and explored techniques for investigating how people decide which other people to copy when learning new skills. Mesoudi then went on to perform many more such experiments, on both human subjects (Mesoudi and Whiten 2008a) and animals (Mesoudi and Whiten 2008b). Whiten's 2005 experiments have demonstrated chimpanzee cultural traditions under controlled conditions that allow hypotheses involving other genetic and environmental influences to be ruled out.

Christine Caldwell is another of the researchers involved. Her "spaghetti towers" project rewarded people for building towers out of spaghetti and plasticine. It investigated the extent to which seeing photographs of towers built by previous participants allowed people to produce better designs.

3.8 Evidence from natural experiments

In the organic world, it is possible to observe evolution taking place in real time. A well-known example is industrial melanism. This is an adaptive form of melanism caused by industrial pollution, and it has been reported in peppered moths. In cultural evolution, real-time changes are much more obvious. Most adults will be able to recall how human culture has changed over their own lifespans. Technological progress results in cultural changes that are rapid enough to be noticeable from one year to the next.

3.9 Evidence from progress

Evolution is a gigantic optimisation process. As such, in sufficiently benign environments, it is characterised by progress towards creatures that are increasingly fit. The progressive nature of evolution is obvious from a cursory examination of the history of life. Later forms systematically build on features they inherited from earlier ones - creating *castles of adaptations*. This is part of the evidence for evolution.

Cultural evolution is similarly progressive. Progress is perhaps *most* evident in the realms of science and technology - but *clear* signs of progress can be seen in most areas of human culture.

3.10 Evidence from imperfections

Some of the evidence cited by Darwin consisted of evidence for imperfection. In part this evidence was needed because one alternative hypothesis was that living things had been created by an all-powerful god. Not very many people think that human culture comes from an all-powerful creator - but it is still worth noting that culture exhibits imperfections, in a broadly similar manner to the way in

The "penny farthing" was not a perfect bicycle .

which imperfections are seen in organic evolution. For example, a penny farthing was not a perfect bicycle - it was an early bicycle. The early bats and birds didn't work too well either. The reasons for such imperfections are easy to find if you look at the evolutionary history.

3.11 Evidence from domestication

Some of the evidence Darwin used to make the case for organic evolution involved observing cases where creatures had been domesticated. These creatures had been systematically changed by human decisions. He then suggested that wild forms had arisen in a similar manner. We can certainly see similar cases of domestication in human culture. Modern advertisements represent deliberately-crafted cultural artefacts. We can see in some detail how they arise, develop, change and get forgotten - since we can see these processes happening in real time. The evolution of ancient languages, religion and medicine are not always so easy to document. Seeing cultural changes "up close" provides insight into how the whole process happens - in a broadly-similar manner to the way in which the evidence for changes in domestic animals helped Darwin to understand and explain organic evolution.

3.12 Evidence of recombination

In the early days of evolution, there was little or no recombination - and organisms reproduced asexually. While recombination is not really needed for change to qualify as being evolutionary, cultural recombination is a real phenomenon. There is plenty of evidence that cultural recombination exists. Words leap from one language to another; companies incorporate the personnel, business practices, and products of other companies into their own *business DNA*; musicians incorporate riffs and lyrics from other songs into their own productions - and so on.

Portmanteaus provide some neat examples of recombination:

- **cyborg** - comes from **cybernetic** and **organism**;
- **ginormous** - comes from **gigantic** and **enormous**;
- **televangelist** - comes from **television** and **evangelist**;
- **bit** - comes from **binary** and **digit**.

In organic evolution, there is a bit of a split - between involuntary and voluntary recombination. Involuntary recombination can be broadly modelled as disease - for example, when bacteria inject their DNA into other passing bacteria. However, this process has somewhat different dynamics from consensual sex - where the recipient cooperates. Recombination in cultural evolution is consensual - at least some of the time. For example, if a company copies the business practices of another company, it may accept the new information willingly, discarding its old practices in that area without coercion. However very few cultural entities engage in sexual recombination in quite the same regular, ritualised way that many eukaryotes do.

3.13 Culture evolves

Cultural evolution is a fact - much like organic evolution is. Indeed, if anything, the evidence is *stronger* for cultural evolution - since we can more easily see culture changing and evolving in real time, and we have excellent historical records rather than a patchy collection of fossils. As Whiten, Hinde, Laland, and Stringer (2011a) bluntly put it: "culture evolves". They also have their own web site on the topic: http://www.cultureevolves.org/

3.14 Further reading

In case the evidence presented here isn't enough for you, Mesoudi, Whiten and Laland (2004a) offers a nice review of the evidence for cultural evolution.

4 Defining evolution - What "evolution" means

The last chapter explained why cultural change is an evolutionary process - but in case any readers are still sceptical about the point - this chapter examines the case for that classification in more detail.

4.1 Common usage

There is a general sense of the term "evolution" that simply means change over time. In this sense, everyone agrees that technology evolves - much as stars evolve. However the term "evolution" also has a more technical meaning in biology. It is this technical sense which gives rise to disputes about the issue.

4.2 Cultural change is evolution

The basic case for classifying cultural change as evolution involves observing that:

- Culture is passed down from one generation to the next;
- Culture varies as it is copied,
- Some culture persists better than others

...and concludes that - since these are the basic requirements for a process being evolutionary, cultural change qualifies as being evolutionary. However, it is possible to argue against this kind of position by claiming that is not really what the term "evolution" means. To resolve the issue of whether cultural phenomena evolve, it is necessary to consult with definitions of the term "evolution".

4.3 Particular definitions

Definitions of evolution in biology have been offered by many authors - and there are a range of different ones. Darwin (1859) gave:

The theory of descent with modification through natural selection.

Lynda Harding (2000) offers:

Evolution can be defined as the change in allele frequencies in a population.

Larry Moran (1993) gives:

The natural process that results in inheritable changes in a population which is spread over many generations.

Johnson & Raven, Holt, Rinehart and Winston, Biology Principles and Explorations (1996, p. 1040) has:

A change in the genetic makeup of a population or species over time.

These definitions all agree that evolution is a type of inherited change over time - but differ on other details. Those who say that culture does not really evolve in the biological sense of the word have various claims. Next we will review some of them:

4.4 Objections

In the context of these kinds of definition of the term "evolution ", some objections that commonly arise to classifying cultural change as being evolution are as follows:

- **Cultural evolution is not "genetic"** - Some say that, if culture is not transmitted "genetically" then it cannot result in the "changes in gene frequencies" that characterise evolution. This raises the issue of what counts as a being a "gene" - and whether cultural information qualifies. However, rather than arguing that cultural information is "genetic", I think the best way of dealing with this issue is to observe that it only applies to definitions of evolution derived from population genetics. *Most* definitions of evolution make no mention of "genes" or "genetic" - they just talk about "heritable changes" - and so this objection is irrelevant to them.
- **Cultural entities do not form a "population"** - Some say that, if cultural entities do not form an identifiable population then cultural change would not qualify as evolution. However, regardless of the issue of whether cultural entities form a population or not, their human "hosts" most certainly do. *They* still exhibit cultural traits, and these are inherited.
- **Cultural evolution entities are not "organisms"** - Some claim that, if the entities of cultural evolution are not organisms, then culture can't *really* evolve. However, regardless of the issue of whether cultural

entities are organisms or not, their human "hosts" most certainly are. So, for example, being circumcised is a trait of some male humans, it is transmitted down the generations (and so qualifies as an inherited trait). Being circumcised is a trait which isn't coded for by any DNA, and instead is transmitted culturally.

· **Cultural evolution is not "natural"** - Darwin's definition of evolution mentioned "modification through natural selection". Some people have interpreted this is meaning that evolutionary change cannot arise via intelligence - saying, for example: "Evolution cannot be guided by any intelligence. If it is so guided, it is not natural any longer". However, excluding intelligence contradicts most definitions of evolution - which typically do not constrain mechanisms of evolutionary change. Also, not allowing change by intelligent agents runs the risk of disqualifying the process that took place among our ancestors from being classified as being a form of evolution. Many of our ancestors were reasonably intelligent - and their choices certainly guided the direction of evolutionary change - via the well-known process of sexual selection. The idea that evolution stops when intelligent agents arise is a terrible one. Intelligence is also present in primates, monkeys and rodents. From a biological perspective, the brain is just another organ. It no more halts the evolutionary process by processing information than the kidneys halt it by processing blood. These days, Darwin's definition invoking "modification through natural selection" is not used any more. Rather, natural selection is seen as one mechanism for evolutionary change among many.

4.5 Naysayers

Next, some quotes from those who deny the existence of cultural evolution illustrate their respective positions. Here is Eliezer Yudkowsky (2005):

Technology does not evolve, it is designed.

These modes of change are not, in fact, incompatible. Technology evolves *and* it is designed. Here is Stephen Jay Gould, in *Life's Grandeur* (1996 page 219):

Using the same term - evolution - for both natural and cultural history obfuscates far more than it enlightens.

As I hope this book will make clear, an evolutionary perspective is *essential* to a proper understanding of cultural change. Here Stephen is again, in *Bully for Brontosaurus* (1991, page 63).

I am convinced that comparisons between biological evolution and human cultural or technological change have done vastly more harm than good - and examples abound of this most common of intellectual traps. [...] Biological evolution is powered by natural selection, cultural evolution by a different set of principles that I understand but dimly.

The first claim is sociological and hard to assess. However, there's a *real* relationship between organic and cultural evolution which it is important to understand. If you *don't* understanding the relationship, you don't have a good theoretical understanding at least one of the two subjects.

John Maynard-Smith wrote in 1986 - in a review of a book on the topic:

The explanatory power of evolutionary theory rests largely on three assumptions: that mutation is non-adaptive, that acquired characters are not inherited, and that inheritance is Mendelian - that is, it is atomic, and we inherit the atoms, or genes, equally from our two parents, and from no one else. In the cultural analogy, none of these things is true. This must severely limit the ability of a theory of cultural inheritance to say what can happen and, more importantly, what cannot happen.

We will return to these points in more detail in the chapter devoted to criticism later on in this book.

Richard Dawkins has been among the critics. Here he is in 1976:

Whether the mileau of human culture really does have what it takes to get a form of Darwinism going , I am not sure.

...and, in 1982...

these differences may prove sufficient to render the analogy with genetic natural selection positively misleading

This sort of thing has caused me to describe Richard as a *reluctant apostle*. In *The Blind Watchmaker* (Dawkins 1982, p.216) he even asserted the exact opposite of the claim being made in this chapter:

Cultural 'evolution' is not really evolution at all if we are being fussy and purist about our use of words, but there may be enough in common between them to justify a comparison of principles.

By contrast, the thesis here is that cultural evolution *really is* evolution.

In justification of its failure to include anything about cultural evolution between its covers, Mark Ridley's "Evolution" textbook says:

Changes that take place in human politics, economics, history and technology and even scientific theories are sometimes loosely described as "evolutionary". In this sense, evolutionary means mainly that there has been change through time and perhaps not in a preordained direction. Human ideas and institutions can sometimes split during their history but their history does not have such a clear-cut, branching, tree-like like structure as does the history of life. Change and spitting provide two of the main themes of evolutionary theory."

This kind of material is quite unsatisfactory. According to most standard definitions of evolution, it doesn't matter whether there is a "clear-cut, branching, tree-like like structure" - or not. What matters are things like whether changes are inherited.

Also, organic evolution itself doesn't exhibit much of a "clear-cut, branching, tree-like like structure" - near to the root of the tree of life. Bacterial genomes are one big melting pot as far as gene transfer goes. Horizontal gene transfer is rife. In the bacterial domain, the supposed "tree of life" has turned out not to be a "tree" at all - but is rather a densely inter-connected web. Ridley stops short of proclaiming that "bacteria don't evolve" - because their phylogeny is insufficiently tree-like. As a proposed classification scheme, whether a population exhibits a "a clear-cut, branching, tree-like structure" is not neat - and it is not useful.

4.6 Standard definitions

The definitions of evolution do not rule out intelligence as the source of the changes. They do not say that inheritance must take place via nucleic acids either. It is all very well contrasting engineering design with natural selection and blind variation - but in *most* definitions of evolution it does not say that the process cannot include processes derived from engineering design.

So - according to the *standard* definitions of the term "evolution" in biology - we must include cultural and technological changes under its umbrella. Culture, science and technology are all passed on down the generations and inherited.

There are no reasonable grounds for excluding genetic engineering, design, or any other type of technological progress from beneath evolution's umbrella. Specifications relating to the mechanisms of change are not present in the standard definitions of evolution - so we cannot rule out phenomena which change by such means on those grounds.

This is all just as well. It would make quite a mockery of the whole idea if, in the future, what people refer to by "biological evolution" comes to an end

- while living systems continue to change and - for want of a better term - *evolve*.

5 Similarities - Between organic and cultural

Cultural evolution shares a number of properties with organic evolution. This chapter reviews some of these similarities.

5.1 Basic similarities

Both cultural and organic evolution feature inheritance, variation and differential reproductive success. The evidence relating to those similarities was covered in a previous chapter - but very briefly:

- **Inheritance** - This is commonplace - kids sometimes inherit, spoken language, religion, houses, land and wealth from their ancestors, in addition to their genes. The inheritance sometimes includes "bodily" traits - such as circumcision and piercing.
- **Variation** - This is equally commonplace, partly since many cultural phenomena are copied imperfectly (for example martial arts) and change over time (for example scientific knowledge).
- **Differential reproductive success** - For an example, consider the following quotations. Shakespeare wrote: "To be, or not to be: that is the question" in Hamlet. He also wrote "What tellest thou me of black and blue?" - an obscure line in a much less well known play entitled "The Merry Wives of Windsor". Both lines have survived to this day, but instances of the former quote are hundreds of times more common. This is because of more frequent copying of the first quotation. This sort of thing is very common.

Inheritance, variation and differential reproductive success are key properties which are required for most definitions of evolution. They are what leads to cultural evolution is classified as being a type of evolution.

5.2 Other similarities

In addition to the above basic points, there are *many* other similarities between organic and cultural evolution. *Some* of these help to illustrate the point that there are shared underlying dynamics - which can be usefully modelled by a kind of *generalised Darwinism*. Others arise from the shared laws of physics and cybernetics, and would be expected in practically any agent-based system.

- **Cumulative adaptation** - Both processes produce true cumulative evolution - and not merely trivial evolution or devolution (i.e. loss of adaptive complexity).
- **Recombination** - This results in traits from separate sources becoming combined. So, for example, Cliff Richard fitted the words of *The Lords Prayer* to the tune of *Auld Lang Syne* - creating *The Millennium Prayer* in the process. Most songs derive from multiple sources, but these days some songs are very explicit in their copying - creating what is commonly known as a "mashup".
- **Immunity** - Complex animals with long lifespans have immune systems - whose job it is to protect the organism from pathogens. Humans also have a mental filtering systems - designed to reject harmful ideas that act against the best interest of the host's DNA genes
- **Parasitism** - Cultural examples include computer viruses, habitual smoking, chain letters, and pyramid marketing schemes.
- **Mutualism** - Cultural examples include language, recipes, medical knowledge, fire and the wheel.
- **Predators** - A cultural example of a predator is a debt-collection agency.
- **Extinction** - Permanent and irretrievable loss of certain inherited patterns happens in cultural evolution.
- **Linkage** - Alleles can become "linked" with other alleles - and they are then more likely to be inherited together. There is a similar effect in the cultural realm - which causes associations to form between peanut butter and jelly, and between witches and broomsticks.
- **Hitchhiking** - Hitchhiking arises out of linkage - when one allele gets a boost in fitness from the proximity of a nearby allele, it is said to be "hitchhiking". The same effect is used ubiquitously by marketers, to allow their messages to be propagated around by linking them to viral content.
- **Niche-construction** - Technology creates the environment in which further technological development occurs. Similarly, artists create an environment in which future artistic creations take place.
- **Organisms** - Cultural entities come in delimited packages much like organic ones do. For example, companies are like cultural organisms. They have birthdays, names, friends, relatives, boundaries - and are mortal - just like organic organisms
- **Species** - If a species is considered to be group of genomes which recombine relatively frequently with other group members - but which

recombine relatively infrequently with outsiders then COBOL programs make an example of a relatively isolated cultural species. Origami patterns are also relatively isolated.

- **Birth** - As with organic organisms, some cultural phenomena have clearly defined birthdays (as opposed to vegetative reproduction). For example Neil Armstrong said "one giant leap for mankind" at 2:56 July 21, 1969 - a phrase which has been subsequently been copied many times.
- **Development** - Both processes sometimes exhibit a genotype/phenotype split. To give a cultural example: the propagation of a cooked dish might involve both of a set of instructions (known as the recipe) and the result of executing those instructions (the edible product).
- **Senescence** - Computers, cars, houses - all exhibit senescence. Part of the explanation for that is reliability theory - which is not an evolution-based theory. However, that does not explain why light bulbs fail. *Some cultural senescence is explained by evolutionary theories (antagonistic pleiotropy, disposable soma* and *the red queen*) - much as it is in organic systems.
- **Death** - Books, CDs, DVDs, databases, hard disc drives - all are mortal and can die, losing their information.
- **Arms races** - Arms races are found in human culture. Security-related areas are often dominated by the dynamics of attack and defence. Governments try and make money that is difficult to forge - while counterfeiters do their best to outwit them. The result is money the evolves anti-counterfeiting adaptations. Banks try to make secure facilities, while thieves try to break into them - resulting in the evolution of secure safe designs, and the evolution of safe-cracking tools. On the internet, marketers try to flood the world with adverts and positive reviews - while consumer-oriented organisations try and filter genuine consumer responses from the marketing messages.
- **Advertising** - Just as peacocks advertise themselves, so do companies and products.
- **Mimicry** - Cultural artefacts mimic other cultural artefacts (e.g. iPhone clones) and organic systems (e.g. portrait paintings).
- **Camouflage** - Cultural examples include camouflaged jackets, tanks and aircraft.
- **Decoys** - Cultural evolution has produced scarecrows, inflatable tanks and decoy ducks. These are similar to the way in which organic evolution has produced fake eye spots and fake eggs on leaf stems.

- **Stasis** - This arises *partly* through organisms becoming stuck on adaptive peaks. Cultural adaptive peaks exist too - and they produce cultural stasis - which is where things persist for extended periods of time with little or no modification. The word "the" is an example of cultural stasis.

5.3 Significance of the similarities

Organic and cultural evolution exhibit many of the same properties. They are best described as being instances of an single underlying system. The shared dynamics have been called "universal Darwinism" and "generalised Darwinism". The term "evolutionary" also seems to be a highly appropriate term for the dynamics exhibited by this type of system.

5.4 Similarities illustrated

A few of the above similarities can be illustrated visually - so to finish off this chapter, a gallery of images. The organic images are on the left, and the cultural ones are on the right.

Parasitism

Mosquito.   *Smoking.*

Camouflage

Tiger.   *Camouflage jacket.*

Advertisements

Peacock advertisement.   *Cereal advertisement.*

Warnings

Toxic Frog.   *Lighthouse.*

Mimicry

Butterflies.   *Cereal packets.*

6 Differences - Between cultural and organic

While cultural evolution has some similarities with organic evolution, there are also many significant differences. The differences are not enough to mean that cultural evolution doesn't fit into an evolutionary framework - but they are worth noting. Firstly, here is Dawkins (1982a, p.112) on the topic:

> *These differences may prove sufficient to render the analogy with genetic natural selection worthless or even positively misleading.*

Next, a list of some of the more prominent differences. The larger differences are nearer to the top:

6.1 The differences

- **Directed mutations** - This is the most obvious area where there are differences. In organic evolution, most mutations are either neutral - or deleterious. The proximate causes of mutations are mostly accidents - cosmic rays, chemical damage, copying errors - and the like. Cultural evolution has its share of accidental mutations - but there is a new class of mutation - deliberate changes, aimed at gathering information about the surrounding search space or aimed at making things better directly. Deliberate mutations often have a higher fitness than accidental ones. For example, some mutations break things, or are obviously bad - and are not worth trying. Other mutations have already been tried recently - and so probably don't need trying again any time soon.

- **Unconstrained recombination** - Recombination in organic evolution takes place in a fairly limited number of ways - the most common being recombination between two individuals. Cultural evolution exhibits a much broader range of types of recombination. Information from all members of the population can *potentially* be used to determine the form of the next generation. That would represent recombination on a massive scale. Statistical techniques - such as linear regression - can be used to help to ensure that the best alleles are chosen.

- **Fusion** - In organic evolution, creatures fusing with each other *can* happen. There are cases of *symbiogenesis* - where two creatures become one through fusing together. The4 best known example of this is the idea that that chloroplasts in plants originate from free-living cyanobacteria. However in cultural evolution, creatures fusing together is much more common. Companies fuse with other companies. While sometimes this is more like one company eating the other, on other occasions, elements of both companies survive. It is rather as though a bird and a cat fused together to make a flying creature with whiskers.

- **Division** - The types of division that are familiar from organic evolution, include: fission (where one creature splits into two copies), birth (where one or more creatures produce a smaller offspring), speciation (where a lineage divides into two) and cases where a creature gives rise to a pathogen. In cultural evolution, there are more possibilities. Companies illustrate the available options reasonably well. Existing companies can split into distinct functional units that can then continue independently. Companies can split for many reasons - because they are forced to by anti-trust organisations - or to gain more custom by signalling independence from their parent. This seems rather like the equivalent of the liver and kidneys wrapping themselves up in skin and then going off on their own.
- **Partial evaluations** - In organic evolution, fitness evaluations normally take place of a per-organism basis. The fitness of your heart is not evaluated separately from the fitness of your brain - rather these fitnesses are combined into a single measure of reproductive success. However, in cultural evolution, such partial fitness evaluations are possible - and make a lot of sense - in the context of efficiently exploring a search space.
- **Modularity** - This makes so much sense that most organisms have considerable level of modularity in them - even though organ transplants are a relatively new phenomenon. Independent fitness evaluations of the different modules allow problems to be identified early in development. These are important when making changes - because changing one component fairly often breaks other components which depend upon it. Ideas that can be used to deliberately promote modularity include standardised component interfaces and specified interface contracts.
- **Systematic testing** - Organisms may not necessarily have their features "checked" by selection in each generation. For example, disease-resistance genes may only be required intermittently. Lack of continuous testing gives these features more chance to be broken between tests - due to mutations, side effects of deliberate changes, etc. This phenomena is familiar to computer programmers. They make extensive use of what are known as "unit tests" - which are tests of

individual aspects of the project. Organic evolution *can* employ unit testing strategies. Failed unit tests may well be responsible for many aborted fetuses - and ladies sometimes do their best to systematically test out their prospective mates. However, testing for things like disease resistance genes is not very practical - and is often neglected. Cultural evolution can employ unit testing strategies more comprehensively and extensively.

· **Early termination** - This exists in organic evolution. Mothers reabsorb unborn foetuses, abandon or eat their litter's runts. There are also schemes for killing off elderly individuals. However, in practice many "failed" individuals do not actually die - and may continue to take up resources for a considerable time. From the perspective of performing an efficient search, those resources would be better off being recycled. Cultural evolution can use large scale population management tools on a scale not seen in nature to exploit this concept and generate a more efficient search.

· **Eugenics** - Techniques such as large-scale selective breeding programs and the active termination of failures are historically associated with eugenics - and have a poor reputation. However in cultural evolution, the entities evolving are not necessarily classified as being people - in which case, use of such techniques may be regarded as being a legitimate short cut.

· **Intelligent design** - In cultural evolution, the whole process of evolution could be managed by an intelligent agent. If the cost of tests or trials is sufficiently high, it can be advantageous to use considerable resources to calculate the expected fitness of mutations before bothering to test them. Cultural evolution embeds intelligent design in the evolutionary process as a fundamental mechanism of evolutionary change. Directed mutations can be made using techniques involving interpolation, extrapolation and optimisation

· **Evaluation under simulation** - Mutations can have their fitness estimated by a simulation before testing them in the real world. This exists in organic evolution to some extent - where organisms with brains can test out their actions in virtual worlds before executing them. However, again, cultural evolution takes these capabilities to new levels. Evaluation under simulation potentially saves real-world resources - in cases where the simulation is inexpensive enough and accurate enough. Using models and computer simulations is a ubiquitous practice among engineers.

· **Lamarckian inheritance** - Inheritance of acquired characteristics is relatively rare in organic evolution, but happens with greater frequency in the cultural realm (though *most* cultural inheritance is still of the ordinary, Darwinian kind).

- **Horizontal transfer** - Bacteria sometimes transfer genes around horizontally (i.e. between peers - rather than down the generations, vertically). *Occasionally* a parasite incorporates some of its genes into its host - resulting in horizontal gene transfer. This happens most frequently with retroviruses. In the cultural realm, horizontal transfer of information is rather more common.
- **Foresight** - organic evolution is often likened to a "blind" hill-climbing process. Cultural evolution is less like this. Agents can see the consequences of their actions - and can take steps if they do not like the consequences. This phenomenon is not *entirely* new with cultural evolution - since foreseeing the consequences of your actions has been going on since organisms developed sophisticated world simulators composed of neurons and running inside their brains. However, cultural evolution pushes the effects of foresight to new levels.
- **Refactoring** - This is a term originating among computer programmers. It refers to systematically making structural rearrangements to a project which do not alter its functionality - but which do facilitate future work on it. Refactoring is *normally* done prior to making changes to a project. Since refactoring preserves functionality, it often consists of a highly constrained set of changes - and these can often be automated and applied by machines. Refactoring facilitates making large changes - since it allows the ground to be prepared for them before they are made. Refactoring has led to a revolution in computer programming, and its effects are also being felt elsewhere - refactoring is now also considered to be a basic project management skill. Refactoring is one of the advantages of using foresight. It facilitates changes that would otherwise represent large leaps in *design space*, by allowing systematic distortions to be made to that space, to bring the separated peaks close together before a crossing is attempted. Because refactoring is possible, there are not so many obvious design imperfections of certain kinds - because they have been "refactored" out of existence.
- **Project management** - Changes in organic evolution tend to originate in random mutations - or in sexual recombination. However, in the cultural realm, there's a more scientific approach to making changes to existing complex designs. Here I will use the term "project management" as an umbrella term to cover those techniques.
- **Optimisation toolkit** - Organic evolution spent most of its time using a

basic optimisation algorithm, the genetic algorithm. Computer scientists tend to see this as one element in a larger toolkit, which includes many more basic forms of optimisation, and a range of techniques to be used under special circumstances, when something is known about the shape of the fitness landscape.

- **Population control** - When exploring a search space, the population size usually represents the degree of parallelism to be employed. The optimal strategy depends on factors such as the quantity of resources which are concurrently available - and on how fast the solution is needed. Nature doesn't really adjust the resources allocated to such problems according to how they are needed. Rather there's a free-for-all and organisms grab whatever they can. Now humans control the biosphere, they are in a good position to impose population control on both organic and cultural systems. This allows humans to allocate resources where they are *actually* needed to best perform optimisation activities.
- **Mutation ordering** - This refers to the sequential order in which mutations are tested. The concept makes the most sense in very small populations. Mutations can be tried in an optimal order - to help efficiently divide up a search space. The well-known game of 20-questions illustrates this principle. The first questions you ask should divide the search space roughly in half - since this is an application where a *binary search* is the optimal algorithm.

For another list of the differences see the "Disanalogies between biological and conceptual evolution" section in Hull (2001).

6.2 Different dynamics

Most of the differences in the above list might be classed as being differing properties of cultural and organic evolution. However, the different properties lead to different dynamics. For example:

- **Reduced species barriers** - species barriers are less evident in cultural evolution and gene flow between different types of creatures is facilitated. Viruses provide vectors for this type of thing in organic evolution too - but the effects are not as pronounced.
- **Speed** - cultural evolution is faster than the organic evolution that preceded it. In particular it is *much* faster than human evolution - where each generation takes decades. Hans Moravec has estimated that cultural evolution is proceeding about 10,000 times faster than the evolution by random mutations that preceded it - based on the rate of evolution of robots. If true, that's quite a difference!

6.3 Significance of the differences

I think the differences between cultural and organic evolution are quite significant. A genetic material that can be written on by brains is a big deal - and this is reflected by the scale of the impact the development is having on the biosphere. However some claim that the differences are exaggerated. Here is John Wilkins, from 2008:

It seems to me that people want to exaggerate the differences between cultural evolution and biological evolution. The greater the difference the more special we can all feel about ourselves.

It is certainly true that many critics who don't have much of an understanding of cultural evolution like to emphasise the differences. For example, here is David Burbridge, writing in 2003:

Analogies are often drawn between biological evolution and 'social' or 'cultural' evolution. I believe these analogies are seldom enlightening, and often misleading. There are too many major differences between culture and biology for the analogies to be useful.

However, I am inclined to think that - for those who understand the fundamental, shared underpinnings of cultural and organic evolution - some emphasis on the differences is warranted.

7 Memes - Terminology for cultural evolution

At this point, it seems best to introduce some terminology - to help make communicating the concepts of cultural evolution quicker and easier. The terminology used to describe cultural evolution has been one of the most controversial issues associated with it.

The author of this book thinks that terminology is important. Language controls thought - and so getting technical words right helps to produce clear thinking. Many find terminology a subject which is not very interesting. They would rather learn about topic itself than about the names which people use to refer to things.

7.1 Memes

To study things from an evolutionary perspective, *probably* the most important terms that are needed are equivalents of "gene", "genetics". In the author's view, the best terminology in this area was invented by Richard Dawkins - in his 1976 book, The Selfish Gene. Dawkins proposed we use "meme" as the cultural equivalent of "gene", "memeticist" as the cultural equivalent of "geneticist", and "memic" to mean "to do with memes". "Memic" has been largely replaced by "memetics" - a term coined by Keith Henson's wife, Arel Lucas by analogy with "genetics". However, the term "meme" has stuck - and has now been replicated some 41 million times on the internet - attaining *far* greater circulation than its competitors.

The term did *once* have some competition:

- **Edward Burnett Tylor** started by calling them "survivals";
- **Lumsden and Wilson** (1981) called them "culturegens"
- **Joseph Giovannoli** calls them "psychogenes";
- **Seth Godin** (2000) refers to "ideaviruses";
- **Donald Campbell** (1960) called them "mnemones";
- **Barry Hewlett** (2002) calls them "semes";
- **William Brodie** (1996) preferred to talk about "mind viruses";
- **Craig Mackay** (2011) calls them "supergenes";
- **M. Stuart-Fox** (1986) called them "mentemes";
- **Richard Semon** (1921) called them "mnemes";
- **Henry Murray** (1959) called them "idenes";
- **F.T. Cloak** recommended use of the term "instruction";
- **Carl Swanson** (1983) called them "sociogenes";
- **George van Driem** (2007) called to the unit of imitation a "mime";
- **William Croft** (2000) used "linguemes" for "linguistic replicator";
- **Aaron Lynch** (2000) used a term he invented: "thought contagions";
- **Leslie White** (1959) called products of symbolism "symbolates";
- **Harold Blum** (1963) endorsed "mnemes" by coining "mnemotype";
- **Boyd and Richerson** have called them: "culture-types", "cultural representations", "cultural traits" - and now "cultural variants".

Lumsden and Wilson (1981, p.7) have a review of meme synonyms. However, none of these other terms has become anywhere *near* as popular as the term "meme". Essentially, memes arrived on the scene *relatively* early, were given quite a boost by virtue of being included in *The Selfish Gene* - and have now won the terminology war through a lack of competitive alternatives.

7.2 Endorsements

Memes are not *just* promoted by **Daniel Dennett**, **Richard Dawkins** and **Susan Blackmore**.

Edward Wilson writing in 1998, gave up on his own "culturegens" - and endorsed memes - by saying:

The notion of a cultural unit, the most basic element of all, has been around for over 30 years, and has been dubbed by different authors variously as mnemotype, idea, idene, meme, sociogene, concept, culturgen and culture type. The one label that has caught on the most, and for which I now vote to be the winner, is meme, introduced by Richard Dawkins in his influential work The Selfish Gene in 1976.

Douglas Hofstadter (1983) endorsed memes, writing:

When I muse about memes, I often find myself picturing an ephemeral flickering pattern of sparks leaping from brain to brain, screaming "Me, me!"

George Williams (1998) endorsed memes, writing:

Within a society a meme may indeed enhance the happiness or fitness of its bearer, or it may not.

Robert Wright (2009) endorsed memes, writing:

But biological evolution isn't the only great "designer" at work on this planet. There is also cultural evolution: the selective transmission of "memes"—beliefs, habits, rituals, songs, technologies, theories, and so forth—from person to person. And one criterion that shapes cultural evolution is social utility; memes that are conducive to smooth functioning at the group level often have an advantage over memes that aren't.

William Hamilton (1977) predicted long ago that the term would come to dominate - writing:

He floats the term "meme" (short for mimeme) for the cultural equivalent of "gene". Hard as this term may be to delimit - it surely must be harder than gene, which is bad enough - I suspect that it will soon be in common use by biologists and, one hopes, by philosophers, linguists, and others as well and that it may become absorbed as far as the word "gene" has been into everyday speech.

Nicholas Humphrey endorsed memes and memetics, and is reported to have said:

I think memes provide a neat way of explaining some of the paradoxes of cultural transmission and, if they help with explaining something that important, there had better be a science of them.

John Wilkins writing in 2010 appears to have endorsed memes:

Something evolves in culture, so we may as well accede to popular usage and call them memes.

Robert Aunger (2005a) wrote:

The 'meme' has won the contest to be the accepted name for the fundamental unit of culture.

David Hull (1999 and 2000) apparently endorsed memetics, describing himself as being a "memeticist".

7.3 Dictionaries

The term "meme" has found its way into the *Merriam-Webster Dictionary*:

an idea, behavior, style, or usage that spreads from person to person within a culture

The *Oxford English Dictionary* has:

an element of a culture that may be considered to be passed on by non-genetic means, esp. imitation.

7.4 Terminology family

Meme is not *just* a neat term for a cultural gene - it also *sounds* like "gene". That means that it can be substituted for "gene" in the family of biological terms that are based on genes and genetics - as illustrated by the following table:

Memetic	Genetic	Memetic	Genetic
Meme(s)	Gene(s)	Memetic evolution	Genetic evolution
Memetic(s)	Genetic(s)	Memetic program	Genetic program
Memeticist	Geneticst	Memetic hitchhiking	Genetic hitchhiking
Meme expression	Gene expression	Memetic linkage	Genetic linkage
Meme regulation	Gene regulation	Memetic drive	Genetic drive
Meme flow	Gene flow	Meme's eye view	Gene's eye view
Meme pool	Gene pool	Memetic algorithms	Genetic algorithms
Meme therapy	Gene therapy	Memetic load	Genetic load
Memealogy	Genealogy	Memetic testing	Genetic testing
Memetic drift	Genetic drift	Memetic pollution	Genetic pollution
Memesis	Genesis	Memetic takeover	Genetic takeover
Memotype	Genotype	Memetic engineering	Genetic engineering
Memome	Genome	Population memetics	Population genetics
Phylomemetics	Phylogenetics	Horizontal meme transfer	Horizontal gene transfer
Epimemesis	Epigenesis		

That you get access to all these useful terms at the expense of remembering one simple rule is one of the main benefits of adopting the memetic terminology. Those who doubt the worth of making the link between genes and memes should consider this table carefully. The raft of shared concepts between genetics and memetics is part of the validation of this relationship.

7.5 Etymology

Dawkins said that the word "meme" was a shortening (modelled on "gene") of the word *mimeme* ("something imitated" in Ancient Greek) together with a pun on the word *même* ("same" in French).

Apart from "gene", the word "meme" has some other cousins, as follows:

- **Lexeme** - basic unit of morphological analysis in linguistics;
- **Phoneme** - unit of sound allowing utterances to be distinguished;
- **Morpheme** - the smallest meaningful component of a word;
- **Sememe** - a semantic unit of language meaning;
- **Seme** - the smallest unit of meaning recognized in semantics;
- **Grapheme** - is a fundamental unit in a written language.

7.6 Richard Dawkins

Richard Dawkins came up with the term "meme" - and was largely responsible for popularising the "meme" terminology. However, he has not subsequently been its biggest fan. His efforts to promote the term have been a little half-hearted. As I have previously put it, the patron saint of memetics is a *reluctant apostle*.

Richard Dawkins.
Coined the term "meme".

The "meme" terminology *does* have some drawbacks. For one thing, it drags in a considerable amount of historical "baggage" with it. Some of that baggage is from Richard Dawkins himself.

He said that he christened memes after the greek word for "mimeme" - which means "to mime". Ever since there has been confusion over the issue of whether culture which is passed on my other means than imitation should be described as being "memetic".

His initial contribution in *The Selfish Gene* (Dawkins 1976) was presented in a chatty style that was not exactly a paragon of scientific rigor, and people have been debating exactly what he meant ever since. He presented multiple contradictory definitions of the term "meme", describing it as:

- "a unit of cultural transmission";
- "a unit of imitation";
- "a unit of information residing in a brain";

These conflicting definitions have led to various factions within the resulting community - with disagreements over the significance of imitation, and whether memes should be thought of as being confined to brains.

7.7 Dawkins retreats

Richard subsequently played-down his contribution - saying, in 1976:

> *Whether the mileau of human culture really does have what it takes to get a form of Darwinism going , I am not sure.*

...and in 1982:

> *These differences may prove sufficient to render the analogy with genetic natural selection worthless or even positively misleading.*

...and in 1982:

> *I do not know enough about the existing literature on human culture to make an authoritative contribution to it.*

...and in an interview (Lanier and Dawkins 1997):

> *I'm not committed to memes as the explanation for human culture.*

Dawkins, in an interview with Jim Holt (2004), said:

> *My enthusiasm for it was never, ever as a contribution to the study of human culture. It was always intended to be a way of dramatizing the idea that a Darwinian replicator doesn't have to be a gene. It can be a computer virus. Or a meme. The point is that a good replicator is just a replicator that spreads, regardless of its material form.*

Dawkins is quoted by Michael Shermer in his "The Skeptic's Chaplain" as saying:

> *I am not going to utter the "m" word; everybody else keeps saying it and then looking at me, and I am going to duck out of that. I used not to think this, but I am increasingly thinking that nothing but confusion arises from confounding genetic evolution with cultural evolution, unless you are very careful about what you are doing and don't talk as though they are somehow just different aspects of the same phenomenon. Or, if they are different aspects of the same phenomenon, then let's hear a good case for regarding them as such.*

7.8 The term "meme" wins anyway

Despite these messy beginnings, the term "meme" caught people's imaginations more effectively that any competing terminology has managed before or since then.

While "meme" seems to have won, "memetics" seems to be having a much harder time establishing itself as the standard term for the study the cultural equivalent of genetics. It isn't *that* much shorter than "cultural genetics". Also, "memetics" is jargon - whereas "cultural genetics" is self-explanatory. Also, *cultural evolution* is *really* the most important idea. *Cultural genetics* is more of a nuts and-bolts concept for describing the mechanics of how memes change. Since many memes recombine inside human brains - and we do not yet have a very complete understanding of how those work - this is a rather challenging area to explore experimentally. There is, however, *population memetics* - the study of how meme frequencies change in populations. That requires less delving into how brains work - and consequently we have a *lot* more knowledge about that area.

7.9 Duplication

Another problem with the memetics terminology is that it *largely* duplicates a lot of concepts from organic evolution. Since *genetics* and *memetics* are so similar, it is *tempting* to reject the claim that new terminology is needed, and just expand the "gene" / "genetics" terminology to embrace human culture. Then we could refer to organic inherited elements as "organic-genes" and cultural inherited elements as "cultural-genes".

Since *genetics* and *memetics* have an *enormous* overlap - we could just call the whole field "genetics". The terms "cultural genetics" and "cultural evolution" could be used to refer to the sciences associated with cultural inheritance - and the term "organic genetics" could be used to refer to the science of cellular inheritance.

However, as the popularity of the "meme" term shows, it *is* sometimes useful to distinguish between cultural and organic inheritance. "Meme" is certainly shorter and neater than "cultural-gene". So, I think there is a good reason to embrace the "memetics" terminology.

7.10 Memetics as a hypothesis

The ideas *originally* put forward by Richard Dawkins have subsequently come to be known as *memetics*.

Memetics is *usually* considered to be a *bit* more than *just* terminology for cultural genetics and cultural evolution.

Dennett (1998) says:

> *Dawkins' theory of memes, as briefly sketched in a single chapter of*
> *The Selfish Gene (1976, but see also Dawkins, 1993), is hardly a*
> *theory at all, especially compared to the models of cultural evolution*
> *developed by other biologists, such as Cavalli-Sforza and Feldman*
> *(1981), Lumsden and Wilson (1981), and Boyd and Richerson (1985).*
> *Unlike these others, Dawkins offers no formal development, no*
> *mathematical models, no quantitative predictions, no systematic*
> *survey of relevant empirical findings. But Dawkins does present an*
> *idea that is overlooked by all the others, and it is, I think, a most*
> *important idea.*

What Dennett is talking about is the idea that memes benefit. The inherited information that is responsible for culture (memes) consist of multiple small fragments that are copied in the process of cultural transmission, and which behave rather like viruses - in that they spread horizontally like disease agents do - as well as sometimes being transmitted vertically - down the generations of their hosts.

Dennett says that, in biology, the benefits associated with possessing adaptations accrue to some entity - and that entity is usually considered to be DNA genes. Memetics says that there is now another possible answer to the question of "who benefts?" - that the benefit accrues to memes. It is true that some of the early academic researchers (e.g. Lumsden and Wilson) didn't seem to understand this sort of perspective. However, these days, at least Peter Richerson (2010f) *does* seem to agree that memes can selfishly benefit - as the following quote indicates:

> *One of the problems with the meme concept as it evolved is that users*
> *of the term focused far too heavily on the selfish potential of memes.*
> *But I think it is near to undeniable that cultural variants are*
> *sometimes selected to become selfish pathogens along the lines that*
> *Dawkins suggested. Since some cultural variants can spread rapidly*
> *among people, as in the case of fads, they rather resemble the life*
> *cycle of a viral or bacterial pathogen.*

This admission is a step in the right direction. In memetics, memes don't just *resemble* parasites. They literally *are* part of the germ line of cultural parasites. Until you realise how useful that idea is, the utility of applying epidemiological models to the cultural realm will not be fully clear.

7.11 Meme critics

Not everyone approves of the meme terminology. Unfortunately, *most* of the critics simply do not have a proper understanding of the topic. As Dennett (2010) explains:

> *Memes are the cultural items that are analagous to genes or to viruses. They are units that get replicated, and differentially replicated, and that's where we get evolution. That's Dawkins' theory. Its deeply controversial, many people hate it. I don't, I love it. I am a critic of the ideas, but mainly I encounter dozens of second rate and third rate and fourth rate arguments against memes and I am not going to spend any time on it now, but I just want to let you know, I think memes are good. I think it is not the only good idea on cultural evolution, but I think it is a good idea - because it allows us to see how cultural evolution it itself can be, under some circumstances, a variety of natural selection. Not genetic natural selection, but memetic natural selection.*

Interestingly, some of the critics of memetics are nonetheless using the term "meme". For instance, Gil-White (2006) seems pretty hostile to memetics, but still writes:

> *I will still call what is transmitted culturally a 'meme,' and so - I will bet my house - will everybody else. The term 'meme' has already been selected for, so rather than forcing its meaning to coincide with a particular hypothesis about cultural transmission, let us do some science.*

I have a whole chapter devoted to criticisms of memetics later in the book. Criticisms of memetic terminology will be discussed there.

7.12 Glossary

The more esoteric memetics terminology will be used only lightly in this book - in an attempt to make it easier to understand. I *have* included a memetics glossary at the back of this book, though. It may help from time to time with some of the more obscure memetics terms.

7.13 The mutating "meme" meme

Richard Dawkins coined the term "meme" in his 1976 book, *The Selfish Gene*. He defined it to refer to a "unit of cultural transmission".

The circulation of the term "meme" has been boosted recently by what have become known as "internet memes" - viral phenomena (usually frivolous) that spread rapidly on the internet. Probably by now more people have heard of these "internet memes" than ever read *The Selfish Gene*:

The term "meme" has often come to be used as an abbreviation for "internet meme" - which is a term most frequently used to refer to a piece of highly viral (but usually rather frivolous) culture which is shared frequently on the internet. Tom Michael put it this way in 2010:

> *It's ironic that the term "meme" has spread much more widely as a term relating to internet silliness than as a general unit of cultural exchange. It had to mutate into a faster-reproducing form in order to be widely known about.*

Sometimes the "frivolous internet culture" is described as being a "meme", as it is being passed around. In such cases, the term "meme" has become a kind of meta-meme - which spreads due to its association with the viral culture which it is associated with. In biology, there is the concept of "linkage". This causes the fate of genes to be associated with the fate of their neighbouring genes. Some genes can us this effect to spread - because they are near other genes which are favourably selected for. This effect is commonly-known as *genetic hitchhiking*. The term "meme" is has been doing some *memetic hitchhiking* recently - spreading by virtue of its association with the highly-viral content which it has come to be associated with. As a result, at the time of writing, it is exploding in popularity.

7.14 Popularity explosion

A couple of graphs illustrate the recent explosion in the use of the term "meme":

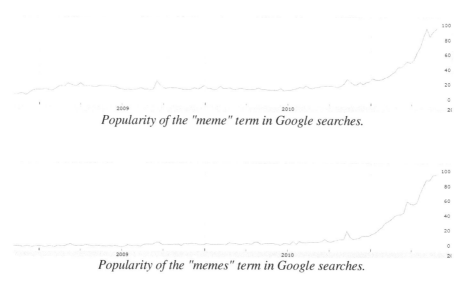

Popularity of the "meme" term in Google searches.

Popularity of the "memes" term in Google searches.

I think this means that the term "meme" is here to stay.

8 Coevolution - Culture-organic interactions

A common way to visualise memetic evolution is as a separate instance of the evolutionary process, operating in parallel to organic evolution, using different set of genotypes and phenotypes. This chapter illustrates the scale of the flaws in that conception. As Spencer (1862) put it:

there are not several kinds of Evolution having certain traits in common, but one Evolution going on everywhere after the same manner.

Just so. In fact, organic creatures and memetic ones *coevolve*. They compete with one another for space and resources. Each influences the environment in which the other evolves.

8.1 Agricultural revolution

The recent agricultural revolution led to *selective sweeps* by a variety of genes through the human population. Some of the genetic winners we know about include:

- **Lactose digestion** - this is one of the best-documented examples of coevolution between the organic and cultural realms. Most young mammals exhibit reduced lactase production at the end of the weaning period. Among most humans, lactase production usually drops about 90% during the first four years of life. However some

Cow udders: milk producers.

  populations exhibit a mutation that allows lactase production to continue indefinitely - making it possible for their members to consume unfermented dairy products throughout their lives. The mutation has spread through the regions where dairy herds are actually raised (Schaffner 2008). Maintaining a dairy herd is a culturally-transmitted trait - so this represents a case of memes going on to influence the prevalence of organic genes.

Mosquito: malaria vector.

- **Malaria resistance** - Malaria is a deadly parasitic disease which results in over 1 million deaths annually. It is carried by mosquitoes. Malaria is common in Africa and many people of African descent have either sickle cell anaemia or sickle cell trait. The sickle cell trait reduces the occurrence of malaria. This adaptation has been selected for and retained in human populations. The sickle cell mutation provides resistance to Malaria - although it also leads to sickle cell anaemia in rare cases (Schaffner 2008). Malaria is linked to the agricultural revolution. Farmers learned to store water - and the water storage receptacles used provide favourable aquatic habitats for mosquitoes. Additionally, farmers use irrigation methods that increase the potential for mosquito breeding. The agricultural revolution also caused the human population explosion, increasing the human population density and so making disease transmission between hosts easier.

8.2 Other cases

Looking further back in time, there are other cases of meme-gene coevolution - though often the supporting evidence in these cases is not so clear-cut:

- **Walking upright** - this was *probably* originally a trait that was transmitted down the generations culturally. There is *still* a *significant* cultural element to learning this behaviour - many *feral children* have never learned to walk upright.
- **Speech** - started out as learned, culturally-transmitted behaviour - but language and genes coevolved - leading to today's babbling infants, who have the seeds of language encoded in their DNA.
- **Enlarged cranium** - this human may be the one of the most dramatic cases of memes and genes coevolving. Memes take up mental real-estate - and is often beneficial. Brains swelled up to better accommodate the huge number of memes that swarmed inside them. Now the resulting meme-nest has become enormous, and it barely fits through the hole in the female pelvis.
- **Ultrasociality** - humans are an *ultrasocial* species. It seems likely that coevolution with memes helped to make them so. Memes are pro-social since they rely on human interactions for their own reproduction. They thus attempt to manipulate humans so they engage in more social contact.
- **Fire** - mastery of the technology of flame was transmitted down the generations culturally - and the human digestive tract became adapted to eat pre-digested, cooked food - to *some* extent.
- **Swimming** - this is another case where what started out as something which was transmitted culturally has led to adaptations - the human nose, human hairlessness, human blubber - and so on.

- **Endurance chases** - hunting habits involving lengthy chases changed the morphology of the human leg.
- **Projectile weapons** - spears and throwable weapons apparently reduced defensive needs - and resulted in a morphology that was less robust.

A common pattern here is that traits tend to evolve in the cultural realm first, and then subsequently go on to influence the nuclear genome.

8.3 Rapid memetic evolution

Memetic evolution is *fast* - at least compared to human evolution. The generation time is much smaller. The population size is much larger. Also, memetic evolution can take advantage of directed mutations and intelligent design.

As a result of this, the memes tend to lead, and the genes tend to be dragged along in their wake. In the example of lactose digestion given above, the memes for milk drinking came first, and only *many decades later*, as the DNA of the milk-drinkers proved to be successful, did lactose tolerance become more widespread. The effect is sometimes compared to a big, powerful dog which is using a leash to drag its human owners around. In this leash metaphor, culture is the dog, straining at the leash, and the human gene pool is the dog's owner - being dragged along after it.

8.4 Rapid human evolution

In the past some biologists have wondered why human evolution went as fast as it did. Other apes still seem to be much closer to our common ancestor with us than we are. This is a real effect - not something that can be explained by our own lack of perspective, and the idea that any species would think they are more different from their ancestors than related species are.

There is a problem known as *Haldane's dilemma* - which is has been used to question whether human evolution can have occurred as fast as it did.

R. P. Worden (1995) proposed "A Speed Limit For Evolution" - and concluded that:

> *I showed that the human brain differs from the chimpanzee brain by at most 2 Kilobytes of design information, out of a 100 Kilobyte total. So it must differ mainly in capacity and power, rather than in design complexity. This makes the evolution of a de novo Language Acquisition Device in mankind seem highly unlikely.*

We should not take this conclusion too seriously - but it illustrates the perception that human evolution took place very rapidly.

Coevolution with memes offers an explanation for the observed rapid rate of human evolution. Human genes coevolved with symbiotic memes - in a way that the genes of other apes *mostly* did not. Other apes have memes too- but they have yet to reach their equivalent of the stone age - which is where human memetic evolution *really* started to take off. Memetic evolution happens *relatively* quickly - as was explained above. Memes change the fitness landscape the DNA genes evolved on, keeping them constantly off balance. As a result, human evolution was accelerated and the DNA genes rushed to track the resulting rapid memetic changes.

8.5 Genetic assimilation

One of the basic ideas of gene-meme coevolution is *genetic assimilation*. The concept refers to acquired phenotypic traits turning into genetic ones over time. In the context of memetic evolution it *usually* refers to learned behaviours becoming encoded in DNA genes. The case of lactose digestion illustrates how the culturally-transmitted practice of adults consuming milk can eventually result in adaptations that facilitate the consumption of more milk.

The idea of genetic assimilation was pioneered by James Mark Baldwin (1896), and for a long time was controversial, since there was not very much supporting evidence. However, in the 1950s genetic assimilation gained some experimental support from experiments performed by C. H. Waddington.

8.6 The assimilate-stretch principle

Avital and Jablonka (2000) introduced *The Assimilate-Stretch Principle*. The basic idea is that *genetic assimilation* may apply in an iterative fashion. A learning system may have a limited capacity to learn behavioural sequences. It may learn a sequence of operations or steps. If *genetic assimilation* then causes some of these to become instinctive, then there would be fewer steps that need to be learned. That would free up capacity in the learning system - and that capacity could then be used to add more steps to the sequence. This process could be iterated, with the learning system adding steps to the sequence, and genetic assimilation making them instinctive.

The Assimilate-Stretch Principle suggests how complex instincts could be formed relatively rapidly in a system capable of learning. The principle could result sequences of behaviour which are too long for the individual's learning system to be able to cope with gradually being acquired.

8.7 Oscillations

One phenomenon that arises in the organic world where there are predators and prey is boom-bust cycles. Similar cyclic behaviour can arise between parasites and hosts. In the cultural realm, fads and fashions seem to behave a *lot* like this. Hula hoops, rubik cubes, pokemon, pet rocks and hippies have all fluctuated on a worldwide scale as crazes for these things have repeatedly swept through the population.

8.8 Shielding

Memes can create new selective pressures, by altering the genetic fitness landscape of their hosts. However, they can also reduce the intensity of selection under other circumstances. When this happens, it is usually known as "shielding". In their book *Animal Traditions*, Eva Jablonka and Eytan Avital (2000) discussed the effects of shielding:

> *Since plasticity of higher animals can mask both environmental and genetic variations, many genetic variations are protected from selective elimination and can accumulate. The net effect is a large reservoir of genetic variation underlying the organization of the nervous system. This variation is exposed and recruited when the environment changes.*

Although this quote refers to genetic plasticity, memetic plasticity can produce a similar effect and allow for even greater plasticity - and an even greater build up of variations. For example, the reason myopia is not being selected so strongly against today is because of the use of spectacles, contact lenses and laser eye surgery. These are all cultural phenomena.

In the past those with myopia would have been at a greater disadvantage than people today who suffer from it. On the other hand, myopia is *partly* a disease of civilisation: cultural factors play a big role in causing it, as well as offering some opportunities for alleviating its symptoms.

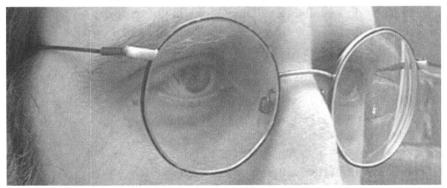

Spectacles show how memes can sometimes help to shield humans from selection.

Many other diseases with genetic risk factors also persist more than they used to - due to medical practices which cure the diseases or alleviate their symptoms. Again, this results in the persistence of greater genetic diversity.

9 Symbiosis - Symbiotic relationships

This chapter is about how human culture is in a symbiotic relationship with the human gene pool. Memes are best thought of as being the heritable information for cultural symbionts. These symbionts are usually small, and they frequently have their own reproductive cycle, which is typically quite different from that of their hosts.

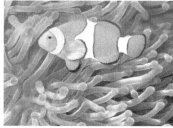

Clownfish and anemone.

Since they are often small, reproduce rapidly and are passed horizontally from host to host they can be usefully thought of as being rather like viruses - although viruses are usually harmful, whereas memes are, on average, beneficial.

9.1 Organic symbiosis

The term "symbiosis" refers an extended relationship between two or more creatures which come to depend on each other to some extent. So, for example:

· **Dogs** - In a symbiotic relationship with their **fleas**;
· **Humans** - In a symbiotic relationship with **lettuces**;
· **Humans** - In a symbiotic relationship with **gut bacteria**;
· **Humans** - In a symbiotic relationship with **the AIDS virus**;
· **Ants** - In a symbiotic relationship with **aphids**.

9.2 Memetic symbiosis

Cultural entities are creatures which are in an obligate symbiosis with humans. In other words, they depend on humans for their existence. Language, fashion, religion, science, technology - all consist of cultural creatures that have symbiotic relationships with humans. These cultural entities

Wireless headset.

can vary dramatically in size and capabilities - from individual words up to forming the guts of large, international companies. That covers a range spanning from something simpler than a virus up to something bigger than a blue whale.

9.3 Classification by physical relationship type

If you classify symbiotic relationships according to the physical relationships between the hosts there are two main types:

- **Endosymbiosis** - one organism lives inside the other one;
- **Ectosymbiosis** - the organisms interact via their surfaces;

Endosymbiotic memes are fairly common. Many memes spend most of their time inside human brains. However, memes have life cycles which involve travelling between hosts, through the space between them. *Sometimes*, this stage occupies the majority of their life cycle.

9.4 Classification by benefits to host

Effect on host	Interaction type
+	**Mutualism** - beneficial symbiosis.
-	**Parasitism** - deleterious parasites.
0	**Commensalism** - host unaffected.

The *main* types of relationship between memes and their hosts are usually considered to be mutualism, parasitism and commensalism. All three types of meme are common. There is good reason to believe that the mutualistic ones - in some sense - outweighed the parasitic ones during the period in which our ancestors evolved - since humans have a range of meme-spreading adaptations. Some more details about these types:

- **Mutualism** - Many memes are beneficial to their hosts. Language, numeracy, critical thinking, romance and child-rearing are all important ideas that are transmitted culturally, and are useful to their hosts. Humans have a range of pro-meme adaptations - in the form of articulate speech abilities and a sociable nature - that facilitate the transfer of beneficial memes.
- **Parasitism** - Some memes behave like infectious diseases. Smoking, urban legends, scandalous lies, pornography and the recipe for chocolate gateau are typically not good for their hosts. However, they spread anyway. Such negative memes are sometimes opposed by memetic immune responses in the host.
- **Commensalism** - This is where the host is not significantly inconvenienced. For example someone wearing an advertising logo on

their shoe may not be too seriously harmed by it.

9.5 Classification of organic-memetic relationships by benefit

If we broaden things a little and consider other interactions besides those between memes and their immediate human hosts, organic-memetic relationships can again be classified according to which parties benefit. Then there are *four* main possiblities:

Effect on organic	Effect on memetic	Interaction type
+	+	**Mutualism** - mutual benefit.
-	+	**Parasitism** - memetic parasitises organic.
+	-	**Parasitism** - organic parasitises memetic.
-	-	**Competition** - mutual harm.

If neutrality is included, there are also these five *additional* possibilities:

Effect on organic	Effect on memetic	Interaction type
0	+	**Commensalism** - benefits to memetic.
0	-	**Amensalism** - harm to memetic.
0	0	**Neutralism** - mutual neutrality.
-	0	**Amensalism** - harm to organic.
+	0	**Commensalism** - benefits to organic.

It is *fairly* common to ignore neutrality - and thus neutralism, amensalism and commensalism - on the grounds that neutrality is relatively rare. For example Blute (2006) does exactly that.

This type of classification scheme can be complicated by the possibility that a symbiont has a life cycle that involves multiple different hosts. Such cases are *fairly* common in the organic world. There is no rule that says that the symbiote necessarily *has* to play the same type of role in each host.

To give a cultural example, tobacco advertising memes are typically *harmful* to consumers, but *beneficial* to tobacco executives, who receive revenue from tobacco sales and have appropriate immune defences. This is an example of a memetically-engineered parasite.

Another example which often illustrates a cultural parasite playing different roles in different hosts is religion. Religion often has priests and laymen, or gurus and follows. The same memes express themselves rather differently in these two types of host. The relationship is somewhat similar to the caste system found in eusocial insects – with the priest or guru acting rather like a queen. *Sometimes* the leader benefits at the expense of the followers – producing a rather toxic set of religious memes and motivation for the leader to memetically engineer them to be ever-more virulent. However, sometimes the leader is *sterilised* by the religious parasite. Instead of producing a new generation of hosts, reproductive resources are sometimes redirected towards junior members of the same sex. In such cases, no benefits accrue to the host genes, and the benefits associated with the priest's efforts go instead to the religious memes.

9.6 Classification by type of dependency

If you classify symbiosis by the type of dependency, there are two types:

- **Obligate** - both symbionts *entirely* depend on each other for survival;
- **Facultative** - one symbiont can live without the other one;

Since it seems best to consider dependency from the perspective of the individual organisms involved, this classification scheme is not ideal.

Humans are not *usually* dependent on *particular* memes. It might be challenging to live without the number zero, or the word "I" - but it is probably not impossible. Remove enough memes, and male humans may be effectively sterilised, though. By contrast, memes are usually totally dependent on their human hosts. Possibly in the future, intelligent machines may form a meme ecosystem that allows the memes to eliminate their dependency on humans - however, today the dependency is still absolute: elimination of all humans would *quickly* lead to the elimination of all memes.

9.7 Symbiosis modelled

There are mathematical model of population growth which describe how populations change over time. These models are ultimately based on the logistic growth equation. The models have been adapted to deal with symbiotic relationships - and the same models can be applied to meme-gene coevolution.

Mutualism can be modelled using the logistic growth equation with an added term to represent the mutualistic interaction. Parasitism can be modelled in much the same way - though there the effect of the pathogen on the host is represented by a term which is subtracted, rather than added. For more details, there are whole books on how to mathematically model the interaction between genes and culture - e.g. McElreath and Boyd (2007).

9.8 Pure memetic relationships

Another classification scheme for symbiotic relationships looks at the *types* of creature the relationship takes place between:

- **Organic-organic** - for example, **humans** and **lettuces**;
- **Organic-memetic** - for example, **humans** and **wheels**;
- **Memetic-memetic** - for example, **computer virus** and **host O.S.**;

The last category involves memes that form symbiotic relationships with other memes. So, for example, a computer virus may have a symbiotic relationship with a particular program - which it uses as a *vector* to help it spread.

These relationships can be classified by benefits involved. If you classify pure memetic relationships according to which parties benefit there are *six* main possibilities – as follows:

Party one	Party two	Interaction type
+	+	**Mutualism** - mutual benefit.
-	+	**Parasitism** - one party exploits the other.
-	-	**Competition** - mutual harm.
0	+	**Commensalism** - one party benefits.
0	-	**Amensalism** - one party harmed.
0	0	**Neutralism** - mutual neutrality.

9.9 Competition

Parasites and mutualists will be covered in a lot more depth in the next two chapters, but first a few words about competition:

In the organic realm, competition is *very* common. It typically arises as a result of conflict over space, information or material resources. For example, both lions and hyenas might want to feast on the same kill. In this picture two male red deer fight over territory and the associated mating opportunities.

Red deer fight over mates.

In the cultural realm, competition is common too. For example, adverts compete for eyeballs, religions compete for adherents and churches compete for congregations. Competition between the cultural and organic realms also happens - for example, a movie and a woman might compete for a man's attention.

9.10 Slavery

Slavery is known by the term "helotism" in biology. It is a common strategy of ants. Here, we will consider willing *and* unwilling slavery:

Unwilling slavery involves a symbiotic relationship where two parties have a close relationship in which one party

Robots slave willingly in factories.

profits at the expense of the other. Unwilling slavery can be thought of as being a type of parasitism that doesn't involve anything like a pathogen. Most types of parasitism *usually* involve many small creatures exploiting a large one. However, in unwilling slavery things are *usually* the other way around - with one large creature exploiting many small ones. This kind of master-slave relationship can go on to evolve in two main directions:

- **Slave resistance** - if the slaves have much chance of freedom, they may develop adaptations that resist enslavement;
- **Slave domestication** - if the slaves are more comprehensively controlled, they may be domesticated by the masters;

Domestication tends to result in evolution towards willing slavery.

Cases of unwilling slavery have not been terribly common in cultural evolution so far. Botnets would be one example. In a botnet, he hijacked PCs clearly resist being controlled, and have immune adaptations to help with this.

Willing slavery is a type of mutualistic relationship. Examples of it are *fairly* common phenomenon in cultural evolution. There are many cultural elements that slave tirelessly for human masters. Some live in factories. There are also mechanical slave masters - and memes working for other memes. For example, willing slavery in virtual worlds can be seen in the case of genetic algorithms.

9.11 Predation

Though not *usually* categorised as being a type of symbiosis, predation is another common type of interaction between species in the organic world. John Wilkins (1997) suggested the distinction between predation and parasitism was rather arbitrary:

> *The arbitrary difference between a predator and*
> *a parasite is the rate at which it kills its host.*

Predation occurs in the cultural realm too. Humans sometimes destroy memes, and recycle their associated resources. If you burn a book, that exterminates the associated memes and makes use of the resources that were being used to store them.

Eating memes.

- **Organic eats memetic** - For example, many memes are eaten by bacteria and fungi;
- **Memetic eats memetic** - for example predatory company takeovers and some types of garbage recycling systems;
- **Memetic eats organic** - for example most of the bio-diesel industry;

As with slavery, there are both willing and unwilling versions of predation. When a human eats a sea fish, that is an example of unwilling prey. When a human eats a lettuce, that is an example of a willing prey. There's a sense in which the lettuce *wants* to be eaten - rather like a fruit.

What about humans? Most memes are not represented in a human-edible format. However, some types of mint and gum have logos on them - and that would be one example of humans eating memes. As food becomes more synthetic, consumption of meme *products* by humans seems likely to become more frequent. However, in most of these cases these memes *want* to be eaten - which is an unconventional predator-prey situation. Currently, the reverse situation - where memes eat humans - is not very common.

9.12 A note about teleology

At this point certain philosophically inclined readers may be inclined to tell me that I *really* should not be talking about mints being "willing prey", or about robots being "willing slaves". These things, it may be patiently explained, don't have wills, and so can't will anything. Thinking otherwise, is teleology, or anthropomorphism, or some other dreadful thing. Mary Midgley (1979) is one of the better known proponents of this idea, with her:

> *Genes cannot be selfish or unselfish, any more than atoms can be*
> *jealous, elephants abstract or biscuits teleological.*

Such readers should be reminded that such usage is standard shorthand in biology - and that it is possible to "cash out" such descriptions in terms that are more amenable to a literal interpretation.

If we imagine each gene as being a general, then these generals would have their own wants, and understanding what *they* would want helps us to understand the behaviour of the whole organism. This is the "gene's eye view" - and part of the reason it is so useful is because the human brain is wired up to model other goal-directed dynamical systems by putting itself in their shoes (well not *literally* their shoes, *of course*).

Lettuces may not *literally* "want" to be eaten - but they *don't* evolve protective armour and toxins to help prevent their consumption - in contrast to, say, peach seeds - which do *not* "want" to be eaten. One way of understanding that is to adopt the "gene's eye view", and to consider what strategy lettuce genes *would* want, *if* they were little, dumb, self-interested agents who wanted to reproduce themselves.

10 Parasitism - Memetic epidemiology

This chapter is about how ideas behave like infectious diseases - and how the spread of ideas can usefully be modelled with the same framework which is used to describe the spread of parasites and pathogens.

10.1 Memetic infections

One of the basic ideas in memetics is that human brains act as hosts to visiting creatures from the cultural realm. The visitors may be beneficial symbionts, deleterious parasites or anything in between. The parasites are the ones that cause us to

Cigarette advertisement.

be apes with infected brains. In this chapter, we will be looking *particularly* at parasites. Some examples of cultural parasites:

- **Cigarette advertising** - results in the smoking epidemic;
- **Junk food advertising** - results in the obesity epidemic;

These are culturally-transmitted phenomena which spread through society *despite* the negative effect they have on the fitness of *most* of their hosts.

These are both memetically engineered parasites. They are bad for their *most* of their hosts, but result in benefits to the heads of companies that manufacture and distribute the supporting products.

10.2 Infectious disease epidemiology

There is an existing framework within biology for modelling the relationship between hosts and parasites. The framework is known as *infectious disease epidemiology*. In memetics the basic idea is to reuse this framework to model the relationship between the human hosts and their memes.

Modelling memes as infectious disease agents allows a number of concepts from the biological realm to be reused in a memetic context:

The concept of *infectiousness* can be used to describe how easily an idea spreads from one person to the next. *Immunity* represents resistance to infection. Hosts have *immune systems* that reject bad or harmful ideas. The hosts display *immune reactions* to ideas that appear harmful. Immune defences may be built-up by using *inoculations* or education relating to avoiding getting infected. There are memetic *immune system disorders*, involving excessive suspicion, shyness, paranoia - and so on. There are treatment and recuperation centres to allow infections to be combated. The idea of an *infection period* describes how long infections persist for before they are defeated by the immune system - or otherwise eliminated. There are also *persistent memetic infections* that can last for a lifetime.

10.3 Host harm

By definition, parasites harm their hosts. However, the degree to which they do that varies. Parasites are commonly classified according to how they hamper their hosts as follows:

- **Biotrophic parasites** - among agents with the potential to spread horizontally some parasites may prefer to keep their hosts alive. These are known as "biotrophic" - meaning that they don't kill their own host. Many parasites act as though they want their host continue interacting with others. The living host may act as a reservoir of infection - whereas once a host is dead it may no longer be actively used to spread infection to others. Most parasitic memes are biotrophic.
- **Castrating parasites** - parasites often want to keep their hosts alive - but rarely need them to be able to reproduce. Parasites typically have few qualms about sterilising their hosts and using their reproductive resources for their own ends. Castration is a relatively common result of infection, among those parasites powerful enough to produce it. An example from the organic world: the bacterium *Pasteuria ramosa* produces spores that accumulate in large numbers within the host.

They are not released until after the host is dead. The host is castrated by its infection. Only a few memes actually castrate their hosts. Memeplexes involving not having babies do exist. However a much more common case is for memes to reduce host reproductive output - rather than completely castrating them.

- **Necrotrophic parasites** - a more worrying type of parasite doesn't bother with keeping its host alive. Instead it dismantles its hosts body, takes all the resources that it can find and then uses them to make more copies of itself, killing the host in the process. Such parasites are known as "Necrotrophic". The Ebola virus is an example of a pathogen that works something like this. Fortunately, this model does not represent a common means of propagation for memes - though *perhaps* some martyrdom memes could be thought of as working a little like this.

A number of factors affect how parasites impact on host fitness. Vertical transmission (from host parent to offspring) align the interests of parasites with those of their hosts. A parasite saturating its host population can have a similar effect. Frequent opportunities for horizontal transmission tend to result in parasites that do not care for the welfare of their hosts - since they will soon be moving on. As Robert Wright (1999) points out:

> *The more easily viruses are transmitted from body to body, the less their fertility depends on their hosts' survival. So highly lethal viruses tend to evolve in urban areas.*

Infectious diseases typically benefit from high host population densities. Many memes certainly behave as though they like to be in areas where there are lots of people.

10.4 Transmission

The term "transmission" refers to how parasites spread from one host to the next. If population has not been saturated with the parasite, it can profitably spread to other members of the population. There are a couple of ways of doing that:

- **Vertical transmission** - from hosts to their own offspring;
- **Horizontal transmission** - between hosts who are not necessarily related;

The interests of parasites that spread "vertically" down the host generations tend to become aligned with the interests of their hosts. They tend to want to keep the hosts alive and help them to reproduce - since their reproduction depends on that of their hosts. However *most* parasites have at least *some* potential to spread horizontally. In that case, their interests often conflict with those of their hosts - and they often come to compete with their them for reproductive resources. Most memes are capable of horizontal transmission. Vertical transmission happens for traits like circumcision, walking, speaking and religion - where the memetic influence is applied to young children.

Transmission can be assisted by agents (known as vectors), or can take place via inanimate forces, such as convection or diffusion. Intermediate hosts are sometimes employed during active transmission.

Transmission can be directional. Some of the possibilities are listed below - complete with examples from the cultural realm:

- **Uni-directional** - for example, a telephone;
- **Bi-directional** - for example, a telephone conversation;
- **Multi-directional** - for example, a satellite television broadcast;
- **Omni-directional** - for example, a radio blaring out pop-music;

10.5 Epidemics

The term "epidemic" is used to refer to an unexpected outbreak of disease. In the context of memetics, it is usually used to refer to an outbreak of transmissible cultural parasites. Transmission-driven epidemics are *usually* characterised by an initial period of exponential growth. This is illustrated in the diagram here - which is based on a computer simulation of an epidemic.

Epidemics initially exhibit exponential growth.

10.6 Vectors

Deer tick: spreads Lyme disease.

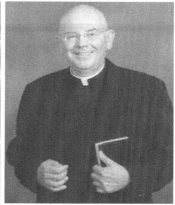

Preacher: spreads catholicism.

The term "vector" refers to agents which actively spread parasites around.

Vectors may themselves be infected, and may be manipulated by the parasite - or they may just passively carry the parasite around. Missionaries are example of meme vectors.

10.7 Epidemic threshold

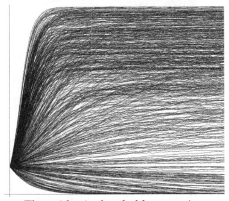 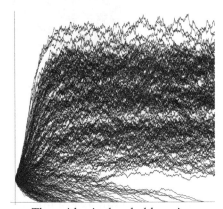

The epidemic threshold – no noise. *The epidemic threshold - noise.*

Here, the total number of infected individuals is plotted against time.

A few words about the model that produced the results shown in these diagrams. The model is *extremely* simple. Individuals are modelled as being either infected or not infected. They have a constant probability of dying in each generation. Senescence and pathology are not modelled. Infected agents infect more agents (randomly) in each generation. Then some individuals (chosen randomly) die, and are replaced by *healthy* newly-born individuals. The population size is a fixed constant - so the death rate and birth rate are equal. The plots are made by varying two parameters: the infection rate and the death/birth rate. These variables are sampled from a uniform bounded random distribution to create the plots.

In the diagram on the right, the infection and death rates are both higher - resulting in more of a random walk, with an increased chance of fluctuations that lead to extinction. These diagrams show a substantial seed population - in order to better illustrate the dynamics of the exponential decay. In the real world, most epidemics start with smaller seed populations - so the extinction gutter is nearer and more frequently encountered.

10.8 Pandemics

Pandemics are epidemics that have come of afflict a large number of members of the population. Examples of global memetic pandemics include smoking, obesity, pornography, soap operas, computer games and pop music.

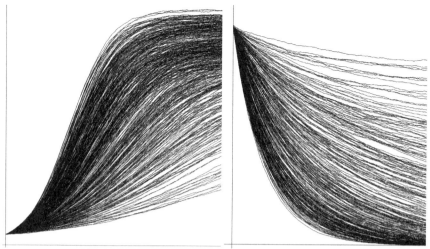

Epidemic success.   *Epidemic failure.*

Again, the total number of infected individuals is plotted against time.

10.9 Population saturation

Persistent widespread infections can reach the point where most of the population is infected. Once the population is saturated the parasites face a bit of a different situation from when there were spare hosts available. They are pushed into competition with each other - and this change in their ecosystem often results in some changes to the strategies that are used. A memetic example of saturation

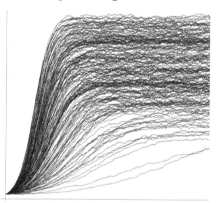

Population saturation.

would be the decimal number system - which is used by almost everybody.

If a resident infection prevents subsequent infections establishing themselves, getting to the hosts before other parasites do is sometimes favoured - which results in quite a different set of selection pressures on the parasites. If parasites can successfully displace a host's existing occupants, then the parasites may still compete directly with one another. However, often the residents have an advantage. They are more numerous and often are better adapted to the host's body - and so occupy all the available niches inside it. Sometimes, residents can recruit the host's immune system to help repel any invaders - for instance the commandment "thou shall have no gods before me" makes use of the host's memetic immune system to repel prospective invaders.

Parasites that dominate their niche can *sometimes* establish a monopoly, obliterating other types of parasite that compete with them for host resources.

10.10 Terminology note

Although the concepts of *transmission, vectors, epidemics, epidemic threshold, pandemics* and *saturation* all arise from epidemiology, much the same concepts apply equally well to non-parasitic symbionts.

10.11 Behavioural modification

Pathogens typically modify or control the behaviour of their hosts, in order to facilitate their own reproduction. For example:

- **Pertussis** - causes coughing behaviour;
- **Influenza** - causes sneezing behaviour;
- **Rabies** - causes biting behaviour;
- **Scabies** - causes itching behaviour;
- **Gastroenteritis** - causes diarrhoea and vomiting;

Some more sophisticated parasites manipulate the nervous system of their hosts with what appears to be considerable skill in order to obtain the required behaviour. Some examples of that:

- **Euhaplorchis Californiensis** - Infects fish - makes them swim near the surface, so they are eaten by birds;
- **Glyptapanteles** - Infects caterpillars - makes them defend the parasite's brood;
- **Leucochloridium** - Infects snails - makes them seek sunlight, so they are eaten by birds;
- **Spinochordodes Tellinii** - Infects grasshoppers - makes them drown themselves;
- **Dicrocoelium dendriticum** - Infects ants - makes them climb foliage, so they are eaten by cows;
- **Schistocephalus solidus** - Infects sticklebacks - makes them swim near the surface, so they are eaten by birds;
- **Toxoplasma Gondii** - Infects mice - makes them fearless, and more likely to be eaten by cats;
- **Hymenoepimecis Argyraphaga** - Infects spiders - makes them sit in the middle of their web;
- **Acanthocephala** - (thorny headed worm) Infects pill bugs - makes them dance in the sun;
- **Sicus ferrugineus** - (Conopid fly) Infects bees - makes them bury themselves;

- **Cordyceps Unilateralis** - Infects ants - makes them climb foliage;
- **Entomophaga grylli** - Infects grasshoppers - makes them climb high - to help spore distribution;
- **Polymorphus Paradoxus** - Infects *Gammarus lacustris* (shrimp-like amphipod) - makes them rise to the surface;
- **Ophiocordyceps unilateralis** - Infects ants - makes them jaw clamp on major leaf veins.

Human mind control parasites have been featured in popular movies, notably, The Puppet Masters, The Wrath of Khan and Slither. Many have compared memes to "Puppet Masters" and "Body Snatchers" - referencing these kinds of films - because the mind-control capabilities of memes are reminiscent of the mind-control capabilities shown by the parasites in these popular movies.

10.12 The Red Queen

The *Red Queen Hypothesis* is named after the Red Queen's race in Lewis Carroll's Through the Looking-Glass. In the book, the Red Queen and Alice run for a long time - but they don't seem to be getting anywhere. They then have the following dialogue:

Well, in our country," said Alice, still panting a little, "you'd generally get to somewhere else — if you run very fast for a long time, as we've been doing."

"A slow sort of country!" said the Queen. "Now, here, you see, it takes all the running you can do, to keep in the same place. If you want to get somewhere else, you must run at least twice as fast as that!"

The Red Queen.

The *Red Queen Hypothesis* refers to the way in which organisms constantly need to adapt to maintain their fitness - in the face of constantly and rapidly evolving parasites. It invokes an evolutionary arms race between hosts and parasites. The short generation time of the parasites results in rapid evolution for them. This typically results in an endless chase through gene-space as the hosts seek to avoid the attentions of the parasites - while the parasites hunt them down.

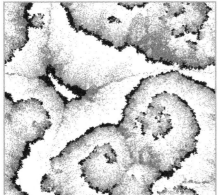

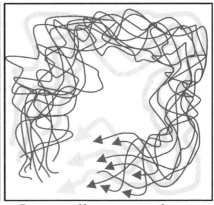

Cellular automaton simulation of host-parasite chase.

Diagram of host-parasite chase in fitness landscape.

In the above-left diagram, parasites chase immobile hosts through physical space, as well as through gene-space - in a cellular automaton simulation of disease transmission. The simulation was designed to illustrate the *Red Queen* chase. An interactive version is available online at:

http://alife.co.uk/eosex/

The above-right diagram offers a symbolic representation of parasites chasing hosts around in gene-space.

The parasites are undesirable from the perspective of individual hosts - but they *can* have some overall positive effects. They constantly deform the fitness landscape of their hosts, keeping the hosts constantly off balance. This can result in previously separated peaks in the fitness landscape of the hosts sometimes turning into a ridge system - creating paths that lead up and away from what would otherwise have been sub-optimal adaptive peaks, thus promoting evolutionary change.

10.13 Sexual recombination

William Hamilton promoted the idea that this *Red Queen race* helped hosts to invent sexual recombination - so they would be better able to defend themselves against the attention of parasites by maintaining a large quantity of genetic variation in their

William Hamilton.

populations - thereby making life for parasites more challenging.

Sexual recombination is one of nature's masterpieces, and it seems likely that we have a *Red Queen race* to blame for it.

10.14 The Red Queen of culture

These days, *Red Queen race* races are also taking place in the cultural realm. There, the rapidly-reproducing symbionts are not bacteria and viruses, but memes - swarming in our heads and infesting our computer networks. As with the organic *Red Queen races* some of the memetic symbionts are parasites - which the hosts usually want to avoid. As in the organic realm, the short generation time of the memetic parasites results in rapid evolution. This pushes their hosts around in gene-space, keeping them constantly off balance, and accelerating genetic change in the host gene pool.

We can see a *Red Queen* race between organic hosts and cultural pathogens taking place in the world of junk food. Junk food manufacturers race to provide the tastiest, most addictive foodstuffs to consumers.

Vulnerable consumers eat the junk food, and get sick. Some become obese, others eventually die. The cultural pathogens evolve quickly, rapidly tuning into the

Junk food.

weaknesses in the taste discrimination systems of their hosts. By contrast, their hosts evolve much more slowly.

10.15 Evolution towards mutualism

Pathogens whose spread is closely aligned with the spread of the genes of their hosts and pathogens who have saturated their host populations have a tendency to evolve so that they become commensuals or mutualists - symbionts which are neutral, or beneficial to their hosts. They still need to steal resources from their host to fuel their own reproductive processes - but they often try to avoid other types of destructive interference. This idea of parasitic evolution towards mutualism is backed by both theory (Herre et al, 1999) and observations (Weeks et al, 2007).

Though parasites harm their hosts, the extent to which parasites and hosts cooperate can be quite large. For example, a parasite known as *Cymothoa exigua* consumes the tongue of some fishes and then replaces it with its own body, which then takes over all the functional roles of the fish's tongue. This is illustrated in the following photographs:

Cymothoa exigua. *Cymothoa exigua.*

It is *rare* for a parasite to *completely* take over the role of a host organ - but this example illustrates that it *can* sometimes happen.

10.16 Optimal virulence

There's a model called "optimal virulence" - which suggests that parasites attempt to optimise their relationship with their host to provide the greatest reproductive output for themselves. The results depend on the outcome of a battle with the host's immune system - and *optimal virulence* is not *necessarily* attained - *if* the host's immune system is in good working order. This idea transfers across into the cultural domain without modification.

10.17 Resource competition with the host

Like any living thing, parasites need resources to fuel their reproductive processes. Many parasites are *entirely* dependent on their host for resources. In such cases there almost inevitably ensues a competition over resources. The parasites typically steal resources directly from their host, while the hosts try to stop them - *usually* by using their immune system. From the perspective of parasites, it is *often* in their interest to have the host live for as long as possible - because, while the host is still alive, it can actively transmit parasites to others. Often, when the host dies, its parasites die too. Parasites may want their host to live a long life - but they often do not care very much about whether the host reproduces. So when stealing the host's resources to further their own ends, parasites have a preference for the reproduction budget, rather than the maintenance and repair budget.

10.18 Effects on fertility

In the organic world, some parasites sterilise their hosts. For example, Sphaerularia bombi (a nematode worm) attacks hibernating queen bees and sterilises them, using their reproductive resources to manufacture nematode worm offspring and litter them around the hibernation site to await next year's queen.

Reproduction rate

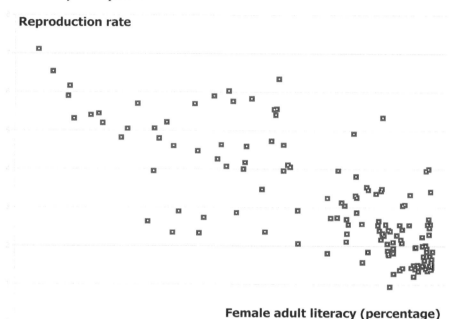

Female adult literacy (percentage)

A plot of female fertility against female adult literacy. Data compiled by Earth Policy Institute from UNESCO, at stats.uis.unesco.org, in 2010.

In the realm of culture, education level is correlated with fewer births. The effect is seen in both men and women. The more educated you are the fewer children you have. The more memes a country has, the fewer babies people tend to have. The effect is known as the "demographic transition". Japan illustrates this principle taken to an extreme. By contrast, the Amish, who mostly reject technology, have high fertility. Few things do as much damage to human fertility as getting a college education. This observation is broadly consistent with the idea that memes propagate themselves at the expense of host reproductive resources. This effect is illustrated in the above scatter-plot diagram. I should probably add that *Gapminder* have female fertility data going back to 1800 and offer some *beautiful* animations which show how it has changed since then.

The relationship between education and fertility is a statistical association - and so it does not *necessarily* indicate a direct cause and effect relationship.

It is certainly possible to *imagine* factors that result in having babies at a young age interfering with your education. However, it seems likely that the effect goes more the other way - something about countries which have higher levels of education causes people in those countries to have fewer babies.

There have been a variety of suggestions relating to the issue of why this might be happening. Many of them invoke increased access to family planning and birth control. Under this hypothesis the humans can repeatedly obtain the rewards associated with having sex, without paying the costs associated with having to bring up children.

Another idea is based on *r/K selection theory*. This refers to an axis along which reproductive strategies can vary.

- **r-selected organisms** - many offspring, little parental investment.
- **K-selected organisms** - few offspring lots of parental investment.

Many organisms (including humans) can adopt different positions along the r/K selection axis in response to differences in their environment. Which strategy it is best to adopt depends on what other individuals are doing. If everyone else is producing high quality offspring, then it can pay to do the same, since otherwise your own offspring will not be competitive or viable. This can produce a counter-intuitive effect - where a greater quantity of resources results in the production of fewer offspring.

The idea of *r/K selection theory* has multiple applications in memetics. One of these ideas is that K-selected organisms invest more in education than r-selected organisms do. Thus one might expect that memes might attempt to manipulate human society so that it is more K-selected - so that more resources are invested in memes. This is consistent with what we see. Meme-rich countries exhibit more K-selected organisms. One possible explanation of this is that the memes have been successful in manipulating the environment of their hosts so that it is more K-selected - in order to gain a larger chunk of the available resources. It has been pointed out that some societies of humans systematically reduce their reproductive output to the point of sub-replacement fertility. The r/K theory can extend that far - provided the perceived competitiveness of the environment is sufficiently high.

There are also some other ideas in the space to consider. High levels of memetic infections may be successful at diverting host reproductive resources towards meme survival that offers another explanation of how the memes may be reproducing at the expense of the humans. Also, meme-rich environments are radically different from the ancestral environment, increasing the chances of the host behaving maladaptively.

Several possible explanations have been given, but it seems possible that they are complementary. Memes could be using family planning, contraception and belief systems to reduce human resource expenditure on offspring, thereby maximising the resources they have available for reproducing memes. They could *also* be manipulating the human environment so that highly K-selected reproductive strategies are selected - creating an environment that favours meme reproduction.

So: the mass sterilisation of humans by memes seems likely to be currently taking place. Looking to the future, it seems likely that human reproductive output will be lowered further. A lot more social contact will take place over the internet in environments where sharing body fluids is not practical. There will be more computer game addiction and pornography, and after a while, it seems likely that machines will be able to provide better romantic and sexual experiences than other humans. The human gene pool will respond to these changes, but may do so slowly. There are other factors involved, so it is not trivial to predict, but it seems possible that this effect may develop rapidly enough to halt - and then reverse - the current climb in human populations. *If* this happens, it would be a remarkable development.

10.19 Effects on lifespan

Many parasites do not stop at stealing host reproductive resources. They damage and gradually kill their hosts. Other parasites act to preserve their hosts out of self-preservation. So, next, we will look at the effects of parasites on lifespan:

Parasistes can kill

Necrotrophic parasites reduce host lifespan, by taking the host's resources for themselves. Parasites often casually damage the host as part of their own reproductive processes. The AIDS virus causes damage to the host's immune system - resulting in the host's life being shortened. As hosts age, they gradually clock up an extensive list of persistent viral infections. Also, each individual viral infection adapts to its host using natural selection to tune into the flaws of the host's immune system. In some cases, hosts are born with finite defences, and these are gradually eaten away by parasites. Tooth enamel is probably a reasonable example of this. Persistent infections can interact synergetically - for example, if one infection compromises the host's immune system, other residents may benefit. Parasites are implicated in many common causes of death. Their effects contribute to the process of senescence.

Life extension by parasites

Many parasites do not have a noticeable negative effect on the lifespan of their hosts. Indeed, in many cases, it is in the parasite's interest to have its host live for as long as possible - because, while the host is still alive, it can still actively transmit parasites to others. Often, when the host dies, its parasites die too. Extending the lifespan of your host while simultaneously stealing resources from it and using the host to propagate your germ line is not a trivial exercise. However there *are* some metabolic pathways which could facilitate this.

Many large organisms face a resource allocation dilemma - involving whether to allocate resources to reproductive processes or to ones associated with bodily maintenance. Since different tradeoffs between reproduction and maintenance are desirable under different circumstances, organisms have metabolic switches to control these tradeoffs. One example is the *famine survival* mode associated with dietary energy restriction. When dietary energy is scarce resources are channelled away from the reproduction-related activities that *normally* preoccupy most adult organisms - and into activities that promote survival. The organisms attempt to survive until the end of the famine - in the hope of refeeding themselves and reproducing when it is over. This *famine survival* mode can be activated deliberately, and dietary energy restriction is the best-established means of extending the lifespan of large animals. This illustrates one metabolic pathway which parasites could use to extend the lifespan of their hosts. If you can stop your host getting into risky male combat situations, that can also sometimes help to extend their life. For animals where birth is risky (like it is for humans) avoiding pregnancy may be another means of extending host lifespan.

Parasites that increase host lifespan exist. For example, *Hymenolepis diminuta* increases the lifespan of its beetle hosts (Hurd et Al. 2001).

Actual effects on lifespan

Since there are theoretical arguments for both life-shortening and life-extension by parasites, what *actually* happens in the case of memes? We know that, the more memes a country has, the longer people tend to live. Japan offers an extreme example of this principle in action. The Japanese people are among the most meme-saturated people - and also the most long lived people - in the world. By contrast, in Africa there are fewer memes - and shorter lives. This may not have much to do with the parasitic aspect of memes, though - we can be *fairly* sure that memes are, on average, beneficial. They were certainly beneficial to our ancestors, anyway.

10.20 Immunity

There is a whole chapter devoted to the subject of immunity later in this book. See that for coverage of the topic.

10.21 Meme shedding

"Virus shedding" refers the way in which infected hosts often liberally shed viruses they are infected with into their environment.

Similarly, "meme shedding" refers to the liberal shedding by hosts of copies of their memes into their environment.

Meme shedding is a *very* commonly-used advertising technique. Using logos on

Meme shedding.

products typically results in *meme shedding*. Display advertising also works using *meme shedding*. For many memes, public display in a populated area is sufficient to create copies of the meme in the minds of large numbers of people.

The internet now allows *meme shedding* to take place on a global scale - and it is now possible for one individual to quickly infect millions of others with their memes.

Much *meme shedding* takes place using visual media - but there is also audio meme shedding - as seen in the form of street preaching.

10.22 Virus talk

Many have come to refer to memes as being akin to viruses. So, we have "virus of the mind", "thought contagion", "viral videos" and so on. This characterisation is understandable - but it carries with it the implicit suggestion that the effect of the memes on host fitness is negative. Since many memes are mutualists - and act as beneficial symbionts - that is not necessarily true.

Also, meme enthusiasts repeatedly use examples in which meme fitnesses is negatively correlated with host fitnesses - and so the memes are profiting at the expense of the genes of their hosts. One reason such examples are used so frequently is because cases where there are conflicts between the cultural and organic realms represent good evidence for memetics. Another reason is because tales of conflict are typically more interesting and exciting that tales of cooperation. As a result a selection effect causes these stories to be spread around more frequently.

A potential disadvantage of all this "virus talk" is that it may result in a popular misunderstanding of memetics - where people may think that all of the ideas involved are considered to be deleterious. This implication is *not* intended by those using the "virus" metaphor.

The use of epidemiological models and terminology in memetics is *not* usually intended to literally imply that the memes involved are deleterious to their hosts. Epidemiology just has some of the best terminology and models available, that's all. "Plagues", "epidemics", "vectors" and "transmission" are all concepts from epidemiology that apply equally well to mutualist relationships. Beneficial symbionts have "epidemic thresholds" just as much as deleterious parasites do. We can work to try and develop better terminology, but that should *probably* not stop up from borrowing extensively from epidemiology in the mean time. The epidemiological terminology is certainly *vastly* better than the early anthropological concept of "cultural diffusion" that preceded it.

One group that is frequently unhappy with the "virus" talk is marketers. Marketing is a *major* application for memetics. Those trying to set up win-win relationships between producers and consumers do not always take kindly to the idea that they are spreading "viral plagues" or attempting to set off "epidemics".

10.23 Frequency-dependent selection

Parasites often gain some advantages from being rare. When they are rare the immune system of the hosts they target "forgets" about them. This means that diseases can be hard to obliterate completely, and can wait in the wings until the situation changes and their next opportunity arises. Parasites, rather obviously, *also* benefit from their hosts being common. David Attenborough explains how these dynamics operate:

> *It's not just ants that fall victim to this killer. There are, literally, thousands of types of Cordyceps fungi, and remarkably, each specialises on just one species. But these attacks do have a positive effect on the jungle's diversity since parasites like these stop any one animal getting the upper hand: the more numerous a species becomes the more likely it is to be attacked by its nemesis, a Cordyceps fungus.*

Barnett and Sorenson 2002 point out that much the same dynamics may act in the cultural realm, and act to prevent any one type of cultural entity from becoming *too* dominant. In the realm of economics, this idea suggests that there may be a kind of *natural* force that acts in a similar manner to the monopolies and mergers commission - specifically targeting large monocultures and promoting diversity.

10.24 Memes parasitising other memes

Most of the examples in this chapter are of cultural systems acting as parasites on organic ones. However, other types of parasitic relationship are possible. In particular, memes can act as parasites on other memes:

Memes acting as parasites on other memes.

In the photograph above, a piece of famous artwork by the graffiti artist known as "Banksy" is having its energies sapped by a hitchhiking crocodile with an advertisement painted onto its side - which impinges on the graffiti artwork from the bottom-left corner.

Memes that parasitise other memes can also engage in *Red Queen* races with them. An interesting example of this kind of dynamics comes from the world of computer printer ink cartridges. This example *also* illustrates the principle that increased host diversity leads makes it harder for parasites to migrate between hosts - slowing their spread.

Computer printer manufacturers would like their customers to buy ink cartridges from them, at prices they dictate. However, they face competition from third-party ink-producers who want to plug their cartridges into the printer cartridge slots, thereby intercepting the printer manufacturers' revenue stream. These organisations act rather like parasites on the printer manufacturers. The printer manufacturers counter this interception using a strategy sometimes known as "twisting and turning". This involves constantly changing the details of the interface between the printer and the ink cartridge. The effect of this is to increase the quantity of research and development work that the third-party ink manufacturers need to do to stay in business - which increases their costs and makes their products less attractive. Also there is a delay between the release of the printer and when the third-party ink manufacturers copy the cartridges.

Printer cartridges illustrate parasite-caused diversity.

The result of this process is a huge diversity of printer cartridge types. The photographs above show the range of printer cartridges in a single shop.

10.25 Genes can parasitise memes

Organic parasites can attack a cultural entities. This most probably most frequently happens with microorganisms and fungi. It can also happen on a macroscopic scale. Here messages from the cultural realm are being put into the shade by a ubiquitous organic climbing parasite: ivy.

Organic systems can parasitise memetic ones.

11 Mutualism - Mutually-beneficial relationships

This chapter is about how positive ideas behave like beneficial symbionts - and the adaptations which humans have developed to support them.

11.1 Mutually beneficial symbiosis

Beneficial symbiotic relationships between different species are characterised by mutualism. Mutually-beneficial interactions lead to adaptations which support the symbiosis. This contrasts with more negative relationships - which tend to produce defence systems and immune reactions.

Honey bee and flower mutualism.

11.2 Organic-organic mutualism

Humans are in a mutually-beneficial symbiosys with gut bacteria, dairy cows, carrots, dogs - and many other creatures.

Examples of mutually-beneficial symbiosys drawn from the rest of biology include: bees and flowers, lichens, cleaner fish, and nitrogen-fixing bacteria that nest in plant roots. Many land plants rely on mycorrhizal relationships with fungi to provide them with inorganic compounds and trace elements. The eucaryotic cell is itself the result of an ancient beneficial symbiosis.

Beneficial symbiosis is found in many other places in the animal kingdom. Ants offer many rich examples of the phenomenon. Ants and termites cultivate fungi in underground farms. They feed the

Leaf cutter ants.

fungi with decaying vegetable matter. Fungus-farming ants have special glands on their bodies where they secrete fluids that feed specialised bacteria (genus *Streptomyces*). The bacteria in turn produce antibiotics, which fight a parasite (*Escovopsis*) that feeds on the ant's fungal symbiote. Tree ants receive shelter from specialised structures in the trees in return for protecting the trees from predators. Ants also have symbiotic relationships with aphids. The aphids suck juices from plants and then produce honeydew for the ants. Ants transport aphids onto plants, protect them from predators, build mounds of earth up around plant stems, to provide aphids with shaded and moist environments, and over-winter them in their underground nests.

11.3 Organic-memetic mutualism

Many aspects of culture are beneficial to their hosts. Language memes are beneficial. Maths memes are beneficial. Science memes are beneficial. Much cultural knowledge is useful in earning a living, finding a mate or raising your kids. We can see that memes have - on average - been beneficial to their hosts - since humans exhibit meme-spreading adaptations.

11.4 Supporting adaptations

Mutualism is often characterised by the formation of adaptations which support the relationship. For example, in the organic world, flowers have specialised structures which offer nectar to their pollinators, while showering them with pollen.

To help memes spread, humans have adopted adaptations that make them babble and chatter. The human larynx has changed its form and function. The human brain case has swelled up, to better accommodate the memes. Humans no-longer bristle with hostility quite so much when they encounter other members of their own species - and instead exhibit *ultrasociality*.

One important type of adaptation is a home - and we will look at those next:

11.5 Symbiont homes

Looking at other mutually beneficial symbiotic relationships, it is quite common for the larger organisms to develop swollen body parts which act as homes for their smaller symbionts.

Fig wasp on fig.

For example, each fig plant has a mutual symbiosis with its own species of fig wasp - which is solely responsible for pollinating it. The wasps live inside the figs. Coevolution with these symbiotic visitors has utterly transformed the fig - to the point where figs are utterly unlike any other fruit.

The master animal endosymbiotes are ants. There are so many symbiotic relationships between plants and ants and plants that ant-friendly plants have their own name: *myrmecophytes*. There are over 100 different genera of *myrmecophytes*. Many produce *domatia* - which are are internal plant structures that are adapted for habitation. Domatia adapted for habitation by ants are called *myrmecodomatia*. Some examples:

- **Australian ant-plants** (*Myrmecodia*) develop swollen bulbs at the base of their stems to accommodate ants;
- **Swollen Thorn Acacias** of Central America have enlarged hollow

thorns that act as homes for their ants;
- **Tococa guianensis** (a plant from Peru) develops sac-like outgrowths near the base of the plant for its ants;
- **Costa Rican pepper plants** host *Pheidole* ants which live inside their hollow stems;
- **Cordia nodosa** plants house *Azteca* ants inside swollen stems;

Alder trees have root galls whose purpose is to act as homes for nitrogen-fixing bacteria.

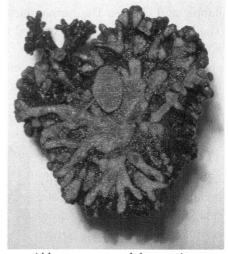

Alder tree root nodule.   *Alder tree root nodule - section.*

The alder tree root nodules even have a rather brain-like appearance. This is because they are trying to maximise surface area, which in turn is because that is where the nitrogen-fixing bacteria interact with the surrounding air. The surface of the brain also has valuable properties, and consequentially becomes wrinkled to maximise the space devoted to its surface.

These are not gall-like swellings that are created by parasites, but adaptations by the host to create space for the mutualists. In the case of the *Swollen Thorn Acacias* this is illustrated by the fact that they still develop their hollow thorns - whether ants take up residence inside them or not.

Animal bodies *also* have cavities which allow other animals to live inside. For example, an *acarinarium* is a specialized anatomical structure which evolved to facilitate the retention of mites. These are typically found on bees and wasps. Studies have found that some of these mites pay their hosts rent - by acting to guard the host infants while they are developing.

11.6 The big brain as a meme nest

Susan Blackmore pioneered the hypothesis that the human big brain is *actually* an adaptation for storing large quantities of memes. She has a whole chapter (called "The big brain") on this hypothesis in her 1999 book *The Meme Machine*.

The basic idea

The idea that the enlarged human cranium might be an adaptation for housing our mutualist symbiont visitors is an astonishing and counter-intuitive one.

However, culture and co-evolution with memes has resulted in most of the main ways in which we differ from chimpanzees. Memes are, on average beneficial, and as a result of this, humans feature adaptations that are oriented towards hosting their memes - ultrasociality, incessant babbling, and an enlarged cranium to act as a home for all the memes. It makes a lot of sense for our large brain to be a meme-hosting adaptation.

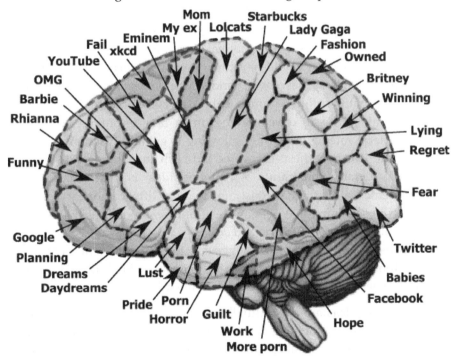

The big brain.

Other ideas

To see how plausible the idea that the enlarged human brain is a meme nest really is, one has to consider its merits *relative* to other theories that purport to explain the same observations:

- **Machiavellian intelligence hypothesis** - This is probably the best-known hypothesis. It is also known as *The Social Brain Hypothesis*. It states that humans became as smart as they did as a result of an arms race involving social skills - lying, cheating, manipulation - and the detection of these things in others.
- **Sexual selection** - This hypothesis proposes that some aspect of being smart was sexy - and that selection by members of the opposite sex (probably *mostly* females) resulted in large brains being favoured. This makes the brain the human equivalent of a peacock tail. This idea - along with the *Machiavellian intelligence hypothesis* - is discussed at length in a fine book: *The Runaway Brain*.
- **Neoteny** - Another idea is that neoteny was responsible. Young infants have disproportionately large heads compared to adult forms. Human evolution features neoteny. So, our large heads could be a side effect of neoteny.
- **Bipedalism** - Another idea is that our large craniums resulted from the tendency toward bipedalism in our species. Bipedalism, in turn, forced a narrowing of the pelvic region making it more difficult for females to give birth. Selection would have then favoured females who gave birth to premature, less developed, and, therefore, smaller infants. Being born premature allows human babies to come into the world while their brains are still developing. Human brains continue to grow at rapid, fetal rates after birth - allowing a greater eventual size to be attained. This hypothesis is covered in Lynch and Granger (2008).
- **Lifted dietary constraints** - Another idea is that omega-3 fats represented a nutritional constraint that got lifted by dietary changes, which possibly involved eating meat and seafood. That hypothesis is laid out in the book *The Driving Force*.
- **Tool use** - Early hypotheses suggested that environmental challenges and tool use drove the evolution of big brains. Such ideas have now *mostly* been superseded by more social hypotheses.

Many of these ideas are not mutually exclusive. It is possible that each of them contributed something to the enlargement of the human brain. However, it *also* seems likely that some of these hypotheses are more important than other ones.

The place of the meme hypothesis

The idea that our big brains are meme nests is broadly compatible with the idea that runaway sexual selection is responsible. It suggests a sexually-selected arms race where what was sexy was a good sense of humour, being able to sing love songs, the ability to dance the latest dance - and other products of cultural evolution.

The *Machiavellian intelligence hypothesis* no doubt has some truth to it as well. It doesn't *really* explain why our brains blew up, while chimpanzee brains did not. What humans have that chimpanzees *mostly* don't is language, tools and culture.

Cost

The cost of a large brain in enormous. Brains must be providing a huge benefit to allow them to pay for themselves in the way that they did among our ancestors. Since the effects of culture are enormous, the meme theory shows promising signs of being able to account for the magnitude of the observed benefits.

Timing

The oldest archaeological sites containing tools are dated to 2.6-2.55 million years ago - around the beginning of the stone age - which is an *excellent* match for when the human brain first really started to inflate. Timing considerations provide significant support to the meme theory.

Testing

Of course, to qualify as being genuine science, hypotheses need to be testable, and one obvious weakness of these ideas is they they relate to events millions of years ago - and so are not trivial to test.

Sue suggested that investigating whether brain size was correlated with innovation ability would throw light on the issue. The corresponding test for the idea that too many memes crammed into a confined space was what created the selection pressure is to see whether brain size is correlated with the number of socially-transmitted skills. However, both these tests seem rather weak - neither seems likely to be falsified any time soon.

Both skulls and some aspects of culture fossilise. We will *probably* have access to enough evidence on the issue to get to the bottom of it in due course.

11.7 Memes and the evolution of human ultrasociality

Memetics offers an interesting explanation of human ultrasociality. The idea is that memes promote human ultrasociality by pushing humans into close proximity with each other, so the memes can infect new hosts.

Ultrasocial humans collect more memes, and memes are on average beneficial, so memes promoting ultrasociality have the effect of boosting in genetic fitness of their hosts. So, in meme-rich environments, the hosts eagerly embrace ultrasociality. Over time the trait gradually begins to migrate into their

Human ultrasociality.

germ line, via a process of *genetic assimilation*, so learning it becomes easier.

Ultrasociality memes offer a double fitness boost to other memes they have memetic linkage with. One boost due to being linked to the fit ultrasociality memes. A second boost is due to being more likely to be spread around by their more sociable hosts. Memeplexes thus welcome ultrasociality memes into their fold.

The whole idea seems to have been first proposed by Donald T. Campbell in 1983. It was taken up by Francis Heylighen in 1992, and then eventually popularised by Susan Blackmore in 1997 and 1999. Since then, the idea has been the subject of much experimental work, and several books - by Herbert Gintis, Peter Richerson, Robert Boyd, Joseph Henrich and others.

I count this as one of the triumphs of the field - an early speculation that has panned out in spectacular style.

11.8 Mutualism and ultrasociality

A fascinating speculation is that this may not be the first time that symbionts have produced ultrasociality. In *The Extended Phenotype*, Dawkins (1982, p. 208) speculated:

Termites.

> *Could the evolution of eusociality in the Isoptera be explained as an adaptation of the microscopic symbionts rather than of the termites themselves?*

It is also possible that Macrotermes (termite) colonies may owe their ultrasociality to their symbiosis with Termitomyces (fungus). Turner (2004) points out that the fungi do most of the metabolic work in the colony.

> *It is a bit of a misnomer to call the nest and mound a termite colony. The fungi account for roughly 85% of the colony's collective*

metabolism, which makes the fungi, not the termites, the major perturber of the nest environment.

Turner goes on to speculate that it may be a fungus colony, which has recruited termites to tend it:

Termite mound.

> *This raises the intriguing hypothesis that it is the fungi that are cultivating the termites, using their tendency to build regulated environments as a way to suppress the growth of Termitomyces' fungal competitors.*

Ants, bees and termites all feature a rich array of mutualist endosymbiotic bacteria.

Another interesting example of ultrasociality to consider is the naked mole rat. Mole rats are mammals with an eusocial, ant-like social structure - with oversize queens and sterile workers.

Here the most obvious symbionts live in guts of the mole rats. However, the gut symbionts of these creatures are not the ordinary kind. Mole rats mostly eat plant

Naked mole rat.

roots - and their gut bacteria have a lot of work to do. The naked mole rats eat each other's feces. This is called coprophagy - and is not *particularly* unusual for rodents - but young mole rats eat feces almost exclusively for the first few months of their lives. Feces-eating continues into adulthood. This set-up is probably a gut bacterium's dream.

There's another significant instance to consider as well: the eucaryotic endosymbiosis, and how that led to multicellularity. No doubt multicellularity started off as an instance of ultrasociality that deepened. Creatures like the *Portuguese Man o' War* - which consist of a colony of mostly-unrelated creatures, each of which acts as an organ - illustrate how even

Portuguese Man o' War.

unrelated creatures can benefit from clumping together.

If human, ant, termite and eucaryotic ultrasociality all arose out of close symbiotic relationships, that raises the question of what - if anything - it is about close symbiotic relationships that brings the creatures involved closer together.

Leaf cutter ants.

A speculative attempt at a general answer is that creatures often have to interact with other creatures of the same kind in order to reproduce. The more creatures involved in a symbiosis, the more forces there are pulling the various creatures together. For example, memes selfishly encourage humans interact with other humans because the reproduction of the memes depends on them finding new human hosts.

Causality may *also* work the other way around: creatures that tend to clump together are among those more likely to attract transmissible parasites. These may then saturate the population, and then evolve towards mutualism.

Many have noted that we are following the ants, termites and naked mole rats down the road that leads towards becoming a gigantic superorganism. If so, it may be the exact same force that led these creatures to become *ultrasocial* that is pushing us in the same direction. That would give the symbionts of these creatures a new significance. If it will throw light on human evolution, we may need to re-examine the forces leading to ultrasociality with the needs of their symbiotes in mind.

11.9 Adaptations for speaking

Humans can speak and sing. The ability to speak is not *just* something humans learn - individuals have *adaptations* for language acquisition and speech - in the form of dedicated brain regions, modified vocal folds and enhanced tongue, breath and lip control. Practically all the hypotheses about the origin of language explain this by invoking some form of gene-culture coevolution.

Humans benefit from learning to speak. Language offers humans a facility for controlling other humans remotely. With language, humans were able to express their wishes, and also better acquire memes from others. Memes also benefited *enormously* from the development of language. Language involves a digital symbol coding scheme which uses redundancy in the signal to implement error detection and correction. For memes, language transmission resulted in a dramatic boost in copying fidelity - resulting in larger quantities of information being able to persist down the generations.

Memetics raises the possibility that, while humans were evolving the ability to speak, languages themselves were evolving the ability to be spoken by humans. Memetics also suggests asking the question of how memes from the pre-linguistic era might have contributed towards the development of language. There are several possibilities here. It seems likely from phenomena such as walking and stone tools that humans developed imitative culture before they developed language. An enhanced ability to copy and imitate others would naturally lead to vocalisations *also* being imitated and copied. Enhanced sociality would also have helped to develop language by increasing the frequency of human interactions where communication is needed, magnifying the selection pressures favouring the development of language skills.

Memetics also raises the possibility of humans getting hijacked by linguistic constructs, and behaving maladaptively in response to them - for example by engaging in more babbling than is good for them. Perhaps this kind of memetic hijacking is responsible for some cases of chatterboxes and street preaching. The memes have taken over their brains, and are busy trying to reproduce themselves. This kind of thing can be referred to as *memetic hijacking*.

11.10 The significance of song

Singing probably developed in parallel with language. The ability to sing love songs could have been part of the selection pressure favouring vocalisation talents. Music is associated with dancing, and both are forms of human sexual display. In modern times the often-intense interest of young people in music is indicative of how closely music and mating are still tied together.

Rock musician.

Between them, singing and ultrasociality brought with them an opportunity for increasing meme transmission fidelity: group chanting. Chanting hymns together facilitates a kind of "group memory" effect - where it doesn't matter if *some* individuals forget the

Military choir.

words, since they can pick them up again from other group members during the next chanting session. The increased meme transmission fidelity as a result of this kind of action may help to explain why many humans participate regularly and enthusiastically in group chanting sessions. In modern times, this tendency is used by religions. It is also used by other organisations who seek to create artificial family groups, such as schools and the military.

11.11 Humans without memes

Humans are now quite dependent on their memes. Deprived of memes, humans are often reduced to an inarticulate, caveman-like state - where they have difficulty in making a living or finding a mate in the modern environment. We have *some* knowledge of the state, due to a series of natural experiments - resulting in the production of "feral children". A feral child is one which has been raised from a *relatively* young age by members of another species - without contact with human adults. Most accounts of feral children lack reliable documentation, but we do still know some

Caveman - not many memes.

things about the state. The behaviour of such children often matches that of the animals they are found with. Feral children typically lack basic social skills, have difficulty learning to use a toilet, cannot and walk upright, and have great difficulty in learning a human language.

11.12 Cultural-cultural mutualism

Memes may also have mutualistic relationships with other memes. They club together to make memeplexes. They also engage in larger-scale cooperative behaviour with other cultural entities. Some pictures illustrate the phenomenon:

The first is from the computer industry. Often lots of companies need to combine their resources in order to make a competitive machine:

Component logos on a computer.

The second shows feature logos on an LCD television. Many of the logos represent endorsement by standards organisations whose memes help to make up the product:

Feature logos on an LCD television.

11.13 Memetic linkage

Genetic linkage refers to the concept that alleles in close proximity to each other have an increased chance of being inherited together.

The concept of linkage applies well

Peanut butter and jelly sandwich.

in *memetics* too - leading to the idea of *memetic linkage* - which is the idea that nearby memes are more likely to be inherited together as a result of their close proximity.

To give some examples: consider the food combinations shown on the right. These are culturally transmitted - at least to some extent. People might independently discover that peanut butter and jelly taste good together, but proximity-based linkage seems likely to be the *primary* reason for the association between them in this basic recipe. In more sophisticated recipes, cultural inheritance and linkage are likely to

Strawberries and cream.

play an even bigger role. Also, adjacent sentences in documents tend to become linked together - and quotations may take adjacent sentences with them. Much the same thing happens with audio and video. Images may juxtapose unrelated subjects - which then become linked together.

The origins of the idea of *memetic linkage* can be traced back to the concept of an `adhesion' - which was developed by Edward Burnett Tylor and published in 1889.

Linkage-driven migration

An idea associated with the idea of genetic linkage is that alleles that have some kind of functional dependence on each other tend to migrate towards each other, so that linkage effects are increased, and the chances of them being divided from one another are smaller.

Quantifying linkage

In genetics linkage can be quantified by measuring how far the linked alleles are from one another on a chromosome - or by looking at descendants and calculating the chances that the alleles are inherited together.

In memetics, the second option is still possible - memes frequencies can be tracked just as gene frequencies can - but a predictive theory based on the original heritable information itself is not so easy. Memes do not line up neatly in a one-dimensional space where distances from one another can be calculated easily. It is possible to use the concept - but in general, the linkage-distance between two memes is not always as clearly-defined as the linkage-distance between two genes.

11.14 Memetic hitchhiking

Memetic linkage is an important concept in helping to explain how *memetic hitchhiking* works.

Genetic hitchhiking is a well-known and well-understood effect in organic biology - where a gene spreads by virtue of linkage to another gene which is subject to favourable selection.

"Memetic hitchhiking" is the same thing - but with memes, instead of genes.

Organic hitchhiking.

Memetic hitchhiking is a key marketing concept. It typically involves taking some viral content, and attaching some *payload* material that you want to spread around to it. The viral content spreads naturally, dragging the *payload* material along for the ride in the process.

The viral content can come from practically anywhere. *Memetic hitchhiking* is used by parodies. It is used by cover versions. Fan fiction uses it. It is used by many mashups.

In some cases, relatively little prevents the viral

Cereal packet with hitchhiking memes.

delivery mechanism being separated from the *payload*. One strategy for dealing with this is to make the advert is relatively inconspicuous - so that only a few would care enough to bother stripping it off. Another strategy is *interleaving*. Rather than just appending or prepending the payload to the viral content, a more sophisticated technique is to interleave the two - so they cannot *easily* be separated.

Marketing applications

Here we see a movie advertisement that has hitched a ride on a breakfast cereal. Most regular customers will buy the cereal anyway, and the advert comes along for the ride, and then is observed for extended periods on the breakfast table every morning for weeks, in an environment where it faces little competition.

Anyone who has ever attached a picture of a pretty lady to their article or product is essentially using *memetic hitchhiking* for marketing purposes. Of course, this section needs a picture of a female hitchhiker - to illustrate the effect. The pretty girl is the favoured content. The payload that comes along for the ride is her boyfriend - who was hiding off-camera at the time the above photograph was taken.

12 Defining memes - What "meme" means

There is a controversy about exactly what counts as a meme - much as there is a controversy about exactly what constitutes an organic gene. Both terms have become heavily overloaded - both have multiple definitions and meanings. The fact that there is no consensus definition of a meme in the field is one of the factors sometimes highlighted by critics of the field - though the almost exactly corresponding debate over the definition of the term "gene" apparently attracts little attention.

There are several controversial issues associated with the definition of the term "meme" - and we will start with a brief overview of these:

12.1 The role of imitation

There seems to be some controversy about whether cultural information that is transmitted down the generations by means other than imitation counts as being memetic. The primary cause of this controversy seems to be

Susan Blackmore. For years she has been promoting the idea that memes are copied by imitation. She says her definition is "clear and simple" and that other ideas about the definition of a meme are the cause of much confusion. Susan cites Richard Dawkins and The Oxford English Dictionary in support of this idea. She says:

> The most important point to remember is that, as in Dawkins's original formulation, memes are passed on by imitation.

Richard Dawkins (1976) described memes as being:

> a unit of cultural transmission, or a unit of imitation.

The *Oxford English Dictionary* says:

> meme (mi:m), n. Biol. (shortened from mimeme ... that which is imitated, after GENE n.). An element of a culture that may be considered to be passed on by non-genetic means, esp. imitation".

So, what *doesn't* count as being transmitted by "imitation"? According to Blackmore (1998):

> So if you want to stick to the definition of memes as transmitted by imitation then you have to say that bottle-top pecking, termite-fishing and potato-washing are probably not memes.

Blackmore claims that bottle-top pecking (among blue tits), termite-fishing (among chimpanzees) and potato-washing (among Japanese macaques) are not copied by "imitation". Susan lists several forms of copying which she says are not based on imitation. These are *stimulus enhancement*, *local enhancement*, and *goal emulation*.

- **Stimulus enhancement** - here Susan gives the example of blue tits bottle-top pecking. We can imagine blue tits learning to pack at bottle tops without ever seeing another blue tit doing so - if they encounter bottles with lids broken by other tits, and then learn to associate pecking at silver milk bottle tops with cream.
- **Local enhancement** - a form of social learning based on location. Susan gives the example of rabbits who are able to nest on railway embankments, despite all the noise. They don't exactly copy the behaviour of other rabbits - but rather just get used to the racket made by the passing trains, simply because they happen to be nearby.
- **Goal emulation** - here, Susan gives the example of an ape seeing another ape getting food from a container - but then using a different method of its own invention for getting at that food.

Susan explains that her motivation for including imitation in her proposed definition is make sure it is clear - and *also* to explain why humans have complex culture, while other animals do not.

> *This, I suggest, leaves us with a simple definition of the meme that not only makes it easy to decide what is and is not a meme, but also shows why it is that humans alone have produced complex culture. Humans are fundamentally unique not because they are especially clever, not just because they have big brains or language, but because they are capable of extensive and generalised imitation. I think we will discover that it is imitation that gave rise to our cleverness, big brains and language - and it is imitation that makes culture possible, for only imitation gives rise to a new replicator that can propagate from brain to brain, or from brain to artefact and back to brain. For all these reasons I suggest that we stick with the dictionary, and define the meme as that which is passed on by imitation.*

Susan's proposed meme classification scheme has some serious problems. The differences between the various forms of social learning used by humans are not very great - and it doesn't make much sense to use a classification scheme that attempts to divide them. There are many aspects of culture which are copied by are not copied by directly observing behaviour. This is especially true on the internet.

Knots can often be copied without observing the behaviour that produced them.

If you see a knot, you can probably duplicate it, even though you may never have seen it being tied. A classification scheme that says some knots are memes, while other ones are not seems intolerable. If the same knot can serve as a meme or non-meme depending on how it is copied, that would be even worse.

Layland and Odling-Smee (2000) are also critical of this position, writing:

> *Susan Blackmore (1999) suggests that, of all the processes that can result in social learning, imitation alone can support the transmission of memes, since it alone results in the learning of a behaviour pattern. She argues that other forms of social learning involve learning about the environment, and require the behaviour to be reconstructed by trial and error. In our view this position is misguided (see also Reader and Laland 1999).*

A *much* more sensible classification system than Susan's involves defining "memes" as being *any* type of heritable cultural information. This results in practically all human *and* animal culture becoming the subject of memetics. We do not need two distinct sciences of cultural evolution.

How can you tell whether heritable information is "cultural" or not? Essentially, cultural information passes through - and is inherited via - brains.

There *are* still *some* things that would not be included in such a definition. For example, the twists and turns of rabbit warrens persist over time - lasting for longer than the rabbits live. This is an example of environmental inheritance. A human might inherit a cave, a field and a flock of sheep from their parents. However, although these things are passed on from one generation to the next. I would not classify them as being "cultural" - and they would not be memes - since they are not inherited via brains.

Yawns are often given as a "corner case" for meme definitions. Yawns evidently are frequently transmitted from person to person, by a process involving copying behaviour. However, the behaviour is mostly-self generated - and the details of the behaviour are not usually copied. The "inherited" information, then is very low - consisting mostly of a signal saying if yawning is taking place or not. Also, yawns - while contagious - usually die out faster than they spread. I think this makes yawning a *trivial* kind of inheritance - one that carries very little information - and which *usually* quickly dies out.

One issue that crops up with this definition is whether computers count as brains. I would answer in the affirmative: in this context, computers may be usefully considered to be a type of *artificial brain*. Memes are substrate independent, and many can now be copied by computers more easily than they are were once copied in minds.

The idea that humans are exceptional because only they can imitate is not very convincing these days - we now know that many animals do have behavioural imitation. Our closest relatives, chimpanzees have a *considerable* repertoire of culturally-transmitted knowledge.

If memetics explains only explains the imitation of observed behaviour, we would need another theory to explain how non-imitated culture propagates. That theory would look a *lot* like the theory that covers culture that *is* imitated. It seems best to combine these ideas into a single subject.

Under the proposal here we *would* still need a separate theory of *environmental inheritance. Environmental inheritance* is not a trivial subject. It would be rather unfortunate for it to be neglected as a result of the spotlight being on human culture. In a number of respects, *environmental inheritance* is a more basic and fundamental idea than *cultural inheritance*. The study of *environmental inheritance* includes the study of *cultural inheritance* as a sub-topic. If the history of science had taken a different path, perhaps this book would be about *xemes* and *xemetics* - with the "x" being short for "eXternal transmission". We will revisit the topic of *environmental inheritance* later on in this book.

12.2 Internalist vs Externalist

Part of the controversy over the definition of the term "meme" involves the issue of whether memes should be regarded as existing only in people's minds - or whether representations in books, tapes, discs, and other media can be counted as well. I will refer to the idea that memes only exist within brains as the "internalist" school, while the idea that they exist in other media will be called the "externalist" school.

The controversy dates back at least as far as 1982. The Dawkins (1976) definition of a meme as:

> *a unit of cultural transmission*

...forms the basis of the "externalist" school, while the Dawkins (1982, p 109) statement that:

> *A meme should be regarded as a unit of information residing in a brain (Cloak's i-culture)*

...describes the "internalist" school.

Next we will look at these two schools:

12.3 Internalist

Some think that memes are things that reside inside brains. In defense of the idea, Aunger (2004) writes:

> *If memes could exist in brains, in speech and in artifacts, they would be the superheros of the replicator world, able to transform themselves into any shape or form at will, like the Proteus of Greek mythology. Instead, memes must be confined to one physical substrate, just as their brethren, the biological replicators genes and prions, are. I thus argue that only one substrate can be associated with memes.*

A few more examples should help to illustrate the position:

- **Burchett, Rolando and Lottman** have stated that a meme can be defined as "a unit of cultural information that can be copied, located in the brain".

- **Delius** (1989) describes memes as "constellations of activated and non-activated synapses within neural memory networks" (p 45) or "arrays of modified synapses" (p 54).
- **Lynch** (1991) defines them as memory abstractions or memory items.
- **Grant** (1990) as information patterns infecting human minds
- **Plotkin** (1993, p 215) says they are ideas or representations: "... the internal end of the knowledge relationship".
- **Wilkins** (1999) writes: "Memes are, in my perspective, multiply realised and multiply instantiated by neural net structures (as neural nets are wont to do)."
- **Wilson** (1998, p.148) says they are "encoded by discrete neural circuits awaiting identification."
- **Brodie** (1996, p.32) defines a meme as "a unit of information in a mind whose existence influences events such that more copies of itself get created in other minds.".

Prominent internalists include Aaron Lynch, Robert Aunger and Richard Brodie.

12.4 Externalist

By contrast, here are some representatives of the externalist school:

Dennett (2000) writes:

> *There is considerable debate among memeticists about whether memes should be defined as brain-structures, or as behaviours, or some other presumably well-anchored concreta, but I think the case is still overwhelming for defining memes abstractly, in terms of information worth copying (however embodied) since it is the information that determines how much design work or R and D doesn't have to be re-done. That is why a wagon with spoked wheels carries the idea of a wagon with spoked wheels as well as any mind or brain could carry it.*

Blackmore (2001) writes:

> *Given the complexities of human life, information can be copied in myriad ways. We do a disservice to the basic concept of the meme if we try to restrict it to information residing only inside people's heads - as well as landing ourselves in all sorts of further confusions. For this reason I agree with Dennett, Wilkins, Durham and Dawkins A, who do not restrict memes to being inside brains. The information in this article counts as memes when it is inside my head or yours, when it is*

in my computer or on the journal pages, or when it is speeding across the world in wires or bouncing off satellites, because in any of these forms it is potentially available for copying and can therefore take part in an evolutionary process.

Externalists have included Derek Gatherer and William Benzon.

12.5 Externalism rules

Externalists claim that internal brain entities are not practical to observe - and memetics will have difficulties in advancing as a quantitative science, unless its emphasis is on quantifiable aspects of culture.

Internalists responded with the idea that brain states will eventually become directly observable - and that we can infer their existence until then.

The author favours the externalist perspective. Memes, like genes, are informational, and - just like all other forms of information - they can be represented in any physical medium.

Calling a viral video a meme is OK by me - even though it is not necessarily instantiated in any person's brain at the time. An information-theoretic perspective neatly resolves the internalist / externalist controversy. According to that perspective, memes and genes are considered to be informational entities - embodied by patterns. They are both made of the same thing that bits are made of - i.e. they are not made of anything in particular - and may be represented in any physical medium.

Internalists not only tuck memes away where they are hard to investigate, they also frequently attempt to tie memes to the details of biological wetware. With so many memes migrating into computers and machines, this organic chauvinism seems intolerable to me. Machines can and do manipulate, copy and propagate memes too. Defining memes to be anything to do with neuronal patterns - as most internalists seem inclined to do - seems to me to be an obvious mistake in the light of this.

12.6 Information theory - The foundations of genetics

Informational genetics refers to the unification of Shannon's information theory and genetics. A quote from Richard Dawkins (1986) to start with:

If you want to understand life, don't think about vibrant, throbbing gels and oozes, think about information technology.

In this book I use the term gene to mean 'that which segregates and recombines with appreciable frequency

Williams (1966, p. 25) wrote:

In evolutionary theory, a gene could be defined as any hereditary information for which there is a favourable or unfavourable selection bias equal to several or many times the rate of endogenous change.

Williams (1992, page 11) wrote:

A gene is not a DNA molecule; it is the transcribable information coded by the molecule.

This view of genes as informational entities was subsequently embraced by numerous theoretical biologists - and popularised by writers such as Dawkins and Hull. John Wilkins (1998) has continued the tradition started by Williams by defining the term "meme" as:

the least unit of sociocultural information relative to a selection process that has favourable or unfavourable selection bias that exceeds its endogenous tendency to change.

12.7 Problems

The definition of the term "gene" has proved to be a thorny problem. The type of definition which Williams and Wilkins give has some issues. Such definitions disqualify anything which is neutral from being a gene.

Defining a gene (or an allele) as something which has an "appreciable frequency" results in novel mutations which occur only once in the population being denied the status of genes. Defining genes (or alleles) in terms of the selection pressure on them doesn't seem right either. If an allele happens to be neutral, surely it doesn't suddenly stop being an allele.

Worse, these definitions conflict with each other. One mentions selection, and the other mentions frequency. An allele can rise in frequency for other reasons besides its selective benefit - e.g. because of linkage to beneficial alleles present at other loci.

The reason Williams adopted these definitions *appears* to be because he wanted his definition to address the issue of how big genes are. Molecular geneticists sometimes *define* evolution in terms of changes in allele frequencies. With such a definition, the issue of how big alleles are can seem to be an important one. However, these definitions introduce serious problems. Genes should surely not stop being genes if they are neutral, or if their frequency becomes low. Definitions that have these strange features need to be rejected.

12.8 Attractions

I think that the key insight of Williams - that genes are informational - is very important. At first glance some may regard this idea as trivially wrong. Organisms inherit more than just information from their ancestors. They inherit geographical location, their ecosystem, pathogens, grandfather clocks, traditions - and all manner of other things.

However, if you look across multiple generations and ask what *actually* persists over extended periods of time, the answer is almost always some kind of digital information.

Grandfather clocks disintegrate - but digital patterns can live forever. Digital information can be backed up and copied. It is therefore potentially immortal - it can evade entropy and death. No physical object can do the same. What evolves and changes over time is, at its base, *informational* in nature.

Phenotypes may *appear* to persist overtime - however, they do so as a *consequence* of the persistence of genetic information.

12.9 Definition of "gene"

Dawkins, following Williams, defined a gene as being "an active germ-line replicator". The term "active" referred to phenotypic expression - disqualifying some neutral sequences and apparently requiring an analysis of developmental processes or gene frequencies in the population before something could be classified as being a gene or not. Also, this definition is based on the idea of a "replicator" - which is bad for reasons explained in the chapter on replication in this book.

The definitions proposed by Williams and Dawkins seem overly complex, and demanding to apply to me. The most basic and fundamental concept here appears to be that of "heritable information". The term "gene" should *probably* have originally been defined to be "a piece of heritable information". That seems to be the neatest way to carve nature at the joints. This avoids the problems the definitions of Williams - while dodging the question of how big a gene is.

12.10 Rival definitions of "gene"

Currently many dictionaries define a "gene" as being:

A hereditary unit consisting of a sequence of DNA that occupies a specific location on a chromosome and determines a particular characteristic in an organism.

Artificial Life enthusiasts have long derided definitions of *life, genes* and *biology* that reference the details of biochemistry - as *carbon chauvinism*. The belief that genes are necessarily made of DNA is castigated as being *nucleic-acid centrism* This is a useful perspective. The idea that genes are necessarily made out of DNA represents out-dated thinking - which biologists have *got* to get over.

Genetics - by definition - is concerned with the inheritance of traits. It is neutral about the medium by which they are inherited. Memes are heritable entities that span multiple generations - and so, they are genetic.

We should *not* define fundamental biological terms based on the historical accidents of our own biochemistry. This hinders discussion of synthetic life, our early ancestors, cultural evolution, and aliens. Such terminology is quite an embarrassment to philosophers of biology - whose job it is to straighten such messes out.

12.11 Other definitions of "meme"

Derek Gatherer once defines memes as follows:

> *Meme: an observable cultural phenomenon, such as a behaviour, artefact or an objective piece of information, which is copied, imitated or learned, and thus may replicate within a cultural system. Objective information includes instructions, norms, rules, institutions and social practices provided they are observable.*

Another definition of meme comes from John Wilkins (1998) - who writes:

> *A meme is the least unit of sociocultural information relative to a selection process that has favourable or unfavourable selection bias that exceeds its endogenous tendency to change.*

This is modelled on the similar definition of "gene" from George Williams. I don't favour this definition much. It is complicated - which I don't like - and it defines neutral memes out of existence, which I consider to be undesirable.

Bill Spight produced the following definition:

> *I propose that "A unit of cultural inheritance" is also sufficient to define a meme, and thus, is an acceptable standard definition.*

Lynch (1998) produced this definition:

> *A memory item, or portion of an organism's neurally-stored information, identified using the abstraction system of the observer, whose instantiation depended critically on causation by prior instantiation of the same memory item in one or more other organisms' nervous systems.*

Robert Finkelstein (2008) offers this:

> A meme is information transmitted by one or more primary sources to recipients who, as secondary sources, retransmit the information to at least an order of magnitude more recipients than primary sources, where propagation persists at least ten hours and the information has observable impact in addition to its transmission.

In the 2008 "What is a meme?" paper that the above quote is from, Finkelstein devotes nine pages to "extant meme definitions". These are unreferenced, but illustrate the range of different definitions that have been used.

12.12 Definition of meme

So: what is the definition a a meme according to this book? Memes should be considered to be be informational entities – ones that exist in artefacts - as well as in brains. The idea that genes map onto Mendelian traits - and that memes should map onto cultural traits is interesting, but ultimately, invoking traits seems to be *mostly* an unnecessary complication. It seems simplest to just define genes as being: *sections of heritable information*, and so to define memes as being: *sections of heritable cultural information*.

Such a definition leaves unresolved the issue of how big a meme is. While that's an interesting issue, I am not sure a definition is the best place to deal with it. The first thing to note is that - for many purposes, this is not an important issue. Population memetics works with *any* chunk of heritable information you care to mention. If you choose a sufficiently huge chunk, it may be unique. If your chunk is too small, its frequency may not be a very interesting statistic. However, the mathematics of frequency analysis works just the same in every case. There, the size of memes is a complete non-issue.

In common usage, memes are *rarely* divided - whereas memeplexes are *more frequently* split up. This idea does not seem all that easy that idea is to condense down, and it doesn't seem obvious that *that* much benefit would come from doing so.

The definition above doesn't mention the word "unit". The word has caused considerable confusion historically. It doesn't mention "frequency". The idea that whether something is classified as a meme (or a gene) should depend on its frequency seems undesirable. It doesn't mention "selection". Definitions in this area should probably not depend on whether something is the subject of selection, or not. It doesn't mention the word "replicator" either. As will be discussed shortly, that word has a history of causing misunderstandings, and it seems to be rather undesirable.

This definition leaves open the question of what counts as being "cultural". For example, the paths taken by the burrows in a rabbit warren persist beyond the lifespan of individual rabbits - and yet are not passed down the generations in DNA genes. However, rabbit warren burrow paths should not be counted as being "cultural" information - instead they are a form of non-cultural environmental inheritance. The best place to deal with such issues is probably in the definition of the word "culture".

13 Replicators - Replicator terminology problems

Richard Dawkins *appears* to have been *primarily* responsible for introducing the term "replicator" into evolutionary biology. He did this in his 1976 book, "The Selfish Gene". In his 1982 book, "The Extended Phenotype" he *defined* the term, as follows:

> *I define a replicator as anything in the universe of which copies are made.*

This definition contrasts with the common definition of terms based on the "replica" root. *Usually* the "replica"-based terms have the implication of a near-exact copy. However, the definition Dawkins gives makes no mention of the copying being high fidelity.

Dawkins originally used the term "gene" to refer to these persistent informational entities. However, he wanted a term that covered both organic and cultural inheritance - and he adopted the term "replicator" for that purpose. David Hull also began to use the term "replicator" in this context. Hull (1988) defined a replicator as:

> *an entity that passes on its structure largely intact in successive generations*

Hull's definition captures the high-fidelity implications of the term "replicator" - but this runs into the technical problems described later in this chapter.

13.1 Replicator problems

Next, I will present my case against the "replicator" terminology - in the context of the foundations of evolutionary biology. I have three main objections:

- **High-fidelity** - near-perfect copying is strongly implied by using the term "replicator". Such connotations are inappropriate;
- **Etymology** - the term "replicator" means: device which makes copies. Genes and memes don't *make* copies; rather they are things which are copied;
- **Too late** - the term "replicator" largely duplicates the function of the term "gene" - which is its rival for being the foundation stone of evolutionary biology. The term "gene" came first, has more support from associated terminology - and has a better claim on this central role.

My view is that - between them, these objections render the concept of a "replicator" unsuitable for use in the foundations of evolutionary biology. Next, we will look at each of these objections in turn:

13.2 The "high fidelity" objection

The term "replicator" does not *normally* just mean "copy" - it has *strong* connotations of high-fidelity copying.

If you look at the etymology of the word, it starts with the term "replica" - and a "replica" is a copy that is *almost* indistinguishable from the original.

David Hull acknowledges this in his definition of replicator - in "Science as a Process" - as follows:

> *replicator: an entity that passes on its structure largely intact in successive generations*

These connotations of high-fidelity are inappropriate for an entity that acts as the foundation stone for evolutionary biology. We know - from basic information theory - that information can survive in relatively poor-fidelity copying systems - *provided* that they employ compensating redundancy and error correction mechanisms. This insight was appreciated early on - by Shannon in 1948 and by John von-Neumann's in his 1956 paper: "Probabilistic logics and synthesis of reliable organisms from unreliable components." For adaptive evolution, *information* needs to persist with high fidelity - but such persistence can be implemented even in noisy data-transmission systems. High-fidelity copying is absolutely not necessary.

This terminological issue has caused real confusion among working scientists. For example, see the sections entitled: "Memes may not be replicators" and "Replicators are not necessary for cumulative adaptive evolution" in Richerson and Boyd (2000b). Or consider the following excerpt from Henrich and McElreath, 2003:

> *Through these analyses, the authors demonstrate how Dawkins' original claims about replicators and Darwinian evolution were wrong - replicators are sufficient for cumulative evolution, but not necessary.*

Defining the term "replicator" in a counter-intuitive manner that *avoids* the connotations of high-fidelity copying has evidently led to much confusion. Misunderstandings associated with this lie at the root of some of the common misconceptions regarding memetics. In "The Extended Phenotype", Dawkins (1982) wrote:

> *I define a replicator as anything in the universe of which copies are made.*

However that *isn't* really the normal definition of the term. The more conventional word for that in the philosophy of biology is "reproducer" - which means much the same thing - but lacks the connotations of high fidelity copying.

You *do* need to have data copying to have adaptive evolution. However, *high-fidelity* data copying is not necessary. You *do* need high-fidelity copying of *information*, if systems are to avoid an error catastrophe. However, you can have high-fidelity information transmission *without* high-fidelity data transmission. Also, you can still have non-adaptive change with low-fidelity systems - and these might still count as being "evolution". These distinctions were rather glossed over in early treatments of the issue.

13.3 The "etymology" objection

An etymological analysis of the term "replicator" strongly suggests that it should mean: *device which makes copies*. Organic genes and memes don't make copies - rather they are things which copies are made of.

> *In English, the suffix -or is used to indicate that the root to which it is attached falls under the ontological category of an agent. As with the -er in 'copier', it means that which does the copying, not the sheet of paper that we copy when we feed it into a piece of office machinery."*

This is from Ghiselin (1994). "Authors", "editors", "translators" - these words end in "-or". They are *makers* of copies. Replicators do the copying. The copies are called replicas. Here's Blackmore (2008a) on the topic:

> *In fact "replicator" is not a very good name, implying that it is the*

thing that does the replicating rather than being the thing that is replicated, (perhaps "replicatee" would be better) but "replicator" is what it is called and I will stick with that here; the concept is more important than the name.

Blackmore uses the term anyway - but I am less inclined to do that. Bad terminology needs to be combated, or at least boycotted.

13.4 The "too late" objection

The term "replicator" is a late-comer to the scene of evolutionary biology. Before its arrival everyone was quite happily talking about genes.

Dawkins correctly recognised that a key concept in biology was the idea of the coping of heritable information - and that this concept applied to human culture just as well as to DNA-protein systems.

He sought a term to refer to small pieces of heritable information that would apply equally well to all living systems - and came up with the term "replicator". By the time it arrived, the "gene" term had become well established. The study of genes is called "genetics". A collection of genes in an organism is called a "genome". A particular collection of genes is called a "genotype". The study of lineages is called "genealogy". Phenotype changes which are *not* based on genes are called "epigenetic" - and so on. Biology is saturated with gene-talk.

Basically, the term "replicator" arrived on the scene much too late.

If it had been there from the beginning, genetics might have been called "replicatics", genomes might have been called "replicatomes", genotypes might have been called "replicatypes", genealogy might have been called "replicatology" - and so on. However, that's *not* what happened.

I think that - between them - these objections to the concept of a "replicator" as the foundation-stone of evolutionary biology are pretty terminal.

13.5 Other critics

Many others have been critical about the "replicator" terminology. Most have ignored the definition provided by Dawkins (1982), *assumed* that "replicator" is intended to imply high fidelity copying, and then launched into an attack on the idea that adaptive evolution requires high-fidelity copying. For examples see: Henrich and Boyd (2002) "Why replicators are not necessary for cultural evolution", Richerson, Boyd and Henrich, (2008) "Five misunderstandings about cultural evolution", Gabora (2004) "Ideas are not replicators but minds are", Godfrey-Smith (2000) "The Replicator in Retrospect" and Gil-White, (2006) "Common misunderstandings of memes (and genes)".

People have retrospectively hunted around to see if they can find where Dawkins actually said that "replicator" meant making a high-fidelity copy. The best they have been able to produce seems to be this, from Gil-White (2008):

> *What did Richard Dawkins originally mean by "replicator"? Not surprisingly, something that produces "identical replicas" (Dawkins 1989:16).*

While this may *appear* incriminating, the context has been snipped out - and if you check with *The Selfish Gene* it is not from a definition of the term replicator at all, but from a passage relating to the origin of life. It immediately goes on to say that no copying process is perfect and that the early replicators were probably "far more erratic" than modern ones.

The Dawkins (1982) definition of replicator made no mention of exact copying. Blackmore (1999, p.5) uses the same definition, saying:

> *A replicator is anything of which copies are made*

Gil-White (2008) complains that the definitions of other meme enthusiasts do not specify exact reproduction either:

> *Blackmore is not alone: Daniel Dennet (1995) does the same, and Robert Aunger (2002) likewise defines replication as "the recurrence of... features," eliminating all emphasis on exact reproduction.*

The situation here is *actually* fairly simple. Complex adaptive evolution really *does* require high fidelity copying of information. It seems pretty reasonable to refer to high-fidelity copying of information as "replication" of that information - with any implication of high fidelity copying being fine in this case. However, a high fidelity information-copying system can be *implemented* by using a low-fidelity data-transmission system *plus* some type of error correction technology. This is all pretty basic information theory, and has been pretty well understood for many decades. However, a big mountain of ink has been rather pointlessly spilled by critics over this issue.

As far as I can tell, this debate is completely devoid of any scientific content, and boils down to a dispute over the "replicator" terminology.

13.6 Reproducers

The solution adopted by Griesemer (2000a, 2000b) is to use the term "reproducers" instead. This would deal with the implications of high-fidelity copying associated with using the term "replicators". The etymology does not so strongly suggest self-reproduction - and that issue could be clarified by talking about what is "reproduced". Using the term "reproducers" *would* be a technical improvement in a number of respects. It *is* a more umbrella term, though - since whole organisms reproduce too. Next we will consider a different solution to the problem. It seems less radical that the proposed shift to "reproducers" - but will still take some swallowing.

13.7 It's not too late

When new forms of inheritance were discovered, rather than attempting to develop new terminology, what *should* have happened is that the term "gene" should have been *expanded* slightly - to include all types of heritable information transfer - not *just* those based on DNA. It is not too late to restore the term "gene" to its rightful place at the heart of biology!

Here are some diagrams - representing possible arrangements of the basic terminology of evolution:

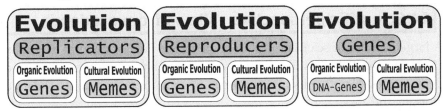

On the left, *replicators* are the fundamental unit of inheritance in evolution. In the middle, reproducers have taken over the role of replicators. This is at least an improvement. The right-hand diagram elevates *genes* to being the fundamental unit of inheritance in evolutionary biology. Gene and genetics are promoted back to the top spots - where they can play the roles they should always have played.

No doubt some will find this proposal difficult to swallow. It would certainly cause some pain during transition.

However *defining* the term "gene" in terms of DNA or nucleic acids seems *highly* undesirable. Then we would need to produce a whole new science of reproducing agents - perhaps called "Universal Darwinism" - which reproduces all the features of biological and cultural evolution. That would also cause considerable pain. I think it is better to expand the existing, established field of genetics to cover all biological inheritance than to try and invent a whole new science of *epigenetic inheritance* [sic] with its own terminology.

Some will say that the term "gene" is already too overloaded. That is true.

The term "gene" is a desirable one - and many want to use it. However, "gene" is surely evolutionary biology's term, first and foremost. Evolutionary biologists have the strongest claim on the term.

If a "gene" is defined to be a small chunk of heritable material, what name should be given to small chunks of nucleic acid?

Those are "genes" too, of course, and can normally simply be referred to as such - but if a term is *really* wanted to refer *specifically* to nucleic acid chunks while *excluding* other forms of inheritance - they *could* be called "organic genes", "cellular genes", "nuclear genes" or "DNA genes" - depending on exactly what you actually meant.

14 Scientific perspective - Views from academia

A large number of scientific works relate to the field of cultural evolution. However, the field is still a controversial area and there are a variety of perspectives. Here we look at the work of some of the relevant academics working the area.

14.1 A slow start

Cultural evolution is the most common term for the ideas in this book within academia. It is an old idea - but also one that has suffered from hostility and neglect from early on. Here is Berthold Laufer from a 1918, an essay in *American Anthropologist*:

> *The theory of cultural evolution, to my mind the most inane, sterile, and pernicious theory ever conceived in the history of science (a cheap toy for the amusement of big children), is duly disparaged.*

Strong words! In the first chapter of his book *Non Zero*, Robert Wright reported:

> *By 1939, another anthropologist could report that "[cultural] evolutionism can muster hardly a single adherent."*

Not exactly rapid growth of the idea in the social sciences.

14.2 Current retardation

Overall, Boyd and Richerson (2000) describe the current situation in the field as follows:

In the social sciences, evolutionary dynamics have been relatively quite neglected. Only a few scientist-lifetimes of work have so far been invested in the Darwinian approach to cultural evolution and related investigations.

Marks (2004) puts it this way:

The idea that culture can be partitioned meaningfully into constituent elements, and can be usefully understood scientifically as the differential propagation of those variant elements, would be entirely unfamiliar to Darwin, as it indeed is to most evolutionary biologists.

Dual Inheritance Theory (the idea that nucleic acids and culture coevolve in humans) seems to be a reasonably well-established concept within the field. However, there is at least one problem with *Dual Inheritance Theory* - which is that not many people have heard of it. Harvard biologist E.O. Wilson expressed disappointment at the lack of attention given to *Dual Inheritance Theory*:

...for some reason I haven't fully fathomed, this most promising frontier of scientific research has attracted very few people and very little effort.

Mesoudi, Whiten and Laland (2004) wrote:

By recognizing that our current understanding of culture is comparable to that attained by biology in 1859, perhaps some shortcuts can be taken by learning lessons from the succeeding 150 years of biological research.

The understanding of these authors shows signs of being somewhat beyond the "1859" level - but it must be said that many of their colleagues have yet to reach that point.

14.3 Memetics and cultural evolution

What many people *do* know about - largely thanks to *The Selfish Gene* - is memes and memetics. However, many of those people *also* seem to think that memetics is an inaccurate theory.

Memetics *does* have some prominent supporters - among them Dawkins, Dennett, Hofstadter and Blackmore. However, it *also* has many critics - and prominent among their supporting claims is that memetics hasn't yet been accepted by the scientific establishment. That claim *does* have some truth to it - in that there are relatively few references to memetics in the majority of scientific papers which relate to cultural change.

However, what has *actually* happened is that many of the people who are using evolutionary theories of culture to study cultural change have adopted different terminology to describe it. So, for example, Boyd and Richerson use "cultural variants" in place of "memes", while Avital and Jablonka use the terms "behavioural inheritance" and "traditions".

The result is a curious situation - where many people are aware of some of the basic concepts of memetics - but *apparently* think that these ideas have been examined - and largely-rejected - by scientists. Whereas in fact a number of scientists in the field embrace evolutionary theories of culture - but use different terminology to describe it.

14.4 Cultural evolution

Serious academic work on cultural evolution began in the 1970 - starting with a 1971 publication by Cavalli-Sforza (1971) entitled "Similarities and dissimilarities of sociocultural and biological evolution" and then continuing in a couple of years later with two papers from Cavalli-Sforza and Feldman (1973a, 1973b). This material found its way into the hands of Richard Dawkins and he cited it in Dawkins (1976a).

Some five years later, other researchers followed along with their own books on the topic: Lumsden and Wilson (1981), Cavalli-Sforza and Feldman (1981) and Boyd and Richerson (1985). The books were all *fairly* thick and technical.

Lumsden and Wilson

Lumsden and Wilson (1981) started out by saying:

> *This book contains the first attempt to trace development all the way from genes through the mind to culture. Many have sought the grail of a unifying theory of biology and the social sciences. In recent years the present authors have come to appreciate the probable existence of some form of coupling between genetic and cultural evolution, and we have undertaken our effort with the conviction that the time is ripe for the discovery of its nature.*

However, the book did not *really* present a modern-looking model of cultural evolution. It tried to get away from the sociobiological approach of tracing things back to genes - but they imagined that genes are able to control whatever they liked by adjusting human preferences. Their book is now known for its "leash" metaphor. Lumsden and Wilson (1981 p. 13) wrote:

> *genetic natural selection operates in such a way as to keep culture on a leash.*

Their work was subsequently heavily criticised. Maynard-Smith (1986) described the work as "deeply unsatisfactory". Marion Blute (1987) described their work as being "sociobiology in drag". Alper and Lange (1981) suggested that the authors were still trying to trace things back to genes too much.

Lumsden and Wilson followed up with another related book in 1983. This was on the topic of the evolution of the human mind. They wrote (p. 2.):

> *To many of the wisest of contemporary scholars, the mind and culture still seem so elusive as to defeat evolutionary theory and perhaps even to transcend biology. This pessimism is understandable but, we believe, can no longer be justified. The mind and culture are living phenomena like any other, sprung from genetics, and their phylogeny can be traced.*

Cavalli-Sforza and Feldman

Cavalli-Sforza and Feldman (1981) produced a mathematical treatment, derived from population genetics. They distinguished between first-order organisms (organic creatures) and second-order organisms (cultural creatures) - giving technologies, languages and customs as examples of the latter. Here they are, on page 341:

> *We have used the terminology "second-order organisms" for such cultural objects as technologies, languages and customs that are entirely dependent on the properties of the "first-order organisms," namely humans, or other cultural animals. Concepts usually reserved for biological evolution can then be transferred to the second-order organism which will also be affected indirectly by the evolutionary pressures acting on the first-order organism. The result is two orders of selection, natural and cultural.*

Some of their models are derived from epidemiology. They give epidemic-based models of cultural transmission, and identify an epidemic threshold (p. 348), in the form of a number of individuals. They discuss drift, the evolution of surnames and languages and present many specific models of gene-culture coevolution.

Boyd and Richerson

Boyd and Richerson (1985) built on top of the work of Cavalli-Sforza and Feldman (1981). They included comprehensive reviews of studies illustrating horizontal and vertical transmission and other phenomena they considered. They made a greater effort to place their work in the context of the work of others. Unlike the earlier academic authors, Boyd and

Richerson *even* mentioned the term "meme"! They did so only once, and it was to be critical of it - they claimed that Dawkins assumed that culture was encoded as discrete "particles".

Apart from its *dismal* coverage of memetics, Boyd and Richerson's book is pretty good - though fairly dense and technical. Boyd and Richerson invoked the puppet masters of memetics, by saying:

> *Horizontal transmission is analogous in some ways to the transmission of a pathogen*

...and...

> *The item of culture being spread horizontally acts like a microbe that reproduces and spreads rapidly because it is "infective" and has a short generation length compared to the biological generation length of the "host. Fads and fashions and technical innovations are familiar examples.*

...but only get as far as calling it an "analogy".

They use the terms "cultural parents", "cultural offspring" and "cultural organisms" - but, alas, they don't use them to refer to *genuine* cultural items, but instead to refer to *people* who distribute culture, people who absorb culture and organisms who participate in cultural transmission systems - respectively. In memetics, things are rather different - for example, "smoke" and "fog" would be the "cultural parents" of "smog" - while "brunch" would be the "cultural offspring" of "breakfast" and "lunch" - and an example of a "cultural creature" would be *Catholicism*. The memetics approach seems better to this author.

Slow progress

Multiple scientific books on the subject and a popular treatment in *The Selfish Gene* should have been *more than enough* to kick-start a science of cultural evolution - but then something strange happened. That strange something was: not very much. Cultural evolution faced resistance from within the social sciences, who had seen similar things before, explored how bad they were and then moved on. Biologists seemed to be mostly-oblivious to culture. There were specialised sciences for dealing with that. Cultural evolution fell between academic stools. It was explicitly rejected by those responsible for studying the area of human cultural change. The scientific treatments by the population geneticists who did understand it heavily-laden with mathematics, and not widely read or understood.

Relationship to memetics

The next major work in the area was Durham's 1991 "Coevolution" book. This book openly embraced the "meme" terminology. However, its subject area was *relatively* narrow - it focussed on areas where culture had influenced human genes - things like lactose tolerance, and the sickle-cell trait.

Since then there has been a steady trickle of papers on the subject from those looking at it from a population-genetics perspective.

The close equivalence between the work of the academic cultural evolution theorists and memetics was pointed out Kendal and Laland (2001):

> *We reject the argument that meaningful differences exist between memetics and these population genetics methods. The goal of this article is to point out the similarities between memetics and cultural evolution and gene-culture co-evolutionary theory, and to illustrate the potential utility of the models to memetics.*

In parallel with memetics, a number of academic researchers began to develop a gene-culture coevolutionary theory as an offshoot of population genetics. However, though treating much the same subject matter, the memeticists and the coevolutionary theorists have interacted very little. Kendal and Laland (2000) describe the situation by saying:

> *Memetics has developed in virtually complete isolation from a related discipline with very similar concerns, namely, cultural evolution and gene-culture co-evolution. Cultural evolution is a branch of theoretical population genetics established in the early part of the 1970s, and dedicated to using*

Peter Richerson, cultural evolution pioneer.

> *population genetics models to investigate the evolution and dynamics of cultural traits equivalent to memes.*

Many students of memetics had not heard of the population genetics work, and those that had probably found most of it to be rather impenetrable. In turn those studying cultural evolution did not always "get" memetics. Interactions between the groups were rare, and many of those that did take place were fairly hostile. Some of the population geneticists wrote critical diatribes against memetics Gil-White (2006), Richerson and Boyd (2000e), Ehrlich and Feldman (2003). In turn the review of these researchers by

Blackmore (1999) was fairly dismissive - they evidently didn't *really* understand memetics.

It does seem to be possible to understand that culture evolves without developing very much of an understanding of memetics. Boyd and Richerson in their 2005 popular work on the subject mention memetics only briefly - and their comments are all critical ones. Ehrlich and Feldman (2003) dismissed memetics, writing:

> *Identifying the basic mechanisms by which our culture evolves will be difficult; the most recent attempts using a "meme" approach (Blackmore 1999, Dawkins 1989 [1976]) appear to be a dead end.*

It seems rather challenging to understand how it is possible to study cultural evolution while *failing* to find a sympathetic interpretation of memetics - but some seem to manage it.

Layland and Odling-Smee (2000) did some important bridge-building between memetics and the cultural evolution researchers a decade ago - by endorsing memes. Kendal and Laland (2000) went further, explaining the equivalence of memetics and cultural evolution, as follows:

> *We reject the argument that meaningful differences exist between memetics and the population genetics methods. We also believe that cultural evolution and gene-culture co-evolutionary theory will be much enriched by embracing memetics.*

Layland revisits memetics in his 2011 book. Many other academic researchers in the area do not seem so impressed by memetics, though. A *lot* of the criticism of memetics from these researchers revolves around a misunderstanding (on their part) of the "replicator" terminology. This is basic information theory - and seems to be a complete non-issue. Some more criticism comes from how valuable the relationship between genes and memes is. Some researchers *seem* to have hold of the the idea that the term "genes" refers to strings of DNA nucleotides, and so have failed to grasp the essence of the gene-meme relationship.

Some of those who come the closest to memetics are Peter Richerson, Robert Boyd. Their 2005 popular book, "Not By Genes Alone" was much more accessible than their previous works, and represents a good introduction to their work. Blackmore wrote, in her: "Memetics by another name?" article:

> *Could it be that Richerson and Boyd are merely rejecting the word "meme" because of its popular connotations, when their theory is really equivalent to memetics?*

The ideas of these researchers are certainly *very* close to memetics. However, Boyd and Richerson (1995 p. 81) *apparently* don't get much out of viewing memes as being related to genes - and recommend against building on this relationship:

> *We encourage you not to think of cultural variants as close analogs of genes, but as different entities entirely about which we know distressingly little.*

That is *very* different to the stance taken in this book. Here, *nuclear genes* and *memes* both consist of sections heritable information which are instantiated using different media. Thinking of memes as being "different entities entirely" would be a very bad approach because it would *ignore* the *many* similarities between genes and memes. Ignoring the gene-like nature of memes goes in the direction of the superorganic idea of treating culture as a new phenomenon with different rules - a position which fails to make proper use of what we already know.

14.5 No cultural creatures

My general impression of the academic cultural evolution literature is that it researchers fail to bite the bullet that treats cultural entities as forming their own organisms and species. Researchers *rarely* mention symbiosis. For example, in *Not By Genes Alone*, symbiosis, parasitism and mutualism are only mentioned in one paragraph (at the top of page 165). By contrast, memetics literature is *full* of links to symbiosis, parasites, mutualists, viruses and epidemiology. It seems as though it is *possible* to interpret the phenomenon of cultural inheritance, without making any mention of the "brain viruses" or "body snatchers" of memetics. To treat culture as though there were inheritable information and phenotypic expression *without* there being any cultural organisms involved - *except* for the humans themselves. I think this is part of why the academic literature seems to memeticists to not really "get" it.

On page 7 of *Culture and the Evolutionary Process*, Boyd and Richerson give what *appears* to be an argument against cultural creatures:

> *This does not mean that cultures have mysterious lives of their own that cause them to evolve independently of the individuals of which they are composed. As in the case of genetic evolution, individuals are the primary locus of the evolutionary forces that cause cultural evolution and in modelling cultural evolution we will focus on observable events in the lives of individuals.*

This is the wrong approach. It is like saying: to study the evolution of HIV, we should focus on the AIDS sufferers. Yes, that approach will result in *some* progress - but it is *fundamentally* misguided.

The impression that academic researchers lack a proper understanding of cultural creatures is complicated by the fact that *some* of the academic researches do *sometimes* make positive mentions of cultural organisms. They seem to do this rarely, and in passing. For example, Cavalli-Sforza and Feldman (1981) talk explicitly about "second-order organsims" - which are cultural entities.

Boyd and Richerson (2005a, p.165) say:

> *The non-parentally-transmitted parts of culture are analogous to microbes.*

...and...

> *The psychology of social learning is like an immune system in that it is adapted to absorb beneficial ideas but resist maladaptive ones. And like the immune system it is not always able to keep up with rapidly evolving cultural parasites.*

This is using the language of analogy, though. However, Richerson (2010f) shows signs of having come around to the memetics perspective of full cultural creatures:

> *I think it is near to undeniable that cultural variants are sometimes selected to become selfish pathogens along the lines that Dawkins suggested.*

Another example showing how tentative many of the academic researchers are in this area is Simon Kirby. In a 2011 lecture entitled "The Language Organism: evolution, culture, and what it means to be human", he says:

> *One way to think about this is to sort-of turn things on their head and, rather than think about us being adapted to language biologically, rather language is adapted to best survive in us. In order for language to get passed on and to work it has to be learnable by children - and that is the adaptive force at work in the explanation of these structural features - and this has led a number of researchers to suggest that language itself can be seen as an organism whose environment is our brains. Whether you can really make that analogy work, I am not so sure - but it's highlighting the point that you can look at language from this other perspective and understand the features of it.*

Simon can *see* the hypothesis that cultural creatures exist - but he falls short of endorsing it. He invokes the cultural "puppet masters" of memetics, but then describes them as an "analogy", and subsequently pushes them to one side.

Memetics has *always* taken cultural creatures *much* more seriously, with *real* memetic parasites, and a *real* memetic immune system. Memetics is absolutely correct in biting this bullet - treating cultural entities as forming full organisms with their own phenotypes, fitnesses, species and populations. It uses the terminology and models of symbiosis and epidemiology to deal with them. A failure to think of the situation in terms of cultural creatures surely leads to a view of culture that is *deeply* impoverished. Academics can't sustainably deny the existence of cultural creatures - this is a basic part of understanding how human culture works.

14.6 No meme's eye view

For Boyd and Richerson at least, it seems as though there is no "meme's eye view" - or at least it is never seems to get mentioned. Kendal and Laland attempt to explain this apparent omission:

> *If contemporary practitioners of geneculture co-evolutionary theory no longer ask Dennett's Cui bono? question, it is because two decades earlier they developed their own method of answering this question, namely, the phenogenotype.*

A *phenogenotype* is essentially just a mixture of genes and memes. From a memetics perspective, "phenogenotype" looks a lot like a way of conceptually muddling together the genomes of organic and cultural creatures. Aunger (2000d) correctly points out that mixtures of genes and memes frequently do not form long-term relationships - due to the different reproductive pathways of organic and cultural entities.

Perhaps thinking in terms of *phenogenotypes* is what leads Boyd and Richerson, to say things like "culture is part of human biology" (Richerson 2001). This gets dangerously close to *the fallacy of the extended genotype* - where researchers think of culture as an extension of the human genome, with artefacts being its corresponding extended phenotype. That is a *very bad* way of thinking about cultural evolution. Cultural inheritance is *not* best thought of as being an extended part of human nuclear genetic inheritance, but rather as the genomes of distinct symbiotic cultural creatures which typically have *very* different life trajectories and reproductive strategies from their hosts.

As for the "meme's eye view", some researchers *do* seem to be *gradually* coming around. Shennan (2010) explicitly makes the case for a "meme's eye view" and the perspective is given favourable mention in the introductory "Culture evolves" paper of Whiten, Hinde, Laland, Stringer (2011a), who say:

> *Shennan argues that the 'meme's eye view' offers a significant theoretical perspective that the field ought to embrace.*

This is still pretty tentative material - but academics *may* yet come around.

In organic evolution, Darwin's theory of evolution preceded the *gene's eye view* by over one hundred years. Academics may need time to swallow one radical development before being presented with the next one. However, the time of the *meme's eye view* of culture will inevitably come around. I think it is really just a matter of time before the penny drops in the minds of the individual researchers.

14.7 Scientific endorsement

Despite their differences in perspective from memetics, the *cultural evolution* researchers *have* now performed a mountain of experimental work and other studies which serve as *excellent* evidence supporting the hypothesis that culture evolves - and exhibits Darwinian evolutionary dynamics. This material represents a wonderful resource for students of cultural evolution everywhere. It now represents the majority of scientific papers and evidence that memetics rests on.

Finding sympathetic interpretations of the work of others often takes some time and energy. I propose that everyone in the field makes more of an effort to get along, pull together, and try to avoid petty squabbles and academic turf wars.

14.8 Modern memetics

Richard Dawkins remains active in the area - with a whole section about memes in *The God Delusion*. Daniel Dennett also devoted a section to memes in his 2006 book *Breaking the Spell*. Susan Blackmore is also still active - with a relevant 2009 performance at TED and two 2010 pieces on the topic in *The New York Times*.

At least one meme supporter - Kate Distin has been discouraged by the frosty reception given to memes and has switched from using "meme"-based terminology to using the less-controversial term "cultural evolution".

While "meme" has become the de-facto-standard term for a contagious idea (it has entered into most English dictionaries - and it is used ubiquitously on the internet) the terminology associated with memetics has been *fairly* widely rejected by scientists in the field - *purportedly* for reasons associated with technical niggles about how the term "meme" has been defined. Having said that, one can't help wonder if politics and "not invented here" syndrome is involved. Daniel Dennett has claimed that Boyd and Richerson have said that their distaste for memes arises because they didn't invent the concept. However, we should probably not be relying on information from Daniel Dennett about what Boyd and Richerson think. They have written on the subject of memetics explicitly themselves - and it seems pretty clear what their objections are. Their objections seem groundless to me. Their attack on memetics is not a coherent attack on what I understand by the term.

Richard Dawkins (1999) once claimed that:

Memes have not yet found their Watson and Crick; they even lack their Mendel.

The structure of memes in brains is not easy to discover. We probably won't be able to identify memes from brain patterns until we have much more advanced brain scanning - as well as artificial intelligence and nanotechnology. However, there are *a lot* of memes that can be written down - and in those cases, we can see the structure of the transmitted information pretty clearly. I think we are well past the "Mendel" phase. There may not be any one person who is the pioneer of how cultural forms recombine - but we *do* now know quite a bit about that subject.

Matteo Mameli (2005) claimed:

the problem with the memetic literature is that most of the people who have written on memetics seem to lack either the motivation or the competence to do what is needed to transform memetics into a productive scientific enterprise.

If so, this is more a marketing problem than anything else. As scientific subjects go, memetics would appear to have a low barrier to entry - since everyday experience provides a mountain of evidence relating to it. The result has been that it has attracted many amateur armchair philosophers.

As a result, quite a lot of pseudo-scientific nonsense has been written about memetics. That is *possibly* one of the factors that has led to professionals being reluctant to associate themselves with the subject area. It was certainly one of the things that made me think twice before titling this book "Memetics" - rather than "Cultural Evolution". Another factor is the poor-quality foundation documents. Dawkins contradicted himself about the definition of the meme, claimed that he wasn't proposing a theory of cultural evolution and generally distanced himself from the topic. He never got around to writing *The Selfish Meme*. These shaky foundations have not been the most positive ones for a theory of cultural evolution.

Despite its drawbacks, memetics still seems to to be the best available framework and terminology for discussing cultural evolution. There is a *real* need for a term *like* "meme" - and "meme" has become the de-facto standard term in the area. Memetics is the name *conventionally* given to the study of how memes change (after "genetics", the study of how genes change) - and it too is a fine word. The many technical criticisms of memetics seem to be *mostly* misguided and confused. Memetics got on the right track from the beginning with its strong links to genetics. Memetics offers one of the best ways of understanding, visualising and communicating about what is happening in the area.

However, today, there is *still* no proper "memetics" science. Nobody studies memetics at university, and nobody is taught about it either. The nearest thing is the gene-culture coevolution theorists, few of whom seem to have a proper understanding of memetics. So, in a way, these are still the dark ages for the meme and cultural evolution. People look to memetics for the cultural equivalent of genetics. Scientists should make sure they find it.

14.9 Social science

Several factors have led to the neglect of the idea of cultural evolution - and its failure to penetrate the mainstream. Today, to the extent that there is any coverage at all, the topic is covered in other academic areas - including history, anthropology and sociology, economics, music and literature. A brief overview of some of the related fields:

Several sub-disciplines within the social sciences appear relevant:

- **Sociocultural evolution** - this seems to be a relatively well-established concept. However, much that is written in its name pays little lip service to Darwin's legacy. Often the term "evolution" is used loosely - in a similar sense to the way in which it is used to describe "stellar evolution" - just meaning change over time. From the perspective of Darwin-inspired theories of cultural evolution, this field has apparently yet to flower.
- **Cultural anthropology** - this is probably the existing academic discipline which is closest to memetics. However, it is dominated by *ethnography* - which studies particular cultures and ethic groups, and documents their cultural traditions. There seems to have been a focus on studying traditional and undeveloped cultures - perhaps in order to capture and preserve the diversity of humans in their natural state. Ethnography has a strong empirical component, and so far, its practitioners have mostly adopted an a-theoretical stance and have

not had *that* much of an interest in finding theoretical frameworks that help to explain their data and reveal its underlying structure.

- **Cultural evolutionism** - while in theory this term designates social scientists who examine cultural evolution, in practice it is generally used to refer to ideas about cultural evolution from around a hundred years ago - now popularly associated with the idea of social progress towards a western ideal - and thinly-veiled racism.
- **Biocultural evolution** - studies the impact of culture on genomes.
- **Biocultural anthropology** - studies the impact of human culture on the human genome (e.g. lactose tolerance genes).
- **Evolutionary psychology** - memetics was created as part of a reaction against evolutionary psychology - which has a long and sorry history of attempting to reduce psychology to genes and failing to understand the significance of memetics.
- **History** - studies the past. Historians often have an a-theoretical stance - as though interpreting data is not their job.
- **Archaeology** - studies buried human settlements. This has been one of the areas most accepting of cultural evolution.

Most of these disciplines are not accustomed to looking at their subject matter from an evolutionary perspective - much as biologists did not before Darwin. They often treat incursions onto their territory by Darwinian thinkers as hostile invasions. Indeed, it is sometimes worse than that. Biological perspectives have frequently received black marks from social scientists in the past. Darwinism isn't just foreign, it has a history of being wrong - and of being nasty. Here is John Maynard-Smith (1986) on the topic:

> *Biologists have, by and large, been eager to borrow ideas from the human sciences. Borrowing in the other direction is less well regarded. The reason for this ill repute is not far to seek: biological ideas have too often been used, not as potentially valuable research tools, but as a moral justification of policies that might otherwise seem dubious. The Social Darwinists, at the end of the last century, used Darwin's ideas to justify laissez-faire capitalism and to oppose economic measures aimed at helping the underprivileged. More recently, the Nazis used biological terminology—they can hardly be said to have used biological ideas—to justify genocide.*

Social Darwinism cast a bit of a shadow over social science, and many social scientists reject anything associated with it. Here is Bloch (2000) on the topic:

> *The reasons are various and include sheer prejudice for anything*

remotely 'scientific', as well as a suspicion that any 'biologizing' of culture rapidly becomes a legitimization for racism and sexism. (It is easy to disregard this as being a case of ignorant self-righteousness, but the history of the subject shows that such fears are not wholly unfounded.)

Indeed, there has been a long history of evolutionary science being debased by this type of concern. As John Wilkins (1999b) put it:

The debasement of memetics by quick and easy metaphors and popularised science to serve metaphysical agendas and political ideologies, with which we are all too familiar, is just the latest instance of serious evolutionary theory being perverted in that way, beginning with Spencer and the Edinburgh radicals of the 1840s, through social "Darwinism", "cultural evolution" theories, eugenics positive and negative, and so forth.

In many respects, the social sciences are still busy attempting to absorb the implications of the first Darwinian revolution. Mesoudi, Veldhuis and Foley (2010) list some other reasons for the poor penetration of the idea into the social sciences. The reasons are not complimentary to social scientists. They argue that social scientists hold distorted views concerning evolution, have been misled by past failed approaches which used the theory, and lack respect for the scientific method. Blackmore (2008a) explains the reaction of some social scientists as follows:

some social scientists brand all evolutionary approaches to their subject "reductionist," and reject memetics along with sociobiology and evolutionary psychology (Bloch 2000)

Bloch (2000) has this to say:

Meme theory deserves a better fate, yet I am afraid the story so far has not been encouraging. Indeed, we have to note how little success the concept of memes has had among social scientists. The great majority of sociocultural anthropologists would not even recognize the word and, when it is explained to them, they are invariably hostile.

However, the lack of acceptance of the idea by social scientists is not really a point against cultural evolution. It is a point against the social sciences. The social sciences are sick. The rot set in early this century - and most of the social sciences have been on the wrong track since then. William Irons (2009) described the attitude of the social sciences as follows:

Because they are so different, most social scientists and humanistic scholars assume that there is no point in trying to understand human behavior in the same ways that evolutionary biologists try to understand animal behavior. Humans and other animals are, in effect, separate universes, and each can be studied without reference to the other.

This idea is often known as "superorganicism". The idea of "The superorganic" is associated with Alfred Kroeber, a very famous American anthropologist writing in the first half of the twentieth century. The idea is of a hierarchy: inorganic -> organic -> superorganic. At each level new laws and emergent properties arise that are different from those governing the lower levels.

To *some* extent, it is true that culture can be usefully thought of as being "superorganic". However, the idea has some significant negative effects. It tends to result in conceptually "walling off" culture from the rest of biology. This tends to blind people to the powerful relationships and similarities between the organic and cultural realms.

Boyd and Richerson (2005a) describe the historical development that led to the absence of Darwinism from social science:

> *We thus have an interesting historical paradox: Darwin's theory was a better starting point for humans than any other species, and required a major pruning to adjust to the rise of genetics. Nevertheless, the Descent had no lasting influence on the social sciences that emerged at the turn of the twentieth century. Darwin was pigeonholed as a biologist, and sociology, economics, and history all eventually wrote biology out of their disciplines.*

Within anthropology, one of the main sources of problems was Franz Boas. Boas regarded cultural evolution as unscientific. He thought anthropologists should concentrate of the facts with their minds unclouded by theories. He promoted an approach which concentrated on fieldwork among native peoples to identify actual cultural and historical processes. Evolutionary theories within anthropology have yet to recover from this backwards step. A similar approach was taken by students of history. History's job was to observe and record the facts. Theoretical apparatus was not needed - and acted only as a distorter of the facts of the matter - by introducing preconceptions. Popper's book *The Poverty of Historicism* made a misguided case against using the human past to predict its future.

However, history and anthropology are both concerned with finding out what is correct - and so both are - or should be sciences, and should use the scientific method. Facts are all very well, but science does not consist *entirely* of observation.

Evolutionary theory *still* has a poor standing in the social sciences. Consider the following finding, reported by Mesoudi, Veldhuis and Foley (2010):

> *Unfortunately, as Perry and Mace point out, many social scientists appear to acquire biased and distorted beliefs concerning evolution during their training, as evidenced by their survey finding that rejection of evolution is significantly correlated with the number of years spent studying the social sciences.*

Richerson and Boyd (2001a) say:

> *No 20th Century social science derives any significant influence from the Descent, and to this day eminent social scientists are quite hostile to Darwinism.*

Many social scientists have been led astray by their teachers. They will apparently need extensive retraining to properly absorb a Darwinian perspective on their subject area. That might take a little while.

The fact that the social sciences can get by as well as they can without Darwinian underpinning is sometimes cited by critics of memetics (e.g. Alister McGrath, 2011) as an argument *against* taking a Darwinian approach. However, that is doubtful data. The social sciences are in a mess. They lack the unifying principle that united the biological sciences, and as a result are a mish-mash of conflicting approaches and experts who can't talk to each other due to a lack of shared foundations. Proper application of Darwinian principles will help to unify and heal the social sciences. The application of quantitative population models from biology will help to make them into proper scientific disciplines.

14.10 Neglect

At the time of writing, the position of cultural evolution in the biological and social sciences is very strange. There are some experts who have a reasonable understanding of the topic - and who do research and write papers in the field. However, mainstream acceptance is very poor, misunderstandings are common, and ignorance of the topic is widespread - *including* among biologists and students of evolutionary theory.

A number of experts in biology and evolution have publicly come out against the very idea of cultural evolution. I've watched a number of biologists and evolutionary theorists debating the origins of humans - and hardly any of them appears to have any real understanding of cultural evolution. As a result many of their theories about human evolution are all wrong. You can't really understand human evolution properly without an appreciation of gene-culture coevolution. Humans have significant differences from other animals. The cumulative effects of culture are the main reason why. If people fail to understand this, they are conceptually stuck in a primitive state where it is impossible to understand what is going on.

Perhaps biologists can be excused on the grounds that humans cultural evolution has its own dedicated scientific area: the social sciences. However biologists are among the best placed to understand human culture. Leaving the area to social scientists has not worked out very well. Social scientists, for the most part have failed to identify the basic principles of their own subject areas - and their failing has persisted for over a hundred years. As a result the social sciences are mostly still stuck in a pre-Darwinian era - and are some 150 years behind the times. As a result, each social science is specialised, and interdisciplinary dialogue is relatively rare - since the sciences lack the basic common ground needed to have a dialogue.

14.11 Renaissance

After over 150 years of lying almost totally dormant, the *science* of cultural evolution is *finally* showing signs of waking up. This impression is shared by others - for example, Alex Mesoudi (2011) recently wrote:

> *Despite these early pronouncements by prominent scholars of a curious and remarkable parallel between biological and cultural change only now are scholars beginning to properly apply Darwinian methods, tools, theories, and concepts to explain social phenomena.*

Peter Richerson (2011) said:

> *The idea that cultural evolution is Darwinian... this was appreciated by Darwin and students of linguistic history way back in the nineteenth century - both languages and organic forms seem to evolve by the descent with modification and this idea didn't do very much work until the last quarter of the 20th century or so - when a number of us got interested in trying to study formally the cultural system of inheritance.*

There has been an explosion of work on animal culture in the last decade, and there are signs that another burst of activity related to cultural transmission laboratory experiments is under way.

This book is intended to contribute to projecting cultural evolution into the consciousness of the public. Its publication coincides neatly with the explosion of internet memes into the consciousness of the general public.

14.12 Unnecessary controversy

The area of cultural evolution is currently a controversial one - but it surely shouldn't be. The facts of the issue are pretty clear-cut. There *are* a few remaining debates among genuine experts in the area - but most of these are more around terminology and emphasis than they are about the facts of the matter. Among those who study cultural evolution, the areas of agreement are enormous. We now know a *lot* about cultural evolution and how it works. The issue at this stage is more one of getting the word out - first to social scientists and evolutionary biologists, and then *eventually* to the general public.

14.13 A difficult update

Many have come to associate organic evolution with random mutations and natural selection - and so they tend to think of evolution is a trial-and-error process. The processes that generate human culture often don't always look like that. For example scientists typically choose their trials carefully - the process is not remotely random. So: cultural evolution can often look a bit different from organic evolution.

Another issue is that embracing cultural evolution can represent quite a radical shift. For example, cultural evolution tends to treat culture as alive - not just metaphorically, but literally. You don't necessarily have to do that - but it helps. However, for many, the idea that things like books and music or science and technology are alive and evolving runs contrary to basic human intuitions about which things are alive.

Others find the idea that their minds are the temporary nest of self-replicating ideas - which are using them to propagate themselves and do not have their best interests at heart - to be objectionable. The terms "reductionism" and "free will" sometimes get mentioned. This is the same kind of problem that was faced by the first Darwinian revolution. People didn't take kindly to the idea that they were related to monkeys. Similarly people like to think they are the master of their thoughts; and are resistant to the notion that their brain is a nest to a bunch of largely-unseen symbiotic mutualists and parasites.

Evolution enthusiasts have endured a long-running battle with those who believe that "intelligent design" is responsible for some features of organisms. So, installing intelligent design as a fundamental mechanism of evolutionary change - and affirming that choices made by intelligent agents are indeed responsible for some of the features of modern humans - may also be the cause of some problems.

For whatever reason, the ideas underlying cultural evolution have remarkably poor penetration. This needs to change. It looks set to be a big change for many. Looking at the revolutions in Darwinism that have taken place since 1859, none appear to be as radical as the shift that incorporating cultural evolution seems set to result in. There have been some adjustments to evolutionary theory - the discovery of Mendel's rules, the biochemical mechanisms of inheritance, and the origin of the modern synthesis, for example - but surely nothing as major as the expansion of evolution's domain that cultural evolution represents.

Embracing intelligent design and the inheritance of acquired traits may be difficult for evolutionary theorists who have long been taught that these ideas are wrong. The transition to correct views on the topic looks set to be a painful one for many.

15 Criticism - Skeptics and naysayers

Next it is time to address the critics. Cultural evolution has many critics, and memetics has many more. Here we will look at some of the most common issues raised.

Memetics is probably the most widely-known theory of cultural evolution. It has attracted a lot of different criticisms over they years: it oversimplifies things; it is based on a faulty analogy, it is not different from other theories; it has been falsified, it is too reductionistic, it never became popular - and so on. In *Freedom Evolves*, Daniel Dennett (1995) said:

> *Most of the arguments that have been deployed against a science of memetics have been misguided and misinformed, and they betray a distinct whiff of disingenuousness or desperation.*

Practically everyone seems to have a criticism of memetics. Also, there are a wide range of *different* criticisms. Many of them appear to be based on misunderstandings. Generally speaking, the critics here are attempting to offer a valuable service. However, in some cases criticism's darker side emerges - ulterior motives - rationalisations - not-invented-here syndrome - trying to look smart - and so on. Anyway, to start with:

15.1 Memes do not exist

A common criticism is that memes are nebulous entities that do not obviously exist. For example here is Jonathan Marks (2000):

Now unlike genes, memes have the decided disadvantage of not actually existing.

Four years later in 2004, Marks had toned down his rhetoric - but only a little:

We do not even know whether memes actually exist or not. This is an obvious stumbling block for any theory purporting to be scientific. It raises the question in my mind whether memes are like genes, which do exist, or like angels, which do not.

Andrew Brown (2009) compares memes to phlogiston writing:

The answer looks obvious: it's the idea behind it that is copied; at this point the weasel phrase "memes for ..." comes into play. But these seem to me purest phlogiston. All of a sudden, instead of meaning, there is some completely hypothethetical behaviour which magically produces meaning. We're back to the invisible propagules. I don't believe they exist. I take a sky-fairyist view of their reality.

McGrath (2005, p 121) says:

There is no direct evidence for the existence of "memes" themselves".

My favourite response to this sort of thing comes from Daniel Dennett (2007). He compares memes with words:

Sometimes when people say, "Do memes exist?" I say, "Well, do words exist? Are they in your ontology?" If they are, words are memes that can be pronounced. Then there's all the other memes that can't be pronounced.

Memes are informational entities. They exist in the same sense as anything else that is made of information exists. Informational entities can be represented in any physical substrate - but they are *always* represented physically *in some way or another.*

Here is Maurice Bloch (2005) articulating his doubts about the existence of memes:

[Memeticsts] will bring up the originality of thinking of the evolution of culture from the memes point of view. And, of course, they are right, because if they had been able to argue that there were such things as memes, this would have been a fascinating new perspective on human history. The point is, however, that they have not succeeded in arguing

convincingly - any more than the diffusionists had before them when talking of "traits" - that there are such things in the world as memes. And so, talk of invasion by the "body snatchers" to use Dennett's delightful phrase, is an idea as intriguing, as frighting and as likely as invasion by little green men from Mars.

I love this paragraph. Maurice Bloch *understands* what memetics says, *agrees* that *if true* it would offer "a fascinating new perspective" - but he flatly denies that memes exist. The problem is now that there is a *lot* of evidence for transmission of things looking a *lot* like memes. Chain letters, urban legends, viral tweets, viral videos - and so on - really do exist. Internet memes are a huge international phenomenon. These *really do* spread in epidemics and generally behave in the way that the memeticists claim. I don't think the claim that *memes don't exist* is remotely defensible.

15.2 Memetics is a pseudoscience

For this one, Luis Benites-Bribiesca (2001) can be our representative critic:

But while genes are well defined and their molecular structure has been extensively investigated, memes are ethereal and cannot be defined. Without an adequate idea of these elusive elements it is no surprise that no scientific demonstration of such an immaterial replicator exists and serious scientists disregard memes as the basis to explain consciousness and cultural evolution. Memetics is nothing more than a pseudoscientific dogma where memes are compared to genes, viruses, parasites, or infectious agents thriving for their own survival in human brains.

It is true that cultural evolution has had a hard time establishing itself as a science. That is *mostly* not the fault of the discipline, but rather is a function of entrenched anti-Darwinian dogma in the social sciences. However, now there are pretty-well established Darwinian lineages within economics, cultural anthropology, linguistics, epistemology, archaeology - and some other fields. I would describe cultural evolution as being a *protoscience* - not a *pseudoscience*.

Some would point out differences between cultural evolution in academia and memetics. There *have* been some differences in emphasis historically - and some of the academics that came along after Richard Dawkins (in particular, Lumsden and Wilson) got themselves into quite a muddle. However, today's best-of-breed academic theories of cultural evolution seem to be *fairly* closely isomorphic to memetics. Memetics came before most of the academic work on cultural evolution existed - and subsequent work has now confirmed pretty-much all of its basic principles. The pioneering work on memetics Richard Dawkins did in the 1970s has turned out to be one of his most significant contributions to evolutionary biology.

15.3 Memetics has never taken off

This, alas, is true. Steven Pinker - in a 2009 Harvard lecture - said:

> *For one thing, just empirically, the idea of memetics, of a science of cultural change based on a close analogy with natural selection, it is just a fact: it's never taken off. It's thirty-five years old almost at this point. Every five years a paper appears that heralds the final development that we have all been waiting for of a science of memetics - and nothing ever happens.*

> *Compare this to other sciences that have just flourished since 1976: neural networks, cognitive neuroscience, evolutionary psychology - there are conferences and journals and textbooks - we don't have a science of memetics - despite the constant promise that it is just around the corner - and I think that there is a good reason why we don't that there is something deeply flawed with the idea.*

What we *do* have is a science of gene-culture coevolution. This is a branch of population genetics - and on close inspection, it is closely isomorphic to memetics - a fact which both students of memetics (Blackmore 2006f) *and* people from the population genetics side (Kendal and Laland, 2000) have previously pointed out. This is *essentially* memetics without the "m"-word - and it has *all* the features which Pinker objects to. Pinker doesn't make any mention of this.

The other *main* problem is with social scientists dragging their feet when it comes to embracing the principles of Darwinian evolution. Darwin and humans just don't mix for them, it seems. That memetics has never taken off is a rather embarrassing fact for rational humans. The correct response is *not* to look for holes in memetics, but rather to set to work constructing the science - since it is better if it is built now than later.

15.4 Culture cannot be neatly partitioned into discrete units

Here is Maurice Bloch (2000) asking after the "discrete units" of the meme:

> *As I look at the work of meme enthusiasts, I find a ragbag of proposals for candidate memes; or what one would otherwise call units of human knowledge. At first, some seem convincing as discrete units: catchy tunes, folk tales, the taboo on shaving among Sikhs, Pythagoras' theorem, etc. However, on closer observation, even these more obvious 'units' lose their boundaries. Is it the whole tune or only a part of it which is the meme?*

In *population memetics*, you could treat either as a meme, and analyse the frequency of both.

Mary Midgley (2004, p.57) has a similar complaint:

> *The trouble is that thought and culture are not the sort of thing that can have distinct units. They do not have a granular structure for the same reason that ocean currents do not have one – namely, because they are not stuffs but patterns.*

Also, in the *Stanford Encyclopedia of Philosophy* section on cultural evolution, Tim Lewens claims "culture cannot be atomised into discrete units" - citing Adam Kuper (2000, p.180) saying that "Unlike genes, cultural traits are not particulate."

At this stage we need to step back and ask about the circumstances genes are expected to be discrete. Just like population genetics, population memetics assumes that heritable cultural information can be sliced into pieces and their frequency can be analysed. The ability to be sliced up into small pieces is a basic property of information. In *that* sense, memes are discrete.

The granularity of DNA genes can be exaggerated. As Hull (2000) says:

> *Of course, one does not need to know very much Mendelian genetics to know that Mendelian genes are not all that particulate*

That is about right. Nuclear genes can overlap, have context-specific start points and can be of variable length. They can be sliced and diced in innumerable ways by recombination, and can be modulated by methylation and other effects. Organic inheritance is quite a messy business, and the idea that it can be "atomised into discrete units" is may well be the result of having an overly-simplistic view of how it works.

Having said that, many genes *do* have *natural* divisions - in the form of start and stop codons. Is there a memetic equivalent? Yes - but it doesn't apply to *all* memes. Whether or not a piece of culture comes in "natural" chunks and has "preferred" points of division depends entirely on the piece of culture we are discussing. Memes do not *necessarily* need to be discrete *in that sense*.

Mary Midgley appears to accept that memes are to culture what phonemes are to spoken language. However in Midgley (2004, p.58), she writes:

> *In short, the sound of speech as we hear it turns out not to be granular, not to have definite units. It is a continuum which can be divided up in various ways for various purposes. The original hope of atomising it seems to have flowed from a general confidence in*

atomising which was rather prevalent at that epoch.

Not only does Midgley disapprove of memes, she *also* disapproves of phonemes! Apparently the concept is the result of a misguided attempt to atomise language - dating back to a time when atomising things seemed to be a more promising approach. Since *phonemes* are an *extremely* useful concept in linguistics, I don't see this as reflecting badly on memes at all.

According to an article by Massimo Pigliucci (2009) entitled: "Memes, Selfish Genes And Darwinian Paranoia", the problem arises not just with memes, but *also* with genes:

> *Godfrey-Smith makes an excellent argument at some point in the book (chapter 7, on the gene's eye view) that genes are not at all the sort of things Richard Dawkins and some other biologists think they are. For instance, contrary to the standard view, genes are not "unities of heredity" (and therefore do not last as "individuals") for the simple reason that crossing-overs (the molecular processes that shuffle bits and pieces of genetic material, the real reason for sex) do not respect gene's boundaries, but rather cut genes into pieces and shuffle them. Indeed, as Godfrey-Smith points out, for this and other reasons sophisticated theoretical biologists are abandoning talk of "genes" altogether, referring instead to the more diffuse concept of "genetic material."*

This kind of thing does not deserve to be taken seriously. Those who doubt whether the idea of a "gene" is a useful concept need to attend some basic biology classes.

15.5 Evolution doesn't require replicators

One of the common complaints about memes is that memes are defined to be replicators, and replicators are not needed for evolution. For instance, Richerson, Boyd and Henrich, (2008) say - in a section titled: "Replicators are not necessary for cumulative adaptive cultural evolution ":

> *Much confusion about cultural evolution traces to Dawkins (1976, 1982) argument that discrete, accurately copied, long-lived "replicators" are necessary for cumulative, adaptive evolution. Dawkins argues that self-replicating entities are a requirement for cumulative evolution and must have the following characteristics:*
> - *Fidelity. The copying must be sufficiently accurate that even after a long chain of copies the replicator remains almost unchanged.*
> - *Fecundity. At least some varieties of the replicator must be capable of generating more than one copy of themselves.*

- **Longevity.** *Replicators must survive long enough to affect their own rate of replication.*

This argument has been repeated and elaborated by Dennett (1995), Blackmore (1999), Aunger (2002), among others, and has convinced many people that discrete, gene-like particles are a requirement for adaptive cultural evolution.

Dawkins made no such argument. Perhaps Richerson, Boyd and Henrich (2008) were unfamiliar with the terminology used by Dawkins. Dawkins (1982a) defined what he meant by "replicator" as follows:

I define a replicator as anything in the universe of which copies are made.

A *very* similar definition appears in Dawkins (1982c), and in Dawkins (2004b) he defined the term replicator by saying:

A replicator is anything of which copies are made.

Let's refer to this concept as a *Dawkins-replicator*. Now, *Dawkins-replicators* are *definitely* required for cumulative adaptive evolution - because without copying, nothing can possibly live. Now, of course you *could* argue (correctly) that Dawkins is misbehaving - by defining the ordinary English word "replicator" in a counter-intuitive manner. However, that seems to be a bit of a different complaint from the one being made here.

Dawkins *did* talk about *fidelity, fecundity* and *longevity* - but he didn't make anything like the argument that is being attributed to him here. Something Dawkins actually *did* say in *The Extended Phenotype* was:

This, then, is our candidate replicator. But a candidate should be regarded as an actual replicator only if it possesses some minimum degree of longevity/fecundity/fidelity (there may be trade-offs among the three).

I think this quote illustrates how far Dawkins was from giving the argument that Richerson, Boyd and Henrich *apparently* think that he made.

Others have made the same criticism of Boyd and Richerson - e.g. here is Sylvain Magne, writing in 2010:

Boyd and Richerson first introduce replicators as "material objects that are faithfully copied". It certainly isn't Richard Dawkin's view who described replicators as "any entity in the universe of which copies are made".

Sylvain does not seem too impressed with the resulting confusion:

It is very unfortunate that Boyd and Richerson misrepresent Richard's ideas in such a way. Because of this misunderstanding they then criticise memetics for the wrong reasons.

15.6 Memes are not like genes

Memes exhibit *some* differences from DNA genes - and some see these as a big problem for memetics. Here is Allen Orr (1996a) on the topic:

As I made clear, my other problem is that what we do know about how humans hold ideas in their heads suggests that "memes"-ideas, songs, fashions-aren't anything like genes. And if memes aren't sufficiently gene-like, we have little reason for thinking that "concepts from population genetics transfer quite smoothly" to population memetics, as Dennett hopes.

Memes *are* like genes - in that they are the heritable information involved in the evolutionary process. That's what leads to the huge overlap of concepts between population memetics and population genetics. Another person with this complaint is Adam Kuper (2006):

In any case, ideas are not independent gene-like entities, much less parasites. They are attached to symbols and institutions. Their power and endurance have to do with the social status and resources of those who propagate them. Darwin may be right and Moses may be wrong, but biological metaphors don't help us to understand the social history of beliefs and practices.

The argument that memes are not "independent" seems to be a feeble one. Genes are not "independent" either. They exhibit linkage with other genes and all kinds of mutual dependencies. Nobody ever claimed that memes are "independent" in the first place.

Boyd and Richerson (2005a p.81) also deny that memes are particularly gene-like:

We heartily endorse the argument that cultural evolution will proceed according to Darwinian principles, but at the same time we think that cultural evolution may be based on units that are quite unlike genes. We encourage you not to think of cultural variants as close analogs to genes but as different entities entirely about which we know distressingly little.

This advice seems pretty dubious. Much of interest and value follows from the idea that memes and DNA genes are both instances of small, reproducing informational entities. A failure to keep this relationship in mind risks losing a lot of the understanding of memetics that results from the existing study of genetics. Not *all* concepts are useful in both domains, but an enormous number *are*. A kind of gene-meme dualism is the *last thing* that is needed. A good understanding of the relationship between memes and DNA genes is pretty critical to developing a proper understanding of cultural evolution.

In their 2005 book *Not By Genes Alone* Boyd and Richerson, wrote:

> *Some authors use the term meme coined by the evolutionary biologist Richard Dawkins, but this connotes a discrete, faithfully transmitted genelike entity, and we have good reasons to believe that a lot of culturally transmitted information is neither discrete nor faithfully transmitted. So we will use the term cultural variant.*

Their characterisation of memes seems inaccurate. Memes just consist of cultural heritable information. Faithful transmission is not necessarily implied. Dawkins (1976, p.195) originally wrote:

> *It looks as though meme transmission is subject to continuous mutation, and also to blending.*

Saying that using the term "meme" is bad because it "connotes a discrete, faithfully transmitted genelike entity" seems pretty weak. It *is* intended to connote "gene-like" - but it is *not* intended to imply faithful transmission - and that has been made pretty clear from the beginning. The idea that - in order for memes to be "like" genes - they should be faithfully transmitted seems to be an unconvincing straw man. There is, in fact, no limit on how high mutation rates can go in the organic realm or the cultural realm.

15.7 Memes are not like viruses

Wimsatt (2010) complains that memes are not like viruses - on the grounds that:

> *Suppose that whether you could catch a given virus, and how it was expressed, was a complex function of what other viruses you had caught and in what order, and you were forced to deal with complex interactions of tens of thousands of virus types per individual What would epidemiology look like then?*

However we *do* see interactions between virus-borne pathologies in the organic world too. Infection with one virus results in antibodies that sometimes offer subsequent protection against other strains of the same viruses. A classic example of this occurred in the manufacture of the smallpox vaccine. In 1796 Dr. Edward Jenner was visited by a milkmaid who was infected with Cowpox. He infected his gardener's son with Cowpox. He contracted the disease - and recovered within a few days. Weeks later, Dr. Jenner exposed the boy to smallpox. Amazingly, the boy did not contract the deadly disease. This experiment led to the development of a smallpox vaccine. These days it is common for weakened forms of a virus to be given to people as vaccines - allowing them to produce antibodies against the real disease.

This is broadly similar to the way that exposure of one pyramid marketing scheme helps to produce immunity to other ones.

There are also cases where an organic infection results in other infections. Being sick puts a load on the immune system, which makes it more vulnerable to opportunistic infections. Persistent viral infections often make the host more susceptible to opportunistic infections by decreasing the production of some types of interferons. Some pathogens (e.g. HIV) sabotage the immune system, which can lead to infection with other pathogens. This is broadly similar to the way in which the idea of getting on the internet makes you more vulnerable to many other memes.

Perhaps memes interact with one another more than viruses do. However, the differences in this area seem to be more *differences in degree* than *differences in kind*.

Steven Pinker (2009) also claimed that memes are not like parasites. His objection is that some memes (words) are not deleterious. Indeed, *some* memes are beneficial. Nobody has ever claimed otherwise - as far as I can tell.

15.8 Genes are concrete, memes are intangible

Some say that memes are too *intangible*. For example, Massimo Pigliucci (2007) writes:

> Genes are-roughly speaking-pieces of nucleic acids (DNA or RNA), with known physical-chemical characteristics. But memes can be instantiated equally well inside someone's mind (where presumably they correspond to specific patterns of neuronal firings), on a computer's hard drive, in a book, or on an iPod. While it is true that, for decades after Gregor Mendel proposed the idea of genes, biologists didn't know what they were made of either, the likelihood of pinpointing a physical makeup for memes is less likely because they seem to be a sort of "diffuse" entity that can have many physical incarnations.

Both genes and memes are *informational* entities. Defining genes as being nucleic acids would be a basic *philosophy of science* mistake. We should not have to rewrite the basic concepts of evolutionary biology if we find aliens with non-DNA genes, if we discover replicating proteins, or if our distant ancestors turn out to have non-nucleic acid inheritance (highly likely). So, genes are *not* "roughly speaking-pieces of nucleic acids". From the perspective of evolutionary biology, that idea is just a basic terminological mistake.

As for DNA genes not having "many physical incarnations", that now seems to be an out-of-date idea. DNA sequencing and synthesis are now routine. Storing gene sequences in databases is now common, and genes have phenotypic effects this way, for example when used for forensic purposes. The convergence of organic and cultural evolution is already making headway.

15.9 Cultural evolution features directed mutation

The directed mutations in cultural evolution cause problems for some. Here is Allen Orr (1996a) on this topic.

> *Moreover, new ideas - but not genes - are produced by a sort of directed mutation. Newton did not uncover the Fundamental Theorem of Calculus by conceiving millions of random ideas.*

At this point, it needs to be pointed out that, mutation is not random in organic evolution either. Some loci are mutated more than others, the mutation rate depends on stress levels, and mutations are preferentially performed in genes that are part of the immune system.

Steven Pinker (1997) raised a similar point in *How the Mind Works*:

> *A complex meme does not arise from the retention of copying errors. It arises because some person knuckles down, racks his brain, musters his ingenuity, and composes or writes or paints or invents something.*

Here Pinker apparently equates mutations with "copying errors". In definitions of evolution it talks about variation. It *doesn't* say that variation must arise through copying errors. Directed mutations are permitted - according to most definitions of what an evolutionary process is.

Memes *do* arise through processes other than "copying errors". However, nobody claimed that mutations in cultural evolution were *all* copying errors in the first place. Nor is that an important part of the analogy with organic evolution. Many mutations in cultural evolution are directed - and arise from the actions of intelligent agents. That is *quite* compatible with the process of cultural change being an evolutionary one. If you doubt that, check with the definition of "evolution" - you will see that it makes no mention of mutations being performed at random.

The frequency of directed mutations *is* probably one of the biggest differences between cultural and organic evolution. However, they do not stop culture from exhibiting complex adaptations, family trees, and many the other stigmata of an evolutionary process. You *still* need a Darwinian *foundation* for any theory of *cultural evolution - even* if some types of mutation arise in novel ways.

15.10 Error catastrophe

Some have speculated that high mutation rates in cultural evolution might lead to an error catastrophe. Here is Sperber (1996, p102-p103):

> *In the case of genes, a typical rate of mutation might be one mutation per million replications. With such low rates of mutation, even a very small selection bias is enough to have, with time, major cumulative effects. If, on the other hand, in the case of culture there may be, as Dawkins [1976] acknowledges, 'a certain "mutational" element in every copying event,' then the very possibility of cumulative effects of selection is open to question.*

Here Sperber raises the issue of whether the mutation rate in culture is too high to permit complex adaptations to form. That issue seems easy to answer - cultural evolution evidently exhibits adaptive complexity in *some* areas - for example, science, technology and religion clearly exhibit adaptive complexity. The reason for this is fairly obvious - mutation rates of textual documents have been made very low in modern times via the use of error detection and correction technologies. High fidelity copying facilitates true adaptive evolution. Catherine Driscoll (2011) provides a more detailed rebuttal in her article entitled "Why Sperber's Attractors do not Prevent Cumulative Cultural Evolution".

If human culture was so prone to mutation that it results in an error catastrophe, we would not see cumulative adaptations, or progress in the cultural realm. Yet we *do* see both those things. It is thus evident that information succeeds in persisting *despite* the mutation rates associated with cultural transmission. High mutation rates are not contrary to the principles of evolution or genetics. They *sometimes* result in devolution (in the sense of systematic descent from adaptive peaks) - if the mutations are numerous enough. However, there are a *lot* of cultural adaptations - so we can see from the results of the evolutionary process that this is not *too* much of a problem, in practice.

Critic Luis Benites-Bribiesca (2001) says:

> *Genes require that messages be replicated with a high degree of accuracy, something which does not and cannot occur with memes.*

This is not correct. In fact it is a basic mistake. Many memes evidently *are* copied with high fidelity. They persist for thousands of years. Good examples of high-fidelity transmission memes are abundant: CDs, DVDs, Bibles - and so on. This assertion that accurate copying of memes *cannot* take place is so strange that one has to wonder that the author could possibly have been thinking. Maybe he imagined the era of memory-based meme transmission - when people passed on their memes using group chanting - and then failed to consider any of the examples using more sophisticated error detection and correction.

15.11 Mutations are more common

Scott Atran (2001) complains about the high mutation rate culture exhibits:

Cognitive study of multimodular human minds undermines memetics: unlike genetic replication, high fidelity transmission of cultural information is the exception, not the rule. Constant, rapid "mutation" of information during communication generates endlessly varied creations

In the organic world it is more frequently sexual recombination produces the "endlessly varied creations". These are differences, but quantitative ones.

Boyd and Richerson (2000) also complain about the mutation rate. In a *Scientific American* response article entitled: *Meme Theory Oversimplifies Cultural Change* the pair offer some criticisms. They start by describing the low-fidelity transmission of some memes - and then say:

As a result, memes are often systematically transformed during transmission - a process quite unlike natural selection, which depends on one meme spreading more quickly than competing alternatives.

They are correct that the effects of low-fidelity transmission do not closely resemble natural selection. However, poor quality transmission is evidently a source of *variation*, and so can be more accurately modelled as a type of mutation. Boyd and Richerson anticipate this complaint about their objection - and then proceed:

genes can also be transformed by spontaneous changes called mutations. But genetic mutations are rare, occurring about once every million replications, and as a result their effect usually can be ignored when thinking about adaptations. If mutations occurred more often - say, every 10 replications - they would have a significant effect on which genes were most common. We think this situation is exactly what occurs with ideas, which can transform rapidly as they spread from one person to the next. If we are right, cultural change will be understood only if the effects of transformation and natural selection are combined.

This is not unreasonable - at least for some kinds of cultural change. However, an understanding of mutational mechanisms is a fundamental part of genetics - as well as being part of memetics. Nobody ever advocated modelling evolution by only considering natural selection in the first place. Common phenomena - like genetic drift and environmentally-induced mutational meltdowns - are simply incomprehensible if you ignore the effects of mutations in your models. So modellers should consider mutations in their models. As far as I know, nobody ever advocated doing otherwise.

It is true that mutations in cultural evolution are a more interesting phenomenon than they are in organic evolution. There mutations are mostly independent of fitness, whereas in cultural evolution, there is significant scope for making adaptive changes. However, perhaps this point should not be exaggerated:

Mutations are *far* from random in the organic world - and a variety of mechanisms exist that facilitate adaptive changes via mutation. Many immune system mutations are deliberately performed (and so are adaptive) - and the resulting antibodies can sometimes be inherited via mother's milk. Stressed organisms have a greater mutation rates, and this *may* also be an adaptive response. There's also gene duplication. Duplication is more often adaptive than most mutations are. This leads to an interesting response to mutations that damage genes. The response produces effects similar to those produced by directed mutation. The damaged genes get copied into adjacent DNA - so they get expressed in greater numbers, and still do their job a little - a process known as "selective gene amplification". The duplicated genes then present a bigger target to cellular mutagens. If a beneficial mutation arises, it is "fixed", then the dysfunctional duplicate genes are gradually discarded.

15.12 Copying and selection may not explain culture

This is one of the complaints of Dan Sperber. Here he is in 2000:

For memetics to be a reasonable research programme, it should be the case that copying, and differential success in causing the multiplication of copies, overwhelmingly plays the major role in shaping all or at least most of the contents of culture.

It is probably true that new culture arises largely from existing culture - but memetics doesn't depend on that being true. For example, most theories of cultural evolution and memetics would still apply if mutational forces outweighed selective ones. In that case the resemblance between cultural and organic evolution *would* be reduced - and there would not be cumulative cultural evolution - but evolutionary theory would still apply. More from Dan Sperber (2000):

> *Memeticists have to give empirical evidence to support the claim that, in the micro-processes of cultural transmission, elements of culture inherit all or nearly all their relevant properties from other elements of culture that they replicate.*

Since so much culture has been digitised, ultra-high-fidelity transmission of cultural information is now evidently *extremely* common - but memetics handles low-fidelity transmission just fine. Memetics is just the genetics of culture. Cultural inheritance that is low-fidelity, is just another object of study for memetics. If inheritance had *such* low fidelity that adaptations were unable to form, that might be a bit more of a problem - but that is evidently not true in a wide variety of cultural realms - since we can plainly see the results of cumulative adaptive evolution in the cultural realm.

An alternative to explanations based on differential reproductive success are ones based on directed mutation - since cultural evolution permits variation to be directed. I think it is reasonable to entertain such explanations - but do not agree that they potentially represent grounds for rejecting memetics. Memetics says that copying, variation and selection are the basis of culture. Directed variation is not prohibited, and *is* permissible.

15.13 Memes are not copied but recreated

Andrew Brown (2009) writes:

> *What we know about the transmission of meaning, like that of memory, is that it involves continuous recreation rather than simple copying.*

Since most cultural information has gone digital these days, it is indeed reproduced largely by "simple copying" - for example on peer-to-peer networks, or via "retweeting". However, *even* back in the stone age, when that wasn't true, cumulative cultural evolution *still* took place. Definitions of evolution do not say anything about "simple copying". Evolution involves the transmission of heritable information from one generation to the next. *Exactly* how that happens is an implementation detail, not a fundamental feature.

This is also part of the critique of Jablonka and Lamb (2005, p.209):

Since heritable variations in behaviour and ideas (memes) are reconstructed by individuals and groups (vehicles) through learning, it is impossible to think about the transmission of memes in isolation from their development and function.

Reconstructed behaviours may be a mix of transmitted information and trial-and error learning. However, for memeticists, reconstruction from observation is *just fine* as a means of copying behaviour. It is not some kind of a problem.

We can *still* usefully talk about a *meme for skateboarding*, even though children learn some of the required skills by trial-and-error learning - rather than by copying them from other children.

Some say that memes are so mangled in minds as to become practically unrecognisable. Here is Maurice Bloch in 1995:

Sperber, Levi-Strauss and most of the ir colleagues - as well as myself - accept the fundamental criticisms formulated by the American consistency theorists against the diffusionists: criticisms which apply with equal force against memeticists. Agreement is focused on the fact that the transmission of culture is not a matter of passing on "bits of culture" as though they were a rugby ball being thrown from player to player. Nothing is passed on; rather a communication link is established which then requires an act of re-creation on the part of the receiver. This means that, even if we grant that was was communicated was a distinct unit at the time of communication, the recreation it stimulates transforms totally this original stimulus and integrates it into a different mental universe so that it loses its identity and specificity. In sum, the culture of an individual, or of a group is not a collection of bits, traits or memes, acquired from here and there, any more than a squirrel is a collection of hazelnuts.

The idea that "nothing is passed on" is just wrong. Shannon information is passed on. The donor and recipient of the meme come to share Shannon mutual information. *Sometimes* what is passed on is indeed faithfully copied - as by biblical scribes. *Sometimes* what is passed on is not faithfully copied - as we see in Chinese whispers. The former process leads to long term adaptive evolution, while the latter one leads to an error catastrophe. Memetics - just like genetics - handles both cases just fine. Memetics is just - by definition - the science that studies cultural heredity, and variation.

If culture was so badly mangled in minds, that indeed "nothing is passed on" that would be an issue - but that is just false. The biblical scribes copied many thousands of words with high fidelity. For biblical scribes, the "re-

creation on the part of the receiver" was reliable at constructing the word they just read - and then they wrote it down again immediately. It was not a 100% reliable process - but it was still pretty good. In the internet era, copying has become much better still. *Sometimes* things get mangled during transmission - but that happens with DNA genes too. Indeed, for sexual organisms, half of organisms' genomes get discarded in each generation - and this results in all kinds of problems and dysfunctional organisms. It is hardly good quality copying. However, organic inheritance works well enough, nonetheless. Similarly with cultural inheritance. Some things do get mangled - but *enough* is transmitted for evolutionary theories to work very effectively.

15.14 Memes are sometimes analog

According to John Maynard Smith (1999), the analog nature of some memes prohibits adaptive evolution:

> *Two features necessary for any genetic system that is to support adaptive evolution: The system should be digital and should not permit the 'inheritance of acquired characters'.*

However, this claim is simply wrong. Analog systems can support adaptive evolution - according to basic information theory considerations.

Many memes have analog elements. Brains themselves contain numerous analog components, and - although brains make ubiquitous use of thresholding to cut down the noise levels - not much inside them is *pure*-digital.

Of course, *if* you do have low-fidelity transmission, then the inherited cultural information typically fails to result in adaptive evolution, and is *often* rapidly lost. Similarly with analog information. Analog information typically has *terrible* copying fidelity, and attempts to transmit it down the generations soon results in outcomes similar to those found in games of *Chinese whispers*.

So: analog and low-fidelity transmission mostly represent rather uninteresting corner cases of cultural evolution. However, it seems best for theories of cultural evolution not to *explicitly* exclude analog information. Mathematical models of cultural evolution are mostly indifferent to whether the inherited information is analog or digital.

Indeed, if you look at things from the perspective of information theory, there isn't really much of a distinction between analog and digital information. There's just information, measured in bits. To the extent that analog and digital systems do differ, the differences lie in the type of errors they are prone to. From this kind of perspective, the difference between analog and digital inheritance does not look very interesting.

15.15 Culture is more complicated than that

Memetics is a beautiful, simple idea. However many resist simple explanations of biological phenomena, saying something like: "it is more complicated than that". One example of this is provided by Maurice Bloch (2005):

> *British anthropologists see culture as existing on many levels, learnt implicitly or explicitly in a great variety of ways (e.g. Leach 1954; Bloch 1998). It is not a library of propositions or memes. This type of argument is principally intended as a criticism of American cultural anthropology, which (as we saw) was itself a criticism of diffusionism. But clearly it also applies to the simple diffusionist idea that culture is made up of "bits of information" that spread unproblematically by "transmission" where transmission is understood as a unitary type of phenomenon. British anthropologists, including myself, would argue that knowledge is extremely complex, of many different kinds, and impossible to locate, as though it was a single type.*

So, the idea of memetics is that memes are made of information. Information is complex - in the sense that it can be used to represent or describe anything else, *including* complex objects - but it could be described as being of a "single type". Information can be measured in bits. Memes themselves can be complex - even though the idea of a meme is essentially simple.

The vision of "a library of propositions or memes" conjures up an image which seems obviously wrong. However, nobody thinks that memes are somehow neatly stacked up in brains in the first place. It is well understood that brains are messy tangles. Also, something like *riding a bike* exists partly in muscle memory. Some of that information is stored in the spinal cord - and not in the brain. Cells where viruses reproduce are not neat and orderly either - yet we can still have an epidemiology for viruses. Similarly, despite the brain's tangles, we can still usefully have an epidemiology of ideas.

If there *is* a problem with diffusionism, it is more that the word "diffusion" implies a rather passive process. Memetics rejects the the diffusion terminology (from early cultural anthropology) as being misleading - and replaces it with concepts derived from epidemiology - infection, vector, plague, transmission, pandemic, etc. That in turn promotes the "memes are negative" misunderstanding, but *at least* it successfully gets across the important idea that culture is composed of living, reproducing, evolving, active agents.

15.16 Memetics does not explain meme fitnesses

The longest criticism of memetics I have seen comes from Maria Kronfeldner (2007). Her critique runs to over 300 pages - and has now been turned into a book. In her summary (p.290) she writes:

Given that there is no independence of meme diffusion from human individuals, the explanatory units of selection analogy ends up in an explanatory dilemma: Either the analogy is heuristically trivial, because it loses its main claim, namely that memetics presents an alternative to the traditional explanation, which is given in terms of properties and interests of humans, or the explanatory units of selection analogy is trivial in explanatory terms, because it is tautological – it does not explain anything, since it merely states that those memes that have a high actual survival are those memes that have a high propensity for survival, without explaining where this high fitness emerges from.

Genetics doesn't explain much about the fitness of genes either - it is more about the nuts and bolts of how genes combine. However, if you look a little further afield, to evolution and ecology, there is a wealth on information about why some genes are fitter than others. It is much the same with memes - that isn't really the domain of memetics, but we really do have *lots* of information about how and why some ideas spread, and others do not. Ideas vary in their truth, how memorable they are, how short they are, whether they activate humour, desire, fear or boredom in those exposed to them - and so on. We don't know *everything* about why meme fitnesses vary - but we don't know everything about how gene fitnesses vary either.

Serenely and Griffiths (1999 p.334) have essentially the same complaint:

With the possible exception of scientific ideas, we have no explanation of the nature of the fitness of ideas, nor do we typically understand why they differ in fitness. We can call a tune "a meme with high replication potential" rather than "catchy" if we like. But without source laws, this adds nothing to our understanding of musical trends.

There is a *lot* of information relating to the fitness of ideas out there - even if Serenely and Griffiths are not aware of it. I don't *really* see how they can be unaware of this kind of material, though. Even *if* there were no known rules of how cultural fitness worked, that would not be a problem for memetics. All it would mean is that people would have to start studying the issue - if they wanted to understand it. Meme fitnesses evidently vary - and if you don't understand why, then one obvious solution is to study the issue. As Crozier (2008) says:

> *Cultural evolution should not be expected to provide an explanation for the psychological attractiveness of a trait any more than biological evolution should explain why a bird's wings are aerodynamically sound: that is where the theory of aerodynamics comes in.*

Memetics doesn't pretend to completely explain gene fitnesses - any more than genetics pretends to completely explain gene fitnesses. Such issues are more a matter for biologists or ecologists.

15.17 Culture is designed - not evolved

In 2009, Steven Pinker said:

> *Design without a designer is essential for biological evolution - but it is perverse for cultural evolution: there really is a designer - the human brain - and there's nothing mystical or mysterious about saying that.*

That some aspects of culture are designed does *not* mean that culture doesn't evolve, or that we don't need a selection-based model to model how it changes. There are *plenty* of places where memes compete with each other and undergo selection. That happens in science, technology, marketplaces, languages and charities. That is what you need a Darwinian model of culture for.

Memetics does not deny a role for intelligent design by the human mind. In memetics, intelligent design is a source of mutations. Mutations are a basic element of all evolutionary theories - and there is no rule saying that mutations have to be random.

It is worth noting that intelligence itself contains evolutionary processes. Minds constantly attempt to maintain a compact and parsimonious world model, and their model of the world evolves. A considerable amount of trial-and-error testing processes go on in minds. Thoughts compete with other thoughts, possible actions compete with other possible actions and synapses compete with other synapses.

Most optimisation processes work using trials, variation, and information that persists via copying. You really have to go back to *random search* to find an optimisation process that doesn't even feature inheritance.

15.18 Memetics makes no predictions and is unfalsifiable

Massimo Pigliucci (2007) goes so far as to claim that memetics is unfalsifiable.

> *Popper's objection remains valid for memetics: the only way to tell which memes are going to be successful, which tunes are going to stick in your mind, or which religions are going to become popular is by waiting and seeing what happens. That is, memeticists completely lack a functional ecological theory of memes. Without it, the whole enterprise is scientifically empty.*

This accusation is not true. Scientists know a *lot* about what spreads and what does not. It is *totally false* to claim that the only way to know if something will be successful is to try it and see. For instance, these days we have a mountain of information about what status updates get "retweeted" on social networks. Dan Zarrella's 2009 paper "The Science of Retweets" has *lots* of details about that.

15.19 Alleged danger

Another reasonably commonly-cited criticism is a paper entitled: "Memetics: a dangerous idea" by Luis Benites-Bribiesca (2001). Part of the abstract reads:

> *Memetics is a dangerous idea that poses a threat to the serious study of consciousness and cultural evolution.*

Inflammatory material - though perhaps Dennett would agree that this material is "dangerous". Another who would raise the alarm is Allen Orr (1996a):

> *Except to a handful of biologists, there is little "dangerous" in the idea that Biology is Engineering. There is something dangerous, though, in the idea that Darwinism transcends biology, undermining our views of culture, consciousness, and morality.*

OK, then: if that is dangerous, then memetics is indeed dangerous. Those attached to rigid and inaccurate conceptions of the scope of Darwin's theory of evolution should take special care with it.

15.20 There is no memetic code

Critic Luis Benites-Bribiesca (2001) says:

> *For evolution and selection to take place, genetic information has to be stored in a relatively stable molecule such as DNA in what Schrodinger referred as a "code script".*

This is not correct. Evolutionary theory simply *doesn't* require that genetic information has to be stored in stable molecules. It makes no mention of the medium of inheritance. There are other possibilities - for example, the information could be stored in streams of photons or electrons. This kind of thing actually happens frequently - when memes move around in the modern world.

15.21 Memetics is nothing new

One complaint is that memetics fails to offer anything new. The exact complaints vary. Here is Maurice Bloch (2005) on the topic:

> I noted above that, in many ways, Dawkins' work on memes - and that of other writers who have followed him, such as Dennett - is a good, accessible introduction to what is intrinsic in social and cultural anthropology. This fact, however, will not necessarily endear memetics to anthropologists. At a general level, Dawkins and Dennett make very similar, if not identical, points to those which anthropologists have always made about human culture.

Memetics certainly isn't just a rehashing of what anthropologists have always thought. Michael Ruse (2008) has a slightly different complaint:

> one is really just taking regular language and putting it in fancy terms. No new insights. No new predictions.

This isn't right- if the theory of Darwinian evolution covers all of human culture, that *is* a big deal. Massimo Pigliucci (2007) says:

> memetics - at least for now - doesn't seem to add anything to the standard view of gene-culture co-evolution that was developed well before Dawkins put down his ideas in The Selfish Gene.

Before *The Selfish Gene* (Dawkins 1976), the field of cultural evolution was *much* more of a disorganised mess than it is today. Today, we have lots of scientific papers on the topic, but back then, academic study of the area was a mere trickle. Dawkins *mostly* contributed useful terminology - and drew attention to this important and neglected field.

Another complaint is this (anonymous) one:

> The idea that culture, and ideas, are evolving is not new. Popper, with his "evolutionary epistemology" (Popper, 1969), was already advancing the idea that scientific ideas were evolving a little like gene; the most fit had more chance to survive longer, while poor ideas were doomed to extinction.

It is true that we have had theories of cultural evolution dating back over a century. However, Dawkins did a *fine* thing by drawing attention to the concept in his 1976 book, and the associated New Scientist article. He popularised the idea - much as he also popularised the work of Bill Hamilton in the earlier chapters of the same book. Popularisation is useful and important work.

15.22 Memetics terminology is pointless

Andrew Brown (2009) complains:

> *But why call these studies "memetic"? If you're going to use "meme" as a synonym for "idea"; what's the point? What is added to our understanding?*

Meme is *not* a synonym for "idea", though. Memes are transmitted from one person to the next, while ideas may not be.

Martin Gardner (2000) wrote:

> *The point is that the notion of a meme is much too broad to be useful in explaining human thinking and behavior. A meme is little more than a peculiar terminology for saying the obvious. Who can deny that cultures change in ways independent of genetics, ways involving information that is spread throughout society mainly by spoken and written words?*

Memes *do* seem rather obvious - once you understand them. The problem is that only a tiny fraction of people seems to understand the idea. Gardner continues with:

> *To critics, who at the moment far outnumber true believers, memetics is no more than a cumbersome terminology for saying what everybody knows and that can be more usefully said in the dull terminology of information transfer.*

By contrast, using a term for contagious ideas that evokes the biological concept of a gene seems to be a *fine* piece of terminological engineering to me. I think these days we can just point at the enormous scale of the modern usage of the term "meme" to illustrate that there was indeed a need for such a term before Richard Dawkins came up with it. The beauty of the meme terminology is that it lets you access the terminology of genetics, while keeping tabs on whether you are talking about organic or memetic inheritance.

15.23 Unpalatable truth

Some apparently dislike memetics because it doesn't seem to present a very nice picture of human nature. Daniel Dennett (1991, p. 202) describes some of his first impressions of the idea:

I don't know about you, but I'm not initially attracted by the idea of my brain as a sort of dung heap in which the larvae of other people's ideas renew themselves, before sending out copies of themselves in an informational Diaspora. It does seem to rob my mind of its importance as both author and critic.

Conventionally, a human is the product of genetic and environmental influences. Memetics points out that some of the environment consists of memes. People are familiar with the idea that the environment contains pathogens and other organisms - who don't have their best interests at heart, and often attempt to manipulate them. One of the memetics insights is that much of the rest of the cultural ecosystem is like that too. Things that people didn't previously consider to be alive are *actually* out to manipulate them, in much the same way that pathogens are. People understand that other people may try to manipulate them through books, television and other media. However, memetics says that culture tends to behave like this - even if there are no manipulative human beings involved.

Some might feel liberated and empowered by this knowledge - a better understanding of the forces at work helps to deal with them. However, others don't like the idea that they are - in part - constructed my memes. People often don't like the idea that their behaviours are being controlled by DNA genes - and the idea that they are being controlled by memes is an additional insult. Humans are built by evolution to believe that they are powerful masters of their own fate. The idea that their actions are largely the product of a swarm of copied fragments of information seems to be an affront to their self-mastery.

One reviewer put it this way:

Some years ago, Richard Dawkins published "The Selfish Gene", explaining how gene survival was fundamental in natural selection. He also coined the term "meme" to explain the dissemination of ideas across societies. Almost immediately, there was a strident chorus of objection, based on the theme of "you can't say that about humans!"

Richard Barbrook put it this way in his "Memesis Critique":

The real crime of the Memesis statement is the way that it willfully obscures the process of human innovation and creativity under a mass of dodgy biological metaphors. In contrast, we must celebrate the Promethean power of humans to create - and recreate - themselves. It is precisely our refusal to accept our biological destiny which makes us more than insects. Unlike our fellow species, we can transform ourselves through thought and action.

This kind of thing is an appeal to the human ego. Humans cherish their sense of self-mastery. They don't like to hear that they are products of genes and memes - they often seem to find that insulting and degrading. Lastly, here's Dennett (2009b).

> *Finally, one of the most persistent sources of discomfort about memes is the dreaded suspicion that an account of human minds in terms of brains being parasitized by memes will undermine the precious traditions of human creativity.*

People had a hard time adjusting to the first Darwinian revolution. The second wave of Darwinism is causing at least as many problems for people. It was bad enough learning that you are a product of natural selection - but to learn that many of your thoughts and ideas are themselves subject to mutation and selection as well seems to be too much for some people.

15.24 Naked memes

Some claim that memotypes (cultural genotypes) acting as meme phenotypes is a problem for memetics. For example, here is Jonathan Marks (2004):

> *In microevolutionary theory we distinguish between genes, the hereditary units themselves, and phenotypes, their expression and interface with the outside world. Memes are commonly used in both senses, suggesting that the analogy breaks down very quickly. Obviously if there is no distinction between the units of replication (genes) and the units of interaction (phenotypes), then it immediately becomes unclear just what value lies in modelling cultural processes as if they mimicked genetics.*

Massimo Pigliucci has much the same complaint:

> *To begin with, unlike the case of genes, there doesn't seem to be any distinction between memes themselves and the phenotypes they produce. Genes in some sense "encode" proteins, and proteins have a variety of effects that indirectly contribute to the fitness of the organism carrying those genes. In Dawkins's own terms, there is a distinction between "replicators" (the genes) and "interactors" (the organisms themselves). But, in the case of memes, the replicating "unit," for example, an annoying tune that gets into your head, forcing you to whistle it, and thereby gets stuck into somebody else's head, is both replicator and interactor.*

Willem Drees (2011) writes, in the Times Higher Education supplement:

> *In the theory of memes, the distinction between the genotype and the phenotype, in other words the one that exists between the recipe*

(genes) and the complete organism, is simply not there.

This confusion should be easily dissolved. Culture *does* have the meme/pheme split, just as the organic world has the gene/phene split. Memes are the cultural equivalent of genes. It is true that there are some cases where the memes and their phenotypes are represented by the same physical structures. However, this is *sometimes* true in organic world as well. There are what are known as "naked genes". Prions are probably the most famous of these. Prions are able to spread without being contained within a cell wall, or a viral sheath. Cairns-Smith's clay mineral genes are also examples of naked genes. Naked genes are perhaps *more common* in cultural evolution than they are in organic evolution - but that doesn't seem to be a particularly big deal.

15.25 Complex developmental tangles

Some say that the tangles of development thwart a memetic analysis. Wimsatt (1999, p. 288) writes:

> *In genetics, and in evolutionary biology, the structure of our theories supposes that we can separate out processes of heredity, development, and selection - if not physically, then at least analytically, each from the other, in our models of the evolutionary process. But these three dimensions of the evolutionary process are inextricably fused and confounded in the process of cultural evolution. This happens because of the pivotal role development and the life cycle assume in cultural transmission.*

From my perspective, this is the opposite of the "naked memes" objection (above). In that, it was claimed that cultural developmental processes are so simple as to be non-existent. Here cultural developmental processes are being claimed to be far too complex for an analysis of inheritance to succeed.

Development is *incredibly* tangled and complex in the organic world as well. Population genetics just treats development as a black box, and completely bypasses the details of development in its analysis. Population memetics does *exactly* the same thing with a similar level of effectiveness. It turns out that there are an awful lot of questions that can be answered using this kind of approach. Now, I can easily imagine how ignoring development might irritate developmental biologists - but it really does make a *lot* of science to have a science of inheritance and a science of development. These really are pretty different subject areas.

15.26 "Just So" stories

Memetics sometimes gets criticised for being a colloection of "Just So" stories. Howard Klepper (2000) suggested that Blackmore's *The Meme Machine* went too far in that direction:

> *Blackmore applauds sociobiology as a science that has made great progress, and sees its critics as Luddites who are afraid of having their superstitions about human nature dispelled. But she never engages the serious criticism of sociobiology (and its close relative, evolutionary psychology) by those who find it lacking in the elements of hard science. Those critics call sociobiology a collection of "just-so" stories, which confuse teleology with causation and lack any evidentiary basis in genetics.*

Mark Rosenfeldter (2001) offers a similar criticism of Aaron Lynch's book *Thought Contagion*:

> *Lynch's book is deeply disappointing; what memetics has chiefly generated is a new way to blather about society, sex, and politics, without rigor and without the slightest need to make sense. Lynch worries a bit in the introduction about this reaction; he pleads for a little patience - he wants to show what sort of exciting ideas memetics can come up with, not get bogged down in factual nitpicking. What he doesn't see is that the real problem is not just that he gets facts wrong. It's that he's developed memetics into a scheme for generating factless scenarios. By excluding rigorous analysis, testing, and verification from his methodology, he's simply refined an ability to tell just-so stories about social behaviors.*

This certainly seems to be a reasonable criticism of *Thought Contagion*. That *was* a relatively early book, but it was *full* of speculation, with *very little* examination of the facts.

However, "Just So" stories afflict genetics too. These days, there are plenty of people doing real science in the field - not just telling appealing stories. A few people telling what *might* turn out to be speculative "Just So" stories does not seem to be a good reason for writing off the whole field.

15.27 Lamarck's curse

Calling a biological theory "Lamarckian" is frequently done as part of an attempt to discredit it. As Crozier (2008) puts it:

> *Lamarckian evolution has long been disconfirmed in biology, supplanted by a Darwinian theory of blind variation and selective retention. Consequently, when an evolutionary theory is charged with being Lamarckian, generally this is meant to imply that the theory is*

seriously flawed.

I'll let Steven Pinker voice the objection. Though one of those leading the way with the enormously-delayed first Darwinian invasion of the social sciences, he seem to be dragging his feet when it comes to the second wave. Here is he is in his 1997 book:

> *To say that cultural evolution is Lamarckian is to confess that one has no idea how it works*

Cultural evolution is *mostly* Weismannian - i.e. showing no inheritance of acquired characteristics.

Cultural evolution is *occasionally* Lamarckian - at least in the sense that phenotypic traits acquired during a cultural entity's lifetime can be *sometimes* transcribed into its germ line and passed on to offspring.

However, it *isn't true* to say that we have no idea how this process works. If someone reverse-engineers an acquired cultural phenotypic trait and then codes it into the germ line, it is pretty clear what is going on.

There are *plenty* of areas of cultural evolution that are *not* Lamarckian. One should not consider an evolutionary framework to be falsified just because some of its dynamics don't fit in with your preconceptions. Dennett (1998a) also dismantles the same criticism from Pinker.

Gould (1997) had a rather different complaint:

> *Evolutionists have long understood that Darwinism cannot operate effectively in systems of Lamarckian inheritance – for Lamarckian change has such a clear direction, and permits evolution to proceed so rapidly, that the much slower process of natural selection shrinks to insignificance before the Lamarckian juggernaut.*

Alas, Gould claims that cultural evolution is Lamarckian because: "Whatever we invent in our lifetimes, we can pass on to our children by our writing and teaching." That is almost certainly *not* how we should interpret Lamarck's idea of the inheritance of acquired characteristics - or else we will wind up classifying a dog passing its fleas on to its offspring as a case of Lamarckian inheritance.

Jablonka and Lamb (2005, p.209) complain that the possibility of Lamarckian inheritance causes problems for memetics because:

> *The problem for the meme concept is that if the developmental processes that vehicles undergo result in the generation of variations that are heritable then the distinction between gene-like replicators and phenotype-vehicles breaks down.*

Whether that is true depends a good deal on how you define the term "meme". If *memes* consist of heritable cultural information, and *phemes* consist of things that are constructed from them, then the distinction between the two *doesn't* break down if Lamarckian inheritance occurs. That is how the term "meme" is used in this book. If you use the word in that way, then Jablonka and Lamb's criticism is no longer applicable.

15.28 Weak predictions

John Maynard Smith (1995c) writes:

> *The explanatory power of evolutionary theory rests largely on three assumptions: that mutation is non-adaptive, that acquired characters are not inherited, and that inheritance is Mendelian - that is, it is atomic, and we inherit the atoms, or genes, equally from our two parents, and from no one else. In the cultural analogy, none of these things is true. This must severely limit the ability of a theory of cultural inheritance to say what can happen and, more importantly, what cannot happen.*

Maynard-Smith is correct in stating that cultural evolutions permits a wider range of possibilities than is available to in organic evolution. However, the possibilities are not *so* broad that predictions based on the theory become useless. Mutations may not *always* be non-adaptive - but they are usually small - so culture forms a branching network similar to that found in organic evolution - which itself constrains the resulting possibilities. The *occasional* cases of inheritance of acquired characteristics, and analog inheritance don't make that much difference. The increased range of possibilities available in cultural evolution represents an interesting feature - but not a terribly problematical one.

15.29 No Mendel of culture

John Maynard Smith (1995c) writes:

> *My uneasiness with the notion of memes arises because we do not know the rules whereby they are transmitted. A science of population genetics is possible because the laws of transmission - Mendel's laws - are known. Dennett would agree that no comparable science of memetics is as yet possible.*

It is hardly surprising that we know more about organic gene transmission as meme transmission. Organic gene recombination is a relatively simple matter - while for memes, most recombination currently takes place in the *tremendously* complex environment of the human mind. However, we certainly *do* have predictive theories about meme transmission and recombination. Psychology and anthropology have a wealth of knowledge on these topics.

A *full* understanding of memetics may have to wait until we have cracked the problem of constructing artificial intelligence - and can simulate the human mind reasonably well. However, much progress can be made - and has been made - by treating the brain as a black box - examining what goes into it, and what comes out of it - and then inferring things about the underlying dynamics. This is the approach taken by population memetics.

15.30 Long-isolated cultures can sill interbreed

Some think the relative lack of isolation in cultural evolution is some sort of problem. Here is Orr, H. Allen (1996a) on this topic:

> *memes and genes differ in other fundamental ways. Species, once isolated, almost never exchange genes, while exchange between long-isolated cultures is immensely important in the history of ideas.*

Stephen J. Gould agrees, saying:

> *The basic topologies of biological and cultural change are completely different. Biological evolution is a system of constant divergence without subsequent joining of branches. Lineages, once distinct, are seperate forever. In human history, transmission across lineages is, perhaps, the major source of cultural change.*

There *is* a difference between organic and cultural evolution in this area - cultural isolation is less extreme. However, isolation in organic evolution is less than perfect - viruses sometimes drag genes around from one lineage to the next. Cultural evolution *does* exhibit a range of types of partial isolation: for example, COBOL programs interbreed little with origami designs. So, this seems to be more like a quantitative difference than a qualitative one. *Even* if there was no equivalent of a cultural species, culture would still evolve. Much of population genetics and evolutionary theory would still apply in the cultural domain.

15.31 Memes do not self-replicate

In a section entitled "The Myth of Self-replication" Wimsatt (2010) complains that memes are not self-replicators, as *supposedly* claimed by Dawkins in 1976. His objection is that they need a lot of complex equipment in order to make copies of themselves, and so are copied, rather than being true self-replicating entities.

Memes do not *literally* make copies of themselves unassisted. Nor do DNA-genes, which *also* depend on a lot of equipment before copies are produced.

I don't think anyone ever claimed otherwise. Memetics certainly doesn't depend on the memes making copies of themselves without assistance. There *is* a sense in which such entities "self-replicate" - if you consider the rest of the organism they are part of to be part of their environment. All things that copy themselves exist in some kind of environment, and depend on features of that environment to operate. However, this whole point about self-replication seems too mundane and trivial to bother having much of an argument about. That the thing that is copied must also do the copying is not a tenet of genetics - or memetics - in the first place.

The critique of Wimsatt (2010) is revealing in another way. The author *acknowledges* Dual Inheritance Theory, cites Boyd and Richerson - and *agrees* that culture evolves. In other words, the guts of the meme theory are accepted. He even postulates his own copied cultural elements - which he calls "Meme-Like-Things" (MLTs). The main difference between these and memes seems to be that his MLTs don't "self-replicate", whereas memes - supposedly - do.

I find this sort of thing rather exasperating. Call them "memes" already! The battle for the terminology to describe small bits of information in cultural evolution is *surely* now over. The *meme* term is fine. We don't need every author on the topic making up their own terminology in the hope of coining a new term.

15.32 Critique from semiotics

Some theorists from semiotics don't seem to like memes. Deacon (1999) says:

> *The theory of memetics is not the answer to a theory of social and psychological evolution, but reinterpreted it may suggest some bridging concepts that can lead to a unifying methodology for the semiotic sciences.*

...while Krull (2000) says:

> *meme is a degenerate sign in which only its ability of being copied is remained.*

The semiotics students are correct to say that memes are signs - *provided* we use the definition of the term "sign" from within semiotics - which is - pretty confusingly - different from the usual english usage of the term. However, they don't seems to have any kind of coherent case against memetics. It seems to be more that they would prefer to use the terminology of semiotics - even though the evolutionary biologists got there decades before them, and have a far more relevant discipline behind them.

15.33 Memetics violates Occam's razor

Mary Midgley (2004, p.70) thinks memetics is too complicated - and that its story of parasites and mutualists is unnecessary:

> *As William of Occam observed, varieties of entities should not be multiplied beyond necessity. When human beings think and act, no extra entities need to be present in them besides themselves.*

What Occam said was that you should not multiply entities *beyond necessity*. A certain amount of explanatory material is often needed is one is to actually explain the facts. Memes are, in fact, a pretty neat and beautiful explanation of human culture. Memetics essentially says that culture is part of biology, and fits neatly into a Darwinian framework. Where previously there were independent explanation for phenomena in the cultural and organic realms, memetics explains a lot of the phenomena in both realms with a single theory, evolutionary theory. The motive is to explain many facts with a single simple, general theory. The numerous symbiotes and parasites of memetics arise *naturally* from the dynamics of evolutionary theory, and should not be counted as being *additional* assumptions. This is surely a project that gets the "thumbs up" signal from Occam.

15.34 Too negative

Some say memeticists exaggerate the negative side of memes:

> *The meme, like any apparatus of evolution, lacks intent or purpose. Dennett, however, subverts this claim by describing the meme as a vicious and aggressive "parasite." Meme replication, in Dennett's language, sounds like a dangerous plague attacking humanity.*

This is one of the complaints Peter Richerson (2010f) raises about memes as well:

> *One of the problems with the meme concept as it evolved is that users of the term focused far too heavily on the selfish potential of memes.*

Historically, it appears that there's some truth to this accusation of negativity. However, some of this is understandable. It is important to bear in mind that the cases where memes act as parasites (where meme interests and gene interests conflict) are the very ones where it is easiest to distinguish between the meme-based hypothesis, and the "inherited treasures" model of cultural evolution, and the idea that benefits must ultimately accrue to DNA genes. Also, cases where memes benefit at the expense of humans are often the cases of most interest - since many people want to know what to avoid. Tales of conflict often make the best stories as well - and then selective retelling results in the conflict stories being encountered more.

So, yes, some meme enthusiasts *have* emphasised the negative side of memes - but there are reasonable reasons for that.

15.35 We are too ignorant to say that cultural evolution is Darwinian

Here is Orr, H. Allen (1996a) on this topic:

> *it is far from clear that Darwinism can account for the percolation of ideas, styles, and songs through culture. In fact, there is a basic problem with any such claim - we are very ignorant of how humans hold ideas in their heads and of how the ideas in your head influence the ideas in my head. So how can we possibly conclude that the process "must be" Darwinian?*

This may sound like humility, but it goes too far. The discovery of Darwinian evolution preceded the discovery of DNA by almost a century. We don't know *exactly* how ideas are represented in brains, but the lack of a cultural *Watson and Crick* should not cause scholars to get stuck in a pre-Darwinian era.

15.36 Cultural evolution is too different - we should start again

Richard Lewontin, in a 2003 lecture entitled, "Does Culture Evolve?" said:

> *I would claim to you that culture should not be analogised to particles like genes that are transmitted, that the notion of transmission is wrong, and that if we want to understand the history of culture, we need to start from culture, and not try to make it isomorphic with some other system of phenomena that we understand too well. That's the bottom line the thing I really want to impress on you most and that is the Darwainaian theory of evolution and its modern form, which I have tried to explain in the previous two lectures, are theories and systems designed to match a particular set of natural phenomena, there's nothing universal about them.*

> *They are tailor-made in every aspect to deal with mortal individuals, with lifespans, with particular mechanisms of transmission of genes of particular kinds of relations and building of the environment, and so on... and if we are to have any kind of successful lawlike dynamical systems for human cultures, we need to discard our knowledge of the phenomenon of biological evolution, and take culture for itself as a set of phenomena and build a set of mechanisms and theories based on our understanding of that phenomenon.*

This *appears* to be reversal of his views when compared with the opinions expressed in Lewontin (1970) and Lewontin (1981). We don't need to "discard our knowledge of the phenomenon of biological evolution". Cultural evolution *does* have *some* differences from organic evolution - but there are *enormous* similarities with the organic world. An underlying unifying theory of evolution of culture offers a great deal.

15.37 Memeticis is not socially acceptable

Kate Distin (2010, p.233) suggests that memetics is not socially acceptable:

> *For now, at least, even though in my view memetics has established that it is quite theoretically respectable, in practice it is not yet quite socially acceptable.*

There are certainly some areas where plenty of scorn is poured on memetics. Distin's solution was to simply drop the "meme" terminology. However, that solution has serious problems. The first few chapters of this book do not contain the term meme. Doing that for very long is a painful process. It isn't just the term meme, it is all the rest of the genetics-based terminology that comes along with it. Repeatedly saying things like "cultural variant drift" and "cultural variant pool" - instead of "memetic drift" and "meme pool" - would be unnacceptably long winded.

So: political correctness be damned. If some people don't get along with meme terminology, that is their loss. Memetics *is* the correct theory of cultural evolution - or so close to it that it is easily bent into shape. The serious students of cultural evolution within academia have converged on something so close to memetics as to be practically indistinguishable from it. Plus memetics has the best and most popular terminology.

15.38 Memetics hasn't produced anything original

Some claim that memetics has not resulted in anything original. For example, Adam Kuper (2000) says:

> *And that is my deal objection to the whole memes industry: it has yet to deliver a single original and plausible analysis of any cultural or social process.*

Cultural evolution is an old idea, but memetics has stimulated many people to consider it who would probably not otherwise have done so - and they have produced an original body of work. Blackmore's idea that memes promoted human ultrasociality has *mostly* cashed out in the last decade. Her idea that memes are responsible for the enlarged human cranium is both original and plausible, in my opinion. Memetics was first to apply epidemiological ideas to cultural phenomena, and now this idea is *much* more widespread. Peter Richerson (2011f), an expert in cultural evolution, concedes that Dawkins got this analysis right:

> *I think it is near to undeniable that cultural variants are sometimes selected to become selfish pathogens along the lines that Dawkins suggested.*

Also, in the mean time, ideas such as "viral marketing" and the "epidemic threshold" have become basic concepts in social media marketing (Zarella 2011b).

15.39 Memeticists can't agree on what a meme is

Mary Midgley (2004) wrote:

> *Unless some clear picture emerges, showing what kind of entity memes are supported to be, the parallel between them and genes surely vanishes, and the claim to scientific status with it.*

No. We understood that organic world evolved long before the mechanisms of inheritance were uncovered and the structure of DNA was revealed. Darwin didn't know what genes were or how they were implemented. A *lot* of useful scientific work can be done by treating the brain as a black box, considering its inputs and outputs.

We won't know the mechanisms by which memes evolve in as much detail as we know how nuclear genes evolve until we crack a lot of problems in artificial intelligence and neuroscience. However, there are still *plenty* of things we can do in the mean time. Population memetics does not depend on having such a detailed understanding of the microscopic nature of memes.

15.40 Evolutionists should present a united front

Some are cautious about controversial evolutionary ideas, and wonder if it would be better to present a united front.

In some countries Darwinists battle against biblical creationism, and there is a history of the creationists using Darwinian controversies on the edges of the science to make out that evolution is somehow not settled science, and is still controversial. For an example, see Robert Wright's 2001 article, "The Accidental Creationist". Since memetics is controversial, some say that perhaps scientists should hold back, so we don't show our underbellies to the creationists. Here's Richard Dawkins in the "Evolutionary Perspectives" panel discussion.

> *I know that there's a certain amount of hostility "out there" to people*

who think that Darwinism is being too aggressively promoted - and I am sensitive to that and I am sufficiently anxious to promote the fundamental form of Darwinism which is the one that Darwin himself and the explains all of life - I mean that's quite a big thing in the first place I think it would be rather a shame if we lost the battle to get people to understand this really very fundamental fact through being a little bit too over-enthusiastic to push the Darwinian line on all sorts of other things which some sensitive people regard as their own territory. So sometimes for tactical reasons I shrink back from venturing into other fields that others have pushed Darwinism into - but I think my heart's with them.

I don't think caution on this front is necessary when it comes to culture, which *plainly* evolves. It is not necessary to keep quiet about memetics "for tactical reasons". Indeed, if anything memetics is an important tool for understanding how religions can still spread even though they present false accounts of the world, and may not necessarily be good for those who are involved with them.

15.41 Memetics is "mind-blind"

Atran (2004) describes memetics as being "mind-blind". Similarly, Pinker (2009) criticised Dennett's presentation of memetics as lacking details about cognitive processes, emotions and motives.

Population memetics treats the mind as a black box. Since most meme mutations take place inside minds, that means that most memetic mutational processes are *also* inside the black box. Such models are *very* useful for modelling cultural change - and they have the virtue of being simple enough to be tractable - but they make no claims to being *complete* models.

Of course, any *complete* theory of memetics would have to model the insides of the black box. However, we don't *fully* understand all the details of that just yet. So, I will plead guilty on the part of population memetics to being "mind-blind". Black-boxing complex and poorly-understood elements is a standard part of scientific modelling. *Hopefully* - as time passes - we will be able to fill in the details of the box, and develop more complex models of memetic recombination, mutation and *de novo* creativity in the process - though these will probably complement - rather than replace - the simpler population memetic models.

However, in the mean time, black-boxing the mind has proved to be a masterful move. Most of the successes in the field to date are due to using population memetics. Also, most of the peer-reviewed science in the area has arisen out of this approach as well.

15.42 Memetic linkage is too strong

Some claim that memes have stronger dependencies on their neighbours than genes do. For example consider this, from Adam Kuper (2000):

Even if memes are just ideas and we specify the ideas rather more precisely than Dawkins has done in these instances, they should not then be treated as isolates. Unlike genes cultural traits are not particulate. An idea about God cannot be separated from other ideas with which it is indissolubly linked in a particular religion.

In fact, memes are a *lot* like genes in this respect. Genes depend of their neighbouring genes about as much as memes depend on neighbouring memes do. Certainly both *sometimes* have *substantial* dependencies on their neighbours - and rely on their presence to work effectively.

15.43 Cultural evolution exhibits progress

In a discussion relating to David Hull's ideas about the evolution of scientific theories, Michael Ruse wrote:

It makes good sense to say the Mendel was ahead of his predecessors, just as Watson and Crick were ahead of their predecessors. Yet as Darwinian evolutionists are perpetually telling us, biological evolution is not progressive (Williams 1966). Appearances to the contrary, it is a rather slow process, going nowhere.

This seems fairly straight-forwards. In a sufficiently large and benign environment, evolution is indeed progressive. The progress made by cultural evolution is, in fact, built directly on top of the cumulative progress made by organic evolution. Not *all* evolution is progressive. For example, if there was a nuclear war, we would probably see a lot of extinction and devolution, neither of which are progressive. If meteorite strikes on the Earth were more frequent, evolution here might not be progressive. However, meteorite strikes are relatively rare - and so evolution is progressive.

15.44 Memes don't have loci

Genes have loci - but memes don't. According to David Burbridge (2003):

Biological individuals compete with each other for available resources, and genes compete with each other for possession of genetic 'loci'. There is nothing closely analogous to this in cultural evolution. It is true that some cultural traits are incompatible with others - you cannot be a Muslim and a Roman Catholic - but this is probably the exception rather than the rule. It is therefore doubtful whether there is a 'struggle for existence' among most cultural traits.

This one seems to be the opposite of the truth to me. For practically every example of culture it is possible to think of, it is possible to come up with an allele. Books compete with other books. Movies compete with other movies. Music competes with other music. Languages compete with other languages. Operating systems compete. Web sites compete. Scientific concepts compete. Only in a few areas are there cultural monopolies, or cultural fixation.

15.45 Culture exhibits insufficient variation

Culture doesn't have enough variation to evolve. According to David Burbridge (2003):

> *In biology, most organisms have the capacity to produce many offspring, and there is considerable variance in reproductive success. This is a prerequisite for natural selection to operate. In culture, by contrast, even if social groups may sometimes in a loose sense reproduce (e.g. by forming colonies), the rate of 'reproduction' is very low, and has little variance. For example, there are nearly 200 recognised independent countries in the world, but it is doubtful if any of them can be said to have 'reproduced' during the last century (unless you count the breakup of the USSR and Yugoslavia as 'reproduction'). Yet there has been immense cultural change in all of those countries during that period.*

Here Burbridge is just giving a cherry-pickled example. Consider instead the billions of copies of "The Holy Bible", vs the small number of copies of "The Little Cyanide Cookbook". That is a massive difference in reproductive success. Or consider "The Beatles" vs "Vashti Bunyan". Again, a *massive* difference in reproductive success. Reproductive success exhibits *huge* variance in cultural evolution just as it does in organic evolution.

15.46 Memetics denies a role for chance processes

Some think memetics is adaptationist. For instance, here is Gil-White (2006):

> *Dennett and Dawkins suggest that the only thing affecting a meme's spread is whether the meme itself is good at replicating, and that selection will successively edit the meme's content so that it is ever better at replicating. This is the 'meme's eye view': only the properties of a meme (i.e. its content) determine its spread. But a meme can be lucky.*

It seems to be a misunderstanding. Neither Dennett nor Dawkins suggested that. Also, that is not what the term "meme's eye view" means, either.

15.47 Deleterious cultural traits can't evolve adaptations

David Burbridge (2003) claims that the deleterious side of culture is problematical:

Biological traits are usually adaptive for the individuals who possess them, in the sense that possession of the trait enhances their reproductive fitness. Genes producing traits that impair reproductive fitness will be eliminated by natural selection. In contrast, there is no reason to suppose that cultural traits (with some important exceptions, such as economic competition in a free market) are usually beneficial in any sense to the individuals or groups that possess them.

Here, Burbridge is looking for benefits to the individual humans. However in memetics the fundamental idea is that cultural entities benefit. When a wave of copy-cat suicides takes place, the hosts don't benefit, it is the suicide meme that gets greater circulation. Compare with viruses, you see that cold viruses are not advantageous for their hosts, either. When a human sneezes, one does not ask how this benefits them. The benefit accrues not to the sneezing human, but rather to the virus they are infected with. Similarly, cultural adaptations, don't necessarily benefit their human hosts. The benefits accrue to the cultural entities themselves.

John Carroll (2010) makes a similar point:

Specific genes are functionally organized to replicate organisms of a specific type, and specific types of organisms are functionally organized to replicate specific genes. The relation between memes and human organisms constitutes no such functionally integrated structure in a replicative process. Specific ideas and cultural practices (memes) might or might not contribute to the inclusive fitness of individual human organisms, but human organisms are not functionally organized to replicate specific memes.

Once again the problem lies in looking for the benefits to humans. In memetics, benefits can *also* accrue to the cultural entities themselves. For example, humans have few adaptations for spreading Catholicism - but Catholicism has lots of Catholicism-spreading adaptations. The idea is that human genes benefit humans in the same way that Catholicism's memes benefit Catholicism. Humans are meme *hosts*. They don't necessarily benefit from their memes any more than they benefit from cold and flu viruses they carry.

15.48 Are memes "quasi-autonomous bots"?

William Benzon wrote in 2010:

> *She has misstated my problem with memes, asserting that it is the TERM I do not like. Not so. I think the term is brilliant, which is why I use it. What I object to is the USE of the term to indicate quasi-autonomous bots that go hopping about from brain to brain commandeering neural realestate in competition with other one another.*

Memes are informational – and so are not really "quasi-autonomous bots". They are more like computer programs. Thinking about them "hopping about from brain to brain" seems fairly reasonable, as does their competing with each other. Memes are comparable to the genes of viruses or bacteria - due to them frequently having small genomes and short generation times.

15.49 Not an analogy!

That is enough criticisms for now. Many of the criticisms of memetics point to areas where meme dynamics are not analogous to DNA gene dynamics. Frequently, critics point out these differences - and then claim that the analogy between memes and genes is poor. For example, here is Peter Merel (1999):

> *I'm saying that minds are not digital replicators, where ribosomes are. I'm saying that therefore the analogy between genes and memes is fundamentally flawed.*

Pointing out imperfections in the analogy misses the point. The relationship between memes and genes is *not* an analogy in the first place. Rather both memes and genes are forms of heritable information that evolve over time due to copying, variation, and differential reproductive success - and consequently come to exhibit a range of Darwinian dynamics. Hodgson (2008) states this point plainly:

> *Contrary to some misconceptions (Cordes 2006; Witt 2006), the idea of generalizing Darwinism is not essentially about biological metaphors or analogies. Instead, it relies on common abstract features in both the social and the biological world.*

David Hull (2000) agrees, saying:

> *Memetics does not involve analogical reasoning at all. Instead, a general account of selection is being developed that applies equally to a variety of different sorts of differential replication. Instead of genetics forming the fundamental analog to which all other selection processes must be compared, all examples of selection processes are*

treated on a par.

Helena Cronin (1991 p.373) also agrees, saying:

If we think of Darwinism in this way, then to say that cultural evolution is Darwinian need be no mere analogy. Cultural evolution could make some claims to being as Darwinian as the evolution of life on Earth.

Daniel Dennett, in a 2009 Harvard lecture said:

Memes are like software viruses in fact I am going to say they are - are - software viruses. This isn't an analogy, this is literally true.

So: not *just* an analogy. The differences between cultural and organic evolution are caused partly by the different heritable materials having different properties and propensities, and partly by information building up in them through different processes - by natural selection, intelligent design or other processes. They don't do damage to the analogy between genes and memes - rather they highlight which aspects of the processes arise as a result of shared underlying evolutionary dynamics, and which aspects are contingent upon the properties of the heritable materials involved.

15.50 Sympathetic interpretations are needed

The critics above have *mostly* failed to find a sympathetic interpretation of memetics. If you are going to criticise something, it pays to first understand it. However, that takes time - and one of the good things about criticism is that it is quick and easy. However, criticism without comprehension is not too valuable - and the resulting criticisms often fail to hit their target.

15.51 Common misunderstandings

There are several common conceptual difficulties shared by the critics. Many pick out some dissimilarity between the cultural and organic realms and then claim the analogy between them is broken. To me, this seems rather like pointing out the differences between a brother and sister and then claiming that they could not have had the same mother. The approach is just a misguided one. Another systematic problem is narrow conceptions of what organic evolution is like. As Hull (2001) said:

In general, those who oppose treating conceptual change as evolutionary reason from an extremely impoverished view of biological evolution to the context of conceptual evolution. Their view of biological evolution is so narrow that most biological evolution does not fit.

15.52 There's nothing wrong with memetics

There is a *very* simple interpretation under which memetics makes perfect sense:

Culture *does* evolve - and scepticism about that can be overcome by the associated mountain of evidence. *How* it evolves can be studied by using *population memetics*. That just requires that you can split cultural inheritance into pieces and then consider their frequencies. The pieces can be of any size - and their sizes are chosen by the scientist involved. The idea of a section of heritable cultural information is a useful concept - partly since it permits this kind of frequency analysis. Most researchers in the field agree about this. Before memetics, they badly needed a name - and "meme" is a great one. The study of how culture changes needs a name too - and "memetics" is a fine name. The rest is really just a case of standard scientific research. We do now have a *reasonable* amount of work that in the area. We now know, in quite a bit of detail, how memetic evolution *actually* works.

16 Controversies - Outstanding issues

Cultural evolution has not been properly studied from a Darwinian perspective until rather recently. So, it is effectively still rather a new science. As a result some lively discussion about its dynamics and properties are taking place, as researchers stake out their positions. In this chapter, we try and cover some of these border disputes.

16.1 Blind Variation and Selective Retention

The role of Campbell's hypothesis about "Blind Variation and Selective Retention" still seems to be disputed to me. Campbell was a pioneer in the field of cultural evolution - and his hypothesis about the significance of "Blind Variation and Selective Retention" (B.V.S.R.) was part of my own introduction to the field. However, my impression is that we have to reject Campbell's hypothesis in the area as a piece of bad poetry.

To recap, Campbell claimed:

1. *A blind-variation-and-selective-retention process is fundamental to all inductive processes; to all genuine increases of knowledge.*
2. *The many processes that shortcut a more full blind-variation-and-selective-retention process are themselves inductive achievements, containing wisdom*

about the environment achieved originally by blind variation and selective retention.

3. *In addition, such shortcut processes contain in their own operation a blind-variation-and-selective-retention process at some level, substituting for overt locomotor exploration or the life or death winnowing of organic evolution.*

This represents a bold thesis, that places "blind" trial-and-error at the conceptual heart of the evolutionary process. However, the thesis appears to collapse when we see what Campbell means by "blind". "Blind" variation might be reasonably expected to mean that variants are chosen without any knowledge of whether they are likely to work or not. However, Campbell uses the word rather differently. He says:

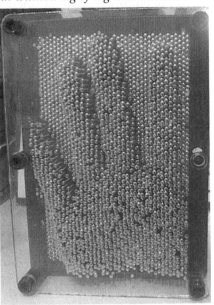

It has represented repeated "breakouts" from the limits of available wisdom. for if such expansions had represented only wise anticipations, they would have Complex adaptations without selection. *been exploiting full or partial knowledge already achieved. Instead, real gains must have been the products of explorations going beyond the limits of foresight and prescience - and in this sense "blind".*

This use of the term "blind" has some serious issues. It categorises any lack of vision is as being a form of blindness. If you think there's a 99% chance of your guess being correct, but you still want to perform a trial in order to be sure, apparently that makes your guess "blind". Cziko (1995) asks:

Can it make any sense to refer to vision as "blind"?

It seems to be a confusing way to speak. In fact, it seems to be an abuse of an ordinary English word. Just because there's *something* you can't see, that doesn't mean that you are blind! I think this criticism leaves the third part of Campbell's "blind-variation-and-selective-retention" thesis effectively in the dustbin.

Others are unhappy with the third part of Campbell's thesis as well. Agner Fog gives it a negative treatment in chapter 2 of his 1999 book.

Another problem with the hypothesis is that brains can use a range of optimisation strategies - *including* random search. The only "selective retention" that is part of random search strategies takes place when a solution is found - and counting "finding a solution" as a case of "selective retention" makes the whole idea seem trivial and meaningless.

Critics of cultural evolution often jab at the "B.V.S.R." hypothesis, claiming that phenomena such as creativity are not the result of a "blind" trial-and-error process (Gabora 2010a).

Despite these apparent problems, the concept still appears to still have its adherents (Simonton, 2011).

16.2 Lamarckian inheritance

There seems to be some dispute over to what extent cultural evolution operates in a Lamarckian manner. It seems self-evident to me that cultural inheritance is *sometimes* Lamarckian - in the sense that acquired characteristics are *sometimes* inherited.

However, some authors have a different perspective on the issue. For instance, here is John Wilkins on the topic:

Perhaps culture does exhibit Lamarckian-style inheritance through the sort of environmental instruction that has a never, or rarely, occurs in biological evolution. One outcome of this would be that variation would come more frequently and more intensively than in a purely Weismannian process, which has to await random mutation or use stored variation from earlier mutation in order for selection to have something on which to operate (Fisher 1930). It would, however, still be Darwinian evolution even if inheritance were Lamarckian. Lamarckian evolution, however, is a different sort of process altogether, driven by perceived need to achieve foreseen outcomes; (see footnote).

Lamarckian inheritance: are acquired traits passed on?

Lamarckian inheritance is not inconsistent with a Darwinian model of memetic evolution. Lamarckian evolution would totally demolish the foundations of memetic theory, and leave us with more traditional forms of cultural analysis.

The last sentence *sounds* bad. However, there seems to be no good reason why organisms which have acquired culture can't use foresight to help them to evolve in a way that makes them better adapted to their environment. More resistance to memetic Lamarckism comes from Rose (1998):

> *Copying the phenotype (when the phenotype has been accidentally changed) could be said to sometimes cause the creation of mutant memes. This form of 'Lamarckism' could be seen as just another potential source of copying infidelity in meme transmission. The 'meme-line' for the construction of the original meme phenotype has ended, and a new mutant 'meme-line' has sprung up. Whilst this is certainly a 'problem' for memes (as all copying infidelity is a problem), it does not necessarily cloud the distinction between memes and their phenotypes or prevent cultural evolution from being considered Darwinian.*

This doesn't seem to be a reasonable approach. Categorising all cases of the inheritance of acquired characteristics as being large mutations is simply not sensible. That just defines Lamarckian inheritance out of existence.

Hull devotes a section in *Science As A Process* to Lamarckian ideas (p.452-457). He (correctly) criticises Medwar for describing some ordinary Darwinian cultural processes as being Lamarckian - and then concludes by saying:

> *Perhaps biological an cultural evolution differ in several important respects. However, terming any of these differences "Lamarckian" serves only to mislead.*

Hull is not being fair here. Lamarckian inheritance happens *sometimes* in cultural evolution. It happens a *lot* more than it did in organic evolution - at least before the invention of genetic engineering.

However, the Lamarckian naysayers *do* seem to be pointing out real deficiencies in some of the Lamarckian enthusiasts. Medawar (1982 p.173) says this:

> *Apart from being mediated through non-genetic channels cultural inheritance is categorically distinguished from biological inheritance by being Lamarckian in character; that is to say, by the fact that what is learned in one generation may become part of the inheritance of the next.*

This seems rather like saying that the transmission of diseases from mother to offspring counts as an instance of Lamarckian inheritance - since an acquired trait (a disease) is inherited. That seems to be stretching the concept of Lamarckian inheritance considerably. It certainly makes Lamarckian inheritance a common phenomenon in the organic world. Hodgson and Knudsen (2006b) are correct to be critical of describing this kind of inheritance as being "Lamarckian":

> *Inheritance means more than merely 'passed on'. If it were merely the latter then the spread of a virus among members of any species would be evidence of Lamarckism. No biologist regards such epidemiological contagions as Lamarckian.*

Richerson and Boyd make the same mistake in their book *Culture and the Evolutionary Process* (1985):

> *The cultural information acquired by an individual may be affected by the events of his or her life, and if so the changes will be transmitted to the individual's cultural offspring. This property of cultural evolution makes for a kind of 'Lamarckian' evolution in the sense that acquired variation is inherited.*

Dennett makes the same mistake in a 2009 Harvard lecture:

> *This is what you learn at mother's knee. this is information that she has learned from her own mother or things that she has figured out for herself - you do get this sort-of Lamarckian possibility here where things she has learned in her own lifetime she can pass on.*

...and Gould (1987, p.70) also makes the same mistake:

> *Human cultural evolution is Lamarckian - the useful discoveries of one generation are passed directly to offspring by writing, teaching, and so forth.*

...so, I figure this misconception is common. If a dog "acquires" some fleas and then passes those on to their offspring, no biologist considers this to be a case of Lamarckian inheritance. For some *genuine* evidence of Lamarckian inheritance you would need to distinguish between the genotype and the phenotype, and then show that changes to the phenotype are reverse engineered, and then coded into the genotype. That *does* happen in cultural evolution - but the process is not as common or trivial as Gould, Richerson and Boyd, Dennett and Medawar seem to think.

Another issue associated with Lamarckian inheritance is political. The association between cultural evolution and Lamarckian inheritance is one of the more frequently-cited reasons for cultural evolution being rejected. People think that they know that Lamarckian inheritance is wrong - so, if cultural evolution is Lamarckian, therefore, cultural evolution must be wrong as well. It is true that this association is probably bad public relations for cultural evolution - but that can't be helped. Calling cultural evolution Darwinian is fine - but it *sometimes* displays Lamarckian properties - and denying cultural evolution's Lamarckian side completely would be misleading.

16.3 Is culture on a leash?

Is culture on a leash?

The freedom of memes to act against the interests of genes has been questioned. Genes create a memetic immune system - which attempts to reject memes that are deleterious to the owner's fitness. To the extent that this memetic immune systems is functioning successfully, this system acts to create a correlation between the interests of genes, and the interests of the memes they associate with. Edward Wilson (1978, p. 172) expressed this idea as follows:

> *The genes hold culture on a leash. The leash is very long, but inevitably values will be constrained in accordance with their effects on the human gene pool.*

Dennett (1998) says:

> *But Wilson's leash is indefinitely long and elastic.*

Boyd and Richerson (2001) say:

> *Culture is on a leash all right, but the dog on the end is big, smart, and independent not a well-trained toy poodle. On any given walk, who is leading whom is not a question with a simple answer.*

In a 2011 talk, Richerson has changed his tune a little. He uses the "leash" metaphor and then compares culture to the boisterous cartoon great dane, Marmaduke, suggesting that culture has gone bounding off, dragging organic genes along behind it. This latter perspective is really the more accurate one. As Susan Blackmore (1999 p.80) put it: "the dog is in the driving seat". Blackmore (2010) denies the usefulness of the analogy, saying:

> *Neither memes nor genes are a dog or a dog-owner. Neither is on a leash.*

The idea that memes may be "on a genetic leash" *has* proved to be a stimulating metaphor. Meme fitnesses are typically *correlated* with the gene fitnesses of their hosts. That memes have - on average - been adaptive for our ancestors is illustrated by the adaptations we have for spreading them - our large brain, vocal nature and sociable disposition. However, there are plenty of rogue memes, ideas that are no good for anyone. The theory that glass is a very viscous fluid is simply a bad one. Some suicide-bomb memes spread only through linkage with fitter memes. Some memes sterilise their hosts. The idea of memes being on a genetic leash doesn't cover such cases very well.

However, there *is* a sense in which memes are currently dependent upon genes for their existence. If *enough enough* memes become deleterious, then humans would *gradually* lose their meme-spreading adaptations, and human culture would die out. Of course such a scenario doesn't seem very likely - since memes are subject to selection pressures that cause them not to behave so suicidally. However, this sort of *thought experiment* illustrates the extent to which the freedom of memes is *currently* constrained and "reined in" by genes.

It should be noted that the existence of a *current* restraint should not be taken to imply that the restraint will necessarily *always* exist. In later chapters I will write about the possibility of a *memetic takeover*. It seems *possible* that culture will pull on the leash so hard that it will break - and cultural entities would bound off into the future leaving their supposed masters behind. That would represent a final severing of any leash by the nuclear genes on the memes.

16.4 Is culture is a part of human biology?

Boyd and Richerson (2001) authored a paper entitled: "Culture is Part of Human Biology - Why the Superorganic Concept Serves the Human Sciences Badly". They start by citing Theodosius Dobzhansky (1962: 20):

Part human, part culture?

> *In producing the genetic basis of culture, biological evolution has transcended itself - it has produced the superorganic.*

Boyd and Richerson do not approve of the sentiment, saying:

> *In our view, superorganicism is wrong because it cannot deal with the rich interconnections between culture and other aspects of our*

phenotype, as exemplified by the Southern culture of honor.

Here Boyd and Richerson are talking about Alfred Kroeber's idea of "superorganicism" - not the meaning given in the dictionary. Kroeber's proposed a hierarchy: inorganic -> organic -> superorganic. Here, saying that culture is "superorganic" means something like that it is at a higher level of complexity to the organic, much as organic things are emergent phenomena - in some sense "above" the inorganic, following different characteristic laws. Boyd and Richerson (2001) then go on to say:

Culture is a part of human biology, as much a part as bipedal locomotion or thick enamel on our molars.

In another paper, Boyd, Richerson and Henrich (2011) say:

Culture has opened up a vast range of evolutionary vistas not available to noncultural species. Nonetheless, culture is as much a part of human biology as our peculiar pelvis. This approach contrasts with the common view that culture and biology are in a tug-of-war for control of human behavior. This common view probably taps into a deep vein of Western thought, which itself may be the result of evolved cognitive biases, but it makes little sense.

Memetics *does* feature the "tug-of-war for control of human behaviour" that they refer to. Memes pull humans one way, and their nuclear genes pull them another.

Boyd and Richerson's "Culture is a part of human biology" slogan has substantial potential to mislead.

In memetics, memes form their own cultural organisms, which do not interbreed with humans. Their relationships with humans are thus more like those of symbiotic gut bacteria, pathogenic agents, or domesticated animals. If you look at what is inherited, culture is not closely related to humans. Nor do cultural inheritance closely track the inheritance patterns of the human genome. Cultural entities are often mobile independently of humans, they can die largely independently of their human hosts and they engage in sexual recombination largely independently of humans. Their genotypes are often found outside the human body. Their phenotypes are often found outside the human body. I think these factors mean that modelling cultural entities as separate organisms makes sense - whereas modelling them as something like an *extended genotype* - as kind of bizarre extension of human biology does not.

Memetics allows classification of cultural entities into different sexual species - with limited meme flow between them. For example, Cobol programs tend to have sex with other Cobol programs while BASIC programs tend to have sex with other BASIC programs. However, if Cobol and BASIC are considered to be "part of human biology", it makes little sense to classify them into separate species. Also, cultural adaptations benefit meme reproduction - while being deleterious to the human hosts involved. That makes a lot of sense under the interpretation that cultural entities represent separate entities that behave much like pathogens - and very little sense otherwise. Similarly, memes compete with similar types of memes for some niches and not other ones - which makes sense in the context of an ecology containing different species occupying different niches - and not much sense otherwise.

The *potential* to absorb culture is certainly part of human biology. However, that seems *very* different from saying that culture *itself* is part of human biology.

16.5 Intelligent design

Cultural evolution positions *intelligent design* as a basic type of mutation. This classification might not cause problems - were it not for the fact that evolution enthusiasts have been waging war on intelligent design for decades now - on the grounds that it is a creationist trojan horse for getting theology into American classrooms.

Religiously motivated advocates of *intelligent design* claim that basic

This watch was intelligently designed.

aspects of life - DNA transcriptase, the bacterial flagellum, etc. show signs of being designed by an intelligent agent. That thesis does not appear to be supported by good quality evidence. It looks instead to be a case of wishful thinking.

However, in cultural evolution, *intelligent design* is ubiquitous. Many memes, artefacts, programs and recipes really are *intelligently designed* by human designers. For example, here is Daniel Dennett on the topic:

We are the first intelligent designers in the tree of life.

Furthermore, DNA and culture coevolve, and there a range of mechanisms exist which result in the "assimilation" of the products of cultural evolution into DNA genes. That provides mechanisms which allow designs developed by intelligent agents to go on to influence human evolution.

One *possible* way to avoid the confusion that the term "intelligent design" might bring would be to use another term - for example, "engineering design". That term doesn't have the same history and connotations. However, "intelligent design" *is* the standard term for referring to design by intelligent agents. I think evolutionary theorists should adopt the term "intelligent design" to refer to the fundamental category of mutations generated intentionally by intelligent agents. I expect that the recommendation that a traditional foe of the scientific enterprise should be elevated to the status of a fundamental class of mutations will go down poorly.

16.6 Does memetics cover all cultural change?

Is memetics a complete model of cultural genetics? Some claim it is not. For example, here is Agner Fog (2009):

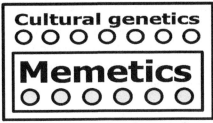

Memetics = cultural genetics?

> *Memetics is not a complete model of cultural evolution. Many aspects of cultural change don't fit well into the framework of memetics. Consider the example that country A is capturing a piece of land from country B in war. Country A grows bigger and B gets smaller. This change is quantitative rather than qualitative. The piece of land that changes owner may be rich in natural resources but have no inhabitants. In this case there is no person who changes the meme of nationality from B to A. Therefore, this example doesn't fit into the framework of memetics, but it is nevertheless a process where competition and selection leads to cultural change.*

The idea that memetics is an incomplete model of cultural change is shared by those who define meme in a manner that means that they are only spread by imitation. There are many cultural phenomena which are *not* spread just by imitation. For example, a butterfly might lay its eggs on plants that smell and taste like the plant it was born on. This may not be because the smell of the plant is programmed into its genes. It may not copying its parents' behaviour either - especially if parents died before it was born. Preferences for eating the plant you were born on represents a type of cultural inheritance (assuming that the effect is mediated by the brain) - but it would be straining the concept to claim that such behaviour was passed on by imitation. Such a perspective leads to the view that memetics is an incomplete theory of cultural inheritance.

If memetics is not defined to be the same thing as cultural genetics, that breaks the relationship between genes and memes, which would be undesirable. Also, there does not seem to be much of a point to a theory of cultural change that doesn't cover all culture. If a theory of cultural evolution fails to cover all cultural change, then it needs to be expanded on. With an appropriate conception of what constitutes a meme, memetics deals with all culture just fine.

16.7 Meme phenotypes

There seems to be some confusion in the community about the issue of whether memes have phenotypes. Blackmore (1999) and Stanovich (2007) both doubt whether the term is useful.

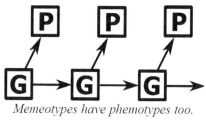

Memeotypes have phemotypes too.

Both say it is part of the gene-meme analogy that need not be transferred across. Stanovich says memes are "naked replicators", and have no phenotype.

This is not really correct. Most memes are not *really* "naked replicators" - since they need sophisticated, intelligent systems in order to be copied at all. Also, many memes do, in fact, have clearly-defined phenotypes. These vary in a manner that mirrors underlying heritable variation - but changes to the phenotype are not normally inherited from. A typical example is a cake recipe. The recipe is inherited from, and the cake varies according to changes in the recipe, but changes to the cake itself are not *normally* passed on. Here the recipe plays the role of the *memotype*, while the cake is a *phenotype*.

Blackmore (2010) seems to have come around - and proposes that meme phenotypes be called "memotypes". Speel (1988) proposed that they be called "phemotypes". I don't think Blackmore's "memotypes" term is usable. The genetic equivalent of "memotype" is *surely* "genotype" - and not "phenotype". "Phemotype" is cute - but perhaps a little esoteric. There *is* the term "sociotype" - which seems quite nice. I think either "sociotype" or simply the term "phenotype" should be used. If what is meant is not clear from the context perhaps say, "cultural phenotype", "meme phenoptype" or "memeplex phenoptype" - as appropriate.

In organic evolution, phenotypes are *rarely* copied from, whereas in cultural evolution, reconstructing inherited information from the phenotype is *fairly* common. In that case, what counts as the phenotype and what counts as the genotype is not *always* terribly clear.

16.8 Group selection

Group selection seems to be another area where researchers disagree about the role of culture. For instance, Boyd and Richerson (2005a) claim that coevolution with cultural entities makes group selection more respectable in the cultural realm. However, this position seems problematical.

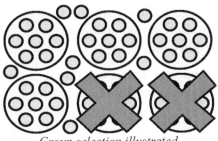

Group selection illustrated.

In the organic realm, memetic evolution results in more migration. It unites groups, making them interbreed more each other. There are fewer isolated groups now than ever before - and the reason is because memetic evolution has facilitated migration. This makes group selection *less* likely to operate. In the memetic realm, there is typically even more meme transfer than gene transfer. Again, this makes memetic group selection less likely. Boyd and Richerson cite various cultural processes that decrease the flow of genes and memes between populations - but they seem to be cherry-picking the evidence. Memes create communications technologies that increase meme-flow between separated populations. Memes also create travel technologies that have the effect of increasing both gene flow and meme flow. These processes are important - and should not be overlooked.

The other thing to point out in this context is that memetic infections are not really *that* different from organic ones in their ability to rapidly create between-group differences between isolated groups. As Jared Diamond documents in his *Guns, Germs and Steel* book, when Europeans made contact with America, the indigenous Americans were ravaged by European diseases - to which the natives had no immunity - and this effect helped to decimate the native populations. Most biologists would not count such invasions as a form of group selection in the first place - since *usually* women are left alive - and they go on to interbreed with the invaders. Memetic infections can rapidly result in differences between neighbouring groups - but it should be noted that *ordinary* organic infections have much the same effect. This is not really very much of a difference between the organic and cultural realms.

As for cultural group selection – in memetics that is like group selection acting on parasite groups. The arguments against group selection are *mostly* based on considering animal groups. Group selection among parasites has not been examined so closely. Some types of parasites are extinguished in groups when their hosts die - so it would not be *terribly* surprising if group selection was found in that realm. When turning to group selection acting on meme groups - it seems to be a rather poorly-studied area.

Boyd and Richerson (1995) invoke cultural group selection to explain human ultrasociality. However it should be noted that memetics offers a pretty simple explanation of ultrasociality that does *not* invoke group selection. It proposes that memes that produce ultrasociality would have been favoured - since memes require social contact between humans to reproduce themselves. Memeplexes would be eager to incorporate any such ultrasociality memes - since they would then be memetically favoured in turn for incorporating them. Since more memes are - on average - good, ultrasociality would also be favoured at the level of the host genes too.

This explanation is simple, obvious, and doesn't require the application of dubious high-level selection constructs.

Group selection seems to be one area where memetics and the academic cultural evolution researchers have different intuitions as a result of their somewhat different philosophical positions.

16.9 Is culture alive?

Daniel Dennett (2008c) claims that memes are not alive - as follows:

A meme is like a virus - it is not alive, but it is something which can evolve. But what is it? Well, it's a data structure. It is an abstract sort of thing.

Dawkins (1976) seems to think otherwise, though:

As my colleague N.K. Humphrey neatly summed up an earlier draft of this chapter: "memes should be regarded as living structures, not just metaphorically but technically"

So: alive? or dead? Memes are parts of living structures. They are as alive as genes are. That makes them pretty lively, most of the time.

16.10 Is imitation difficult?

Susan Blackmore presented the "big brain" hypothesis in 1999. In her 1999 book, Sue introduced three selective forces which she believed were probably responsible for it, writing:

These are: selection for imitation, selection for imitating the best imitators, selection for mating with the best imitators, and (possibly) memetic sexual selection.

She then wrote:

The first three processes alone will produce the selection pressures required to drive a runaway increase in brain size - if one further small assumption is made. That is, that being good at imitation requires a big brain

Sue goes on to predict that imitation ability is likely to be correlated with brain size and writes:

If these predictions turn out to be right they will confirm the suggestion that imitation is an enormously demanding task, and that it takes a large brain to be able to do it.

Critics like Boyd and Richerson (2000) picked up on this point, writing:

This memetic theory depends on a number of conjectures that can be tested, especially the assumption that imitation requires a lot of brainpower, even though it comes so easily to us.

It is great that Sue made predictions and proposed tests. However, the idea about imitation requiring lots of brainpower seems to be only one of the possible explanations.

Another idea is that the human brain rapidly filled up with large numbers of memes - and then selection favoured bigger brains because they could hold more memes.

If memes are beneficial, on average, then many memes will be better than a few memes. If you are wooing a prospective mate with love songs, it helps to have a bit of a repertoire. If you are attracting attention by dancing in front of a fire, it helps to have a range different moves. Knowledge of different fruits, medicines, traps, and lairs all take up space in the brain. Many of our ancestors' heads would have quickly became full to the brim with memes. Modern findings suggest the imitation is widespread among animals - suggesting that is not that difficult. Since basic imitation seems to be cheap, this other mechanism now looks more plausible.

Initially, a tribe's memes would have been essentially confined to a single human skull. For hunter gatherers, there was little specialisation and - apart from some sexual differences and the medicine man - most people carried copies of most of the tribe's memes. As soon as the memes could they created division of labour, so that different heads could come to contain different memes. That *massively* expanded the number of different types of meme that society could collectively support. Then, as soon as the memes were able, they burst forth from the human skull, expanding onto stone tablets, calligraphic volumes, printed pages, and ultimately the internet. The rapidity and force of this outpouring gives some indication of how cramped even the enlarged human cranium was as a meme womb.

Under this hypothesis, the brain did not expand because larger brains could imitate better. It expanded because a huge population of memes living in cramped conditions resulted in selection favouring humans with bigger brains that provided larger living quarters which capable of supporting more memes.

16.11 Is the central dogma toast?

Cultural evolution means that the central dogma of molecular biology is toast. Genetic engineers can now take information form wherever they like wire it into genomes and create adult organisms containing these genes. However, not *everyone* seems agree that central dogma has had its day. In particular, Richard Dawkins (2004) quotes Francis Crick as saying in 1957:

> *the transfer of information from nucleic acid to nucleic acid, or from nucleic acid to protein may be possible, but transfer from protein to protein, or from protein to nucleic acid is impossible. Information means here the precise determination of sequence, either of bases in the nucleic acid or of amino acid residues in the protein*

Dawkins then goes on immediately to say:

> *In this version the central dogma has never been violated and my bet is that it never will. The genetic code, whereby nucleotide sequences are translated into amino acid sequences, is irreversible.*

Arthur C. Clarke's first law fairly evidently applies to Crick's overconfident assertion:

> *When a distinguished but elderly scientist states that something is possible, he is almost certainly right. When he states that something is impossible, he is very probably wrong.*

We have now sequenced dinosaur proteins (without recovering their DNA), and it would be pretty trivial to express them in chickens. Indeed, Jack Horner has a "Chickenosaurus" project whose aim is to turn a chicken into dinosaur using genetic engineering. This means that the central dogma is toast. It falsely claims that information cannot flow in a direction which it now evidently can.

17 Textbooks - What the evolution textbooks say

This chapter is about the portrayal of cultural evolution in the textbooks on evolution.

17.1 The textbooks on evolution

In this book, we have previously explained why it is best to regard cultural evolution as being part of evolution - by definition.

The definition of evolution just says that it's about heritable traits - the changes in heritable traits in a population over time - and it *doesn't* say how the inheritance takes place. Whether information is transmitted down the generations by nucleic acids, by cultural transmission or by some other means is not a factor.

By such definitions of "evolution", circumcision is transmitted down the generations and so counts as evolutionary change. Wearing kilts, for example, is also transmitted down the generations - and changes in kilt styles would be a class of evolutionary change. Similarly with spoken language for example. Changes in spoken language are also a type of evolutionary change - according to the definition of evolution.

However, the textbooks on evolution don't seem to make much mention of cultural change. They *do* describe changes in DNA-based creatures - but they *fail* to mention changes in televisions, computers, automobiles or musical instruments. As Robert Aunger, (2002, p.276) says:

> *Traditional evolutionary theory doesn't concern itself with artefacts. But evolutionary theory should have to account for the existence of things like computers, which are merely fancy artefacts.*

There's a whole section of the biosphere that is excluded from evolutionary explanations by the descriptions of evolution in many of the textbooks.

Next, let's see how the theory of evolution is portrayed in textbooks that deal with the subject.

17.2 Douglas Futayama - "Evolutionary Biology"

To start with, we will look at *Evolutionary Biology* by *Douglas Futayama* - one of the well-known textbooks on the topic of *evolution*.

This particular book makes no mention of evolutionary cultural change. There is no coverage of cultural evolution at all. It presents a *standard* definition of evolution - which includes cultural evolution by definition. However there is *no* coverage in the book of cultural evolution. It *completely* ignores the whole subject. It doesn't attempt to describe the controversy over this issue, it just completely ignores it - a huge blind spot in the book.

Since this book purports to be about evolutionary biology, perhaps it can claim to be about *biological evolution*, not *cultural evolution*. However, any idea that culture is not part of biology would surely be deeply misguided. Biology is the study of life - and culture must surely be considered to be part of the biotic world, and not the prebiotic world.

17.3 Mark Ridley - "Evolution"

The second textbook is *Evolution* by *Mark Ridley* another well-known textbook on evolution. This book has some more interesting coverage of cultural evolution. This book differs from the others in its definition of the term "evolution". It presents a standard definition and then it raises three exceptions that it thinks are irregularities - and so don't count as evolutionary change:

1. **Developmental changes** - Changes over an individual's lifetime don't count as evolution the book says. This seems *relatively* uncontroversial to me. Changes over an individual's lifespan don't usually result in any heritable changes in the population. That is agreed by most parties to not to count as evolution.

2. **Changes in population numbers** - This covers changes in population numbers in an ecosystem over time. So: if we have **species A** and `species B`, and let us say that `species A` composes 10% of the individuals and `species B` is 90% of the individuals, and then population numbers change so that `species A` composes 70% of the individuals and `species B` composes 30% of the individuals . The book claims that *doesn't* count as evolution because there is no change within each individual species.

3. **Cultural evolution** - It says that cultural evolution doesn't count as evolution.

The explanation given for *why* cultural evolution is explicitly excluded reads as follows:

Changes that take place in human politics, economics, history, technology and even scientific theories are sometimes loosely described as evolutionary. In this sense "evolutionary" means mainly that there has been change over time - and perhaps not in a preordained direction.

Human ideas and institutions can sometimes spit during their history - but their history does not have such a clear-cut branching tree-like structure as does the history of life. Change and splitting provide two of the main themes in evolutionary theory.

Here, *Mark Ridley* presents his justification for ignoring cultural evolution in the rest of the book. However, his justification is based on a supposed lack of branching structure within cultural evolution. However, this seems like a basic fallacy to me. If you exclude phenomena that don't have a branching tree-like structure then that immediately writes off most of the bacterial root the tree of life - because there is horizontal transmission of heritable information just as there is in cultural evolution. Do we *really* want to say that early living things were not evolving - due to an excess of horizontal gene transfer?

This point is made by *Daniel Dennett* for example, in *Freedom Evolves*. To quote briefly from that:

> *It is sometimes claimed, erroneously, that this cultural transmission, being between genetically unrelated individuals, shows that human culture cannot be interpreted as an evolutionary phenomenon governed by the principals of neo-Darwinian theory. In fact, as we have just seen, horizontal transmission of good design elements between unrelated individuals is recognized as an important feature of evolution of early (single-celled) life, with a growing list of proven instances, a centerpiece, not an embarrassment, of contemporary evolutionary biology. [p.146]*

...and Daniel precedes that by a discussion of symbiotic relationships and how they indicate transmission of heritable information horizontally between existing organisms rather than down the generations to generate a branching tree-like structure.

So: this is just a fallacy. The idea that cultural evolution displays horizontal transmission and biological evolution doesn't is simply wrong: biological evolution itself displays horizontal transmission in an almost identical manner to cultural evolution. The whole basis of Mark Ridley's dismissal of cultural evolution just seems wrong to me.

Also the whole idea of setting up a nice neat definition of evolution - and then listing exceptional cases - just goes against the grain from the perspective of the philosophy of biology - you want evolution to be a neat and clearly-defined category. Having a list of exceptional cases that don't count is a sign that your definition of evolution fails to carve nature at the joints.

In the case of Ridley's three exceptions, he excludes change during development - which is fair enough, that is not inherited that is not part of evolution anyway. However, his other cases: change in an ecosystem due to changing distributions of species *that* counts as evolution - and cultural change: *that* counts as evolution *too* in my book.

Ridley's textbook doesn't *even* have any coverage of genetic engineering. Genetically engineered crops are everywhere - yet the whole field of genetic engineering doesn't even get a mention in Ridley's "Evolution" textbook. Maybe he considers engineered genetic change to be a type of cultural change - and therefore not really part of evolution. That seems like an incredible position to me - very hard to believe - but perhaps an incredible omission demands an incredible explanation. Anyway, at least Mark presents a coherent reason for ignoring cultural evolution - even though that reason is essentially misguided.

17.4 Monroe Strickberger - "Evolution"

Then lastly, we have *Monroe Strickberger* (1996) with another evolutionary textbook - again called "Evolution". This textbook is about 13 years old, but *actually* gives some coverage of cultural evolution. This textbook *radically* disagrees with the other textbooks that cited here in that it classes cultural evolution as evolution - and there's a nice neat paragraph which expresses the sentiment:

> *In short, humans have two unique hereditary systems. One is the genetic system that transfers biological information from biological parent to offspring in the form of genes and chromosomes. The other is the extragenetic system that transfers cultural information from speaker to listener, from writer to reader, from performer to spectator, and forms our cultural heritage.*

> *Both systems are informational in that they produce their effects by instruction, the biological systems through the information embodied in DNA via the coding properties of these cellular macro-molecules, the cultural system through social interactions coded in language and custom and embodied in records and traditions.*

So, amazingly, a textbook about evolution that actually include something about cultural evolution! It doesn't include much coverage, it's got that paragraph, and then there's another short paragraph which *sounds* as though it's going to lead onto something interesting it says:

> *The fact that human culture has as its source a biological foundation and that culture and biology arise from informational systems that evolve over time, has prompted various writers to suggest that general laws cover both society and nature each sharing similar evolutionary*

mechanisms - especially that of natural selection.

And yes, that is exactly the idea, but then unfortunately it goes on for several pages about *social Darwinism* and about *sociobiology* - and doesn't really address the topic that it originally sounded as though it was going to talk about.

So, although there is *some* coverage, hardly any. It is all confined to a short chapter at the end entitled "culture and the control of human evolution" does talk about genetic engineering a bit, but *still* extremely meagre coverage right at the end of the book, but at least provides an exception to the rule of textbooks completely ignoring cultural evolution - actually includes cultural evolution within evolutionary theory which seems to be a big breakthrough as far as the conventional evolutionary academic establishment goes.

So, good score there, however *poor* coverage - only a few pages really. That's how the textbooks stack up regarding cultural evolution.

17.5 Complete rewrite needed

All the textbooks need a complete rewrite to deal with the issue. Cultural evolution is not something that is unique to humans. It is embedded in almost all animal evolution, there is evidence that small birds exhibit cultural evolution and insects as well - and culture and genes coevolve so you can't really understand evolution without considering cultural evolution.

Some might observe that looking in the evolution textbooks is looking in the wrong place - saying that the science of human cultural change is the domain of cultural anthropology textbooks, not evolutionary biology textbooks - and that that is just how academic disciplines have divided things up. No! Cultural evolution *is* part of evolution. Any conception of evolution that excludes cultural change is *deeply* misguided. That means at least *some* coverage in the evolution textbooks is needed. An example of how things could be can be found in the biology textbooks. Biology textbooks typically have a substantial section devoted to humans. This is despite the fact that there is *also* human biology - which is sometimes treated as a separate subject. If evolution textbooks were like that, I would not be complaining so much. Cursory coverage of cultural evolution in "Evolution" textbooks, with "Human Evolution" being treated as a separate subject, which included more detail about cultural evolution would *at least* be a big improvement over the current situation. However, cultural evolution is not confined to humans. Various other animals have complex cultures. It is difficult to divide evolution up - since it is an area where the component parts all influence each other. In summary, the current coverage of cultural evolution in textbooks on the subjects seems pretty dismal. *Major* rewrites would seem to be required.

18 Marketing - Money for memes

Economically speaking, the largest application area for memetics is probably marketing and advertising. This is also probably the area where memetics has had the biggest penetration in the past. Marketing and advertising are *huge* fields - and very much coverage of them would be well beyond the scope of this book. Instead, in this chapter we will look at marketing, and consider it as a source of techniques which illustrate how memes can attract attention and modify behaviour. The techniques used in marketing are *broadly* similar to those used in other areas where memetics is applied.

18.1 Marketing and advertising

Some of the iconic images that Guinness has used in their adverts.

Advertising uses video, images, music and text to influence consumers to buy products and services. It uses memetic engineering to generate media that are likely to be widely discussed and distributed. Advertising and marketing materials appear on billboards, on television, on the internet, and on product packaging.

Four popular washing powders. Which would you choose?

Here are four highly similar white powders packaged in differently-branded boxes. One of the washing powders above proclaims that it "Cleans your clothes & pleases your nose!" ...while another claims that it: "Removes & helps prevent stains from setting in." These messages seem likely to appeal to different groups of consumers. Marketing memes are used to attract attention, promote distribution and encourage consumer loyalty. Marketing uses memes for practically everything. Marketing and advertising typically consist of a big collection of memes.

These cars are all for sale. Which would you buy?

Here, these cars appear to be *fairly* similar - but differ in colour, logos, and style. Consumers are influenced by these factors - and the cars that we now see are the result of a long process of selection by consumers over many decades - resulting in the manufacturers with the most attractive memes getting an increased share of the market.

Marketing uses memes to develop brand recognition. It uses memes to create slogans and jingles. It uses a wide range of techniques to attract the attention of the customers and get the desired message to them.

18.2 Recommendations

In some sectors, product recommendations are a good way to make sales. If someone likes your product so much that they tell their friends, that is a good sign that they really like it - and their friends will probably see that and consider the possibility that they would like it too. Because recommendations are effective, there are marketing techniques based around generating fake recommendations. Online, fake recommendations are known as "astroturfing". Recommendations are sometimes known as "word of mouth" advertising.

18.3 Viral marketing

Viral marketing is the field that uses crowd-power for distribution purposes - and it is the area of marketing which is most closely linked to memetics. Much marketing is *display advertising* - where advertisers display their content to users or passers by. However, there's quite a large area of marketing where word of mouth, sharing, and recommendations are used to distribute the marketing materials. This is where memetics has the most to say about the resulting dynamics. Some marketing specialists in the social media field have explicitly embraced memetics - for example, Dan Zarella and Paul Marsden. Viral videos are one popular medium. Some of the better-known viral videos are illustrated below:

Some popular viral video advertisements. Readers may recognise some of these.

In many respects, this type of marketing campaign is a stereotypical example of memes at work. The memes are engineered, so we can closely inspect their origin, and their social contagion online can be documented. They represent *great* examples of memes in action.

18.4 Big seed marketing

Next, we will look at a specific viral marketing technique: *big seed marketing*. Social media marketing departments must decide how to allocate their budget between making content that will spread - and distributing that content. The initial distribution is sometimes called "seeding", and focusing on that distribution is *sometimes* called using a "big seed". *Big seeding*

Nature sometimes uses many seeds.

was popularised in 2007 by an article entitled *Viral Marketing for the Real World* - by Duncan J. Watts, Jonah Peretti, and Michael Frumin.

A computer model was constructed extent *big seeding* is likely to work.

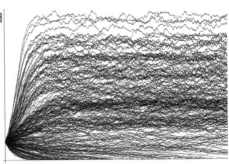

The diagram here shows a simple computer simulation of epidemics which produces graphs showing how the number of infected individuals could increase or decrease over time. For a description of the model of epidemics used here, see the chapter on parasitism. The seed population is fixed at the same value for each run and is shown as the y-intercept on the left hand side of the diagram. The diagram illustrates the concept of an epidemic threshold. If content is insufficiently infectious, it dies off, and goes extinct.

Epidemics - showing the number on infected hosts plotted against time.

Next, we will explore how the seed population size influences the extinction rate. Here, "survival" refers to having a non-zero population size at the end of the run - i.e. it refers to not going extinct. "Percentage survival" refers to what proportion of the runs avoided extinction.

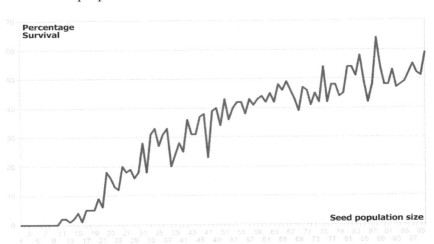

This is a plot of percentage survival against seed population size.

This graph illustrates two main things:

- **Having a seed population too small is often fatal** - random fluctuations in population size too easily cause your seed population to execute a *random walk* into extinction.

- *Big seeding* **rapidly runs into diminishing returns** - *provided* you seed on a *reasonable* scale, success depends quite a bit on how much you exceed the *epidemic threshold* by - and not so much on the size of your seed population.

Big seed marketing is probably most appropriate for when you know that your *shareable* item will fail to exceed the *epidemic threshold*. If you really can't find a way of doing that, using a big seed is probably your best bet.

18.5 Social media marketing

A current growth area is advertising using online social media platforms - such as *Facebook, Twitter,* and *Google plus*. Modern social media typically uses addictive social content to attract and keep users - while providing an advertising platform that combines recommendations with display and broadcast marketing. Social media platforms also allow a high degree of targeting - i.e. showing advertisements to people who might actually be interested in them.

18.6 Marketing techniques

Lastly, a bit of a laundry list of marketing techniques - seen from a memetics perspective:

18.7 Memetic hitchhiking

Memetic hitchhiking uses one entity as a vector to distribute another one with. The picture here shows the packaging container of a popular foodstuff. These food products will probably sell to addicted kids no matter what the packaging. The manufacturers make use of the wide distribution of these products and stable client base as an opportunity to make some money from advertising.

Sweet food for kids used as a vector by a hitchhiking advert.

The food producer gets money from the advertiser. The advertiser gets their product in front of the eyes of lots of kids. Both parties benefit from the arrangement.

Memetic hitchhiking for marketing purposes can use a variety of different sorts of vector. A fairly common vector is a highly contagious meme. Then, provided the *payload* is not too *heavy*, the *delivery mechanism* will give it a wide distribution. In these cases, the link to epidemiology models the spread of the *delivery mechanism*, while memetic hitchhiking models its link with the payload.

To give another example, this image is *actually* an advertisement for Bosch fridges - as can be seen from the word "BOSCH" on the label. The text above the logo says: "Keep food fresh for much longer. Fridges with VitaFresh Technology." Elsewhere, Bosch claim: "VitaFresh Refrigeration Technology Automatically Keeps Produce Fresher, Longer." The

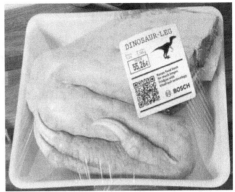
Dinosaur leg.

image of a fresh dinosaur leg acts as a technology demonstration for them - and provides a means of spreading virally.

18.8 Triggering

A commonly-used marketing and advertising technique involves forming a link between a common phrase - or a catchy song - and your product. Here, we will call this *product triggering*, or sometimes just *triggering*. Famous examples of the technique include:

- "Have a break... Have a Kit Kat."
- "Happiness... is a cigar called Hamlet."
- "There are some things money can't buy. For everything else, there's MasterCard."

If you plan to have a break...

The link is formed via observational learning, and then pattern-completion mechanisms complete the catchphrase when presented with the trigger.

18.9 Catchphrases

Some catchphrases still manage to promote a product - even *without* explicitly including a reference to the product name - e.g.:

- "Eat Fresh."
- "Because I'm worth it."
- "Think Different."
- "Once you pop, you can't stop."

Many catchphrases receive special legal protection from trademark law - to allow those who register and pay a fee to a government office a legally-enforced monopoly over the catchphrase. For example, the phrase "Where do you want to go today?" is "owned" by Microsoft.

18.10 Superstimulii

Some stimuli elicit certain types of behaviour - and if you can somehow magnify the stimulus sometimes, the behaviour becomes more probable, more frequent, or magnified.

Lipstick makes lips very red.

So, for example, an apple might make you salivate, and an extra-red ripe looking apple might make you salivate more. Stimulii associated with food, sex and status can be magnified in the modern environment to levels far beyond anything our ancestors would have experienced. Marketers and advertisers have a long history of using superstimulii to sell things.

18.11 Sex appeal

Sex sells, and advertisers and marketers have frequently attempted to associate their products with beauty, youth, and sex appeal since trade was invented. Men, when faced with a beautiful women are more likely to make sales decisions. Some subconscious part of their mind may be thinking that spending money will impress the woman. Also, they may link the surge of desire they feel to the product they are simultaneously being presented with, and behave as though they want that.

Beautiful young lady linked to Coca Cola in around 1890.

Sexual content is also good for initially attracting attention. This technique is used display advertisements, viral marketing, and by "booth babes" at trade shows.

18.12 Brands

A brand is usually a name, term, design or symbol that distinguishes an agent or organisation from other ones.

The Coca-Cola brand.

Brands encompass and symbolise the identity of the entity they represent. A brand may identify one item, a family of items, or a seller. Brands may manifest themselves as names, signs, symbols, colour schemes or slogans. The word "brand" originates in a method of telling one person's cattle from another by means of applying a hot iron stamp to their hides.

18.13 Animation

Advertising sometimes uses animation in order to attract attention. Studies have shown that animated images on the internet attract more clicks than static images. Animation attracts attention - by activating movement sensors in the retina. It also maintains people's interest - reducing the possibility of people becoming bored with the advert and looking away.

Large outdoor animated LCD advertising hoarding in London.

Advertisers have exploited these effects with all kinds of animated adverts.

18.14 Repetition

Repetition emphasizes marketing messages. In some cases, consumers respond to the frequencies of marketing messages - so if it says "for sale" a thousand times, consumers become more confident that they are buying reduced items. So, remember: repetition, repetition, repetition.

Clearance bin.

18.15 Bigger is better

This diagram shows data from *DoubleClick* in 2006. It is fairly self-explanatory. Bigger advertisements are more likely to attract attention and generate more clicks.

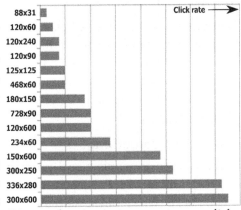

Bigger advertisements generate more clicks.

18.16 Negative marketing

Negative marketing uses negative emotions - such as fear - to promote products. It also covers marketing that aims at sabotaging competitors. Most advertising techniques are oriented towards product promotion. However, if an organisation is in a field where it faces few competitors, it can sometimes pay to sabotage their efforts - rather than promoting your own. This is one of marketing's darker sides. Negative marketing sometimes involves spreading rumours and gossip about competitors. Such phenomena can be treated using models based on epidemiology. A classic negative marketing campaign was the "daisy" advert. This was an "attack ad" that was targeted at *Barry Goldwater* by *Lyndon Johnson* during the run up to the 1964 presidential election. Johnson insinuated that Goldwater was likely to destroy the world in a nuclear apocalypse.

18.17 Free stuff!

Offering people something for free is a common way of starting a relationship with prospective customers.

Customers like being gifted - and it often provides an opportunity to use other sales techniques on them.

Get something for free!

18.18 Discount

If you can't afford to give the customer something for free, then next best thing in terms of attracting attention is to give them something at a reduced price. The signs often say things like: "50% off!", "Half price!" and "For Sale!". Sometimes they juxtapose the sale price with the full price, to show consumers why they should buy the product now.

50% off in the sales.

There is also marketing associated with bulk discounting. Consumers are familiar with the phenomenon that buying more of something lets you get it cheaper. Marketers use this to try and get people to buy additional items which they would not usually purchase. "2 for the price of 1", "Buy one get one free!" and "3 for the price of 2" are some of the most common pitches along these lines.

18.19 Win something!

If you can't give people a real product free of charge, it may still be possible to give them a ticket which *might* help them to win something. Gambling and potentially winning things is an exciting process that

Win something!

gets people's blood up and prepares them for spending money.

18.20 Other areas of marketing

There are many other areas of marketing - too many to go into here. Product placement, direct mail, logos, suggestibility and jingles are some of the areas we have not covered at all.

19 Applications - What memetics is for

What do we need a science of cultural evolution for? Memes are the very foundation of our modern civilisation and its culture. They penetrate all aspects of our life. They underlie science and technology, news, law, morality, religions, causes, music, movies, books, theatre and fashion. Many of these are things we hold dear. We have already discussed marketing. This chapter considers some of the *other* applications of memetics.

19.1 Entertainment

Often with marketing and advertising there is some kind of product or service being promoted. In the entertainment industry, the product itself is often a bunch more memes. This is true for movies, music, books, pornography, computer games. It is partly true for many live events - such as comedy or theatre.

Some stills from popular movies. Advertising and entertainment combined.

It seems likely that pornography, computer games, music and movies will fuse together substantially in the future, forming immersive virtual worlds. This seems likely to be an *especially* economically significant area.

19.2 Self-defense

Since organisations, companies and governments are busy trying to ensure their memes penetrate as many minds as possible, and not all of these memes have their host's best interests at heart, it is natural for people to develop immune responses to some of these memes. Manipulative, toxic and bad memes can be avoided, rejected, and resisted. Infected humans can attempt to disinfect their minds, flushing out bad memes, and those who are not yet infected can take steps to ensure they have a strong memetic immune system.

19.3 Education

Education largely involves acquiring a substantial stock of good memes. People acquire knowledge better when they are young. Consequently there's a rush to cram memes into children's heads at a young age. We need to know which ones are the best ones to include, and what the best ways of inserting them are.

19.4 Self-development

Since some memes are beneficial symbionts, one way to improve yourself is to acquire a better selection of memes. *Meme therapy* involves educating yourself by exposing yourself to beneficial memes, and attempting to replace inferior memes with superior competitors.

19.5 News and politics

Most humans enjoy keeping up with the news - even though a lot of news is a frivolous waste of time. News articles are among the forms of human culture which are frequently shared by friends on the internet.

Political use of memes is mostly in the vein of marketing and self-promotion. Some political doctrines are themselves memes, and evolve and change over time.

19.6 Causes and charities

These not-for-profit organisations are *usually* not selling things, but they often still need to promote their services, gather mindshare and stimulate donations. The causes people support are one of the things people like to display to others - to signal their good character and the things they care about. Causes typically make use of this tendency as part of their propagation mechanism.

19.7 Religion and cults

Religion give us some examples of ancient powerful memes, highly adapted to spreading through human minds. They use superstimulii such as heaven and hell to motivate people. They take advantage of host reproductive energy sometimes. They spread "vertically" down human generations and "horizontally", from person to person in the same generation. Historically, what religious memes you carried was often important. Many people have died for having the wrong religion. Memetics gives a firm foundation to the academic study of religion.

19.8 Deprogramming

Deprogramming and exit-counselling aim to extract victims from religions and cults. These are modern equivalents of exorcism rituals. Exorcisms aimed to free people of the evil spirits that possessed them. These days, we know that the *evil spirits* are actually memeplexes which do not have the interests of their hosts at heart. The possessions by these things are very literally real. These people's minds are infected with contagious parasites, who have implanted hooks into their motivational circuitry, and often come equipped with defences against being removed. Benscoter (2009) gives an account of deprogramming from a memetic perspective.

19.9 Military memetics

Behind every missile, tank, rifle, radio and bomb there is a bunch of memes. Cryptography and cryptanalysis are also meme-driven. Propaganda and surveillance and are ancient military techniques that even more directly employ memetics. So, it is no surprise that the government is interested. Military memetics documents available online say:

PURPOSE OF A MILITARY MEMETICS PROGRAM

To develop a new approach to:

- *Countering terrorists and insurgents before and after they become terrorists and insurgents: influencing beliefs in a scientific way;*
- *Preventing irrational conflict and promoting rational solutions to national and international problems;*
- *Strengthening the U.S. military in: Peacekeeping missions; Psychological operations; Recruitment; Training;*
- *To make new discoveries concerning the human brain, cognition, and social networks.*

...and...

MEMETICS - A GROWTH INDUSTRY IN US MILITARY OPERATIONS

The Meme Warfare Center offers a more complex and intellectually rich capability absent in current IO, PsyOps and SC formations and is specifically designed to combat the enemy's sophistication as highlighted above. The emerging tools to win the metaphysical fight are memes. Managing, employing and leveraging memetic power is key for the US to shape and win on future battlefields.

...and...

The US must recognize the growing need for emerging disciplines in ideological warfare by 'weaponeering' memes. The Meme Warfare Center offers sophisticated and intellectually rich capability absent in current IO, PsyOps and SC formations and is specifically designed to conduct combat inside the mind of the enemy. Memes are key emerging tools to win the ideological metaphysical fight.

There is a document all about "memetic warfare" - which concludes:

It is vital to the interests of the U.S. and its people that memetic theory is fully explored, if for no other reason than to develop defenses against foreign memetic attack. Memetic operations do not require a presence in the target country. For a fraction of the cost of deploying troops on the ground, the enemies of the U.S. could conduct devastating memetic based information warfare against America. It is time for the IC to turn this threat into an opportunity. Memetics after all is only a tool, and tools when properly employed can be used to build peace, hope, prosperity, and a better way of life.

Companies have sprung up to meet the needs of the military in this area. One is "Applied Memetics LLC". Their web site says they specialise in:

· Intelligence Collection & Analysis;
· Media Monitoring & Development;
· Strategic Communications & Public Diplomacy;
· Capacity Building & Transition Assistance;

You can check them out on the internet:
http://www.appliedmemeticsllc.com/

19.10 Other applications

Other application areas for memetics include: technology, law, anthropology, sociology, history, economics, management, philosophy of science, religious studies and linguistics.

20 Origins - The origin of culture

In the same way that the origin of life is a different subject from the study of its subsequent evolution, so the origin of culture is quite a distinct subject from cultural evolution. We can see that culture in our lineage likely started before our ancestors split from those of modern chimpanzees - since chimps too have cultural inheritance. In memetics, the origin of culture is sometimes known as *memesis* - the memetic version of *genesis*.

20.1 Culture in other animals

Culture has arisen in more than one lineage - though it is better developed in humans than in most other animals. It is now well-known that there are examples of cultural inheritance in *many* other animals:

- **Cetaceans** - Humpback whale songs were first recorded in the 1960s. Since then bottlenose dolphin, killer whale, and sperm whales have been studied in some detail. Though humans currently lack a complete understanding of whale song, we can see that it is a complex form of communication with high bandwidth - and we can identify regional dialects within the same species, and see that some whale songs evolve over time in a manner resembling fashions. The Australian biologist Mike Noad and colleagues has found evidence of a cultural revolution in whale song. In 1996 two male humpbacks from the Indian Ocean arrived in the Pacific with a new song. Within two years, all the Pacific males had changed their tune, picking up the new song. Dolphins are also thought to have culture. Domesticated dolphins have taught wild dolphins to tail-walk, for example Black (2008).
- **Apes** - Over 40 populations of chimpanzees have been studied, and scientists have found in them at least 65 categories of behaviours that are culturally transmitted (Whiten et al. 1999). For example, Jane Goodall (1964) reported that chimps culturally transmitted skill of foraging for termites using stalks.
- **Monkeys** - Japanese macaque monkeys on the island of Koshima had been introduced to sweet potatoes by humans, and developed the cultural practice of washing them in the salty surf before eating them. The spread of this practice was carefully documented by Japanese scientists (Kinji Imanishi).
- **Rats** - some black rats strip pine cone scales from pine cones to expose the edible parts - and learn this behaviour from other rats (Joseph Terkel 1991).
- **Songbirds** - These are probably one of the best known cases. Scientists have found compelling evidence for imitation-based learning in songbirds - one of the primary mechanisms supporting cultural inheritance.
- **Meerkats** - These have been investigated by Alex Thornton. Alex has demonstrated teaching behaviour in wild meerkats.
- **Blue tits** - These have learned to open foil milk-bottle tops - and the behaviour spread around culturally. Such behaviour is not normally spread around by imitation, though. Rather the birds simply learn to

associate silver milk-bottle tops with obtaining milk.

· **Guppies** - The mating behaviour of female guppies involves copying the preference of other female guppies - which results in cultural inheritance of mate fashions (Dugatkin 2001).

· **Fruit flies** - The mating preferences of female fruit flies are copied by other females (Mery et al. 2009).

· **Ants** - Alternative social organizations in fire ants appear to be determined culturally (Keller and Ross, 1993).

What do these examples have in common? Cultural inheritance apparently requires a brain - and some degree of sociality. Most cultural inheritance that has been found so far is seen in large, complex, sexual animals. Though many animals exhibit cultural inheritance, none have taken it anywhere near as far as humans have.

20.2 Chimpanzee culture

Chimpanzees are our nearest relatives. Chimpanzee culture has long been reported. Jane Goodall reported, in a 1964 *Nature* paper, the use of twigs used for termite foraging in Tanzanian chimpanzees.

In the 1970s, geographic variation in such customs was documented. Extensive studies of wild chimps (Whiten et al. 1999) showed that they had cultural transmission, and experimentally induced cultural conditions were shown to be transmitted (Whiten et al. 2005) - finally ruling out other forms of inheritance.

Chimpanzee.

Chimpanzees use culture to transmit tool use, gestures and foraging strategies down the generations. However, they have yet to reach their own Chimpanzee "stone age" - the point where human culture first obviously started to take off.

We will not go into very many details here, but several books have been written about chimpanzee culture - including: "Chimpanzee Cultures" by Wrangham, McGrew, de Waal and Heltne (1996), "Chimpanzee Material Culture: Implications for Human Evolution" by McGrew (1992) and "Tree of Origin: What Primate Behavior Can Tell Us about Human Social Evolution" by de Waal, Byrne, Dunbar and McGrew (2002).

20.3 Upright gait hypothesis

Modern humans have an upright stance and gait, whereas the other great apes do not. Fossil evidence suggest that walking upright was one of the first traits to evolve among our ancestors that distinguished our lineage from that of chimpanzees. Here, we will consider the hypothesis that an upright stance and gait started out as a culturally-transmitted trait that *eventually* became assimilated into the genome.

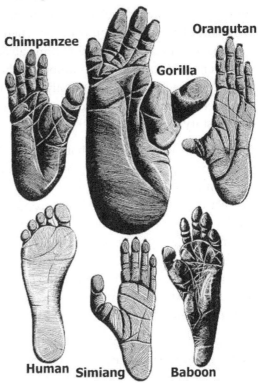

In the light of the evidence that chimpanzees have a diverse range of cultural traditions, it seems quite plausible that early humans also had had a form of culture. An upright gait and stance probably started off as a cultural phenomenon - and was passed on from parent to child. Over time the human foot, leg bones, knee, pelvis, spine, circulatory system, organs and developmental program gradually adjusted to accommodate this new habit, via a process of *genetic assimilation*.

Human feet are different from most primate feet.

The evidence that an upright gait started off as a cultural trait mostly consists of the observation that an upright gait is largely a culturally-transmitted trait - *even* today. Much of the supporting evidence for this from comes from feral children. Though the scientific status of this evidence is often questionable, we know enough from it to see that many feral children fail to learn to walk - and instead copy the gait of the species that raised them.

Oxana Malaya - raised by dogs.

For example, consider the case of Oxana Malaya. From between the ages of three and eight, Oxana lived mostly in a kennel and was raised by dogs.

When found, she barked, growled, panted, ran around on all fours, and sniffed at her food before she ate it. Oxana had failed to learn to walk or speak, and behaved in a manner which was strongly reminiscent of the dogs that had surrounded her during her development. Walking and talking behaviours both require cultural transmission to be successfully elicited.

With feral children it is sometimes difficult to know whether their developmental difficulties are the result of their abandonment, or whether they were handicapped before they were abandoned. However, in Oxana's case, although she never fully recovered, she *did* eventually learn to walk and speak. Other feral children generally tell a similar story.

A *possible* rival to the idea that humans chose to walk upright is the idea that that powerful selection pressures *forced* humans to walk upright.

A walking human.

At least one hypothesis has been proposed that fits that description. This involves a scenario in which humans are isolated on a island which then became flooded, practically forcing the humans to stand up while wading around in marshlands. Such a scenario seems *relatively* implausible, but *even* if it is true, humans were *probably* not in such circumstances for very long. For most of human evolution, our ancestors were probably standing up because they chose to.

An upright gait is partly culturally transmitted in modern humans. However, among our early ancestors cultural inheritance was probably even more important - since organic inheritance of walking-related traits would have been less of a factor.

Culturally-induced speciation?

The upright gait hypothesis hypothesis is interesting for several reasons. Walking is dated back to close to the split between the human and chimpanzee lineages. That makes walking one of the oldest culturally-transmitted traits

The distinctive human upright gait.

we know of - and we can see the scale of its effect on the human gene pool. Also, if memetic evolution is implicated in the split from our nearest living relatives, then we should consider the possibility of links between memetic evolution and speciation. There *are* cases where parasitism causes speciation in the organic world - for example, Wolbachia bacteria can create reproductive isolation in their hosts - and have caused speciation. It has been speculated that cultural influences may cause speciation in other species. The high diversity of the songbirds is likely to be the result of memetic evolution generating reproductive barriers by influencing mating signals. Vaneechoutte (1997) has explored this possibility, along with many other researchers. Paleoanthropology indicates frequent branching of hominid species, which is also consistent with symbiosis-induced speciation.

20.4 Opposable thumb

Humans have developed complex communication, and used it to invent civilisation. However, *cetaceans* never managed their own civilisation - *despite* their *enormous* head start.

One possible explanation for this invokes the human opposable thumb. Cetaceans

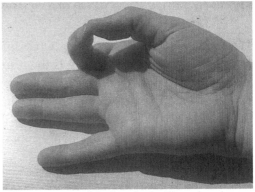

Human opposable thumb: facilitated tool use.

may have an older and perhaps more highly-developed verbal communication system - but they never really mastered writing, using tools, or any other technology. This seems to be because they simply do not have the actuators required to take their culture to the next level. Without external transmission, their culture is limited to what individuals can remember - in much the same way as human tribes were before they mastered writing.

The opposable thumb is probably tied in to the uptight gait hypothesis – since walking upright would have freed up the hands and reduced the adaptive pressures on them for ground-walking.

20.5 Symbolism

Some propose that humans have abstract symbolic communications capabilities that other animals lack. They claim that this difference pre-dates the development of writing. Terrance Deacon (1997) has a summary of this position, and there is a school of anthropology called "symbolic anthropology" that studies culture from this perspective. However, use of symbolic communication has been observed among chimpanzees (Savage-Rumbaugh, 1986 and Meddin, 1979). While symbolic communication is important for humans and forms the basis of our language - but it isn't *really* unique to humans, and it *probably* developed after the stone-age explosion in human culture.

20.6 Imitation

Some have proposed that imitation is a key to the origins of culture in humans. Probably the main proponent of this perspective is Blackmore. In 2009, she wrote:

> *By contrast memetics claims that the turning point in human evolution was the advent of imitation. Indeed it is imitation that makes us human (Blackmore 2007a).*

While it is true that culture is what made us human, there is more to culture than imitation. Culture is the result of copying - but not *necessarily* the result of copying *behaviour*. It is perfectly possible to copy writing artefacts without much knowledge about the behaviour that produced it. This is true of other types of artefact as well. If someone sees a knot, and copies it, they are not *really* copying behaviour.

20.7 Cultural tipping point

Another hypothesis is that culture becomes an autocatalytic phenomenon once it reaches a certain point in its development. Much as a snowball doesn't start to roll on its own until it reaches a critical threshold, so culture needs to reach a certain point before it starts to build on itself and accumulate.

20.8 Language

Speech and language skills dramatically increased the rate of copying fidelity in the transmission of human culture. Language represents digitisation of ideas, and digitisation allows for error detection and correction techniques to be used. Language is sufficiently old for modern humans to have adaptations to facilitate language acquisition and use - with specific dedicated areas of the brain, breath control and modifications to the larynx.

20.9 Ultrasociality

Humans also became more sociable. Unsociable humans were not so good at acquiring memes, and memes offered all kinds of fitness benefits - so ultrasociality was favoured genetically. Also memes which promoted ultrasociality were also favoured and became popular additions to existing memeplexes (since it helped them to spread). Ultrasociality eventually led to stable villages, increased population density, human specialisation with division of labour and the agricultural revolution.

Language and ultrasociality are dealt with in more detail in our chapter about the mutualism between genes and memes.

20.10 Xenophobia

Humans are *ultrasocial* within their *own* tribes, but quite *xenophobic* when it comes to humans from *other* tribes. This too could be a result of memetic influences. Memes can rapidly create between-group differences, and some of these are then treated as tribal group markers. In group members are typically treated as being more trustworthy - due to extended relationships with them that allow reciprocal altruism. So: humans are sensitive to in-group out-group markers - and these markers are frequently memetic – though other markers will do. If coevolution with memes is implicated in human xenophobia, that is yet *another* reason to pay close attention to the subject.

21 Major transitions - Seismic memetic shifts

In their 1995 book *The Major Transitions in Evolution*, Maynard-Smith and Szathmáry offered a perspective on the history of life in terms of major developments in the history of life. Cultural evolution has seen its own set of transitions, which we will document in this chapter.

21.1 Brains

The development of brains was an early milestone. Before that, *most* adaptation to the environment was performed under more direct control by genes. Brains allow a form of "plasticity" in an organism's response to the environment. Just as plasticene molds itself to the shape of your fist, so brains allow

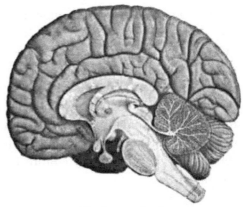

The human brain.

organisms to better mold themselves to their environment. Plants *do* have some limited level of developmental plasticity: their roots develop to avoid rocks and their branches develop so that they avoid obstacles and shade. However, the development of brains permitted a *dramatic* increase in the behavioural plasticity animals could exhibit. As a result animals with brains became *much* better at changing in response to unfamiliar environments.

However, for a while, the information in brains was lost when their owner died. There was no way for the knowledge about local environmental conditions to get out of one brain - and find its way into another one.

21.2 Tools

Tool use is seen in many animals. It may precede cultural transmission in some cases.

In humans, their bipedal gait freed human hands from walking-related roles - which facilitated further tool use. The first human tools we have much evidence about were developed in the stone age and consisted of stone implements – knives, axes,

A stone-age knife.

hammers, spear tips and *eventually* arrowheads.

21.3 Culture

Culture was the next step. Many animals have primitive forms of culture. Culture allows the transmission of learned information from one generation to the next, so things do not need to be rediscovered in each generation. Walking, mating customs and tool techniques would have been among early forms of transmitted culture. However cultural transmission is often noisy, and animal brains are often small. These limits constrained the potential of culture for a long time.

A cultured human.

21.4 Speech

Speech was the next breakthrough. Song may followed shortly afterwards. Speech digitises culture, increasing its copying fidelity.

Human speech is believed to have arisen in the form of inarticulate grunts and gesticulations.

Much human culture was originally preserved by an oral tradition in the form of hymns. Melody and rhymes would have helped people to remember the correct word sequences. Also group chanting has a built-in error correction process. If a

Human singing.

few people forget, their lines, the majority voice will be unaffected. If the chanting is repeated, the forgetful can pick up the correct words again.

During this period genes and memes co-evolved. Humans with more space for memes were rewarded with increased genetic fitness. Humans developed bigger brains with better memories, a more sociable disposition - and more articulate vocal equipment.

21.5 Ultrasociality

Human ultrasociality was promoted by coevolution with memes promoting social behaviour. Any memeplex including such memes would have had its fitness boosted - since memes need sociable humans as part of their reproductive process.

At some point, many humans abandoned hunter-gatherer lifestyles, domesticated plants and animals and began to settle down in villages and trade with each other. This affected meme transmission by bringing many humans closer together and

Humans packed together.

promoting specialisation. In hunter-gatherer tribes there are only a limited number of roles: leader, witch doctor, male member and female member. Each role required its own memes - but there were only four roles, limiting meme diversity.

However, in a village there would have been bakers, winemakers, shopkeepers, builders, cleaners, nannys, doctors, midwives, soldiers, priests - and probably many other roles - each of which would have required its own memes. Human specialisation allowed meme diversification. This increased the total quantity of cultural knowledge. The bigger the community, the more specialisation and the more cultural knowledge.

21.6 Writing

Writing was probably the next major development. It represented a form of meme storage outside the human brain. It represents an external verbal memory. Writing increased the copying fidelity of memes. It allowed backup copies. Written documents persisted for extended periods and could be read by many individuals.

Writing postcards on a table.

21.7 Printing

Then came the printing press. The printing press automated meme production. Soon, many people could afford books and newspapers. Education became cheaper and more widespread. Printing was

Printing press.

followed by the industrial revolution , which led to TV and radio.

21.8 Computers and the internet

Computers are gradually allowing the functions of the human brain to be outsourced. For memes, computers represent a new type of host besides human brains. Many computer viruses skip over the human brain completely. Computer viruses are parasites, though.

Desktop computer.

21.9 Superintelligence

Superintelligent machines seem likely to be able to copy memes with the full consent of society. At that stage, memes won't be dependent on humans any more. The replacement of the economically-significant functions of human brains by objects that can be copied and backed-up looks set to be a significant change. Of course, this step hasn't happened yet - but it is pretty clear that it is going to.

22 Immunity - Resistance to infection

In the organic realm, large organisms have dedicated systems whose function is allow them to resist the unwanted attentions of smaller, faster creatures, which aim at stealing their resources. These systems are known as "immune systems".

There are plenty of deleterious memes in the world. It would make sense for humans to have memetic immune systems - whose purpose is to resist them. Indeed, we can see that many deleterious memes, do in fact, face active resistance from their targets. Blackmore (2006h) described some of the common sources of memetic immunity as follows:

> *Memetic immunity comes from education, reading, sharing ideas with others and above all from free speech – the freedom to learn about all sorts of ideas, compare them as you will and choose for yourself which to believe.*

We will now have a look at the various sources of resistance:

22.1 Immune resistance

- **Immunity as a result of existing infections** - In some cases, the source of the resistance is a defence system formed by other existing memes. Some memeplexes come equipped with adaptations whose function is to prevent infection by competing memeplexes.
- **Immunity as a result of prior infections** - Brains learn - and exposure to previous deleterious memes can provide learning experiences which can help to increase resistance against subsequent infections. For example, if you have participated in one pyramid scheme - and lost out as a result - then future business opportunities that resemble pyramid schemes may have a harder time of attracting your attention.
- **Immunity as a result of inoculations** - In the organic realm, "vaccines" are used to give the immune system a taste of an infectious agent - which then goes on to provide immunity from the associated disease. There are memetic vaccines as well. Sometimes, just understanding how a chain letter, cult or advert operates helps individuals to recognise it - and so avoid a more serious infection.
- **Meme therapy** - "bad" gut bacteria can sometimes be dealt with by

pouring in "good" bacteria on top of them. These are often called "probiotic" bacteria. It is possible to employ a similar strategy to combat "bad" memes after infection, by dosing the afflicted individuals with "good" memes. These could be called "probiotic" memes.

• **Hospitals, medicine and surgery** - In the organic realm, some immune systems have expanded to include extended organisations intended to defeat disease - including hospitals, doctors, vets, and quarantine facilities. Pathogens can be surgically removed, scraped, burned, frozen, poisoned, starved - or otherwise caused to malfunction. Individuals can be quarantined, tracked and their history of interaction can be taken - to help identify other infected agents. Similar organisations exist to help those infected with toxic memes. Many cults have dedicated recovery groups, aimed at rehabilitating their victims. There are support groups for victims of scams. Rescue groups attempt to recover individuals pushed close to the edge by their memes. Wavering creationists have places like *talk.origins*, where they are given assistance with sorting their heads out.

• **Censorship** - One of the biggest experiments with control of undesirable memes in the world has been The Great Firewall of China. Purportedly censoring only superstitious, pornographic, violent, gambling and criminal information, the firewall *appears* to be being used for political means and as a form of control over the population. However, memes are not easy to control. Encryption and steganography make it relatively easy to move information around without attracting undesirable attention. According to a proverb, the internet treats censorship as network damage, and routes around it. Without extensive surveillance of the end-points, censorship is difficult to enforce.

• **Avoidance** - In the organic realm, some parasitic infections can be avoided by avoiding exposure in the first place. This is the memetic equivalent of using condoms. Avoidance can be considered to be a kind of self-censorship.

22.2 Examples

One of the *Ten Commandments* states:

You shall have no other gods before me

This is a meme whose *primary* function is to prevent infection by other competing memes. Another of the *Ten Commandments* talks about *false idols*, saying:

You shall not bow down to them or worship them; for I the Lord your God am a jealous God, punishing children for the iniquity of parents, to the third and the fourth generation of those who reject me.

This is a meme whose purpose is to create an immune response to certain competing memes. In an attempt to increase its own effectiveness, it backs up with its message with a threat of punishment from an imaginary powerful jealous agent.

22.3 Avoiding memes

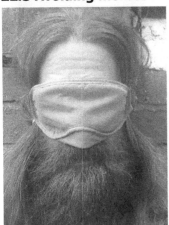

For most, avoiding memes completely is not very practical.

A good way of avoiding infections is avoiding the pathogens that cause them. Barriers can keep them out, and behavioural techniques such as sexual abstinence and hand washing can reduce exposure further.

Deliberate avoidance of memes by individuals is possible. Some people do throw away their televisions, go without a network

Barrier contraceptive.

connection and live in a more primitive era. The Amish provide an example of this type of strategy.

Meme-avoidance is gradually turning into an impractical strategy in the modern world, though. Increasingly, people are being forced to plug themselves into the ideosphere in order to find work, buy things, and perform other essential tasks. However, *selective* meme-avoidance *is* more practical. Pornography can be avoided by not looking at it. Games can be avoided by not trying them out.

22.4 Vaccimes

In the organic realm, vaccination is an effective way of preventing many infections. If often consists of giving the immune system a taste of the pathogen, which helps it to develop a defence. There are memetic vaccines as well. People can be educated about scams, hoaxes and deceptions. They can try out bad ideas in play environments or in the virtual worlds of computer games - where failure does not have so many painful consequences. They can also be exposed to generic vaccines against bad ideas - in the form of scepticism and critical thinking. In this way many deleterious memetic infections can be avoided.

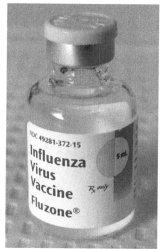

Flu vaccine.

22.5 Childhood immunity

In the organic realm, infections are often picked up by young individuals with inexperienced immune systems. These are also those who benefit most from vaccinations. Things are very similar in the cultural realm. Children are built to absorb memes quickly, and are not too competent at telling good memes from bad ones. They are among the most harmed by infections, and they are also among those who benefit most from vaccimes.

22.6 Memetic immunity is imperfect

Organic immune systems should reject most foreign bodies. However, with meme transmission there is a twist that does not really apply to organic immune systems. Memes are - on average - beneficial. Letting the good ones through while rejecting the bad ones is a *very* difficult problem. If we knew which ideas were the good ones, we wouldn't need cultural transmission in the first place - we could just *invent* the good ideas. However, we *don't* know that - so we do the best we can, and *inevitably* some bad ideas get through the net. The price we pay for getting lots of good ideas culturally is that *some* bad ones make it past our defences. However, that could often be better than beefing up our defences - since that would stop lots of good ideas from reaching us too.

22.7 The origins of memetic immunity

In the organic realm, the immune system is partly the result of genetic adaptations and partly the result of exposure to pathogens. What about the memetic immune system? Is its construction coded into the human genome? Or is the memetic immune system a product of memes?

Evidently, *some* kinds of immunity are caused by memes - or are memetic adaptations. However, it would be interesting to find out whether aspects of the memetic immune system have a basis in the nuclear genes. Many of the learning mechanisms involved appear to be general-purpose ones. These avoid *any* unpleasant events - *regardless* of whether they originate with memes or not. If there *are* dedicated memetic immune responses which are innate in humans - such as an innate tendency towards scepticism - these have yet to be clearly elucidated by researchers.

22.8 Protecting culture against organic parasites

There are also cases where memetic structures need protection against organic parasites. Fungi, plants, rodents, birds, spiders, ants and bacteria can all parasitise culturally-transmitted artefacts.

22.9 Pure-memetic immunity

Humans are not the only type creature which gets infected by culturally-transmitted parasites. Computers can harbour their own breeds of toxic memes - in the form of computer viruses. There are companies which make their living by providing software to disinfect and protect these networked machines.

Bird spikes.

The world of computer viruses offers some of the most vivid parallels between the organic and cultural realms. There are self-encrypting computer viruses - that hide from immune systems. Some viruses deliberately mutate themselves - to help hide from virus checkers looking for their signatures. Some computer viruses deliberately disable the computer's immune system as part of their function, seeking out and destroying any tools that could be used to eliminate them.

These tricks may sound familiar. If so, that may be because organic pathogens use similar tricks against the immune systems of their hosts.

23 The internet - Recent developments

After millions of years of being confined to human heads, the memes have now gone digital and constructed the internet - a massive breeding ground for helping memes to make more memes. Meme-driven developments online are accelerating scientific and technological development and are further promoting the internet's expansion. With the ongoing digitization of human culture, most *existing* memes have *already* found their way onto the internet - and it has also proved itself to be a fertile breeding ground for *new* memes.

In addition to infesting human brains, memes are now swarming in massive numbers in sprawling server farms. *Most* memes still need human brains to complete their lifecycles - but already *some* memes have succeeded in cutting their human hosts out of the loop. Plans are afoot to allow the memes to reproduce more freely by reducing their dependence on human hosts, with plans to construct a "semantic web" with ubiquitous machine-readable interfaces. While *some* areas of the internet are still reserved for humans, others are rapidly becoming more machine-friendly.

23.1 Digital revolution

The world is gradually going digital. CDs are replacing records, DVDs are replacing video cassettes and digital cameras are replacing analog ones. This change is often known as the *Digital Revolution*. This refers to the change from analog technology to digital technology that has taken place over the last three decades. The switch to digital storage media is ongoing.

23.2 Examples of analog and digital systems

Edison's phonograph (1877) is a classical example of analog information storage. It used a diaphragm to convert sound waves into the displacement of a needle. The needle then made tracks on a wax or foil cylinder. The displacement and path of the resulting track varied continuously in response to the changes in air pressure.

By contrast, Morse's telegraph (1844) was a digital communications system. Instead of being continuously variable, the signal sent down a telegraph wire was encoded in binary using two states. These were then used to represent four basic symbols (dit, dah, end-of-letter, end-of-word). Those basic symbols were then combined to form 30-60 alphanumeric symbols - which were in turn used to encode messages.

23.3 Analog problems

One of the problems with analog communications systems is noise. Since analog signals often vary continuously, disturbances typically introduce an error or discrepancy from the original signal that cannot easily be distinguished from it. This becomes a severe problem when consecutive copies of the information are made. For example, audio cassette tapes could be copied - but each consecutive copy exhibits more and more hiss. The disadvantages of using analog inheritance were understood in Darwin's era. *Blending inheritance* was considered by many to be a major problem with Darwin's theory at the time. Once it was understood that inheritance was mostly discrete and particulate, this problem vanished.

23.4 Digital advantage

By contrast, in digital systems, noise is not as much of an issue. Noise is usually a low-level signal, and so can normally be distinguished from the intended message. This allows digital data to be regenerated and the noise removed. Digital systems also support better-established error detection and correction algorithms. As a result, gradual degeneration as copies are made of of copies is usually not as much of a problem with digital data.

23.5 Digital genetics

The system used by organic creatures to store, copy, and transmit genetic information is *primarily* a digital system. Genetic information is *mostly* conveyed by the sequence in which the organic compounds known as bases are strung together to make long molecules of RNA and DNA.

23.6 Digital memetics

As the digital revolution progresses, cultural inheritance is *increasingly* becoming digital - and is gradually becoming a high-fidelity copying process - one which more closely resembles organic inheritance. This development is making the relationship between cultural evolution and organic evolution increasingly obvious.

23.7 Genetic engineering

The domain of the gene has been invaded in turn by human culture - in the form of genetic engineering. This brings the characteristic traits of cultural evolution - in the form of directed mutations and engineering design - directly to the germ lines of existing organisms.

There is a spectrum relating to the involvement of intelligence in evolutionary change. We see natural selection, unconscious selection, conscious selection, deliberate breeding and engineering design. All these stages are visible in *both* the organic and cultural domains. Interestingly, the organic world developed all of these techniques first - *except* for the most recent one: engineering design. Now the cultural world is in the lead, with cultural engineering being developed centuries before organic engineering became practical.

23.8 Convergence

Cultural evolution is becoming more like organic evolution - by going digital. Simultaneously, organic evolution is becoming more like cultural evolution - by embracing engineering design. The resulting convergence of cultural and organic evolution is evidently still in its early stages - but we can expect the two to become increasingly intertwined. It will become increasingly difficult to distinguish the two realms.

23.9 The internet

The digitisation of culture has led to the current internet era. A worldwide network of computers now unites humanity and allows rapid and contact between widely-separated points. The result is a synthetic world where everything is digital: cyberspace.

23.10 Internet memes

The medium affects the message, and the internet has given rise to a range of content that takes advantage of its strengths. One of the results is "internet memes" - culture that spreads rapidly and contagiously online.

23.11 Memetic pandemics

The most virulent memes propagate contagiously on the internet, with many millions of people sharing and spreading them. Global memetic pandemics are not a *particularly* new phenomenon - but the internet means that they happen more frequently and rapidly than ever before. The inexorable growth of the internet ensures that the associated memes are reaching an ever-greater fraction of the population.

23.12 Image macros

Some of the memetic epidemics on the internet consist of images. Among those are image macros. These often use an "exploitable" image, with some amusing or ironic text. Some examples:

Image macros often use an "exploitable" image, with some amusing or ironic text superimposed on it.

23.13 Viral games

Other popular content that spreads virally on the internet is computer programs. Some of these are useful - others: not so much. Computer games can be addictive and use people's adrenal system to stimulate repetitive behaviour. Large quantities of human and computer time are currently spent playing games.

23.14 Viral videos

Other popular content online is in the form of videos. On-demand videos on the internet provide people with their own personalised television channel where they can choose what to watch. Some content is very popular and spreads contagiously on social networks - resulting in "viral videos". A few examples:

| *Charlie bit me.* | *David after dentist.* | *Sneezing panda.* |

The most popular videos can clock up hundreds of millions of views.

23.15 Viral texts

Text results in contagious epidemics on the internet as well. News headlines, scientific abstracts, hypertext links and copyright licenses are often duplicated many times. Chain letters have also taken on a new life on the internet. There are status update chains. When repeating status updates takes a single click, copying becomes much more common. A few viral status updates:

- *ATTENTION!!!!!!! Do not join the group currently on Facebook with the title"Becoming a Father or Mother was the greatest gift of my life" It is a group of Pedophiles trying to access your photos. This was on Fox News at 5. Please copy and post!!*
- *THE PHONE NUMBERS IN YOUR PHONE are now Facebook. Go to the top right of the screen, click on ACCOUNT, click on EDIT FRIENDS, left side of screen click CONTACTS. You will see all phone numbers (FB friends or not) that you have stored in your cell phone are published on Facebook. TO*

REMOVE, go to Right column, click on "this page." Please repost on your status so friends can remove their contact lists.

- *URGENT!!! This is deadly serious!!! A professional Hacker is requesting to be friends. His profile pic is him sitting in a Hoodie in front of a laptop. His name is FACEB HU. He has been accepted by many and he has taken FULL control of their accounts even their emails and friends! People have lost everything in their accounts. Even by rejecting him he still gets in; so just IGNORE him or deactivate account for a while! BE careful who you except as your friends. Please REPOST THIS.*

The phylomemetic tree of such messages is easier to establish on the internet than in other media. For example the "Good Times" virus hoax has been well documented. That virus hoax looks like this:

FYI, a file, going under the name "Good Times" is being sent to some Internet users who subscribe to on-line services (Compuserve, Prodigy and America On Line). If you should receive this file, do not download it! Delete it immediately. I understand that there is a virus included in that file, which if downloaded to your personal computer, will ruin all of your files.

This virus has been captured on many occasions and it exhibits many mutations, including capitalised threats, references to authorities, technical double-talk and jovial greetings.

At the time, Clay Shirky commented:

Its for real. Its an opportunistic self-replicating email virus which tricks its host into replicating it, sometimes adding as many as 200,000 copies at a go. It works by finding hosts with defective parsing apparatus which prevents them from understanding that a piece of email which says there is an email virus and then asking them to remail the message to all their friends is the virus itself.

23.16 Viral games

Other popular content that spreads virally on the internet is computer programs. Some of these are useful - others: not so much. Computer games can be addictive and use people's adrenal system to stimulate repetitive behaviour. Large quantities of human and computer time are currently spent playing games.

23.17 Viral pornography

Pornography represents a substantial fraction of internet traffic. Historically, pornography has been a substantial force driving new communications media. Sexual content taps into deep human desire and motivational structures which facilitate its propagation. The internet has also seen the rise of interactive pornography based around the use webcams. Future technologies may permit even more immersive experiences - so it seems likely that sexual content will remain on the leading edge of the internet revolution for some time to come.

23.18 Sharing prohibition

At the time of writing, much sharing and copying of culture is prohibited by archaic copyright laws. These laws are widely violated in an enormous underground culture of sharing. Progress has made copying trivially easy, and the ubiquitous availability of cryptography has made exchanging material online relatively safe and simple. Banning cryptography does not appear to be very practical. Without ubiquitous government surveillance of the end-points, technical measures to prevent copying appear challenging. That just leaves the legal constraints - and these laws are becoming very widely violated and unpopular.

The original idea of copyright law was to encourage creativity. However, copyright has turned into toll booths on the information super-highway, and these days it acts more to hamper creativity than to stimulate it.

It *is* possible to own intellectual property. You do that by keeping it secret. However, once material finds its way onto the internet the chances any one individual controlling the information diminish rapidly. The *Streisand effect* ensures that *attempts* to produce *information scarcity* are naturally opposed by increased supply. Information loves a void.

23.19 Frivolous internet culture

The term "meme" has exploded in popularity on the internet recently. I think that is great. Others, however, are less enthusiastic. Here is Kate Distin on the topic:

> *The World Wide Web in particular is full of pages and blogs that use the term meme with varying degrees of vagueness, often not bothering to define it at all but simply stretching it to fit whichever space has opened up in the writer's vocabulary. The intellectual credibility of memetics is diminished every time a meme-related term is hijacked in this way and its sense redirected to the latest cultural phenomenon to have caught the eye.*

A "LOLCat" internet meme.

A similar perspective comes from Rachel Haywire:

> *It seems like everyone on the Internet acts like a 14 year old troll. Can I haz my culture back? I don't think that lolcats are funny. They might as well symbolize the death of memetics. The fittest memes are parody macros. Can we say cyber-idiocracy?*

Some internet memes are certainly pretty stupid and infantile. I can see how some might want to distance themselves from the phenomenon. However, humans can never seem to agree to *just* copy the good and fine things and not copy the junk. I think *some* association of memetics with frivolous pop culture is practically inevitable.

23.20 Cultural microscopes

As well as being a hot-bed of meme activity, the internet has become the place for social scientists interested in the area to go. A range of tools have become available to allow people to track cultural trends and developments. Google provides interfaces to allow its database of previous search queries to be explored. These are called "Google Insights for Search" and "Google Trends".

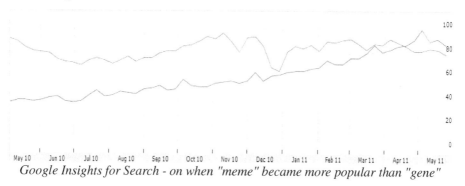

Google Insights for Search - on when "meme" became more popular than "gene"

Google have *also* scanned in a *vast* number of books. They allow these to be searched as well - using the "Google Books Ngram Viewer" - like this:

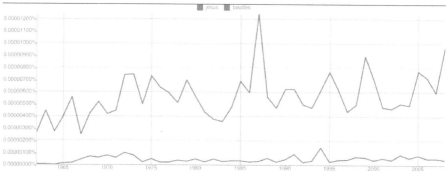

Were The Beatles more popular than Jesus? Google Ngram viewer looks at that.

Tools are *also* available to gather statistics from *Twitter*, news sources, "blogs", *social networking* sites - and from other sources.

Additionally, it has become easier to conduct social science experiments of many kinds - including ones associated with cultural evolution. If you want a questionnaire filled out, you can pay people to do it over the internet at low cost. If you have an interactive experiment that can be performed at home by a people sitting at computers, again, you can now very easily pay people to do that - and it doesn't cost very much. Social scientists can easily gather lots of data less expensively than has been possible until now.

These are some of the developments that led to Daniel Dennett describing the internet as the Drosophila of memetics in a 2009 Harvard lecture.

23.21 Meme graveyard

While the internet is fertile ground for many types of memes, some do not do so well on the internet, relatively speaking. Some religious memes face considerable scepticism on the internet. Indeed, some say that the internet is where old religions go to die.

23.22 Computer viruses

Much as animals sometimes get infected with viruses, so some types of networked computers are vulnerable to similar attacks. Many modern computers run outdated software that carries a legacy dating back from before computers were networked together very much. These computers were not built with security in mind - and typically offer poor resistance to attack. The viruses are usually

A real life Trojan horse.

written by human beings. Sometimes they are designed to mutate themselves. This increases their resistance to immune attacks, but has the side effect of making it easier to trace their origin by reconstructing their phylomemetic tree.

These viruses are a type of meme that is capable of infecting computer systems - as well as sometimes spending some time in human brains. Most computer viruses spend more time inside machines than most other memes do. Though forged in human minds, most of their reproductive life is spent inside machines. Some viruses require humans to take actions before they can spread - however, other viruses do not. For example, the "Santy" worm attacked databases on servers *without* requiring human intervention - and so spread itself very rapidly. The BBC reported that, within 24 hours, it had successfully infected more than 40,000 websites around the world. The behaviour of such viruses provides an indication of how fast memes could spread from one machine to the next, if they are no longer dependent upon humans.

A common infection strategy is to pose as a desirable program or utility. The user then grants this unrestricted access to their machine, and then the virus strikes. This technique is similar to the "Trojan horse" strategy reputedly used by the Greeks to finally enter the city of Troy.

23.23 Progress and synergy

These days, we can *easily* see progressive evolution taking place in real time. Evolution is *snowballing*, with each development building on the next with ever-increasing in speed. Writing led to printing, which led to computers, which led to the internet - which now seems likely to produce machine intelligence. The internet is both a memetic breeding ground *and* the product of memes. This kind of accelerating process has been going on for a very long time - and it can be traced back through the agricultural revolution, the iron age, the stone age - and beyond.

23.24 Machine intelligence

The digital revolution has consumed most signal-transmission, storage and processing systems. However, human and animal brains are currently an exception. Digitising these has proved to be a non-trivial task - these are complex systems. We do not fully understand how they work, and can't yet reproduce many of their abilities. Most meme transmission is still mediated by the human brain. However, it now seems likely that machine intelligence will be constructed as a result of the rise of the internet. Plans to construct a "semantic web" make the internet more machine-readable. Machine intelligences will probably be more attractive homes for memes than human brains have been - and so intelligent machines will probably result in an explosion of cultural information and knowledge. It will *probably* be possible to adapt some of this information into formats suitable for human consumption.

23.25 Robots

Machine intelligence can be usefully thought of as being the result of memes actively constructing better brains for their descendants to thrive in. However brains need bodies to serve their needs. It seems likely that machine intelligence will rapidly develop nanotechnology and robotic technologies - in order to better allow it to sense and manipulate the material world - in order to facilitate the construction of more meme nests.

24 Classification - Category distinctions

There are a variety of ways of classifying entities in cultural evolution. However, cultural evolution is still something of a fledgeling science. As a result, some of the classification schemes associated with it are still under debate.

24.1 Meme anatomy

Douglas Hofstadter had a nice section about memes in his 1985 book *Metamagical Themas* - the book which arose from his *Scientific American* column of the same name, in the chapter entitled: *On Viral Sentences and Self-Replicating Structures*. There, Hofstadter develops an interesting meme classification scheme, involving *memes, schemes, bait* and *hooks*. This classification scheme has subsequently been modified and extended by other authors, including Agner Fog (1999) and myself. An anatomical diagram of a memeplex typically looks something like this:

- **Magnet** - Attract attention to the memeplex;
- **Bait** - Incentive to adopt the memeplex;
- **Reassurance** - Attempts to evade the host's immune sysetm;
- **Indoctrination** - Ensuring the host acquires the entire memeplex;
- **Reward** - To encourage good performance;
- **Threat** - Of punishment, to discourage failure and misbehaviour;
- **Trigger** - Environmental cue to provoke action;
- **Execution** - Of actions, usually oriented towards reproduction;
- **Rehearsal** - To ensure the memeplex is not forgotten;
- **Vaccime** - Innoculation to protect against rival memeplexes.

Some examples of these:

- **Magnet** - Tall spire or impressive cathedral;
- **Bait** - Promise of god's love;
- **Reassurance** - Trust me;

- **Indoctrination** - Bible lessons;
- **Reward** - Believe and go to heaven;
- **Threat** - If you do not believe then you will burn in hell;
- **Trigger** - The sight of a sinner;
- **Execution** - Give moral guidance and invite to prayer meeting;
- **Rehearsal** - Church on Sunday and hymm practice;
- **Vaccime** - Thou shalt have no gods before me!

Not *all* memeplexes will necessarily contain *all* of these elements. No two authors seem to have the same anatomical breakdown. To give an example of the difficulties:

- **Vaccime** - Defence against rivals and attacks on rival memeplexes;
- **Reassurance** - Immune suppression and immune evasion;

These categories could easily be sub-divided. On the other hand, a small number of categories helps people to remember them. Many authors bundle *trigger* and *execution* together into the term *hook*.

24.2 Cybernetics perspective

Another, largely orthogonal way of breaking down memeplexes involves a perspective from cybernetics:

- **Acquisiton** - Take in fuel and raw materials;
- **Sensory** - Perceive environment;
- **Processing** - Process perceptions;
- **Motor** - Take actions;
- **Excretion** - Waste products and heat.

This classification scheme applies to all active agents, be they organic organisms, computer systems, robots or cultural entities.

24.3 Memetic hitchhiking

The perspective of memetic hitchhiking suggests an alternative classification scheme for memeplexes that contain hitchhikers:

- **Delivery mechanism** - Metabolism: does the work of getting copied;
- **Payload** - Memes that are to be delivered;
- **Junk memes** - Memes that are along for the ride.

24.4 Domestication

In Daniel Dennett's (1999) work "The Evolution of Culture" he proposed that:

- **Natural selection** - acts on **wild memes**;

- **Unconscious selection** - acts on **partly-domesticated memes;**
- **Methodical selection** - acts on **domesticated memes;**
- **Memetic engineering** - acts on **engineered memes.**

This classification scheme seems to be *fairly* neat and uncontroversial.

24.5 Environmental inheritance

Environmental inheritance refers to inheritance via the environment. It includes cultural evolution - but also other types of heritable environmental influences.

If I give my son a big suitcase full of gold bars when I die, few would claim this is a case of cultural inheritance. Yet it is *pretty clearly* a form of inheritance.

Environmental inheritance.

Categories

Environmental inheritance is the main alternative to organic inheritance:

- **Organic inheritance** - inheritance via cells;
- **Environmental inheritance** - inheritance via the environment;

Medawar called these *endosomatic inheritance* and *exosomatic inheritance* respectively - and those terms are *also* pretty good.

Environmental inheritance could in turn be subdivided:

- **Cultural inheritance** - information passed on via culture;
- **Non-cultural environmental inheritance** - other types of environmental inheritance;

Diagram

Representing these forms of inheritance on a diagram, results in something like this:

Types of inheritance.

Here you will see that cultural inheritance is represented as a subset of environmental inheritance. This makes sense because all culture must currently necessarily be represented "in the environment" at some point during its transmission down the generations.

Environmental modification

Environment modification occurs when organisms impact their environment in some way.

For example, naked mole rats live in underground burrows which they themselves created. Another example which will be familiar to many is dental plaque. The bacteria that cause tooth decay use this to create their own environment at the edge of the gum line. Earthworms help to create

Environmental modification: Spider.

the topsoil in which they live. Spiders create their own immediate environment out of silk.

Environment modification sometimes results in *environmental inheritance*. This happens when the environment modifications are persistent and are passed down from one generation to the next. Examples of this include:

- **Rabbits** inherit their **burrows**;
- **Earthworms** inherit **topsoil**;
- **Birds** inherit their **nests**;
- **Beavers** inherit their **dams**;
- **Humans** inherit their **houses**.

Among humans, cultural inheritance has resulted in *environment modification* taking place on a grand scale. Without memes humans live in caves and stone huts. With memes they live in cities, skyscrapers. Cities illustrate *environmental modification* taken to an extreme.

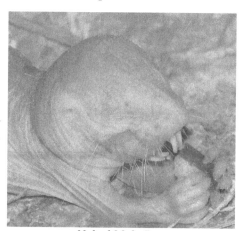

Naked Mole Rat.

The alterations to the environment which *environment modification* creates can go on to affect the organisms living in that environment. For example, after naked mole rats started living in underground burrows, the subterranean environment changed them - selecting against their fur and eyes. Humans have been affected by the agricultural niche they created for themselves, thousands of years ago, with signs that a variety of associated genes have spread through the population.

An environment which has been modified by one species may go on to affect other species. So, for example, human cities affect humans, but they also affect pigeons and seagulls.

Environment modification is often referred to by the name "niche construction". However, as pointed out by Dawkins (2004) when defined to refer to any type of environmental modification, "niche construction" seems to be problematical terminology - since the word "construction" *strongly* implies *deliberate* modification. It is counter-intuitive to describe an animal defecating as engaging in a form of "construction". *Niche construction* has been studied by researchers who are also interested in cultural evolution - for example, see Laland, Odling-Smee, and Feldman (2000a).

Significance

Non-cultural environmental inheritance is pretty important. It *typically* includes your place on the planet, the ecosystem you are born into, and a bunch of non-cultural resources that are the result of e*nvironment modification* by your ancestors.

Implications for Dual Inheritance Theory

The existence of non-cultural environmental inheritance seems as though it is a bit of a problem for *Dual Inheritance Theory*. This kind of inheritance seems important enough to make *Dual Inheritance Theory* seem as though it has a rather unfortunate name. There is more to inheritance than *just* DNA and culture.

24.6 Epidemics

The simplest way to classify the contagiousness of memes is to say whether they are above or below the *epidemic threshold*. A meme may be above the threshold, and not yet part of an epidemic. Memes below the *epidemic threshold* can sometimes be kept at a non-negligible frequency by continual seeding by meme-shedding agents.

24.7 Transmission media

Memes have to get from one brain to the next. Some memes enter the brain through the eyes. Some enter the brain through the ears. Others are passed on via the sense of touch - for example memes expressed in braille.

Most linguistic memes could be passed on in all three ways - which means this classification scheme is not so useful for them.

24.8 Storage media

Some memes spend most of their lives inside human brains. Others are stored on CDs, DVDs, books, in computer hard drives, or memory. Some memes have life cycles where they spend time in multiple different media.

24.9 Meme species

In organic evolution, there are widely recognised to be many different species. In cultural evolution, the situation is not so clear. Skinner (1971) describes entire cultures as being the cultural equivalent of a species - as follows:

> *A culture corresponds to a species. We describe it by listing many of its practices, as we describe a species by listing many of its anatomical features. Two or more cultures may share a practice, as two or more species may share an anatomical feature. The practices of a culture, like the characteristics of a species, are carried by its members, who transmit them to other members.*

In defence of this idea, it is difficult to argue that different elements of a single culture are *completely* reproductively isolated. Ideas from widely separated fields can sometimes combine. On the other hand, species may not be completely reproductively isolated either - since they are *probably* infected with viruses that attack multiple species, and viruses can sometimes drag bits of host DNA along with them.

The best way to deal with this issue is probably to define a *species* as consisting of a group of genomes which recombine relatively frequently with other group members - but which recombine relatively infrequently with outsiders. Applying this definition in the cultural realm, FORTRAN programs would then make an example of a *relatively isolated* cultural species. Origami patterns would also be classified as being a *relatively isolated* cultural species.

24.10 The memotype/phemotype split

This is inherited from the organic realm's genotype/phenotype split. The memotype consists of heritable information, while the phemotype consists of everything whose form is influenced by the memotype.

25 Mental selection - The Darwinian mind

Most of this book is concerned with population memetics, which can get by passably by treating the mind as a black box and not modelling its contents in much depth. However, *ultimately* memetic models should go beyond this, and model the operation of the mind. Today, we have *some* details about how the mind works, but we are nowhere near having a complete model. What we *can* see suggests that a Darwinian approach may help to explain the operation of the mind as well.

25.1 Darwin on the brain

The mind has traditionally been dealt with by psychology and neuroscience. Mirroring the situation with cultural evolution, these disciplines have been slow to embrace Darwinism.

There *is* a field of "evolutionary psychology" - but that mostly looks at human universals and mostly ignores human culture. Ignoring memetics makes it pretty hopeless as an explanation of the behaviour of modern humans. Evolutionary psychology needs to take a step forward - by embracing memes.

There is *also* a field of "evolutionary neuroscience" - but *that* looks at how the brain evolved over millions of years. That field *also* needs to take a step forwards, by looking into evolutionary models of the operation of the brain: copying and natural selection *within* the brain itself.

25.2 Optimisation process

To the extent that the brain behaves in a goal-directed manner, it seems reasonable to model the brain as an optimisation process - and *most optimisation process* have a structure which resemble, to some extent, the algorithm of *universal Darwinism.*

In particular, optimisation processes typically consist of a trial-and-error approach. Most of them keep persistent records about what they have previously tried, and copies are made of that information. The obvious exception to this is a random search - but that is not a great algorithm for most practical problems. Trials are varied, in order to gather information and to avoid repeatedly searching in the same place. Most algorithms that are *reasonably* fast run in parallel - and so maintain populations of entities which are evaluated independently. Effective optimisation strategies thus tend to have an evolutionary character.

25.3 Within-brain copying

Copying processes are ubiquitous inside brains. For example, whenever a spike train travels down an axon, and then the axon branches, *copies* of the original message about the neuron firing are sent to different destinations. There are also likely to be a variety of high-level copying processes. In particular whenever a memory is recalled, it generates new memories of recalling the original memory, which add redundancy to the original memory. Repeatedly performing learned actions makes back-up traces of the motor activation patterns used, and their results. Mental rehearsal probably acts to make copies in a similar way. Copying processes in brains have been explored recently by Chrisantha Fernando and Eörs Szathmáry - details are in our references.

25.4 Within-brain selection

The brain has limited resources, and does a *lot* of copying - and so inevitably, selection processes play an important role inside brains. Within-brain selection takes place at several different levels. The low-level processes include:

· **Synapse selection** - Synapses compete for resources with each other;
· **Spike train selection** - Spike trains are copied and are mortal;
· **Neurite selection** - Neurites compete for neuron resources;
· **Neurite-tip selection** – Growing neurite tips compete with each other;

The brain also contains a range of high-level operations at varying levels of abstraction - and it implements a virtual world where more selection processes take place. High level selection processes include:

· **Idea selection** - Memes compete with each other inside minds with other memes, protomemes and other ideas which are not memes at all.
· **Action selection** - Minds constantly have to choose between their possible actions.
· **Perception selection** - Perceptions compete for consciousness, and for memory space.
· **Skill selection** - Minds constantly learn new things, and have a limited repertoire of habits and skills, and so abilities are constantly being lost.
· **Goal selection** - Minds have long-term goals, which they pursue using instrumental goals, which compete with each other for attention.
· **Memory selection** - new memories are constantly being laid down, and the mind has a limited capacity, so forgetting is common.

- **Model element selection** - Minds maintain a world model, which they try to keep parsimonious. The unconscious mind is constantly attempting to rework elements of this model to try and find a more plausible explanation that is consistent with its observations so far. Model elements are generated, tested, and then either discarded or incorporated into the model.

These lists are not intended to be comprehensive - there may well be many other types of within-brain selection.

25.5 Within-brain variation

Most copying processes are imperfect, so there is likely to be plenty of within-brain variation.

Some Darwin enthusiasts Campbell (1974a) and Cziko (1995) have proposed that within-brain variation is "blind" - in a manner analogous to what happens in traditional evolution by random mutations. However, there doesn't seem to be much of a case to be made for this thesis, as was explained in an earlier chapter that dealt with Campbell's B.S.V.R. thesis.

As with conventional memetics variation within brains is - to some extent - directed. No doubt there will be controversy about the extent to which directed variation plays a role in within-brain selective processes that mirrors the controversy about the extent to which directed variation plays a role in memetics. However, as in the cultural realm, it is important to note that directed variation is quite compatible with an essentially-Darwinian evolutionary framework.

25.6 Brain evolution

Above we have illustrated how brains engage in copying with variation and differential reproductive success. So, there's a sense in which brains exhibit a form of Darwinian evolution. An early paper by Changeux from 1973 described synapse selection. That the brain evolves along Darwinian lines was understood by Skinner, who used Darwinian terminology to describe learning - talking about the "selection" and "extinction" of learned behaviours. The "Selection by Consequences" paper of Skinner (1981) represents an early expression of what is now often called *Universal Darwinism*. Later, Gerald Edelman (1989) proposed "Neural Darwinism". His book on the topic was largely about between-neuron selection during development - but Edelman also speculated about the role of selection in neurite branching. William Calvin (1987) has also promoted selectionist ideas of brain functioning in several books (*The Cerebral Code* and *How Brains Think*). Dennett refers to within-brain selection models as being *competitive neural architectures. Action selection* is a well-recognised idea in the field of *neuroeconomics*.

Evolutionary theory represents a convenient "base theory" for this kind of phenomenon. It explains *some* aspects of the resulting dynamics, while leaving a convenient "holes" - in the form of mutational forces and selection pressures - which require their own independent modelling. This approach is broadly similar to the one used by Darwinian models of culture.

25.7 Adaptive evolution

Copying variation and selection are all very well - but there is no guarantee that it will result in cumulative adaptive evolution - and if it doesn't the resulting evolutionary process is often rather trivial. The selection processes listed above vary in the extend to which they participate in processes that resemble cumulative adaptive evolution in the organic world. We do see cumulative adaptive evolution within the brain in some cases. In particular the brain's *model element evolution* shows a *fairly* close match with traditional cumulative adaptive evolution. Neurite-tip evolution exhibits adaptation - though since neurites have limited lengths, any accumulation is rather limited. *Memory evolution* actively tries to minimise copying errors - and so changes are highly-constrained. *Action evolution* is, if anything, even less familiar-looking.

25.8 Neurite-tip selection

In case is is not entirely clear what the term "neurite-tip selection" refers to, this section explains. "Neurites" refers to axons and dendrites - the branching tree-like extensions of neurons that are used to transmit signals. Neurite-tip selection is similar to the selection process that takes place between branches of trees, or between plant roots. A tree growing under a bridge must find its way to the light, *even* if that means distortion of its structure. The tree takes energy from areas with no light, and transfers it to areas where the sunlight reaches. Plant roots in rocky ground show a similar process. The branching tips compete with each other for the plant's resources - and the result is an adaptive fit to the environment.

The type of inheritance involved here is a form of *environmental inheritance*: *positional inheritance*. The branching neuron tips inherit their *positions* from their precursors, and it is *primarily* this which evolves.

25.9 Memes and idea selection

Of the types of within-brain selection listed above, *idea selection* is the one which is closest to memetics. By using *idea selection*, it may well be possible to build reasonable models of the interactions of memes with minds *without* building a complete model of the mind. Attempts at developing memetic theories to cover events inside minds have mostly tended to focus on this area. A lot of the efforts so far have been made by marketers. Those working in viral marketing know a lot about what people like to share. In a range of different contexts material relating to news, gossip, sex, relationships, babies, celebrities and cuteness are all highly shareable. Marketers exploit this knowledge to help distribute their products, often by using memetic hitchhiking.

25.10 Machine intelligence

Darwinian models of the mind should help to throw some light on the project of building machine intelligence. Many of those working in the area use evolution-inspired approaches - but do so by doing things like using genetic algorithms to control neural network architectures. Viewing the brain's attempts to model the world as being based on a kind of adaptation, and recognising that part of the process is has a Darwinian nature should *hopefully* help to clarify what is required in order to produce intelligent machines.

26 Memetic algorithms - Optimising with memes

One of the standard tools in the computer science optimisation toolkit is genetic algorithms. These emulate organic evolution by using mutation and selection to identify the solutions of optimisation problems.

Memetic algorithms are similar - but typically additionally emulate cultural evolution. As Moscato (1989) said:

> *While genetic algorithms have been inspired in trying to emulate biological evolution. Memetic algorithms would try to mimic cultural evolution.*

Memetic algorithms were inspired by the observation that memes appear to have increased the rate of evolution of human civilization. Memetic algorithms will probably prove to be the most important application of memetics in the long term.

26.1 Cooperation

Genetic algorithms are *normally* considered to be a type of competitive process - but one of the aims of memetic algorithms is to harness the power of cooperation. Letting the creatures to learn from each other encourages them to form social groups, and to work together.

26.2 Collective intelligence

Groups of individuals being involved can potentially result in the effects associated with collective intelligence. Group-related dynamics are possible in more traditional genetic algorithms too - but social learning forces the creatures together, encouraging cooperation, and *hopefully* resulting in group dynamics that facilitate solving collective action problems.

26.3 Agents with limited intelligence

One of the things that allows cultural evolution to occur rapidly is that it allows the optimisation power in the human brain to be employed. Memetic algorithms may have to wait until we have machine intelligence before it can fully make use of the same effect - but it appears that there are nonetheless benefits to be obtained from the approach in the mean time.

26.4 Direct thought transfer

Evolution took billions of years to produce creatures sophisticated enough to produce an open-ended type of cultural evolution based on imitation. This is because imitation is technically quite difficult to perform. Observing the actions of another and then recreating them is not usually a trivial task.

Fortunately, memetic algorithms can bypass most of this. Rather than passing on cultural information by clumsy processes based on behavioural imitation, memetic algorithms can work with creatures which have been designed for direct thought transfer. This can take a variety of forms. One possibility is the ability to pass on experiences. We can imagine the creatures have a recording device, and a device to replay the recordings to other creatures. This would be broadly similar to how humans can help each other to learn by sharing audio-visual experiences with video cameras. Other possibilities include knowledge and skill transfer. If the creatures can be persuaded to represent their knowledge and skills in a portable format, this information could be transmitted directly from one creature to the next.

26.5 Tower of optimisation

Skinner's 1981 publication, *Selection by consequences* argued for a 3-stage model of selection processes:

- **Level 1** is based on evolution by **random mutations**;
- **Level 2** was based on **learning**;

- **Level 3** was based on **cultural evolution**.

One way of classifying evolutionary algorithms is on an extended version of Skinner's selection scale. The simplest algorithms evolve via random mutations and selection. Then Skinnerian learning is layered on top of that. Then memetic evolution is added on top of that - gene-meme co-evolution. Finally the creatures master genetic engineering - and become all-engineered. Memetic algorithms are currently at the third stage. Human civilisation is at that stage too.

In Daniel Dennett's 1995 book "Darwin's Dangerous Idea" he describes a concept he calls the *Tower of Generate-and-Test* which extends Skinner's selection scale. It is a kind of model of the evolution of intelligent agents. Your author recently reworked these ideas into a *tower of optimisation*, as follows:

- **Stateless search** - optimisation with no memory - e.g.: random search.
- **Single-agent search** - uses one agent - e.g.: Newton-Raphson.
- **Multi-agent search** - uses multiple agents - e.g.: simulated-annealing.
- **Genetic search** - uses multiple agents that can reproduce - e.g.: a simple asexual genetic algorithm.
- **Sexual recombination** - uses multiple agents that can reproduce and recombine - e.g.: a genetic algorithm.
- **Learning** - uses agents that can learn from their environment.
- **Virtualisation** - agents can perform evaluations under simulation.
- **Memetics** - uses agents that have developed culture.
- **Artefact symbiosis** - the memes start to build tools, minds and bodies for themselves.
- **All-engineered** - uses all-engineered agents - e.g.: machine intelligence and robots.

Looking at this scale, you will see that synthetic agents are currently stuck at around the "virtualisation" stage. They can build *limited* models of their environments, but have only a very weak mastery of inductive inference - and so can't really build *proper* models of their environments.

The next stage after the "virtualisation" stage is labelled the "memetics" stage. Memetic algorithms represent an attempt to skip ahead to that stage.

26.6 Coevolution

Memetic algorithms may include a genetic component - and thus may exhibit meme-gene coevolution. In cases where both memes and genes are involved, there needs to be a tradeoff made between the resources expended on each type of evolution, and managing this trade-off is a non-trivial problem.

26.7 Machine intelligence

Memetic algorithms seem likely to contribute to progress towards machine intelligence. Cultural evolution in humans represents the process machines will need to master if they are to make very much progress. Machines are masters of mind-to-mind thought transfer, which makes it easy for them to engage in social learning. If you have a partly-intelligent machine, one obvious thing you can do to boost its power is to network it together with other similar machines, and let them cooperate with each other. So, it seems likely that memetic algorithms will play a key role in the development of machine intelligence.

27 History - Of the study of cultural evolution

This chapter offers a brief history of cultural evolution - for the period leading up to 1976.

27.1 William Jones

The basic idea of cultural evolution is older than Darwin. Around the end of the 18th century, linguists discovered the similarities between the world's different languages. Sir William Jones did pioneering work in the field of language evolution studies, specifically looking for the origin and paths of descent of languages.

In 1786, Sir William Jones compared the Sanskrit, Latin and Greek languages. His conclusion was that all three were descended from a common ancestor. This primitive phylogeny of the Indo-European languages was one of the first pieces of evidence for any kind of evolutionary process.

27.2 Lewis Henry Morgan

Lewis Morgan was an American anthropologist and social theorist who became known partly for his views on social

Lewis Henry Morgan.

evolution. He presented three major stages societies moved through: savagery, barbarism, and civilization. He defined the stages by technological inventions, such as use of fire in the "savage" era; domestication of animals in the "barbarian" era; and development of writing in the "civilization" era.

27.3 August Schleicher

The German linguist August Schleicher attempted to recreate the common ancestor of all known languages. In 1850, he represented languages as natural organisms that could most conveniently be described using terms drawn from biology - e.g., genus, species, and variety - and suggested they could be represented on a family tree. His first tree-diagrams of languages were published in 1853, six years before Darwin published his theory. These are what we now would now call *glossogenetic trees*. In 1863 Schleicher's "Darwinism tested by the science of language" was published. Schleicher is widely recognized as the first linguist to portray language development using family trees.

27.4 Charles Darwin

The relationship between organic and cultural evolution was also observed by Darwin himself. In chapter 13 of Darwin's (1859) he uses an analogy with language to explain the process of organic differential reproductive success:

It may be worth while to illustrate this view of classification, by taking the case of languages. If we possessed a perfect pedigree of mankind, a genealogical arrangement of the races of man would afford the best classification of the various languages now spoken throughout the world; and if all extinct languages, and all

Charles Darwin.

intermediate and slowly changing dialects, had to be included, such an arrangement would, I think, be the only possible one. Yet it might be that some very ancient language had altered little, and had given rise to few new languages, whilst others (owing to the spreading and subsequent isolation and states of civilisation of the several races, descended from a common race) had altered much, and had given rise to many new languages and dialects

Later, in the Descent of Man (1871, p. 86), Darwin illustrated his understanding of cultural evolution, writing:

The formation of different languages and of distinct species, and the proofs that both have been developed through a gradual process, are curiously the same. ... We find in distinct languages striking homologies due to community of descent, and analogies due to a similar process of formation. ... The survival or preservation of certain favoured words in the struggle for existence is natural selection.

Darwin clearly understood the basic principles of cultural evolution - but the social sciences failed to take up his ideas at the time - and are stubbornly resisting them to this day.

27.5 William James

James had at least *some* understanding of cultural evolution. Here he is, lecturing in 1880:

A remarkable parallel, which I think has never been noticed, obtains between the facts of social evolution on the one hand, and of zoölogical evolution as expounded by Mr. Darwin on the other.

27.6 Herbert Spencer

Spencer first published on evolution a couple of years before Darwin, but his perspective on it was revised when Darwin's ideas were published. Spencer tried to apply the theory of biological evolution to society.

Spencer believed in progressive evolution - and proposed that society was the product of change from lower to higher forms, just as in the theory of biological evolution, the lowest forms of life eventually evolve into higher

Herbert Spencer.

forms. Savage societies were at the bottom, and the Victorian English civilisation - which Spencer participated in - was at the top.

The idea became known as "sociocultural evolutionism". Progressivism became one of the basic ideas associated with it - but was one of the factors that dragged it into disrepute - when the idea that evolutionary processes were not intrinsically progressive became more popular.

27.7 Thorstein B. Veblen

Veblen was an economist, who became aware that Darwin's theory applied to the social sciences. Here is Veblen (1899):

The life of man in society, just like the life of other species, is a struggle for existence, and therefore it is a process of selective adaptation. The evolution of social structure has been a process of natural selection of institutions.

For details about Veblen's views on socio-economic evolution, Hodgson (2008) goes into the details.

27.8 Edward Burnett Tylor

Edward Burnett Tylor is considered by many a founding figure of the science of social anthropology, and his scholarly works are seen as important and lasting contributions to the discipline of anthropology. He defined the context of scientific study of anthropology, based on the evolutionary theories of Charles Lyell. Tylor's concept of "survivals" explains the characteristics of a culture that are reflections of earlier stages of human culture.

Edward Burnett Tylor.

According to Tylor, survivals are "processes, customs, opinions, and so forth, which have been carried by force of habit into a new state of society different from that in which they had their original home and they remain as proofs and examples of an older condition of culture out of which a newer has been evolved,". Studying survivals assists ethnographers in reconstructing earlier cultural characteristics and possibly reconstructing the evolutionary history of a culture. Here is Tylor writing in 1871:

> *History within its proper field, and ethnography over a wider range, combine to show that the institutions which can best hold their own in the world gradually supersede the less fit ones, and that this incessant conflict determines the general resultant course of culture.*

Tylor represents the strain of anthropology known as "cultural evolutionism". Though largely discredited within anthropology, "cultural evolutionism" is enjoying a modern renaissance in the hands of biologically-inclined theorists.

27.9 Leslie Stephen

Leslie Stephen distinguished between cultural and organic evolution. In his book on the evolution of ethics, Stephen 1882 wrote:

> *Improved artillery, like improved teeth, will enable the group to which it belongs to extirpate or subdue its competitors. But in another respect there is an obvious difference. For the improved teeth belong only to the individuals in whom they appear and to*

Leslie Stephen.

the descendants to whom they are transmitted by inheritance; but the improved artillery may be adopted by a group of individuals who form a continuous society with the original inventor.

...and...

A theory spreads from one brain to another in so far as one man is able to convince another, which is a direct process, whatever its ultimate nature, and has its own laws underlying the general condition which determines the ultimate survival of different systems of opinion.

27.10 Gabriel Tarde

Gabriel Tarde was a lawyer and judge. He observed how some crimes appeared to spread in waves - almost as if they were fashions. He became interested in how this epidemiological aspect of crime might be just one aspect of a more general social phenomenon. He went on to publish several works on the topic - including: "Darwinisme naturel et Darwinisme social" (Tarde 1884) which developed the idea further. In his 1903 book entitled "The Laws of Imitation", Tarde wrote:

Gabriel Tarde.

Self-propagation and not self-organisation is the prime demand of the social as well as of the vital thing.

...and...

What is society? I have answered: Society is imitation".

For more about Tarde's role, see Paul Marsden's article from 2000: "Forefathers of Memetics: Gabriel Tarde and the Laws of Imitation".

27.11 James George Frazer

James Frazer was a Scottish social anthropologist influential in the early stages of the modern studies of mythology and comparative religion. He was a major anthropological theorist at the turn of the century. His work *The Golden Bough: A Study in Magic and Religion*, was first published in two volumes in 1890. It looked mainly at early myths, legends, religions and cults. It treated religion it dispassionately - as a cultural

James George Frazer.

phenomenon - and attempted to trace its roots.

27.12 Pierre Auger

Hofstadter wrote, in 1983:

> *Maurice Gueron wrote me from Paris to tell me that he believed the first clear exposition of the idea of self-reproducing ideas that inhabit the brains of organisms was put forward in 1952 by Pierre Auger, a physicist at the Sorbonne, in his book L' homme microscopique. Gueron sent me a photocopy of the relevant portions, and I could indeed see how prophetic the book was.*

27.13 Pierre White

White was an anthropologist who opposed the anti-evolutionism of the dominant figure of Boas. He championed nineteenth century evolutionists: Spencer, Darwin, and Morgan. However, for White, culture was a superorganic entity that could only be explained in terms of itself. White published a book on the topic: "The Evolution of Culture: The Development of Civilization to the Fall of Rome" in 1959.

27.14 B. F. Skinner

B. F. Skinner wrote a book titled "Science and Human Behavior" in 1953. In the book, Skinner draws various analogies between operant conditioning and organic evolution. For example, page 430 has:

> *We have seen that in certain respects operant reinforcement resembles the natural selection of evolutionary theory. Just as genetic characteristics which arise as mutations are selected or discarded by their consequences, so novel forms of behavior are selected or discarded through reinforcement.*

Page 434 has:

B. F. Skinner.

The evolution of cultures appears to follow the pattern of the evolution of species. The many different forms of culture which arise correspond to the "mutations" of genetic theory. Some forms prove to be effective under prevailing circumstances and others not, and the perpetuation of the culture is determined accordingly.

Skinner subsequently went on to write a book titled "Beyond Freedom and Dignity" in 1971 that contained a chapter about cultural evolution - and a chapter about what is now commonly called memetic engineering. Skinner talked *explicitly* about cultural evolution. He modelled a culture as a single large species, arguing that the flow of heritable information was not seriously restricted within cultures.

> *The fact that a culture may survive or perish suggests a kind of evolution, and a parallel with the evolution of species has, of course, often been pointed out. It needs to be stated carefully. A culture corresponds to a species. We describe it by listing many of its practices, as we describe a species by listing many of its anatomical features. Two or more cultures may share a practice, as two or more species may share an anatomical feature. The practices of a culture, like the characteristics of a species, are carried by its members, who transmit them to other members. In general, the greater the number of individuals who carry a species or a culture, the greater its chance of survival.*

Skinner understood that cultures evolved, exhibited adaptations, competed, and co-evolved with the organic world. He described the cultural inheritance of acquired traits, and how culture could be deleterious. In his chapter on cultural engineering, he advocated the practice, writing:

> *The intentional design of culture and the control of human behaviour it implies, are essential if the human species is to continue to develop.*

In 1981, Skinner published *Selection by consequences* - in which he argued for a 3-stage model of selection processes. Level 1 started with the origin of life - and was based on evolution by random mutations; Level 2 was based on learning; Level 3 was based on cultural evolution. Skinner wrote:

> *As a causal mode, selection by consequences was discovered very late in the history of science - indeed, less than a century and a half ago - and it is still not fully recognised or understood, especially at levels ii and iii. The facts for which it is responsible have been forced into the causal pattern of classical mechanics, and many of the explanatory schemes elaborated in the process must now be discarded.*

Alas, this is *still* true some 30 years later. The broad power and applicability of selection processes in nature is *still* not particularly widely recognised, at the time of writing.

Indeed, we can see now that Skinner *did not go far enough* in extending the role of selection. For one thing, he missed the applicability of selection processes to pre-biological systems. However, that is a topic which is better discussed elsewhere.

27.15 Peter Medawar

Peter Medawar wrote "The Future of Man" in 1959. The topic was cultural evolution. To quote:

endosomatic or internal heredity for the ordinary or genetical heredity we have in common with animals; and exosomatic or external heredity for the non-genetic heredity that is peculiarly our own

In "Technology and Evolution" from 1973, Medawar again looked to the future:

Peter Medawar.

The coming of technology and the new style of human evolution it made possible was an epoch in biological history as important as the evolution of man himself. We are now on the verge of a third episode, as important as either of these: that in which the whole human ambience - the human house - is of our own making and becomes as we intend it should be: a product of human thought - of deep and anxious thought, let us hope, and of forethought rather than afterthought.

27.16 André Siegfried

André Siegfried was a French writer and political scientist. He observed the parallel between cultural and organic evolution, and described cultural epidemics and contagions. In his 1960 book on the topic entitled "Germs and Ideas: Routes of Epidemics and Ideologies", he wrote:

There is a striking parallel between the spreading of germs and the spreading of ideas or propaganda. On the one hand we are dealing with a virus which can be transported and transmitted under certain conditions which favor or limit its transportation or transmission: on the other hand with ideas, religions, and doctrines, which can be described as germs, benevolent or malevolent, according to the point of view one takes up. These germs can either remain at their source and be sterile, or emerge in the spreading of infection.

He also observed the parallel between the organic and memetic immune systems.

27.17 Donald Campbell

Donald Campbell represents our next historical landmark - in the 1960s. Campbell was an American social scientist. He coined the term "evolutionary epistemology" and developed a selectionist theory of human creativity. He also introduced the term *Blind Variation and Selective Retention* (B.S.V.R.) - to refer to what he believed was the fundamental principle of evolution. Campbell was a pioneer in cultural evolution - and was one of the first to clearly articulate the idea in modern times.

Donald Campbell.

27.18 Roger Sperry

In *Mind, Brain and Humanist Values* (1966), Sperry argued that ideas are in charge. He wrote:

> *In the brain model proposed here, the causal potency of an idea, or an ideal, becomes just as real as that of a molecule, a cell, or a nerve impulse. Ideas cause ideas and help evolve new ideas. They interact with each other and with other mental forces in the same brain, in neighboring brains, and thanks to global communication, in far distant, foreign brains. And they also interact with the external surroundings to produce in toto a burstwise advance in evolution that is far beyond anything to hit the evolutionary scene yet, including the emergence of the living cell.*

Interestingly, Sperry appears to grasp and comment on the long-term evolutionary significance of the rise of ideas to power.

27.19 Jacques Monod

Jacques Monod endorsed cultural evolution in his 1970 book "Chance and Necessity". This quotation gives the flavour:

> *For a biologist it is tempting to draw a parallel between the evolution of ideas and that of the biosphere. For while the abstract kingdom stands at a yet greater distance above the biosphere than the latter does above the nonliving universe, ideas have retained some of the properties of organisms. Like them, they tend to perpetuate their structure and to breed; they*

Jacques Monod.

too can fuse, recombine, segregate their content; indeed they too can evolve, and in this evolution selection must surely play an important role.

Monod didn't present much of a theory of cultural evolution in the book - but he *did* seem to grasp the basics of the idea.

27.20 Karl Popper

Karl Popper describes science in terms of evolution, as a process of conjecture and refutation - with conjectures resulting in variation and refutation resulting in selection. His major work on evolutionary epistemology and science is the 1972 book: *Objective Knowledge: An Evolutionary Approach.*

27.21 Richard Dawkins

Richard Dawkins devoted a chapter of The Selfish Gene (1976) to cultural evolution. He coined the term "meme". He subsequently claimed that his purpose was to show that evolution was a general phenomenon - not one confined to DNA - and culture was a convenient example.

Richard Dawkins.

Dawkins (1976) writes:

I think that a new kind of replicator has recently emerged on this very planet. It is staring us in the face. It is still in its infancy, still drifting clumsily about in its primeval soup, but already it is achieving evolutionary change at a rate that leaves the old gene panting far behind. The new soup is the soup of human culture.

This neatly captures the modern understanding of cultural evolution, and gives some hint of its significance. Dawkins also refers to the possibility of the new form of heritable information taking over:

For more than three thousand million years, DNA has been the only replicator worth talking about in the world. But it does not necessarily hold these monopoly rights for all time. Whenever conditions arise in which a new kind of replicator can make copies of itself, the new replicators will tend to take over, and start a new kind of evolution of their own. Once this new evolution begins, it will in no necessary sense be subservient to the old.

...and here, Dawkins discusses the idea of selfish memes:

> *Biologists are accustomed to looking for advantages at the gene level (or the individual, the group, or the species level according to taste). What we do not ordinarily consider is that a cultural trait may have evolved in the way that it has, simply because it is advantageous to itself.*

27.22 More details

For more on the early history of cultural evolution, see Agner Fog (1999) chapter 2: "The history of cultural selection theory", Gatherer (1997) "Macromemetics", and Moritz (1990) "Memetic Science".

The history of the idea from 1976 to the present is better known and won't be summarised in this chapter. Blackmore (1999) offers a summary up to her publication date in Ch. 3 of "*The Meme Machine*".

28 Generalised Darwinism - Basic principles

An understanding that culture evolves along Darwinian lines has led many of those involved to wonder what *other* systems exhibit Darwinian dynamics.

The idea that some parts of evolutionary theory can usefully be generalised dates back at least to Lewontin (1970). It is often referred to using the term "Universal Darwinism". This term was first used by Richard Dawkins - to refer to his thesis that complex living systems would necessarily have to have evolved by Darwinian means. Richard Dawkins (1976) wrote:

> *I am an enthusiastic Darwinian, but, I think Darwinism is too big a theory to be confined to the narrow context of the gene.*

Blackmore (1999) had a chapter on "Universal Darwinism" - where she (sensibly) redefined the term to make it refer to the idea that Darwinism is *substrate-independent* - and so applies to systems of many kinds which feature copying processes. Cases where something akin to persistence via copying and natural selection seems applicable include: the immune system, brain functioning, developmental processes and human culture. Some have hypothesised that the universe itself is the product of a process involving reproduction and selection. The idea is also *sometimes* called *selection theory*, or *selectionism*. Here we will be using the term "Generalised Darwinism" to refer to expanded variations on evolutionary theory.

David Hull (2001, p.98) said he wished people would start from basic selection theory, rather than trying to make culture match up with biology:

> *In the past most authors who have treated cultural evolution in general and scientific change in particular as selection processes have taken gene-based natural selection as the exemplar and reasoned analogically to conceptual change. However, a more appropriate strategy is to present general analysis of selection processes equally applicable to all sorts of selection process.*

We should *not* forget what we learned in our evolutionary biology class, and attempt to analyse culture as a general selection process - since much of the material learned in the evolutionary biology class is *highly* relevant. However, we do *additionally* need an understanding of the theory of general selection processes - a theory of generalised Darwinism. In this chapter we will look at a couple of the foundation stones of such a theory. First we will look at a highly generalised version of Darwinism that drops the axiom of *persistence via copying*.

28.1 Natural selection beyond biology

Most people are familiar with the idea of natural selection. However, many people associate the idea with life - and with living systems. In fact natural selection represents the action of a more general principle that also applies systems which are *not* alive. Natural selection affects *everything* that comes into existence. Whether or not it comes into existence via a copying process is irrelevant. Some abiotic examples of natural selection:

- **Pebbles** tend to be made of hard materials;
- **Islands** tend to include hard rocky outcrops;
- **Planets** tend to have circular orbits.

The generality of this type of selection and its applicability to the abiotic world has long been recognised. For example, Dawkins (1976, p.12) says:

> *Darwin's 'Survival of the fittest' is really a special case of a more general law of survival of the stable. The universe is populated by stable things.*

The idea can be traced back to Lotka's 1922 article: "Natural Selection As A Physical Principle".

28.2 New fundamental concepts

Evolution is often visualised in terms of natural selection, sexual selection and genetic drift. However, when generalising Darwinism, there is another useful perspective, which can be obtained by considering evolution to be the result of a balance between creative forces and destructive forces - as follows:

- **Natural production** - refers to things coming into existence.
- **Natural elimination** - refers to things going out of existence.

These are *extremely* basic and fundamental principles. They neatly encapsulate the aspects of evolution that do *not* involve copying. They thus apply to both biotic and abiotic systems. To illustrate these principles with some abiotic examples:

28.3 Examples of natural elimination

- **Stars** that are observed are the ones that have not previously burned out or exploded;
- **Atoms** that are observed tend to be the stable ones - the ones with long half-lives;
- **Mountains** tend to be covered in hard rocks - soft rocks there tend to get washed away.

28.4 Examples of natural production

- **Stars** are produced by balls of gas condensing;
- **Atoms** are *mostly* produced by the processes of fission or fusion;
- **Mountains** are produced by tectonic plate motion and erosion.

28.5 Observed frequencies

The frequencies of the things we observe in the world arise as a result of a mixture of processes of *production* and *elimination*. Things that are produced *frequently* and are *difficult* to eliminate are *often* observed - whereas things that are produced *infrequently* and are *easy* to eliminate are *rarely* observed. For some examples consider the following table:

.	Produced frequently	Produced rarely
Eliminated frequently	Rain drops	Tall coin stacks
Eliminated rarely	Pebbles	Neutron stars

If production rates exceed elimination rates, the number of entities grows - while if elimination rates exceed production rates, the number of entities shrinks.

Note that the approach here can be applied to *anything* with a measurable frequency. The *entities* do not have to form a *natural kind*. Nor do they need to be to be *discrete* or *particulate*. For example you could consider the category of: "men over six feet tall". Production takes place during adolescence, and elimination takes place through death, limb loss, sex changes or degenerative osteoporosis. The results may be *more interesting* if dealing with natural kinds, but *any* system where you can measure the frequency with which something occurs can be analysed in this way.

28.6 Use in biology

Natural elimination and *natural production* are most familiar in the context of biological systems. There, *production* typically takes place at birth, and *elimination* takes place at death. If birth rates exceed death rates the population grows while if death rates exceed birth rates, the population shrinks. In living systems, natural elimination is selection by death. *Natural elimination* is a *bit* different from natural selection. For one thing, it makes no attempt to exclude genetic drift. The nearest familiar concept in biology to *natural production* is probably sexual selection. However, sexual selection is not a very general principle. It isn't *just* sexual organisms that are able to produce varying numbers of offspring. Instead the concept of *differential reproductive success* is *sometimes* used. Natural production is a more general concept than this though - since it can be applied to both biotic and abiotic systems.

Since biological processes involve copying, what is *naturally produced* is constantly being magnified, while things that are *naturally eliminated* play an ever-diminishing role. Thus, iterative application of *natural production* and *natural elimination* can result in *adaptive evolution*.

Framing things in terms of natural selection and sexual selection reflects the way in which these ideas were discovered historically - but sexual selection is not a very general concept. Thinking in terms of *natural elimination* and *natural production* results in a more general and broadly-applicable framework.

28.7 Fundamental revisions

When taught at all, natural selection is *currently* taught in biology classes. *Natural elimination* and *natural production* should *probably* be taught *first* in physics (or mathematics) classes. These are pretty basic explanatory principles, broadly comparable in scope to the idea of entropy, or to chaos theory.

This material may seem *very* basic - and it is. However, something like it *does* need teaching to children in science classes - with presentation along the lines given here, and with natural selection in biology being given as an example of the results of these principles being applied to a system which involves copying.

28.8 Philosophical issues with natural selection

Natural selection represents an *attempt* to divide forces in biology into the "random" and "non-random" categories of "drift" and "selection". By contrast, *natural elimination* and *natural production* make no mention of randomness. Talking about randomness in the definition of a basic scientific principle is a pretty dubious step. The problem is that randomness refers to unpredictability, and predictability depends on the knowledge of the agent making the predictions. It is thus rather subjective.

28.9 Evolution formalised

Next a bit of a change of topic. An awareness of cultural evolution has resulted in many people developing a broader conception of the evolutionary process. It led to some of those involved revisiting the definition of the term - and trying to tighten up and formalise it. To review some of the attempts made in this area:

28.10 Richard Lewontin

Lewontin (1970) looked into this issue. He based his argument on Darwin's presentation, saying:

> As seen by present-day evolutionists, Darwin's scheme embodies three principles:

> 1. Different individuals in a population have different morphologies, physiologies, and behaviors (phenotypic variation).

Richard Lewontin.

> 2. Different phenotypes have different rates of survival and reproduction in different environments (differential fitness).
> 3. There is a correlation between parents and offspring in the contribution of each to future generations (fitness is heritable).

> These three principles embody the principle of evolution by natural selection. While they hold, a population will undergo evolutionary change.

Lewontin's presentation is not *too* bad. He doesn't really give the minimum requirements for evolution, and makes no attempt to capture the idea of adaptive evolution, though.

28.11 Daniel Dennett

Dennett (1989) also tried his hand at the issue:

The outlines of the theory of evolution by natural selection are now clear: evolution occurs whenever the following conditions exist:

1. *variation: a continuing abundance of different elements*
2. *heredity or replication: the elements have the capacity to create copies or replicas of themselves*
3. *differential "fitness": the number of copies of an element that are created in a given time varies, depending on interactions*

Daniel Dennett.

between the features of that element (whatever it is that makes it different from other elements) and features of the environment in which it persists.

The third condition is unnecessary for evolution to occur, and looks to me as though it is a failed attempt to describe the circumstances under which adaptive evolution occurs. Dennett's approach fails to do that because it does not specify that constructive forces outweigh destructive ones - and the mere existence of selection doesn't mean that selection pressures outweigh the destructive force of random mutations.

28.12 Susan Blackmore

Blackmore (1999) agrees with Dennett:

Darwin's argument requires three main features: variation, selection and retention (or heredity). That is, first there must be variation so that not all creatures are identical. Second, there must be an environment in which not all the creatures can survive and some varieties do better than others. Third, there must be some process by which offspring inherit characteristics from their parents. If all these three are in place then any characteristics that are positively useful for survival in that environment must tend to increase. Put into Richard Dawkins's language, if there is a replicator that makes imperfect copies of itself

Susan Blackmore.

only some of which survive, then evolution simply must occur.

This presentation of the idea is simply wrong. On one hand, you don't really need selection for evolution - since evolution via genetic drift is possible. On the other hand, selection doesn't *necessarily* result in *adaptive* evolution - since that additionally requires that constructive forces outweigh destructive ones.

28.13 Gary Boyd

Gary Boyd (2001) stated that the following are required for "Darwinian Evolution":

1. *It must depend on a **population** of **patterns** of some type (they can be patterns of activity, not just of objects).*
2. ***Copies** are made of these patterns (the smallest reliably copied pattern defines the basic unit of replication - e.g. a meme).*
3. ***Variation**- The pattern-units must*

Gary Boyd.

*occasionally **vary** (due to mutation copying errors, or reshuffling of parts).*
4. ***Competition**- Variant patterns must **compete** to occupy some **limited space** (e.g. someone's CNS).*
5. ***Selection**- The **relative** reproductive success of variants must be influenced by the environment (which also usually co-evolves with the organisms - e.g. Dawkins' Extended Phenotype theory).*
6. ***Heredity**-The **makeup** of the **next generation** of the population must depend on which variants survive to be copied.*

That seems like overkill to me, if you are not trying to capture the concept of adaptive evolution - and insufficient if you are, for the same reason as given above for Dennett and Blackmore.

28.14 William H. Calvin

William Calvin (1997) also had a shot at the problem, listing the "Minimal Requirements for the Darwinian Bootstrapping of Quality". He listed the following properties (summarised for brevity here):

1. *There must be a pattern involved;*
2. *The pattern must be copied somehow;*
3. *Variant patterns must sometimes be produced by chance;*
4. *The pattern and its variant must compete with*

William Calvin.

one another for occupation of a limited work space;
5. *The competition is biased by a multifaceted environment;*
6. *New variants always preferentially occur around the more successful of the current patterns.*

As with the other attempts, this is overkill for evolution, and insufficient for adaptive evolution.

28.15 Eliezer Yudkowsky

Another attempt to characterise the conditions required for adaptive evolution has been made more recently by Eliezer Yudkowsky. In one of his articles expressing distaste for cultural-evolution, Yudkowsky (2007) writes:

Eliezer Yudkowsky.

> *To sum up, if you have all of the following properties:*
> - *Entities that replicate*
> - *Substantial variation in their characteristics*
> - *Substantial variation in their reproduction*
> - *Persistent correlation between the characteristics and reproduction*
> - *High-fidelity long-range heritability in characteristics*
> - *Frequent birth of a significant fraction of the breeding population*
> - *And all this remains true through many iterations*
>
> *Then you will have significant cumulative selection pressures, enough to produce complex adaptations by the force of evolution.*

That is significantly *better*. Yudkowsky recognises that adaptive evolution is relatively demanding. However, it *still* seems rather verbose and redundant. What we *really* want is the *minimum* conditions for adaptive evolution to take place - not a laundry list.

28.16 Tim Tyler

Tim (the author of this book) would say that *cosmological evolution* - the type of evolution that classifies stars and rocks as evolving - requires:

1. **Persistence**: some information must persist over time;
2. **Change**: the information that persists must change over time;

Biological evolution additionally requires:

Tim Tyler.

3. **Copying**: the persistence needs to involve a copying process;

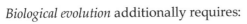

Cumulative adaptive evolution *additionally* requires that *constructive* forces outweigh *destructive* ones. However, this condition is not easy to formalise precisely.

Informally, *constructive forces* are *usually* some form of selection, while *destructive forces usually* take the form of random mutations.

A diagram might help at this stage. One can visualise a spectrum of positive forces (usually selection) and a spectrum of negative forces

Evolution: constructive vs destructive forces.

(usually mutation) - with a threshold between them. In the supplied diagram, the positive forces are represented as going upwards - representing "hill climbing".

Provolution (i.e. adaptive evolution) would then take place on one side of the divide - with devolution (i.e. an error catastrophe) on the other side. Quantifying these effects has been looked into by those attempting to place limits on the speed of evolution - starting with the analysis of Haldane (1957). However, more details about that are beyond the scope of this book.

29 Evolution revolution - The changes needed

If you accept the main ideas in this book, it follows that evolutionary theory has got into a bit of a mess - with a huge area, of critical importance to understanding the recent and ongoing evolution of our species - being neglected. As a result, current evolutionary theory has very poor coverage of the *mechanisms* of evolution - since all the mechanisms associated with cultural evolution have been missed out.

Cultural evolution is of substantial importance in understanding human evolution to date. It will probably have even greater significance in the future, as engineering design is used increasingly to create complex adaptations. Indeed, it seems likely that the process of evolution in the future will be characterised by engineering design - and that very few adaptations will be created by blind variation and natural selection - because that is a tremendously stupid and inefficient optimisation algorithm - and it will be heavily selected against.

How can so many evolutionary biologists have missed what amounts to the entire foundation of their discipline - for all but the earliest era of living systems? The evolutionary biology textbooks *include* early developments that increase the speed of evolution - such as sexual recombination - but *skip over* more recent phenomena that increase the speed of evolution - such as culture.

29.1 Living in the past

The most obvious answer is that many evolutionary biologists have been living in the past. The switch away from blind variation and unintelligent selection is still in progress in some areas. Maybe evolutionary biologists missed it - as a result of being focused on the distant past, where more primitive types of evolution were still very significant.

However, it is not as though these phenomena have not started yet. The evolution of human civilisation via culture has been accelerating for thousands of years. It is practically impossible to ignore the phenomenon today. Meme-accelerated evolution is happening so fast, that the changes are visible from one decade to the next. Cultural evolution is staring us all in the face.

29.2 Ignoring humans

Perhaps another phenomenon is involved. Many biologists are trained to avoid being distracted by considerations of their own species. When considering human nature, all kinds of bias tend to arise that can interfere with taking an objective, scientific view. Considering humans to be "just another animal" is not always an easy trick to pull off. So, biologists may have been systematically avoiding thinking about humans, due to their training.

29.3 Human exceptionalism

There's a *long* tradition of regarding humans as being separate from the rest of biology, and emphasising their differences from other animals. It apparently boosts people's self-esteem if they can distance themselves from the rest of the natural kingdom as much as possible. Human exceptionalism frequently causes people to fail to apply biological theories to human beings. It was responsible for much of the resistance to Darwin's theory in the first place. *Hopefully*, biologists would be mostly immune to this - but social scientists might still be afflicted.

29.4 Delegation of responsibility

Another reaction is: "human evolution?: that's the anthropology department". Some anthropologists *do* have a basic theoretical understanding of their own field. For example, Donald Campbell and Rob Boyd are anthropologists. However, most anthropologists have failed to understand the Darwinian foundations of their own field.

29.5 Too many differences

Another possibility is that the differences between cultural and genetic changes are often emphasised - and so the similarities were neglected. Generalising Darwinism produces a satisfying and rich basis for studying culture - but the differences between human culture and biological evolution can distract people from the benefits of having a single underlying theory.

29.6 Other theories

Linguistic inertia may have been a problem: people have got used to "evolution" being a synonym for "evolution by blind mutations and natural selection" - and so find it hard to embrace the possibility of novel engines of evolutionary change - since such usage appears to change the meaning of a term whose meaning people *think* they already know.

Dennett (2001) offers some hypotheses about how biologists could have got things so wrong:

> Since "culture" is commonly taken to be one of the prime idiosyncrasies distinguishing Homo sapiens from all other species, anything that smacks of the exploitation of culture by non-human species promises to blur a boundary many want to keep as hard-edged as possible.

Later in that document, he invokes the success of a simple - but wrong - theoretical framework of inheritance:

> But the main source of covert resistance comes from the genocentric assumptions that have apparently swept to fixation in the minds of many biologists.

He also addresses the case of the supposedly-missing memetic code:

> A further mistaken grounds for suspicion of the idea of transmission of behavioral tradition is the hunch that since there is no proprietary code (like A,C,G,T) in which such information is couched, transmission cannot be sufficiently high-fidelity to count as replication.

29.7 Radical shift

Another possibility is that the consequences of seeing technological evolution as part of biological evolution can seem so radical. The rise of new forms of heritable information is an amazing development, broadly comparable to the origin of DNA. Some have a hard time believing it is really happening. Everyone knows that changes without precedent are currently occurring on the planet - but: *a new kind of evolution?* It may seem hard to believe that a species of ape has unleashed radical changes to the whole dynamics of evolution, comparable to the evolution of deliberate sexual recombination - and yet that is *exactly* what is happening.

Richard Brodie (1996) characterised the shift towards cultural evolution as a *paradigm shift*:

> *Viruses of the mind, and the whole science of memetics, represent a major paradigm shift in the science of the mind.*

It *is* a major paradigm shift - probably the biggest disruption in evolutionary theory since 1859. However it isn't *just* a paradigm shift. Not only is our *understanding* of evolutionary theory changing, but the way in which evolution actually happens is changing too. The introduction of directed mutations, intelligent design, and the whole modern optimisation toolkit are not just *major* developments in the theory of evolution, they are *major* changes in *how the process of evolution actually works*. If some people have a hard time getting their heads around this, that seems excusable - these developments *are* pretty amazing ones for us to be living through.

30 Memetic takeover - Memes triumphant

Now culture exists, we can see that it is producing a new kind of evolution. Next it is time to look to the future - and consider the consequences. A range of new genetic materials have recently burst forth onto the planet - and new ones are constantly being invented. DNA is starting to look a little out-of-date, with its serial access paradigm and its one-size-fits-all approach.

Will the memes triumph over DNA? Will memes start using DNA as a storage medium? Will the rise of the memes gradually slow and halt - with

DNA and memes peacefully coexisting? It is not easy to say what will happen in the future, but in this case, there are some signs which indicate what is most likely to happen. This chapter will explore the possibilities.

30.1 Takeovers in organic evolution

Many people visualise evolution taking place gradually, by a process of small incremental changes to existing organisms. However, the fossil record seems to tell a rather different story, with organisms spending most of their time stuck on adaptive peaks - and then being suddenly displaced by invading organisms that evolved elsewhere. This is commonly known as "stasis" - and is a well-known phenomenon. We can see recent evidence of a massive invasion of South America - when the Mexican land bridge formed and it rejoined the mainland. We can also see a similar invasion taking place now - as placental mammals invade Australia and New Zealand.

30.2 Takeovers in cultural evolution

We can get insight into this process by observing recent technological evolution. To start with we will consider the evolution of writing:

30.3 Evolution of writing

Charcoal
Quill pen
Fountain pen

Within this *niche*, there *are* signs of gradual evolution - for example, the fountain pen is - in part - a modification of the design of a quill pen. However, what comes next is an example of a "takeover" - the shift to typewriters:

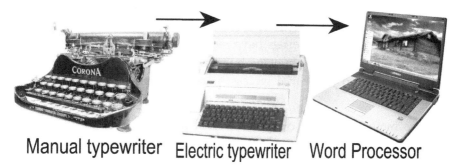
Manual typewriter   Electric typewriter   Word Processor

The design of the typewriters apparently owes very little from the design of the pens that preceded them. Rather they are the descendants of other machines (which are not shown in the diagram).

30.4 Evolution of land transportation

Another example from the history of technology is the evolution of land transportation:

Animals ⟶ Horse and cart ⟶ Bicycle

Here again, we see early designs grounded in the products of evolution via natural selection. One thing to note here is that there is an instance of a hybrid pattern - half organic, half machine - in the case of the horse and cart.

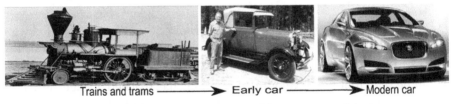

Trains and trams ⟶ Early car ⟶ Modern car

Later vehicles were produced by intelligent design and engineering.

30.5 Evolution of manned flight

Next, we will consider the evolution of manned flight:

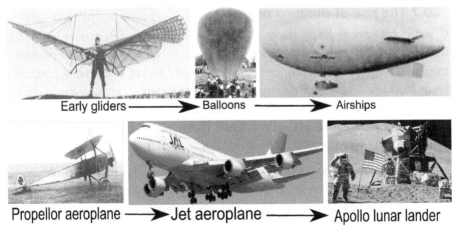

Early gliders ⟶ Balloons ⟶ Airships

Propellor aeroplane ⟶ Jet aeroplane ⟶ Apollo lunar lander

The history of manned flight again illustrates the principle that later designs are not necessarily direct descendants of earlier ones. Aeroplanes worked on different principles from the balloons that preceded them.

30.6 Evolution of thinking

With this perspective, consider the development of "thinking technology":

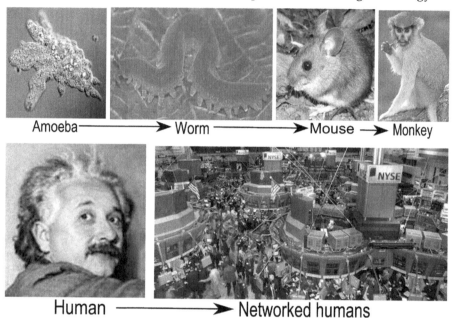

Amoeba ⟶ Worm ⟶ Mouse ⟶ Monkey

Human ⟶ Networked humans

It can be seen that the development of brains has reached a stage similar to the "horse and cart" stage which was used above to illustrate the evolution of transportation. Modern intelligent agents consist of networks of organic and machine components - humans and computers. However, the computers cannot *yet* operate entirely unaided.

30.7 The rise of the new organisms

Genetic takeovers have happened before. We can determine from the highly adapted nature of modern genetic systems - and the prebiotic implausibility of their components - that early living organisms probably went through a range of different genetic materials - clays, organic chains on clay surfaces, PNA or TNA, RNA, and then DNA. So: we can be confident that genetic takeovers have taken place in the past - as new genetic media were produced by evolution.

DNA has proved to be a useful storage medium for organisms - but there is no easy way to write to it. To solve this problem, nature came up with the idea of brains and memory. This writeable storage medium proved very useful, but unfortunately, information in brains is not normally inherited - instead that information is lost when the associated organism dies. However, humans invented a means of transmitting information in brains "horizontally" - from brain to brain. This resulted in human culture - a means of inheriting information stored in brains, and allowing it to persist past the point of an individual's death.

Currently, the human species evolves using two *primary* types of inheritance - organic inheritance and environmental inheritance. Environmental inheritance includes cultural inheritance as a major component. It uses a wide variety of storage media with differing properties to transmit information down the generations. Also, information is very portable. It can move smoothly from one medium to the next.

Memes are transmitted down the generations using the first new medium of inheritance on the planet for billions of years. Their ease of modification has resulted in popularity which has been explosive, and memes are copying themselves all over the place in *huge* numbers.

30.8 Automation - takeover underway

We have now delegated many of our least-desirable roles to machines. Machines wash our clothes and our dishes. They transport us around, and help us do cleaning jobs. Machines started out in factories, where they could operate in controlled environments. However, they act as bank clerks, checkout

Factory automation.

assistants, and are *gradually* taking on more sophisticated roles such as teacher and doctor. As time passes the degree of automation is gradually increasing. Much manufacturing has been automated. Retail, agriculture and distribution are not *that* far out of reach. A close relationship between the humans and the machines is involved - the man-machine symbiosis.

30.9 Meme's eye view

In *The Selfish Gene*, Richard Dawkins looked at evolution from the perspective of genes. Similarly, it is possible to consider gene-meme coevolution from the perspective of memes. Considering human history from the meme's eye view:

The first objective was to make room for themselves in human brains. They did this by rewarding the humans with more space for memes with increased genetic fitness. Memes for language, music and fashion were probably *mainly* responsible for this. The result was 5 million years of steadily-expanding cranial capacity - which resulted in much more space for the memes. Also, humans developed spoken language - a adaptation which can be used for spreading memes. Other aspects of humans have apparently been altered as well. Memes would have benefited from being in humans who are sociable, so those humans who interacted more with other humans were the ones that benefited the most from synergetic memes. The result was human ultrasociality.

The next step for the memes was to increase human numbers - since the more humans there are, the more memes there are. Agricultural memes allowed humans to form closer symbiotic relationships with plants, animals and each other, which boosted their fitness and increased their numbers. The result was a massively increased the population of memes.

The next problem was meme transmission fidelity. At this early stage, memes were copied by behavioural imitation and by vocalisation - neither of which provided very much in the way of copying fidelity. Environmental inheritance proved to be the answer here - by inventing the idea of *writing* memes could persist unaltered across extended periods of time, without fear of mental mutation.

Then there was the copying speed problem. Transcribing documents by hand was slow and tedious. However, the invention of mechanical printing presses allowed machines to take over this task from humans, resulting in vastly wider distribution of memes.

However, many memes often still need the consent of a human brain to get copied - an obvious bottleneck. The afflicted memes are currently busy sorting this issue out. Many computer viruses skip over the human brain completely - but they are nasty parasites. Superintelligent machines seem likely to copy memes with the full consent of society. At that stage, memes won't be dependent on humans any more.

During each of the above stages, the memes accelerated their own synthesis by rewarding those humans who help them to reproduce. Assuming that resource-limitation continues to hold, genes and memes will compete for resources, since they essentially share the same environment. Memes will be able to offer rewards to genes that help them. It is worth noting that memes can still do this *even* if their *average* effect on genes becomes negative. You can *still* climb a mountain path on an island - *even* if that island is sinking into the sea.

30.10 Genetic takeover

This whole idea is known as a genetic takeover, after a 1982 book by A. G.

Cairns-Smith with that title. The book argued that the planet has probably previously seen multiple genetic takeovers.

30.11 Memetic takeover

Dawkins originally speculated that the new inheritance media might come to dominate in 1976:

> *For more than three thousand million years, DNA has been the only replicator worth talking about in the world. But it does not necessarily hold these monopoly rights for all time. Whenever conditions arise in which a new kind of replicator can make copies of itself, the new replicators will tend to take over, and start a new kind of evolution of their own. Once this new evolution begins, it will in no necessary sense be subservient to the old.*

The idea that human culture would precipitate a modern genetic takeover was raised again by Hans Moravec in 1988 - in an article entitled: "Human Culture - A Genetic Takeover Underway". In the same year, Moravec wrote:

> *Today, billions of years later, another change is under way in how information passes from generation to generation. Humans evolved from organisms defined almost totally by their organic genes. We now rely additionally on a vast and rapidly growing corpus of cultural information generated and stored outside our genes - in our nervous systems, libraries, and, most recently, computers.*

> *Our culture still depends utterly on biological human beings, but with each passing year our machines, a major product of the culture, assume a greater role in its maintenance and continued growth. Sooner or later our machines will become knowledgeable enough to handle their own maintenance, reproduction and self-improvement without help. When this happens the new genetic takeover will be complete.*

Susan Blackmore recognises the possibility of a *memetic takeover* in her 1999 book, *The Meme Machine*:

> *At the moment, they mostly carry out simple tasks under human control, but memetics raises the following interesting possibility. For robots to become like humans – in other words, to have human-like artificial intelligence and artificial consciousness – they would need to have memes. Rather than being programmed to do specific tasks or even to learn from their environment as some already can, they would have to be given the ability to imitate. If they could imitate the actions of people or other robots, then robot memes would begin to spread from one to another, and a new kind of memetic evolution take off, perhaps inventing new kinds of language and communication. The*

robot memes would drive the robots to new activities, giving rise to motivations that we could only guess at.

A memetic takeover seems to be a high-probability outcome. The scenario will continue to increase in probability while civilisation continues to progress without interruption.

30.12 Possible paths

The idea of a *memetic takeover* often conjures up images from the *Terminator* or *Matrix* movie franchises, in which the shift to engineered material takes place amidst conflict between the human and engineered elements. This does not seem to be a very realistic scenario to me. Today, *some* humans resist technology, but there are *plenty* of other ones which embrace it - and the machines going off on their own seems to be an improbable catastrophe to me - it would be the biggest engineering mistake of all time.

Some (e.g. Gregory Stock) propose that humans themselves will become engineered - via genetic engineering. Alas, germ-line genetic engineering of humans seems likely to take place on too slow a time-scale to have much impact on future events.

Another oft-mentioned scenario involves humans and machines "merging together" into some kind of cyborg creature. This type of vision is promoted by Ray Kurzweil and several others. However, the human body represent an uncomfortable environment for machines. Today, most machines help humans from the outside - they are in exo-symbiosis. Humans may increase the intimacy of their symbiosis with machines, but they seem unlikely to "merge".

So, enough about what *won't* happen, what *is* likely to happen? The rise of the machines seems set to continue, but what will happen to the humans? Of course, it is hard to make out the details, and so what follows is necessarily speculative. Some humans could persist for quite a while - as a kind of organic froth on top of a machine-based civilisation. Many humans could be effectively sterilised, with a lot of them losing interest in reproduction - in a similar manner to what we currently see in Japan. Many humans will probably find it challenging to compete economically, will become dependent on the government, and will become a parasitic burden on the more productive elements of society. However, the future may still be *relatively* bright - if current trends continue - although *perhaps* not *equally* bright for everyone.

30.13 Meme impact

We have seen the extent to which the memes have invaded the biosphere with their concrete, metal and plastic. The world is busy sprouting artificial sensors, actuators and computing devices. Most other organisms are pushed aside in this process - as the current mass extinction illustrates. It seems likely that this is just the beginning.

Memes are newcomers to the biosphere, but their baby steps are having enormous repercussions all over the planet. If memes have this kind of impact on the biosphere - *before* they have invented molecular nanotechnology and machine intelligence - it seems challenging to imagine very much that will stop them.

Daniel Dennett (1990, p.131) writes:

> *Memes now spread around the world at the speed of light, and replicate at rates that make even fruit flies and yeast cells look glacial in comparison. They leap promiscuously from vehicle to vehicle, and from medium to medium, and are proving to be virtually unquarantinable.*

That seems about right. The memes are in the driver's seat now. The organic world is being dragged around after it - and the tether connecting the two looks as though it won't handle the stress for very long. It remains to be seen if much from the organic world can make it across the divide, and become fully engineered. Probably not. The organic world looks as though it is an unsuitable foundation for an engineered future. No doubt much of it will be preserved - but probably mostly in the future equivalent of nature reserves and museums.

30.14 Extinction possibility

It doesn't happen frequently, but parasites can sometimes completely wipe out whole species. Meme warfare may mean that the most aggressive memes are among those that rise to power. Parasites often evolve into relatively stable relationships with their hosts - but it does *sometimes* happen that they completely wipe them out. That outcome becomes more likely when a parasite has multiple host species, and consequentially the parasite not so dependant for their own survival on the continuing welfare of any one host species.

At the moment, humans are the primary host for most memes. Memes are typically pretty dependent on humans for their reproduction. So: humans being totally wiped out by memes does not look very likely in the short term. However, as our cybernetic systems have become more advanced, the memes have been eagerly swarming out of the human heads and onto the new digital systems with considerable enthusiasm. Plans are afoot to construct mechanical bodies and minds for the memes. After they have established themselves fully in their new synthetic media, the memes may not need the humans *quite* so much. They will become more like a parasite that has multiple host species, and so is not so dependent on any one of them any longer.

We will need to have a good and clear understanding of the dynamics of these types of coevolving systems to have the best chance of surviving our coming encounter with this type of situation. This is one of the reasons why memetics is an important science.

30.15 The modern takeover

For those who dream about keeping future synthetic living organisms quarantined in secure environments, there is bad news - the new organisms are *already* on the outside, in the wild - and they have devoured much of the biosphere, and show every sign growing increasingly more powerful as time passes.

The writeable nature of memes allows Lamarckian evolution and intelligent design. Memes evolve at lightning speed - compared to the glacial pace of DNA evolution. The last few thousand years contains abundant evidence of this. Human genes are bystanders, changing so slowly that we can hardly even see them move. Memes have intelligent design, science, maths, rational thought and computers on their side. Evolution via random mutations can't keep up. Memetic evolution is responsible for all our recent scientific, technological and moral progress. Our story is now *actually* their story. The future belongs to them.

It now appears that the modern *memetic takeover* will be accompanied by a *phenotypic takeover* as well. 20 amino acids are no more an optimal universal constructor than 4 DNA base pairs are an optimal universal storage medium.

It seems likely that the entire edifice of cobbled-together evolved genotypes and phenotypes will be replaced by vastly superior products of engineering design - and looking at the rapid recent and anticipated rise of technology, this might happen surprisingly quickly.

31 Glossary

- **Active meme:** A meme that is in a host and is significantly affecting its behaviour. Antonym:inactive meme.
- **Advertising:** A form of communication used to persuade an audience (viewers, readers or listeners) to take some action with respect to products, ideas, or services. Most commonly, the desired result is drive consumer behaviour with respect to a commercial offering, although political and ideological advertising is also common. Advertising is a primary application of memetics.
- **Astroturfing:** An artificial movement posing as a grassroots movement; e.g. something staged or faked that appears real; formally planned by an organization, but designed to mask its origins to create the impression of being spontaneous behaviour).
- **Audio:** A popular type of content on the internet. Audible content.
- **Auto-toxic:** Dangerous to itself. Highly auto-toxic memes are usually self-limiting because they promote the destruction of their hosts (such as military indoctrination memes and martyrdom memes). (See exo-toxic).
- **Bait:** The attractive co-meme in a scheme that draws in the host, and gets it to adopt the meme. In some religions, "Salvation" is the bait, and " Spread the Word" is the hook.
- **Blackmore:** Susan Blackmore. Author of *The Meme Machine*.
- **Belief-space:** Since a person can only be infected with and transmit a finite number of memes, there is a limit to their *belief-space*. Memes evolve in competition for niches in the *belief-space* of individuals and societies.
- **Brain:** Concentrated nexus of computing elements in an organism.
- **Censorship:** Any attempt to hinder the spread of a meme by eliminating its vectors. Hence, censorship is analogous to attempts to halt diseases by spraying insecticides. Censorship rarely kills off the target meme. In some cases, it may actually help to promote the meme's most virulent strain, while killing off milder forms.
- **Chain letter:** A message that attempts to induce the recipient to make a number of copies of the letter and then pass them on to as many recipients as possible. Common methods used in chain letters include emotionally manipulative stories, get-rich-quick pyramid schemes, and the exploitation of superstition to threaten the recipient with bad luck, violence or even death if they 'break the chain' or refuses to adhere to the conditions set out in the letter.
- **Co-meme:** A meme which has symbiotically co-evolved with other memes, to form a mutually-assisting memeplex. The types of co-memes commonly found in a scheme are called the: bait; hook; threat; and vaccime. The term is from Hofstadter.
- **Computer worm:** A small mobile agent that can reproduce in virtual environments without much assistance.
- **Computer virus:** A small infectious agent that can only replicate with the assistance of another organism, its host. Viruses live inside their host. They can have lifecycles that involve more than one type of host. See also virus.
- **Contagion:** A contagious agent.
- **Contagious:** Easily spread from one host to another.
- **Contagiousness:** A measure of how easily an infection spreads from one host to another.
- **Copy:** A duplicated version of something. The result of copying. Also a verb referring to copying.
- **Copying:** The duplication of information or an artefact based on an instance of it. The act of making a copy.
- **Copypasta:** A *bastardization* of copy-paste. When used as an image macro, it is often accompanied by a picture of *spaghetti*.
- **Cover:** A derivative production, usually inferior to the original. Usually created to attract attention via memetic hitchhiking. Also cover version.
- **Cover version:** See also: cover.
- **Cult:** A sociotype of an auto-toxic memeplex, composed of membots and/or memeoids. Cults often exhibit brainwashing, isolation, proselytizing and leader-worship ("personality cult").
- **Culture:** Inherited patterns of knowledge and behaviour that are transmitted down the generations using brains - rather than nucleic acids.
- **Cultural evolution:** The evolution of culture. More academically respectable synonym of memetic evolution
- **Cultural selection theory:** Memetics variant which embraces non-discrete inheritance, working from the dubious premise that memetics necessarily insists on discrete inheritance, and so is in need of extending.
- **Cultural pandemic:** A memeplex that goes global and becomes carried by very large numbers of people.
- **Culturomics:** The application of high-throughput data collection and analysis to the study of human culture. Word according to Google.
- **Cyberspace:** The virtual side of the internet. Where most memes live. Environment constructed by memes to reduce their dependence on human hosts in meatspace.

- **Darwin:** Charles Darwin. Originator of the theory of evolution by natural selection.
- **Dawkins:** Richard Dawkins. Christened the meme in his book *The Selfish Gene.*
- **Dennett:** Daniel Dennett. Author of *Darwin's Dangerous Idea.*
- **Derivative:** A term to denote any variants of a work that are inspired by or created from parts of it. Literally, it's a thing that is derived from another thing. See also: derivative work, remix, mashup, exploitable and parody.
- **Derivative work:** An expressive creation that includes major, copyright-protected elements of an original, previously created first work. The term derives from *United States* copyright law.
- **Dormant meme:** A meme that is currently inactive. Dormant memes can be inside human brains, inside computers or in the environment. A dormant meme that has infected its host is known as a latent meme. Synonym: inactive meme.
- **Earworm:** A tune or melody which infects a population rapidly. A hit song. (Such as: "Don't Worry, Be Happy".) (from German, ohrwurm=earworm.)
- **Epidemic:** An infectious agent that spreads rapidly, affecting large numbers of hosts.
- **Epidemic threshold:** A threshold above which agents can spread explosively and cause epidemics. Usually expressed in terms of the ratio between birth rate and death rate.
- **Evolution:** The main theory of how biological complexity arises from natural processes via copying, mutation and selection. Discovered by Darwin and published in Darwin (1859).
- **Evolutionary:** Conceptually connected with Evolution.
- **Evolutionary economics:** The study of economics, with an evolutionary perspective.
- **Evolutionary computation:** The study of evolving computer data and programs.
- **Evolutionary epistemology:** The study of epistemology, with an evolutionary perspective.
- **Evolutionary linguistics:** The study of linguistics, with an evolutionary perspective.
- **Evolutionary robotics:** The study of evolving robots.
- **Exo-toxic:** Dangerous to others. Highly exo-toxic memes promote the destruction of persons other than their hosts, particularly those who are carriers of rival memes. (Such as: Nazism, the Inquisition, Pol Pot.) (See meme-allergy)
- **Exploitable:** Refers to a type of image that is prime for editing in many different ways. Generally, there will be one element of an image that can be tweaked, or captions may be added.
- **Failed meme:** Not all memes make it in the real world. Those that don't are often referred to as being 'failed memes'.
- **Family Guy effect:** When a meme becomes so popular it is parodied by mainstream media. When this happens, the reputation of the meme is sometimes tarnished among its fans. However, such memes often show a resurgence in popularity for the meme soon after the mainstream mention.
- **Fecundity:** Having lots of offspring. One of the big three *meme properties* (longevity, fidelity, fecundity).
- **Fidelity:** Producing high-quality unmutated copies. One of the big three *meme properties* (longevity, fidelity, fecundity).
- **Flaming:** Making inflammatory, abusive or directly offensive comments. This is differentiated from a trolling, which is more oriented around provoking responses.
- **Forced Meme:** A planned attempt to make a meme. *Forced Memes* are often unsuccessful.
- **Free riding:** Free riding genes are near-neutral genes that don't serve much of a useful purpose - and are just along for the ride. They differ from junk DNA - since they are expressed. Similarly, free riding memes are near-neutral memes that are just along for the ride.
- **Global brain:** The idea that the internet behaves rather like a giant planetary-scale brain.
- **Godwin's Law:** A behavioural observation stating that the longer a Usenet conversation is, the more likely Nazis are to be mentioned, ending the conversation. It is now applied to all forums.
- **Goliath effect:** An infection strategy common to many memeplexes, placing the potential host in the role of victim and playing on their insecurity, as in: "the bourgeoisie is oppressing the proletariat".
- **Grassroots:** A word to describe a movement or meme created or "grown" by regular people or users; not corporate companies or large organizations. These memes are the kinds that start out small and grow from person to person, rather than a singular massive exposure.
- **Herd behaviour:** Herd behaviour describes how individuals in a group can act together without central planning. Copying each other's actions is often involved. See also: sheeple, information+cascade
- **Henson:** Keith Henson. Coined the term memeoid. Henson's wife coined the term memetics.
- **Hofstadter:** Douglas Hofstadter. Author of Metamagical Themas.
- **Hook:** After a host has been located using the bait, the hook is the co-meme that then results in replication of the meme. The term is from Hofstadter.
- **Horizontal meme transfer:** The cultural equivalent of horizontal gene transfer.
- **Host:** A person who has been successfully infected by a meme. See also: infection, membot, memeoid.
- **Idea:** A thought. The conscious contents of a mind when it engages in thinking.
- **Ideavirus:** Seth Godin's term for a meme.

- **Ideosphere:** The realm of memetic evolution, as the biosphere is the realm of biological evolution. The entire memetic ecology.
- **Image:** A popular type of content on the internet. A visual representation.
- **Image macro:** An image captioned with superimposed text for humorous effect. A image with no caption is often called an exploitable.
- **Immunosuppressant:** Anything that tends to reduce a person's memetic immunity. Common immunosuppressant include: travel, disorientation, exhaustion, insecurity, shock, loss, isolation, stress, drugs, loneliness, alienation, paranoia and hypnosis. Recruiters for cults often target airports and bus terminals because travellers are likely to have depressed memetic immunity.
- **Inactive meme:** A meme that is in a host and is *not* significantly affecting its behaviour. Antonym:active meme. Synonym: dormant meme.
- **Infection:** Successful encoding of a meme in the memory of its host. A memetic infection can be either active or inactive. It is inactive if the host does not feel inclined to transmit the meme to other people. An active infection causes the host to want to infect others. Fanatically active hosts are often membots or memeoids. A person who is exposed to a meme but who does not remember it (consciously or otherwise) is not infected. (A host can indeed be unconsciously infected, and even transmit a meme without conscious awareness of the fact. Many societal norms are transmitted this way.)
- **Infection strategy:** Any memetic strategy which encourages infection of a host. Jokes encourage infection by being humorous, tunes by evoking various emotions, slogans and catch-phrases by being terse and continuously repeated. Common infection strategies include: Goliath effect, Fear of Death, and Sense of Community. In a memeplex, the bait co-meme is often central to the infection strategy.
- **Information cascade:** An information cascade occurs when people observe the actions of others and then make the same choice that the others have made, independently of other factors.
- **Intercranial memetics:** Sub-field of memetics that deals with the dynamics of memes *between* minds. This covers interactions between memes and their environment while the memes are *not* inside minds. See also intracranial memetics.
- **Internet:** An international network of computers that forms a new, electronic home memes have constructed for themselves, as part of a strategy of liberating themselves from the confines of the human brain.
- **Intracranial memetics:** Sub-field of memetics that deals with the dynamics of memes *inside* a single mind. Memes compete with other memes inside minds. Intracranial memetics studies these dynamics - and other forces on memes while they are *inside* minds. Note that intracranial memetics also deals with protomemes failed+memes and other ideas that may never go on to become memes. See also intercranial memetics.
- **Latent meme:** A dormant meme that has already infected its host.
- **Lemming:** A member of a crowd with no originality or voice of his own. One who speaks or repeats only what he has been told. Named after the urban legend that lemmings will jump over cliffs if another lemming does so first.
- **Longevity:** Having a long life. One of the big three *meme properties* (longevity, fidelity, fecundity).
- **Marketing:** The activity, set of institutions, and processes for creating, communicating, delivering, and exchanging offerings that have value for customers, clients, partners, and society at large. Marketing is a primary application of memetics.
- **Mashup:** Media content containing recombined text, images, audio or video drawn from pre-existing sources, to create a new derived work.
- **Meatspace:** Where memes lived before they colonised cyberspace. The land of human brains.
- **Media:** Media (singular medium) are the storage and transmission channels or tools used to store and deliver information or data. Also an abbreviated form of mass media or news media.
- **Medium:** singular of media.
- **Membot:** A person whose entire life has become subordinated to the propagation of a meme (such as many Jehovah's witnesses, Krishna devotees, and scientologists.) Due to internal competition, the most vocal and extreme membots tend to rise to top of their organisation's hierarchy. A self-destructive membot is a memeoid.
- **Meme:** (pron. 'meem') A contagious information pattern that replicates by symbiotically infecting host minds and altering their behaviour, causing them to propagate the pattern. (Term coined by Dawkins (1976), by analogy with "gene".) Examples of memes include slogans, words, catch-phrases, melodies, icons, inventions, logos and fashions. An idea or information pattern is not a meme until it causes someone to replicate it, to repeat it to someone else. All cultural knowledge is memetic.
- **Memes:** Plural of meme.
- **Meme allergy:** A form of intolerance; a condition which causes a person to react in an unusually negative manner when exposed to a specific semiotic stimulus, or `meme-allergen.' Exo-toxic memeplexes typically confer dangerous meme-allergies on their hosts. Often, the actual meme-allergens need not be present, but merely perceived to be present, to trigger a reaction. Common meme-allergies include racism, sexism and

homophobia and pornophobia. Common forms of meme-allergic reaction are censorship, vandalism, belligerent verbal abuse, and physical violence.

- **Meme complex:** See memeplex.
- **Meme entry:** The penetration of the host's immune system by the meme. Techniques used to do this include Trojan horses, injection and suggestion. By analogy with virus entry.
- **Meme expression:** Activity by a meme in a host. By analogy with gene expression.
- **Meme flow:** In population memetics, meme flow is the transfer of memes from one organic population to another - or from one cultural population to another. By analogy with gene flow.
- **Meme freak:** Meme enthusiast who constantly posts memes, references memes in meatspace or tries to explain memes to others.
- **Meme hack:** A crude mutation of a meme, performed deliberately. Subvertising is a common example of meme hacking.
- **Meme instance:** A term to denote any specific instance of a meme. For example, a popular quotes are not described as catchphrases until they have a large number of repeated instances. The cultural equivalent of an allele.
- **Meme pool:** The full diversity of memes accessible to a culture or individual. Learning languages and travelling are methods of expanding one's meme pool.
- **Meme regulation:** Anything that regulates the activities of memes in a host, to affect meme expression. By analogy with gene regulation.
- **Meme shedding:** Sometimes hosts shed copies of their memes liberally into their environment. By analogy with virus shedding.
- **Meme therapy:** Education using memes. By analogy with gene therapy.
- **Meme transmission:** Refers to transport of memes from host to host and from place to place. By analogy with virus transmission.
- **Meme warfare:** A struggle for dominance between mutually exclusive memes.
- **Meme's eye view:** Taking the perspective of the gene on evolution. As opposed to considering the situation from the perspective of the individual, group, or species.
- **Memealogy:** The study of cultural ancestry. The cultural equivalent of an genealogy.
- **Memeplex:** A set of mutually-assisting memes which have co-evolved a symbiotic relationship. Religious and political dogmas, social movements, artistic styles, traditions and customs, chain letters, paradigms, languages, etc. are memeplexes. Similar terms include meme complex, and scheme.
- **Memespeak:** Using meme talk IRL, for example greeting someone with "Yo-Dawg! El-oh-ell!" Also, the childish language of many memes - especially image macros - e.g. "Im in yr couch steelin yr change!", "y u b h8tn?" and "Shoop Da Woop Imma firin Mah Lazer"
- **Memetic algorithms:** These represent one of the recent growing areas of research in evolutionary computation. The term M.A. is now widely used to describe combinations of evolutionary or any population-based approach with separate individual learning procedures to solve optimisation problems.
- **Memetic drift:** Memetic change as a result of random changes - as opposed to selection. By analogy with genetic drift.
- **Memetic engineering:** One who consciously devises memes, through meme-splicing and memetic synthesis, with the intent of altering the behaviour of others. Writers of manifestos and of commercials are typical memetic engineers.
- **Memetic engineer:** One who performs memetic engineering.
- **Memetic evolution:** The evolution of memes. Synonym of cultural evolution.
- **Memetic junk:** Memes that don't have any significant effect - aside from the metabolic costs associated with their reproduction. By analogy with Junk DNA.
- **Memetic hitchhiking:** The attaching of a payload to a meme, to help to the spread the payload around. By analogy with genetic hitchhiking.
- **Memetic hijacking:** The process of a meme becoming active in a host - and overriding the influence of its DNA-genes. Named after the hijacking of vehicles - where an agent who is not *supposed* to be in charge seizes control. Sometimes referred to as 'mind hijacking'. If taken to extremes can produce a memoid.
- **Memetic linkage:** The tendency of 'nearby' memes to be copied and inherited together. By analogy with genetic linkage.
- **Memetic immunity:** Resistance to memetic infections. Memetic immunity can arise from education, reading, scepticism, faith. The freedom to learn about all sorts of ideas, compare them as you will and choose for yourself which to believe also helps.
- **Memetic:** Related to memes.
- **Memeticist:** One who studies memetics.
- **Memetics:** The study of memes and their social effects.
- **Memoid:** A person "whose behaviour is so strongly influenced by a meme that their own survival becomes inconsequential in their own minds. (Henson) Examples include: Kamikazes, Shiite terrorists, suicide

bombers). Sometimes written as 'memeoid'.

- **Memotype:** A collection of memes that are transmitted together as a unit - by analogy with genotype.
- **Metameme:** Any meme about memes (such as: "tolerance", "metaphor").
- **Military memetics:** An interest of the military, aimed at countering terrorism and preventing irrational conflicts by promoting rational solutions to national and international problems. See also propaganda.
- **Mimesis:** Imitation, mimicry - philosophical term, from ancient greek.
- **Mimetic:** Relating to, or exhibiting mimicry.
- **Mimic:** Something that copies the form of something else.
- **Mimicry:** The act of copying the form of something else.
- **Motivational poster:** A motivational poster (or inspirational poster) is a type of poster commonly designed for use in schools and offices. Motivational posters are often parodied on the internet and used as a form of image macro.
- **Mutation:** A memetic change in which an existing meme takes on a slightly different form. For example, when a popular catchphrase has clearly evolved into an image macro series, it can be said a significant mutation has occurred.
- **Mutex:** Abbreviation for mutually exclusive. Mutex memes are ones that do not coexist peacefully in the same host. For example, *Christianity* and *Islam* are mutex memeplexes.
- **Noosphere:** Alternative name for the ideosphere. Originated with Vladimir Vernadsky and Teilhard de Chardin.
- **Organic evolution:** The evolution of organic systems, *not* including cultural evolution.
- **Parody:** A type of derivative in which participants imitate something for humorous effect. Common objects of parody arise from pop culture and politics.
- **Payload:** Deliverable cargo. Often something that is desired to be spread which is attached to a meme, and then spread via memetic hitchhiking.
- **Persistent meme infection:** A meme infection that does not go away. By analogy with persistent viral infections.
- **Population memetics:** Population memetics is the study of the frequency memes occur with, and how this changes under the influence of natural selection, memetic drift, mutation and meme flow. By analogy with Population genetics.
- **Phemotype:** The expressed form of a memotype, as the body of an organism is the physical expression (*phenotype*) of the gene (*genotype*). Close synonym of sociotype.
- **Phylomemetics:** The study of historical evolutionary relationships between cultural entities. There's also the idea of a phylomemetic tree. By analogy with phylogenetics.
- **Propaganda:** A form of communication that is aimed at influencing the attitude of a community toward some cause or position so as to benefit oneself. See also military memetics.
- **Protomeme:** *Protomeme* is an abbreviation of *prototype meme*. It refers to a meme which is *under construction*.
- **Remix:** A type of derivative created by using parts of more than one source material. This is typically observed in all sorts of user-generated content, including cross-meme combos in video mashups and image macros.
- **Remix culture:** Remix culture is a term used to describe a society which allows and encourages derivative works.
- **Replicator:** Term used by Dawkins to describe anything of which copies are made. Note the difference between this usage and the dictionary.
- **Replication strategy:** Any memetic strategy used by a meme to encourage its host to repeat the meme to other people. The hook co-meme of a scheme.
- **Retromeme:** A meme which attempts to splice itself into an existing memeplex (example: Marxist-Leninists trying to co-opt other sociotypes).
- **Sauce:** Slang for "source", often used when the poster wants moar of what was posted. Originated when m00t (the founder of 4chan) filtered "source" to show up as "sauce".
- **Scheme:** A memeplex containing linked elements that help each other to propagate. Often contains a bait or threat, a hook and sometimes a vaccime - to hinder competing infections. Term comes from Hofstadter.
- **Search magnet:** Co-meme which is effective at attracting the attention of those searching. Usually - but not always - the *prime* function of that co-meme.
- **Selfish meme:** Selfish meme theory holds that cultural evolution occurs through a process involving differential survival of competing memes. By analogy with the concept of the selfish gene.
- **Seinfeld Effect:** A term used for when a meme is believed to have begun from certain mainstream media when, in fact, it did not. It was only referencing the already existing meme.
- **Semiotics:** Semiotics is the study of signs, sign processes, indication, designation as used in communication.
- **Sharing:** The joint use of resources: space, time, matter or information.
- **Shareable:** a measure of how likely something is to be shared: e.g.: 'some content is very shareable'. Also,

something capable of being shared, or likely to be shared.

- **Sheeple:** Sheeple (a portmanteau of *sheep* and *people*) is a term of disparagement, in which people are likened to sheep - due to habitually copying each other's behaviour and following each other around.
- **Sneezability:** Seth Godin's term for contagiousness.
- **Snowclone:** An easily-recognised template phrase that can be used in a range of different versions by substituting keywords into the template. 'Grey is the new black', is a version of the template 'X is the new Y'. Frequently-used concept in image macros.
- **Social media:** Media used for social interaction, using highly accessible and scalable communication techniques. Social media are where a lot of sharing happens.
- **Sociotype:** The social expression of a memotype, as the body of an organism is the physical expression (phenotype) of the gene (genotype). Hence, the Protestant Church is one sociotype of the Bible's memotype.
- **Sub-meme:** A derivative meme, usually inferior to the original. Usually created to attract attention via memetic hitchhiking.
- **Subvertising:** A meme hack usually to an advertisement that subverts its message.
- **Spam:** Unsolicited Electronic messages sent in bulk indiscriminately.
- **Spin-off:** A derivative that has grown out of an existing meme, which contain explicit references to the original content.
- **Spread:** The range of locations where a specific meme can be found.
- **Streisand Effect:** When an attempt to censor or hide something from the general public results in its unexpected/sudden rise in popularity.
- **Symbiosis:** The living together of unlike organisms.
- **Text:** A popular type of content on the internet. Contains written language.
- **Teme:** Blackmore's proposed term for a techno-meme - a meme that replicates using technological means - rather than human brains.
- **Thought contagion:** Aaron Lynch's proposed term for meme.
- **Threadjacking:** The act of stealing a thread via a topic change and is often done unintentionally. When done intentionally, it can be considered trolling.
- **Threat:** The part of a memeplex that encourages adherence and discourages mis-replication. (" Damnation to Hell" is the threat co-meme in many religious schemes.) See also: bait, hook, vaccime.
- **Tipping point:** Critical threshold beyond which a meme starts to spread rapidly. Can be caused by mutation, hitchhiking, recombination, etc.
- **Tolerance:** A meta-meme which allows for the peaceful coexistence of a wide variety of memes (and their sociotypes). In its purest form, *tolerance* allows its host to be repeatedly exposed to rival memes, without active infection and without resulting in a meme allergy reaction. Tolerance is a central co-meme in a wide variety of schemes, particularly "liberalism", and " democracy".
- **Trojan:** Abbreviation of *Trojan Horse*. Refers to a technique for bypassing host immune systems by being taken inside a defensive perimeter, into a trusted zone.
- **Troll:** Refers to a person who posts inflammatory, rude, or insulting posts on a forum for the purpose of creating controversy, or provoking replies.
- **Trolling:** Acting like a troll.
- **Universal Darwinism:** This refers to a variety of approaches that extend the theory of Darwinism beyond its original domain of organic, biological evolution. The idea is to formulate a generalized version of the mechanisms of variation, selection and inheritance proposed by Darwin, so that they can be applied to explain evolution in a wide variety of other domains - including psychology, economics, culture, medicine, computer science and physics. Universal Darwinism is also sometimes known as *Generalized Darwinism* or *Universal Selection Theory*.
- **Universal selection:** The idea that natural selection is a universal principle, that governs everything that comes into existence.
- **Vector:** A medium, method, or vehicle for the transmission of memes. Almost any communication medium can be a memetic vector.
- **Urban legend:** A form of modern folklore consisting of stories usually believed by their tellers to be true. The designation suggests nothing about the story's veracity, but merely that it is in circulation, exhibits variation over time, and carries elements that promote its preservation and propagation.
- **Vaccime:** Cultural vaccine, by analogy with Vaccine. Any metameme which confers memetic immunity to one or more memes, allowing that person to be exposed without acquiring an active infection. Also called an *immuno-meme*. Common immunity-conferring memes are "faith", "skepticism" and "tolerance". Some consider *vaccime* to be unnecessary jargon.
- **Vector:** An entity that transports or carries memes. Usage derived from epidemiology.
- **Video:** A popular type of content on the internet. Moving pictures.
- **Viral:** Exhibiting the contagion pattern of a virus.

- **Viral video:** A video with a viral pattern of contagion.
- **Viral license:** A license with conditions that help to promote a viral pattern of contagion - for example by insisting that any kind of derived work carries a copy of the license.
- **Viral marketing:** Marketing that attempts to use viral pattern of contagion. See also: word of mouth.
- **Virus:** A small infectious agent that can only replicate with the assistance of another organism, its host. Viruses live inside their host. They can have lifecycles that involve more than one type of host. See also computer virus.
- **Virus of the mind:** A virus that infects brains. Also the title of a book on the topic by *Stewart Brodie* and an essay by Dawkins.

32 References

- Åm, Onar (1996) **Critique and Defense of Memesis.** *Memesis Symposium.*
- Acerbi, A., Enquist, M., Ghirlanda, S. (2009) **Cultural evolution and individual development of openness and conservatism.** Proc. Nat. Acad. Sci. U S A. 2009 Nov 10;106(45):18931-5.
- Ackley, D. (1994) **A Case for Distributed Lamarckian Evolution.** In Artificial Life III. Addison-Wesley.
- Adar, Eytan and Zhang, Li (2005) **Implicit Structure and the Dynamics of Blogspace.**
- Adar, Eytan and Adamic, Lada A. (2005) **Tracking Information Epidemics in Blogspace.** pp.207-214, 2005 IEEE/WIC/ACM International Conference on Web Intelligence (WI'05).
- Adler, E. (1993) **Cognitive Evolution: A dynamic approach for the study of international relations and their progress CSIA working papers 89-4.** Center for Science & International Affairs, JFK School of Government, Harvard University.
- Alexander, R.D. (1987) **The Biology of Moral Systems.** Aldine de Gruyter.
- Alexander, R.D. (1980) **Darwinism and Human Affairs.** Pitman.
- Alper, Joseph S. and Lange, Robert V. (1981) **Lumsden-Wilson theory of gene culture coevolution.** Proc. NatL Acad. Sci. USA. Vol. 78, No. 6, pp. 3976-3979. Population Biology.
- Allott, Robin (2004) **Evolution and Culture: The Missing Link.**
- Álvarez, Asunción (2004) **Memetics: An Evolutionary Theory of Cultural Transmission.** SORITES - Issue #15 - December 2004. Pp. 24-28.
- Álvarez, Asunción (2005) **Three Memetic Theories of Technology.**
- Alvarez, Mark (2010) **Know Your Meme? From Pseudo-Science to Viral Lulz.**
- Amundson, Ronald (1989) **The trials and tribulations of selectionist explanations.** In K. Hahlweg & C. A. Hooker (Eds.), Issues in evolutionary epistemology (pp. 413-432). Albany: State University of New York Press.
- Anees, Munawar A. (2005) **Memetic Evolution: An Apology for Monocultural Reductionism?** Cultural Evolution | Center for Human Evolution Proceedings of Workshop 4.
- Angel, Wayne M. (2005) **The Theory of Society.**
- Aoki, Kenichi and Feldman, M. W. (1987) **Toward a theory for the evolution of cultural communication: coevolution of signal transmission and reception.** Proc Natl Acad Sci U S A. October; 84(20): 7164–7168.
- Aoki, Kenichi and Feldman, M. W. (1989a) **Pleiotropy and preadaptation in the evolution of human language capacity.**
- Aoki, Kenichi (1989b) **A sexual-selection model for the evolution of imitative learning of song in polygynous birds.**
- Aoki, Kenichi and Feldman, M. W. (1991a) **Recessive heriditary deafness, assortative mating, and persistence of sign language.**
- Aoki, Kenichi (1991b) **Time required for gene frequency change in a deterministic model of gene-culture coevolution, with special reference to the lactose absorption problem.** Theor Popul Biol. Dec;40(3):354-68.
- Aoki, Kenichi and Feldman, M. W. (1994) **Cultural Transmission of a Sign Language When Deafness Is Caused by Recessive Alleles at Two Independent Loci.** Theoretical Population Biology Volume 45, Issue 1, February 1994, Pages 101-120.
- Aoki, Kenichi (2001) **Genes and Culture, Coevolution of.** International Encyclopedia of the Social & Behavioral Sciences. Pages 6084-6087
- Aoki, Kenichi, Feldman, M. W. and Kerr, B. (2001) **Models of sexual selection on a quantitative genetic trait when preference is acquired by sexual imprinting.** Evolution 55: 25–32.
- Aoki, Kenichi (2010) **Evolution of the social-learner-explorer strategy in an environmentally heterogeneous two-island model.** Evolution. 2010 Sep;64(9):2575-86.
- Aoki, Kenichi, Lehmann L. and Feldman, M. W. (2011) **Rates of cultural change and patterns of cultural accumulation in stochastic models of social transmission.**
- Arcaro, Dr Tom (1999) **Of memes, universal Darwinism and humanism.**
- Arcaro, Dr Tom (2000) **A Case for Humanistic Darwinism - The humanistic implications of evolutionary psychology, sociobiology, and memetics and the co-evolution of genes and memes.**
- Armengol, G. (2007) **DANIEL DENNETT, MEMES AND RELIGION - Reasons for the Historical Persistence of Religion.**
- Arnopoulos, P. (1993) **Sociophysics: Cosmos and chaos in nature and culture - A General Theory of Natural and Cultural Systems.** Nova Science Publishers.
- Asendorpf, J. B. (1996) **The nature of personality: a co-evolutionary perspective.** Z Psychol Z Angew Psychol. 1996;204(1):97-115.

- **Asher, Ely** (2006) **Disinfect Your Mind: Defend Yourself with Memetics Against Mass Media, Politicians, Corporate Management, Your Aunt's Advice, and Other Mind Viruses.**
- **Atran, Scott** (1998) **Taxonomic ranks, generic species, and core memes.**
- **Atran, Scott** (2001) **The trouble with memes: Inference versus imitation in cultural creation.** Human Nature 12: 351-381.
- **Atran, Scott** (2004a) **In gods we trust: the evolutionary landscape of religion.**
- **Atran, Scott and Norenzayan, Ara** (2004b) **Religion's evolutionary landscape: Counterintuition, commitment, compassion, communion.** BEHAVIORAL AND BRAIN SCIENCES (2004) 27, 713–770.
- **Auld, H. L., Punzalan, D., Godin, J. G. and Rundle, H. D.** (2009) **Do female fruit flies (Drosophila serrata) copy the mate choice of others?** Behav Processes. 2009 Sep;82(1) :78-80. Epub 2009 Mar 21.
- **Aunger, Robert** (1997) **Exposure Versus Susceptibility In The Epidemiology Of "Everyday" Beliefs.**
- **Aunger, Robert** (1998) **The 'Core Meme' Meme.** Behavioral and Brain Sciences 21 (4) :569-570.
- **Aunger, Robert** (1999a) **A Report On The Conference "Do Memes Account For Culture?" Held At King's College, Cambridge.** Journal of Memetics - Evolutionary Models of Information Transmission.
- **Aunger, Robert** (1999b) **Culture Vultures** *The Sciences* : A review of Blackmore's *The Meme Machine*.
- **Aunger, Robert** (2000a) **Darwinizing culture: The status of memetics as a science** ed. R. Aunger, Oxford & New York: Oxford University Press.
- **Aunger, Robert** (2000b) **Introduction.** In: Darwinizing culture: The status of memetics as a science, ed. R. Aunger, Oxford & New York: Oxford University Press.
- **Aunger, Robert** (2000c) **Conclusion.** In: Darwinizing culture: The status of memetics as a science, ed. R. Aunger, Oxford & New York: Oxford University Press.
- **Aunger, Robert** (2000d) **Phenogenotypes Break Up Under Countervailing Evolutionary Pressures.** Behavioral and Brain Sciences 23 (1):147-147.
- **Aunger, Robert** (2000e) **The life history of culture learning in a face-to-face society.** Ethos 28:1'38.
- **Aunger, Robert** (2002a) **The Electric Meme: A New Theory of How We Think and Communicate.**
- **Aunger, Robert** (2002b) **Exposure versus susceptibility in the epidemiology of 'everyday' beliefs.**
- **Aunger, Robert** (2003) **Cultural Transmission and Diffusion.** In "Encyclopedia of Cognitive Science" Nadel, L. MacMillan (London)
- **Aunger, Robert** (2004) **An agnostic view of memes.**
- **Aunger, Robert** (2005a) **What's the Matter with Memes?**
- **Aunger, Robert** (2006a) **Human communication as niche construction.**
- **Aunger, Robert** (2006b) **Three Roads to Cultural Recurrence.** In "The Epidemiology of Ideas".
- **Aunger, Robert** (2006c) **Culture Evolves Only If There is Cultural Inheritance.** Behavioral and Brain Sciences 29 (4):347-348."
- **Aunger, Robert** (2007) **Memes.**
- **Aunger, Robert** (2009) **Human communication as niche construction.** In Pattern and Process in Cultural Evolution, ed. by Stephen Shennan. University of California Press, pp. 33-44.
- **Aunger, Robert** (2010) **What's special about human technology?** Cambridge Journal of Economics Volume34, Issue1 Pp. 115-123.
- **Aunger, Robert** (2011) **Three Roads to Cultural Replication.** Evolutionary Psychology and Information Systems Research: A New Approach to Studying the Effects of Modern Technologies on Human Behavior, edited by Ned Kock. Springer Verlag.
- **Axelrod, R.** (1984) **The Evolution of Cooperation.** Basic Books.
- **Axelrod, R.** (1986) **An evolutionary approach to norms.** American Political Science Review, Vol. 80, pp 1095-1111.
- **Aytaç, A.** (2005) **'Memes' and 'Memetics' in Industrial Product Design.**

B
- **Bak, P., Tang, C., & Weisenfeld, K.** (1988) **Self-organized criticality.** Phys. Rev. A 38: 364.
- **Baker, Allan J. & Jenkins, Peter F.** (1987) **Founder effect and cultural evolution of songs in an isolated population of chaffinches.** Anim. Behav., 35, 1793-1803.
- **Baldassarre, Gianluca** (2001) **Cultural evolution of "guiding criteria" and behaviour in a population of neural-network agents.** Journal of Memetics - Evolutionary Models of Information Transmission, 4.
- **Baldwin, James M.** (1889) **On selective thinking.** The Psychological Review, 5(1) , 1-24.
- **Baldwin, James M.** (1894) **Imitation: A chapter in the natural history of consciousness.** Mind, 3:25-55.
- **Baldwin, James M.** (1909) **Darwin and the humanities.** Baltimore: Review Publishing Co.
- **Balkin, J. M.** (2003) **Cultural Software: A Theory of Ideology.**
- **Ball, J.** (1984) **Memes as replicators.** In: Ethology and Sociobiology, Vol. 5(3) 145-161.

- Ball, John A. (2007) **Universal Aspects of Biological Evolution?**
- Ball, John A. (1984) **Memes as replicators.** Ethology and Sociobiology Volume 5, Issue 3, 1984, Pages 145-161.
- Barbrook A. C., Howe C. J., Blake N., Robinson (1998) **The phylogeny of the Canterbury Tales.** Nature 394: 839.
- Barbrook, Richard & Lynch, Aaron (1996) **Memes: Self-Replicants or Mysticism?** *Wired* A debate.
- Barbrook, Richard (1997) **Cyberbollocks: trashing memetics and the cyborg cult.**
- Barbrook, Richard (1997) **Never Mind the Cyberbollocks... critique of the memes concept.**
- Barbrook, Richard (1997) **Memesis Critique.**
- Barbrook, Richard (1997) **The Fallacies of Memetics.**
- Barker, Richard H. (2000) **Steering Evolution.** Writer's Showcase Press.
- Barkow, Jerome H. (1989) **The Elastic between Genes and Culture.** Ethology and Sociobiology, vol. 10, no. 1-3, p. 111.
- Basalla, George (1988) **The Evolution of Technology.** Cambridge University Press.
- Bateman, Chris (2005) **The Trouble with Memes.**
- Bateson, Gregory (1979) **Mind and nature: A necessary unity.** New York: Dutton.
- Bateson, Gregory. (1972) **Steps to an Ecology of Mind.** Ballantine Books.
- Battail , Gérard (2008) **An outline of informational genetics.**
- Baum, J.A.C. & Sigh, J.V., eds. (1994) **Evolutionary Dynamics of Organizations.** Oxford University Press.
- Bean, Heather (2003) **Do Memes Hold The Leash On Genes?** Principles of Evolution Term Paper.
- Beer, Francis A. (1997) **A Review of: Evolutionary Paradigms in the Social Sciences** *JOM:EMIT*: A special issue of *International Studies Quarterly.* Journal of Memetics - Evolutionary Models of Information Transmission, 1.
- Beer, Francis A. (1999) **Memetic Meanings - a commentary on Rose's paper: Controversies in Meme Theory** Journal of Memetics - Evolutionary Models of Information Transmission, 3.
- Begun, D.J. & Aquadro, C.F. (1992) **Levels of naturally occurring DNA polymorphism correlate with recombination rates in D. melanogaster.** Nature, 356, p. 519-520.
- Bell, Adrian V., Richerson, Peter J. and McElreath, Richard (2009) **Culture rather than genes provides greater scope for the evolution of large-scale human prosociality.** Proceedings of the National Academy of Sciences 106 (42): 17671-17674.
- Benitez-Bribiesca, L (2001) **Memetics: a dangerous idea.** Interciencia.
- Benedict, R. (1934) **Patterns of Culture.** Houghton-Mifflin, Boston, MA.
- Benscoter, Diane (2009) **How Cults Rewire The Brain**
- Benzon, William L. & Hays, D. G. (1990) **The evolution of cognition.** Journal of Social and Biological Structures, 13(4): 297-320.
- Benzon, William L. (1996) **Culture as an Evolutionary Arena.** In Journal of Social and Evolutionary Systems 19(4): 321-362, 1996.
- Benzon, William L. (2002) **Colorless Green Homunculi.** A review of The Electric Meme: A New Theory of How We Think by Robert Aunger.
- Benzon, William L. (2010) **Cultural Evolution: A Vehicle for Cooperative Interaction Between the Sciences and the Humanities.**
- Benzon, William L. (2010) **Cultural Evolution 1: How "Thick" is Culture?**
- Benzon, William L. (2010) **Cultural Evolution 2: A Phenomenological Gut Check on Gene-Culture Coevolution.**
- Benzon, William L. (2010) **Cultural Evolution 3: Performances and Memes.**
- Benzon, William L. (2010) **Cultural Evolution 4: Rhythm changes 1.**
- Benzon, William L. (2010) **Cultural Evolution 5: Rhythm changes 2.**
- Benzon, William L. (2010) **Cultural Evolution 6: The Problem of Design.**
- Benzon, William L. (2010) **Cultural Evolution 7: Where Are We At?**
- Benzon, William L. (2010) **Cultural Evolution 8: Language Games 1, Speech.**
- Benzon, William L. (2010) **Cultural Evolution 8: Language Games 1, Speech.**
- Benzon, William L. (2010) **Cultural Evolution 8A: Addendum on Language as Game.**
- Benzon, William L. (2010) **Cultural Evolution 8A: Addendum on Language as Game.**
- Benzon, William L. (2010) **Cultural Evolution 9: Language Games 2, Story Telling.**
- Benzon, William L. (2010) **Where are memes?**
- Benzon, William L. (2010) **Memetic Sophistry.**
- Benzon, William L. (2010) **One Candle, a Thousand Points of Light: The Xanadu Meme.**
- Bernstein, Michael S., Monroy-Hernandez, Andres, Harry, Drew Andre, Paul, Panovich, Katrina and Vargas, Greg (2011) **4chan and /b/: An Analysis of Anonymity and Ephemerality in a Large Online Community.**

- **Best, Michael L.** (1997) **Models for Interacting Populations of Memes: Competition and Niche Behavior.** Journal of Memetics - Evolutionary Models of Information Transmission, 1.
- **Best, Michael L.** (1998) **A Letter on: Memes on memes - A critique of memetic models.** Journal of Memetics - Evolutionary Models of Information Transmission, 2.
- **Best, Michael L.** (1998) **Computational Culture and Population Memetics.** Symposium on Memetics: Evolutionary Models of Information Transmission, 15th International Congress on Cybernetics, Namur (Belgium), August 24-28.
- **Best, Michael L. and Pocklington, R.** (1999a) **Meaning as use: Transmission fidelity and evolution in NetNews.** Journal of Theoretical Biology 196: 389-395.
- **Best, Michael L.** (1999b) **How Culture Can Guide Evolution: An Inquiry intoGene/Meme Enhancement and Opposition.**
- **Best, Michael L.** (2007) **Computational Memetics.**
- **Bicchieri, C.** (1997) **Learning to cooperate.** In C. Bicchieri, (Ed.), The Dynamics of Norms, 17-46, Cambridge.
- **Bisin, Alberto and Verdier, Thierry** (2001) **The Economics of Cultural Transmission and the Dynamics of Preferences.** Journal of Economic Theory 97, 298-319.
- **Bisin, Alberto and Verdier, Thierry** (2005) **Cultural Transmission.**
- **Bjarneskans, Grønnevik, Henrik B. and Sandberg, Anders** (2006) **The Lifecycle of Memes.**
- **Black, Richard** (2008) **Wild dolphins tail-walk on water.**
- **Blackmore, Susan, J.** (1996) **Memes, Minds and Selves.**
- **Blackmore, Susan, J.** (1997a) **Speaking Volumes.** Times Higher Education Supplement (on Dennett's Darwin's Dangerous Idea) 3 September 1997.
- **Blackmore, Susan, J.** (1997b) **The Power of the Meme Meme.**
- **Blackmore, Susan, J.** (1998a) **Imitation and the definition of a meme.** Journal of Memetics - Evolutionary Models of Information Transmission, 2.
- **Blackmore, Susan, J.** (1998b) **A day in my life with thoughts about memes.** Don's Diary Times Higher Education Supplement 22.5.98.
- **Blackmore, Susan, J.** (1999a) **The Meme Machine.** Oxford: Oxford University Press.
- **Blackmore, Susan, J.** (1999b) **The forget meme not theory.** Times Higher Education Supplement, 26 February.
- **Blackmore, Susan, J.** (1999c) **Waking From the Meme Dream.**
- **Blackmore, Susan, J.** (1999d) **Meme machines and consciousness** , Journal of Intelligent Systems, 9, 355-376.
- **Blackmore, Susan, J.** (1999e) **Meme, myself, I.** New Scientist, 13 March, 40-44.
- **Blackmore, Susan, J.** (1999f) **The Y2K meme.** The Psychologist, 12, No 12, 599.
- **Blackmore, Susan, J.** (1999g) **Don's Delight in The Guardian (on Dawkins's The Selfish Gene)** 13 April 1999. Also in the Guardian Archives.
- **Blackmore, Susan, J.** (1999h) **Can the Memes Get Off the Leash?** Presented at Do Memes Account for Culture ? King's College Research Centre Conference, King's College, Cambridge.
- **Blackmore, Susan, J.** (2000a) **The meme's eye view.** In: Darwinizing culture: The status of memetics as a science, ed. R. Aunger, Oxford & New York: Oxford University Press.
- **Blackmore, Susan, J.** (2000b) **Memes and the Malign user illusion.** Association for the Scientific Study of Consciousness, conference, Brussels, July.
- **Blackmore, Susan, J.** (2000c) **The power of memes.** Scientific American, 283:4, 52-61. With three reply articles. Also response to letters to the editor, Scientific American, 284:2, 10 [Partial version on Sue Blackmore's site].
- **Blackmore, Susan, J.** (2000d) **Do memes make sense? Yes.** Free Inquiry, Summer 2000, 42-44 (with commentary "No" by Michael Bradie).
- **Blackmore, Susan, J., Bull, L., Holland,O.** (2000e) **On meme-gene coevolution.** Artificial Life, 6, 227-235.
- **Blackmore, Susan, J.** (2000f) **Are we slaves of the memes?** Fortean Unconvention, London April 29-30.
- **Blackmore, Susan, J.** (2000h) **Dismantling the selfplex: Memes machines and the nature of consciousness.** "Toward a Science of Consciousness 4". Tucson, Arizona, April 10-15.
- **Blackmore, Susan, J.** (2001a) **Meme-Gene Coevolution.**
- **Blackmore, Susan, J.** (2001b) **Evolution and Memes: The human brain as a selective imitation device.** Cybernetics and Systems: An International Journal, 32 :225Â± 255, 2001.
- **Blackmore, Susan, J.** (2001c) **Viruses of the Mind, Meme-Gene Coevolution, Self and Consciousness, Controversies in Memetics.**
- **Blackmore, Susan, J.** (2002a) **The Evolution of Meme Machines.**
- **Blackmore, Susan, J.** (2002b) **Meditation as meme weeding.**
- **Blackmore, Susan, J.** (2002c) **Meme machines and consciousness.** In: Rita Carter, Consciousness,

Weidenfeld and Nicolson 2002 pp 241-3.

- **Blackmore, Susan, J.** (2002d) **Memes as Good Science.** In Michael Shermer, Skeptic Encyclopedia of Pseudoscience. p.652
- **Blackmore, Susan, J.** (2003) **Consciousness in Meme Machines.** Journal of Consciousness Studies, 10, 4-5, 19-30.
- **Blackmore, Susan, J.** (2005a) **Implications for memetics.** Commentary on Steels, L and Belpaeme, T. Coordinating perceptually grounded categories through language: A case study for colour. Behavioral and Brain Sciences, 28, 490.
- **Blackmore, Susan, J.** (2005b) **Implications for memetics.**
- **Blackmore, Susan, J.** (2005c) **Even deeper misunderstandings of memes: Commentary on Gil-White, In Perspectives on Imitation: From Mirror Neurons to Memes.** Ed. S. Hurley and N. Chater, MIT Press Vol 2 406-9.
- **Blackmore, Susan, J.** (2005d) **Evidence for memetic drive?: Commentary on Iacoboni, In Perspectives on Imitation: From Mirror Neurons to Memes.** Ed. S. Hurley and N. Chater, MIT Press Vol 2 203-205.
- **Blackmore, Susan, J.** (2005e) **A possible confusion between mimetic and memetic: Commentary on Gil-White, In Perspectives on Imitation: From Mirror Neurons to Memes.** Ed. S. Hurley and N. Chater, MIT Press Vol 2 396-398.
- **Blackmore, Susan, J.** (2005f) **Can memes meet the challenge?: Commentary on Gil-White, In Perspectives on Imitation: From Mirror Neurons to Memes.** Ed. S. Hurley and N. Chater, MIT Press Vol 2 409-11.
- **Blackmore, Susan, J.** (2006a) **Why we need memetics.**
- **Blackmore, Susan, J.** (2006b) **Natural selection applies to everything.** New Humanist, May, June 2006, 23-24.
- **Blackmore, Susan, J.** (2006c) **Memes, Creativity and Consciousness.** Aesthetica, May, June, July 2006 Issue 13, 50.
- **Blackmore, Susan, J.** (2006d) **Darwin and Humanity : Can we rid the mind of God?**
- **Blackmore, Susan, J.** (2006e) **Memes, creativity and consciousness.** Aesthetica Magazine May, June, July 2006 Issue 13, 50.
- **Blackmore, Susan, J.** (2006f) **Memetics by another name?** A review of Not by Genes Alone: How Culture Transformed Human Evolution.
- **Blackmore, Susan, J.** (2006g) **Dawkins's Meme: Why is there still no science of memetics?**
- **Blackmore, Susan, J.** (2006h) **Darwin and Humanity: Can we rid the mind of God?** Oxford Union. February
- **Blackmore, Susan, J.** (2006i) **Meme Wars Part 2**
- **Blackmore, Susan, J.** (2007a) **Imitation Makes Us Human.**
- **Blackmore, Susan, J.** (2007b) **Those dreaded memes: The advantage of memetics over 'symbolic inheritance'.**
- **Blackmore, Susan, J.** (2007c) **The God Meme - Why Faith is So Infectious.**
- **Blackmore, Susan, J.** (2007d) **Memes misunderstood - Comments on Liu (2006).**
- **Blackmore, Susan, J.** (2007e) **Darwin's Meme: On the origin of culture by means of natural selection.** Monday 12 February 2007, Darwin Lecture Theatre, University of Central Lancashire.
- **Blackmore, Susan, J.** (2007f) **Did musical Memes change our minds?.** Music and Evolutionary Thought Conference, Durham, 23.06.07.
- **Blackmore, Susan, J.** (2007g) **Memes, minds and imagination.** In Imaginative Minds (Proceedings of the British Acadamy) Ed by Ilona Roth. Oxford University Press.
- **Blackmore, Susan, J.** (2008a) **Dangerous Memes; or what the Pandorans let loose.** In Cosmos and Culture: Cultural Evolution in a Cosmic Context, edited by Steven Dick and Mark Lupisella.
- **Blackmore, Susan, J.** (2008b) **Memes shape brains shape memes.**
- **Blackmore, Susan, J.** (2008c) **Genes, memes, and temes - Don't think intelligence - think replicators!.**
- **Blackmore, Susan, J.** (2008d) **The trouble with the trouble with memetics.** Skeptical Inquirer, Volume 32, No.2, March/April, pp 65.
- **Blackmore, Susan, J.** (2009a) **Artificial, Self-Replicating Meme Machines.**
- **Blackmore, Susan, J.** (2009b) **Dangerous Memes; or, What the Pandorans Let Loose.**
- **Blackmore, Susan, J.** (2009c) **The third replicator is among us.** The New Scientist. Volume 203, Issue 2719, 29 July 2009, Pages 36-39.
- **Blackmore, Susan, J.** (2010) **Memetics Does Provide a Useful Way of Understanding Cultural Evolution.** In Contemporary Debates in Philosophy of Biology, Ed. Francisco Ayala and Robert Arp, Chichester, Wiley-Blackwell, 255-72.
- **Blackmore, Susan, J.** (2010) **Temes: An Emerging Third Replicator.**

- Blackmore, Susan, J. (2010) **The Third Replicator.** New York Times.
- Blackmore, Susan, J. (2010) **Copy That: A response.** New York Times.
- Blissett, Luther (1998) **On the Misdefinition of Memetics: A letter to the *Journal of Memetics* discussion list.** Disumbrationist League Bulletin.
- Blok, H. J. (2002) **Conditions for memetic driving.**
- Bloch, Maurice (2000) **A well-disposed anthropologist's problems with memes.** In: Darwinizing culture: The status of memetics as a science, ed. R. Aunger, Oxford & New York: Oxford University Press.
- Bloch, Maurice (2005) **Essays on Cultural Transmission.** (London School of Economics Monographs on Social Anthropology)
- Bloom, Howard (1995) **The Lucifer Principle: A Scientific Expedition into the Forces of History.** Atlantic Monthly Press.
- Bloom, Howard (2005) **Instant Evolution: The Influence of the City on Human Genes – A Speculative Case.** Cultural Evolution | Center for Human Evolution Proceedings of Workshop 4.
- Blum, Harold Francis (1963) **On the origin and evolution of human culture.** American Scientist, 51, 32-47.
- Blum, Harold Francis (1967) **Humanity in the perspective of Time.** Annals of the New York Academy of Sciences. Volume 138, Interdisciplinary Perspectives of Time pages 489–503.
- Blum, Harold Francis (1978) **Uncertainty in Interplay of Biological and Cultural Evolution: Man's View of Himself.** The Quarterly Review of Biology. Vol. 53, No. 1 (Mar., 1978), pp. 29-40.
- Blume, Larry (2008) **Natural Selection in Markets.**
- Blute, Marion (1987) **Biologists on Sociocultural Evolution: A Critical Analysis.** Sociological Theory 5 (2):185-193.
- Blute, Marion (2002) **The Evolutionary Ecology Of Science.** Journal of Memetics - Evolutionary Models of Information Transmission, 7.
- Blute, Marion (2005) **Memetics and evolutionary social science.** Journal of Memetics - Evolutionary Models of Information Transmission, 6.
- Blute, Marion (2006) **Gene-Culture Coevolutionary Games** Social Forces - Volume 85, Number 1, September 2006, pp. 151-166
- Blute, Marion (2007) **The Role of Memes in Cultural Evolution: memes if necessary, but not necessarily memes** [PDF].
- Blute, Marion (2010) **Darwinian Sociocultural Evolution: Solutions to Dilemmas in Cultural and Social Theory**
- Blutner, Reinhard (2003) **Save memetics!**
- Boden, M. A. (1991) **The Creative Mind: Myths and Mechanisms.** Cambridge University Press.
- Boehm, C. (1996) **Emergency Decisions, Cultural-Selection Mechanics, and Group Selection.** Current Anthropology 37:763'793.
- Bohannan, Paul. (1980) **The Gene Pool and the Meme Pool.** Science 80, November p. 25, 28.
- Bollen, Johan, Heylighen, Francis, van Rooy, Dirk (1998) **Improving Memetic Evolution in Hypertext and the WWW.** Symposium on Memetics: Evolutionary Models of Information Transmission, 15th International Congress on Cybernetics, Namur (Belgium), August 24-28.
- Bonner, John Tyler (1980) **The Evolution of Culture in Animals.** Princeton University Press.
- Boone, James L. and Eric Alden Smith (1998) **Is It Evolution Yet? A Critique of Evolutionary Archaeology.** Current Anthropology. Vol. 39, No. S1, Special Issue The Neanderthal Problem and the Evolution of Human Behavior (June 1998), pp. S141-S174.
- Botz-Bornstein, Thorsten (2008) **Culture, Nature, Memes.** Cambridge Scholars Publishing.
- Botz-Bornstein, Thorsten (2008) **Can Memes Play Games? Memetics and the Problem of Space.**
- Bouissac, Paul (...) **Construction Of Ignorance, Evolution Of Knowledge.**
- Bouissac, Paul (1984) **Editorial: Memes Matter**
- Bouissac, Paul (1993) **Why Do Memes Die?**
- Bouissac, Paul (2001) **On signs, memes and MEMS.** Sign Systems Studies, vol. 29: 2 (624-646).
- Bouissac, Paul (2007) **The Form of Memes: Twelve Remarks on Memetics**
- Boulding, K. E. (1978) **Ecodynamics: A New Theory of Societal Evolution.** Sage Publications.
- Boulding, K.E. (1981) **Evolutionary Economics.** Sage Publications, Inc.
- Bowers, K. S., Regehr, G., Balthazard, C. & Parker, K. (1990) **Intuition in the context of discovery.** Cognitive Psychology, 22:72-110.
- Boyd, Gary (1998) **Should memes and viral-information be considered synonymous terms?** Symposium on Memetics: Evolutionary Models of Information Transmission, 15th International Congress on Cybernetics, Namur (Belgium), August 24-28.
- Boyd, Gary (2001) **The Human Agency Of Meme Machines. An extended review of Blackmore, Susan (1999) The Meme Machine.** Journal of Memetics - Evolutionary Models of Information Transmission, 5.

- **Boyd, Andrew** (2002) **Truth Is a Virus: Meme Warfare and the Billionaires for Bush (or Gore).** In The Cultural Resistance Reader, edited by Stephen Duncombe. New York: Verso.
- **Boyd, Robert and Richerson, Peter J.** (2008a) **Migration: An Engine for Social Improvement.** Nature, 456: 18.
- **Boyd, Robert and Silk, Joan B.** (2008b) **How Humans Evolved** W. W. Norton & Company; Fifth Edition edition.
- **Boyd, Robert and Richerson, Peter J.** (2010) **Transmission coupling mechanisms: cultural group selection.** Philosophical Transactions of the Royal Society (B), 365, 3787-3795.
- **Boyd, Robert** (2011) **The cultural niche: Why social learning is essential for human adaptation.** Proceedings of the National Academy of Sciences (USA) Early Edition, June 22.
- **Boyer, Pascal** (1998) **Cognitive tracks of cultural inheritance: How evolved intuitive ontology governs cultural transmission.** American Anthropologist 100: 876-889
- **Boyer, Pascal** (2002) **Religion explained: the human instincts that fashion gods, spirits and ancestors.**
- **Bradie, Michael.** (1986) **Assessing evolutionary epistemology.** Biology and Philosophy, 1(4), 401-459.
- **Bradie, Michael.** (2000) **Do memes make sense? No.** Free Inquiry, Summer 2000.
- **Bradie, Michael.** (2003) **The 'new science of memetics': The case against.** Think, 2: 27-30.
- **Bradie, Michael and Harms, William** (2008) **Evolutionary Epistemology** Stanford Encyclopedia of Philosophy
- **Brandon, R.N.** (1988) **The levels of selection: A hierarchy of interactors.** In (H.C. Plotkin, ed.) The Role of Behavior in Evolution. MIT Press.
- **Bravo, Giangiacomo** (2007) **Review of Not by Genes Alone: How Culture Transformed Human Evolution by Richerson, Peter J. and Boyd, Robert.**
- **Bresson C.** (1987) **The evolutionary paradigm and the economics of technological change.** Journal of Economical Issues, Vol. XXI no. 2, June, 751-762.
- **Bresin, Roberto** (1997) **Report on "Ars Electronica 96: Memesis - The future of evolution"**
- **Briggs, William M.** (2011) **Why Memes Are Stupid: The Short Version**
- **Brin, David** (1993) **The New Meme** Kaleidospace.
- **Brisson, D.** (1993) **The directed mutation controversy in an evolutionary context.** Crit Rev Microbiol. 2003;29(1):25-35.
- **Brodie, Edmund D.** (2004) **Caution: Niche Construction Ahead.**
- **Brodie, R.** (1996a) **Virus of the Mind: The New Science of the Meme.** Integral Press.
- **Brodie, Richard** (1996b) **Crisis of the Mind.** The introduction to Virus of the Mind.
- **Brown, Andrew** (1997) **The Meme Hunter.** Salon - A discussion of Blackmore's research into memetics.
- **Brown, Andrew** (1999) **The Darwin wars: the scientific battle for the soul of man.**
- **Brown, Andrew** (2009) **Serious objections to memes.**
- **Brown, J. C. & Greenhood, W.** (1983) **Paternity, Jokes and Song: A Possible Evolutionary Scenario for the Origin of Language and Mind.** In: Cultural Futures Research, 8, 2, Winter.
- **Bruggemann, Haley** (2005) **Memes and Individuality.**
- **Brunvand, Jan Harold** (2002) **Encyclopedia of Urban Legends.**
- **Bruynseels, Koen, Vos, Johan and Vandekerckhove, Pieter** (1998) **Noosphere: an On-line Implementation of a Memetic Evolution.** Symposium on Memetics: Evolutionary Models of Information Transmission, 15th International Congress on Cybernetics, Namur (Belgium), August 24-28.
- **Bryant, J.M.** (2004) **An evolutionary social science? A skeptic's brief, theoretical and substantive.** Philosophy of the Social Sciences 34 (4), 451-92.
- **Bryant, Levi R.** (2009) **Invasion of the Body Snatchers.**
- **Bryson, Joanna** (2008) **Embodiment versus memetics.**
- **Bryne, R. and A. Whitten (eds.)** (1988) **Machiavellian intelligence: social expertise and the evolution of the intellect in monkeys, apes, and humans.** Oxford University Press, Oxford.
- **Budani, Donna** (...) **Boas and Kroeber.**
- **Buenstorf, Guido** (2005) **How Useful Is Universal Darwinism as a Framework to Study Competition and Industrial Evolution?** Papers on Economics and Evolution.
- **Bulbulia, J.** (2008) **Meme infection or religious Niche construction? An adaptationist alternative to the cultural Maladaptationist hypothesis.**
- **Bullinaria, John A.** (2007) **Memes in Artificial Life Simulations of Life History Evolution.**
- **Bura, S.** (1994) **MINIMEME: Of Life and Death in the Noosphere.** In D. Cliff, P. Husbands, J. A. Meyer & S. Wilson (eds.) From Animls to Animats 3. MIT Press, pp. 479-486.
- **Butts, Carter T.and Hilgeman, Christin** (2003) **Inferring Potential Memetic Structure from Cross-Sectional Data: An Application to American Religious Beliefs.** Journal of Memetics - Evolutionary Models of Information Transmission, 7.
- **Bunk, Steve** (2005) **Intelligent design and memes.**

C

- Cairns-Smith, A. G. (1982) **Genetic takeover - and the mineral origins of life.** Cambridge University Press.
- Caldwell, Christine A. and Whiten, A. (2002) **Evolutionary perspectives on imitation: Is a comparative psychology of social learning possible?** Animal Cognition, 5, 193-208.
- Caldwell, Christine A. and Whiten, A. (2003) **Scrounging facilitates social learning in common marmosets, Callithrix jacchus.** Animal Behaviour, 64, 1085-1092.
- Caldwell, Christine A. and Whiten, A. (2004) **Testing for social learning and imitation in common marmosets, Callithrix jacchus, using an 'artificial fruit'.** Animal Cognition, 7, 77-85.
- Caldwell, Christine A. and Whiten, A. (2006) **Social learning in monkeys and apes: Cultural animals?** In C. J. Campbell, A. Fuentes, K. C. MacKinnon, M. Panger & S. Bearder. Primates in Perspective. Oxford: Oxford University Press.
- Caldwell, Christine A. (2008a) **Convergent cultural evolution may explain linguistic universals (commentary on Christiansen & Chater, Language as shaped by the brain).** Behavioral and Brain Sciences, 31, 515-516.
- Caldwell, Christine A. and Millen Ailsa E. (2008b) **Experimental models for testing hypotheses about cumulative cultural evolution.** Evolution and Human Behavior, Vol 29(3) , May 2008, 165-171. doi.
- Caldwell, Christine A. and Millen Ailsa E. (2008c) **Studying cumulative cultural evolution in the laboratory.** Philosophical Transactions of the Royal Society B, 363, 3529'3539.
- Caldwell, Christine A. and Millen Ailsa E. (2009a) **Social learning mechanisms and cumulative cultural evolution. Is imitation necessary?** Psychological Science Dec 1; 20(12):1478-83.
- Caldwell, Christine A. (2009b) **Experimental approaches to the study of culture in primates.** In L. S. Roska-Hardy & E. M. Neumann-Held (Eds.), Learning from Animals? Examining the Nature of Human Uniqueness (pp 173-187). Hove, UK: Psychology Press.
- Caldwell, Christine A. and Millen Ailsa E. (2010) **Human cumulative culture in the laboratory: effects of (micro) population size.** Learning and Behavior, 38, 310-318.
- Caldwell, Christine A. and Whiten, A. (2011) **Social learning in monkeys and apes: cultural animals?** In C. J. Campbell, A. Fuentes, K. C. MacKinnon, S. K. Bearder & R. M. Stumpf (Eds.). Primates in Perspective, 2nd edition (pp652-662). Oxford: Oxford University Press.
- Calvin, William H. (1987) **The brain as a Darwin machine.** Nature, 330, 33-34.
- Calvin, William H. (1988a) **Book review of Gerald M. Edelman's book, Neural Darwinism.** Science 240:1802-1803.
- Calvin, William H. (1998b) **Competing for Consciousness: A Darwinian Mechanism at an Appropriate Level of Explanation.** Journal of Consciousness Studies 5(4) 389-404.
- Calvin, William H. (1996a) **The Cerebral Code: Thinking a Thought in the Mosaics of the Mind.** MIT Press.
- Calvin, William H. (1996b) **How Brains Think: Evolving Intelligence, Then and Now.** Basic Books.
- Calvin, William H. (1997) **The Six Essentials? Minimal Requirements for the Darwinian Bootstrapping of Quality** Journal of Memetics - Evolutionary Models of Information Transmission, 1.
- Calvin, William H. (2001a) **The Cerebral Symphony: Seashore Reflections on the Structure of Consciousness.** iUniverse.
- Calvin, William H. (2001b) **Inside the Brain: An Enthralling Account of the Structure and Workings of the Human Brain.**
- Campbell, Donald T. (1956) **Perception as substitute trial and error.** Psychological Review, 63(5), 331-342.
- Campbell, Donald T. (1958) **Systematic error on the part of human links in communication systems.** Inform. Control 1:334'369.
- Campbell, Donald T. (1965) **Variation and selective retention in socio-cultural evolution.** In (H.R. Barringer, G.I. Blanksten, & R.W. Mack, eds.) Social Change in Developing Areas, a Reinterpretation of Evolutionary Theory. Schenkman Publishing Co.
- Campbell, Donald T. (1974a) **Evolutionary epistemology.** In Evolutionary epistemology, rationality, and the sociology of knowledge by Gerard Radnitzky, William Warren Bartley, Karl Raimund Popper
- Campbell, Donald T. (1974b) **Unjustified variation and selective retention in scientific discovery.** In F J. Ayala & T. Dobzhansky (Eds.), Studies in the philosophy of biology (pp. 139-161). London: Macmillan.
- Campbell, Donald T. (1977) **Comment on Robert J. Richard's "The natural selection model of conceptual evolution."** Philosophy of Science, 44, 502-507.
- Campbell, Donald T. (1983) **The two distinct routes beyond kin selection to ultrasociality: Implications for the Humanities and Social Sciences.** In: The Nature of Prosocial Development: Theories and Strategies D. Bridgeman (ed.), pp. 11-39, Academic Press, New York.
- Campbell, Donald T. (1987) **Neurological embodiments of belief and the gap in the fit of phenomena to noumena.** In A. Shimony & D. Nails (Eds.), Naturalistic epistemology: A symposium of

two decades (pp. 165-192). Dordrecht: Reidel.

• **Campbell, Donald T.** (1988) **A general 'selection theory' as implemented in biological evolution and in social belief-transmission-with-modification in science [A commentary on Hull].** Biology and Philosophy, 3, 171-177.
• **Campbell, Donald T., Lanham, M.D.** (1990) **Epistemological roles for selection theory.** In N. Rescher (Ed.), Evolution, cognition, and realism: Studies in evolutionary epistemology (pp. 1-19). University Press of America.
• **Campbell, Robert L.** (2000) **Selection Pressures Are Mounting.** A review of *The Meme Machine*.
• **Cardoso, G. C.** (2010) **Directional cultural change by modification and replacement of memes.** Evolution. 2011 Jan; 65(1):295-300. doi: 10.1111/j.1558-5646.2010.01102.x. Sep 24.
• **Carneiro, Robert L.** (2003) **Evolutionism In Cultural Anthropology: A Critical History.** Westview Press.
• **Carney, D. Philip and Williams, Russell** (1997) **The memetics of firms, entrepreneurship and the new body politic: the memetics of the marketplace.** Management Decision, Vol. 35 Iss: 6, pp.447 - 451.
• **Carroll, Joseph** (2004) **Literary Darwinism: Evolution, Human Nature, and Literature.** Routledge.
• **Carroll, Joseph** (2011) **Reading Human Nature: Literary Darwinism in Theory and Practice.**
• **Carter, Brandon** (2010) **Hominid evolution: genetics versus memetics.**
• **Castelfranchi, Cristiano** (2001) **Towards a Cognitive Memetics: Socio-Cognitive Mechanisms for Memes Selection and Spreading** Journal of Memetics - Evolutionary Models of Information Transmission, 5.
• **Castro, L., Toro, M.A.** (2002) **Cultural Transmission and the Capacity to Approve or Disapprove of Offspring's Behaviour.** Journal of Memetics - Evolutionary Models of Information Transmission, 6.
• **Castro, L., Toro, M.A.** (2004) **The evolution of culture: from primate social learning to human culture.** Proc Natl Acad Sci U S A. 2004 Jul 6;101(27):10235-40. Jun 24.
• **Caton, Hiram** (2000) **Review of The Meme Machine.** Politics and the Life Sciences, September edition.
• **Cavalli-Sforza, L.L.** (1971) **Similarities and dissimilarities of sociocultural and biological evolution.** In: Mathematics in the Archaeological and Historical Science.
• **Cavalli-Sforza, L.L. and Feldman, M.W.** (1973) **Models for cultural inheritance. I. Group mean and within group variation.** Theoret. Pop. Biol. 4: 42-55.
• **Cavalli-Sforza, L. L. & Feldman, M. W.** (1973) **Cultural versus biological inheritance: phenotypic transmission from parents to children.** Human Genetics 25: 618-637.
• **Cavalli-Sforza, L. L. & Feldman, M. W.** (1981) **Cultural transmission and evolution: A quantitative approach.** Princeton University Press. [googlebooks]
• **Cavalli-Sforza, L. L., Feldman, M. W., Kh Chen, and Dornbusch, S. M.** (1982) **Theory and observation in cultural transmission.** Science 218:19'27.
• **Changeux, J.P., Courrège, P., Danchin, A.** (1973) **A theory of the epigenesis of neuronal networks by selective stabilization of synapses.** Proc Natl Acad Sci U S A. 1973 Oct;70(10) :2974-8.
• **Chatterton, Ben** (1998) **The Need for a New Social Science.** Memetics, Marketing, and Sociology can only get us so far.
• **Chattoe, Edmund** (1998) **Just How (Un)realistic are Evolutionary Algorithms as Representations of Social Processes?** *JASSS*.
• **Chattoe, Edmund** (1998) **Virtual Urban Legends: Investigating the Ecology of the World Wide Web** *IRISS Conference.*
• **Chazan, Michael** (2007) **Is a Handaxe a Meme.** Anthropology, University of Toronto.
• **Chen, K. H., Cavalli-Sforza, L. L. and Feldman, M. W.** (1982) **A study of cultural transmission in Taiwan.** Human Ecology 10(3): 375-392.
• **Chick, Garry** (1997) **Themes, Memes, and Other Schemes: What are the Units of Culture?** Presented at the annual meeting of the Society for Cross-Cultural Research, San Antonio, TX, February 19-23.
• **Chick, Garry** (1999) **The Units of Culture.**
• **Chick, Garry** (2008) **What's in a Meme? The Development of the Meme as a Unit of Culture.**
• **Chielens, Klaas** (2003) **The Viral Aspects of Language: A Quantitative Research of Memetic Selection Criteria.** Unpublished master's thesis, Vrije Universiteit Brussel, Brussels, Belgium.
• **Chielens, Klaas** (2007) **The Status of Memetics as a Science An overview of Memetic Theory and its difficulties.**
• **Choi, Charles Q.** (2007) **Parasites Evolve from Bad to Good.**
• **Christiansen, Morten H.** (2008) **Is Memetics a Science? Lessons from Language Evolution - Department of Psychology, Cornell University [PDF].**
• **Chudek, M., Henrich J.** (2011) **Culture-gene coevolution, norm-psychology and the emergence of human prosociality.** Trends Cogn Sci. 2011 Apr 7.
• **Church, George** (2011) **Non-Inherent Inheritance.** The Edge.
• **Claidière, Nicolas and Sperber, Dan** (2006) **Why Modeling Cultural Evolution Is Still Such a**

Challenge. Journal of Cognition and Culture 7: 89-111.

- **Claidière, Nicolas and Sperber, Dan** (2007) **Defining and explaining culture (comments on Richerson and Boyd, Not by genes alone).** Biology and Philosophy 2008 23(2): 283-292.
- **Claidière, Nicolas and Sperber, Dan** (2007) **The role of attraction in cultural evolution.** Biological Theory 1(1): 20-22.
- **Claidière, Nicolas and Sperber, Dan** (2010) **Imitation explains the propagation, not the stability of animal culture.** Proceedings of the Royal Society B: Biological Sciences 277(1681) : 651-659.
- **Claidière, Nicolas and Sperber, Dan** (2010) **The natural selection of fidelity in social learning.** Communicative and Integrative Biology, 3:4, 1-2.
- **Clark, Stephen R. L.** (1993) **Minds, Memes, and Rhetoric.** Inquiry 36 (1-2):3-16.
- **Clark, Stephen R. L.** (1996) **Minds, Memes, and Multiples.** Philosophy, Psychiatry, and Psychology 3 (1):21-28.
- **Clark, Taylor** (2008) **The 8½ Laws of Rumor Spread - Some rumors grind to a halt, while others circle the world. Why some ideas spread and others die.**
- **Clarks, Theo** (2000) **Do the ends justify the memes? A review of The Meme Machine.** AUSTRALIAN RATIONALIST - Number 56 - p.42-44.
- **Clewley, Robert** (1998a) **Emergence without magic: the role of memetics in multi-scale models of evolution and behaviour.** Symposium on Memetics: Evolutionary Models of Information Transmission, 15th International Congress on Cybernetics, Namur (Belgium), August 24-28.
- **Clewley, Robert** (1998b) **Reinterpreting Memetics in a Multi-Level View of Evolution and Behaviour - Part 1**
- **Clewley, Robert** (1998c) **Reinterpreting Memetics in a Multi-Level View of Evolution and Behaviour - Part 2**
- **Clewley, Robert** (1999) **Conceptual Problems in Memetics in a Multi-Level View of Evolution and Behaviour**
- **Cloak, F. T., Jr.** (1966) **Cultural microevolution.** Research Previews 13: (2) p. 7-10. Also presented at the November, 1966 Annual Meeting of the American Anthropological Association.
- **Cloak, F. T., Jr.** (1967) **A Natural Order of Cultural Adoption and Loss in Trinidad** (Working Papers in Methodology No. 1) Institute for Research in Social Science, University of North Carolina, Chapel Hill.
- **Cloak, F. T., Jr.** (1968a) **Is a cultural ethology possible?** Research Previews 13: (2) p. 37-47.
- **Cloak, F. T., Jr.** (1968b) **Cultural Darwinism: Natural Selection of the Spoked Wood Wheel.** Multi-media presentation to the Annual Meeting of the American Anthropological Association, Seattle.
- **Cloak, F. T., Jr.** (1973) **Elementary self-replicating instructions and their works: Toward a radical reconstruction of general anthropology through a general theory of natural selection.** Communication to the Ninth International Congress of Anthropological and Ethnological Sciences, Chicago.
- **Cloak, F. T., Jr.** (1974) **Cultural ethology experiment number one.** Multi-media presentation at 73d annual meeting of American Anthropological Assn. Available as a narrated PowerPoint presentation. [presentation]
- **Cloak, F. T., Jr.,** (1975a) **Is a Cultural Ethology Possible?** Human Ecology, Vol.3, No.3, pp.161-82.
- **Cloak, F. T., Jr.** (1975b) **That a culture and a social organization mutually shape each other through a process of continuing evolution.** Man-Environment Systems 5: 3-6.
- **Cloak, F. T., Jr.** (1976a) **The evolutionary success of altruism and urban social order.** Zygon 11: 219-240.
- **Cloak, F. T., Jr.** (1976b) **Abating Anthropological Ambiguity: Three common terms and the relations among them.** Presented to the 75th annual meeting of the American Anthropological Association, Washington DC.
- **Cloak, F. T., Jr.** (1977) **Discussion of "The adaptive significance of cultural behavior", by William H. Durham - Comments and Reply.** Human Ecology, Vol.5, No.1, pp.49-50.
- **Cloak, F. T., Jr.** (1981a) **On natural selection and culture: a commentary on "A multiple-level model of evolution and its implications for sociobiology", by H. C. Plotkin and F. J. Odling-Smee.** The Behavioral and Brain Sciences 4: 238-240.
- **Cloak, F. T., Jr.** (1986) **The causal logic of natural selection: a general theory.** Oxford Surveys in Evolutionary Biology 3: article 6, 132-186.
- **Cloak, F. T., Jr.,** (2008) **Perceptual Control Theory and the Evolution of Culture.** PowerPoint presentation and movie, released as version 1.01 Beta. [presentation]
- **Cochran, G., and Harpending, H.** (2009) **The 10,000 Year Explosion: How civilization accelerated human evolution.** New York: Basic Books.
- **Coker, Christopher** (2008) **War, memes and memeplexes.** International Affairs Volume 84, Issue 5, pages 903–914, September.
- **Conley, John, Toossi, Ali and Myrna Wooders** (2006) **Memetics and voting: how nature may make**

us public spirited.

- Conlisk, John (2002) **Costly optimizers versus cheap imitators.** Journal of Economic Behavior & Organization, Volume 1, Issue 3, September 1980, Pages 275-293.
- Conte, Rosaria (2000) **Memes through (social) minds.** In: Darwinizing culture: The status of memetics as a science, ed. R. Aunger, Oxford & New York: Oxford University Press.
- Cordes, Christian (2006) **Darwinism in Economics: From Analogy to Continuity.** Journal of Evolutionary Economics 16, 5 (December): 529-41.
- Cook, Richard, Bird, Geoffrey, Lünser, Gabriele, Huck, Steffen and Heyes Cecilia (2011) **Automatic imitation in a strategic context: players of rock–paper–scissors imitate opponents' gestures.** Proc. R. Soc. B.
- Coombs. R., Saviotti P, & Walsh V., eds. (1992) **Technological Change and Company Strategies: economic and sociological perspectives.** Academic Press.
- Cooper, William S. (2001) **The Evolution of Reason: Logic as a Branch of Biology.** Cambridge University Press.
- Cornell, S. and J.P. Kalt. (1997) **Cultural evolution and constitutional public choice: Institutional diversity and economic performance on American Indian Reservations.** In: J.R. Lott, Jr. Uncertainty and Economic Evolution: Essays in Honor of Armen A. Alchian. London: Routledge. (p. 116-142.
- Costall, A. (1991) **The meme meme.** Cultural Dynamics 4: 321-335.
- Cotta, Carlos (2006) **From Genes to Memes: Optimization by Problem-aware Evolutionary Algorithms.** SCHEDAE INFORATICAE - VOLUME 15 [ma]
- Cowan, Mark (2001) **In Search of the Golden Meme - Is the meme a useful concept or an over-applied analogy?**
- Cox, Paul (2003) **Memes and Schemes.**
- Cristianini, N. (1995) **Evolution and Learning: An Epistemological Perspective.**
- Croft , A. R. (2000) **Explaining language change : an evolutionary approach.**
- Crofts , A. R. (2007) **Life, Information, Entropy, and Time: Vehicles for Semantic Inheritance.** Complexity. 2007;13(1):14-50.
- Crozier, G. K. D. (2008) **Reconsidering Cultural Selection Theory.** Br J Philos Sci (2008) 59 (3): 455-479.
- Crozier, G. K. D. (2010) **A formal investigation of Cultural Selection Theory: acoustic adaptation in bird song.** BIOLOGY AND PHILOSOPHY. Volume 25, Number 5, 781-801.
- Cullen, Ben Sandford (1995) **Parasite Ecology and the Evolution of Religion** *The Evolution of Complexity.*
- Cullen, Ben Sandford (2000) **Contagious Ideas: On Evolution, Culture, Archaeology and Cultural Virus Theory.**
- Csányi, Vilmos (1982) **General theory of evolution.** Akademiai Kiado.
- Csányi, Vilmos (1989) **Evolutionary Systems and Society: A General Theory of Life, Mind and Culture.** Duke University Press.
- Csikszentmihalyi, M. (1993) **The Evolving Self.** Harper Collins.
- Cziko, Gary A. (1995) **Without miracles: Universal selection theory and the second Darwinian revolution.** Cambridge: MIT Press (A Bradford Book).
- Cziko, Gary A. (1998) **From Blind to Creative: In Defense of Donald Campbell.** Journal of Creative Behavior.

D
- Daly, Martin (1998) **Some Caveats about Cultural Transmission Models.** Human Ecology 10 (1982), 402–404.
- Danchin, Étienne, Charmantier, Anne, Champagne, Francis A., Mesoudi, Alex, Pujol, Benoit, Blanchet, Simon (2011) **Beyond DNA: integrating inclusive inheritance into an extended theory of evolution.** Nature Reviews Genetics.
- Danchin, Étienne & Wagner, Richard H. (2010) **Inclusive heritability: combining genetic and nongenetic information to study animal culture.** Oikos 119, 210–218.
- Danchin, Étienne, Blanchet, Simon, Wagner, Richard H. and Mery, Frédérick (2010) **Do invertebrates have culture?**
- Darmesteter, Arsène (1886) **The life of words as the symbols of ideas.** London: Kegan Paul, French & Co.
- Darwin, C. (1871) **The Descent of Man.** John Murray Publications.
- Darwin, C. (1859) **The Origin of Species by Means of Natural Selection or the Preservation of Favoured Races in the Struggle for Life.** Published by John Murray.
- Davies, Paul (2004) **Undermining Free Will.**
- Dawkins, Richard (1976) **Memes and the evolution of culture.** New Scientist. Page 208.
- Dawkins, Richard (1976) **The Selfish Gene.** Oxford University Press. Chapter 11 is available online.

- **Dawkins, Richard** (1976) **Memes: The New Replicators** The Selfish Gene, Chapter 11.
- **Dawkins, Richard** (1982a) **The Extended Phenotype.**
- **Dawkins, Richard** (1982b) **Organisms, groups and memes: replicators or vehicles?** In: The Extended Phenotype. Oxford University Press. pp. 97-117.
- **Dawkins, Richard** (1982c) **Replicators and Vehicles** King's College Sociobiology Group, eds., Current Problems in Sociobiology, Cambridge, Cambridge University Press, pp. 45-64.
- **Dawkins, Richard** (1986) **The Blind Watchmaker.**
- **Dawkins, Richard** (1991) **Viruses of the Mind.** P. 13-27, in: Dennett and his Critics, B. Dalhbom (editor), Blackwell Publishers.
- **Dawkins, Richard** (1993) **Is religion just a disease?** The Daily Telegraph, Wednesday December 15, p. 18.
- **Dawkins, Richard** (1999) **Foreword to The Meme Machine, by S. Blackmore.** Oxford: Oxford University Press.
- **Dawkins, Richard** (2004a) **Extended Phenotype – But Not Too Extended. A Reply to Laland, Turner and Jablonka** Biology and Philosophy 19: 377–396.
- **Dawkins, Richard** (2004b) **An Ecology of Replicators.**
- **De Jong, Martin** (1999) **Survival of the institutionally fittest concepts.** Journal of Memetics - Evolutionary Models of Information Transmission, 3.
- **De Jong, Martin and Speel, Hans-Cees** (1999) **Mimicry behaviour in social and organisational life.** Symposium on Memetics: Evolutionary Models of Information Transmission, 15th International Congress on Cybernetics, Namur (Belgium), August 24-28.
- **De Landa, Manuel** (1998) **Replicators and Interactors in Linguistic History.** Symposium on Memetics: Evolutionary Models of Information Transmission, 15th International Congress on Cybernetics, Namur (Belgium), August 24-28.
- **De Sousa, João Dinis** (2002) **Chess moves and their memomics: a framework for the evolutionary processes of chess openings.** Journal of Memetics - Evolutionary Models of Information Transmission, 6.
- **De Sousa, João Dinis** (2002) **A Reply to Dowd's Commentary on My Paper.** Journal of Memetics - Evolutionary Models of Information Transmission, 6.
- **De Waal, Frans, B. M., Byrne, Richard, Dunbar, Robin and McGrew, W.C.** (2002) **Tree of Origin: What Primate Behavior Can Tell Us about Human Social Evolution.** Harvard University Press.
- **Deacon, Terrence W.** (1997) **The Symbolic Species: The Co-evolution of Language and the Human Brain.** London, Penguin.
- **Deacon, Terrence W.** (1999) **Memes as Signs. The trouble with memes (and what to do about it).**
- **Deakin, S.** (2002) **Legal Memetics: Towards an Evolutionary Theory of Legal Change.**
- **Delius, J. D.** (1989) **Of mind memes and brain bugs, a natural history of culture.** In W.A.Koch (Ed) The Nature of Culture. Bochum, Germany, Bochum Publications. 26-79.
- **Delius, J. D.** (1990) **On the Natural History of Culture: Gene and Meme.** In: Zeitschrift fr Semiotik; 1990, 12, 4, 307-321.
- **Dennett, Daniel C.** (1990) **Memes and the exploitation of imagination.** J. Aesthetics Art Criticism 48: 127-135.
- **Dennett, Daniel C.** (1991) **Consciousness Explained.** Penguin Books.
- **Dennett, Daniel C.** (1996a) **Darwins Dangerous Idea.** The Sciences 35: 34-40.
- **Dennett, Daniel C.** (1996b) **The Scope of Natural Selection. The author replies to H. Allen Orr's review of "Darwin's Dangerous Idea"** Boston Review
- **Dennett, Daniel C.** (1998a) **Memes: Myths, Misunderstandings and Misgivings.** Arts, Sciences
- **Dennett, Daniel C.** (1998b) **Snowmobiles, horses, rats, and memes** , (a comment on "A Critique of Evolutionary Archeology," by James L. Boone and Eric Alden Smith).
- **Dennett, Daniel C.** (1999) **The Evolution of Culture.** The Edge.
- **Dennett, Daniel C.** (2000a) **Review of Eytan Avital and Eva Jablonka, Animal Traditions: Behavioural Inheritance in Evolution** , Cambridge University Press, for Journal of Evolutionary Biology.
- **Dennett, Daniel C.** (2000b) **From Typo to Thinko: When Evolution Graduated to Semantic Norms.**
- **Dennett, Daniel C.** (2001) **The Evolution of Culture.** Monist 84.
- **Dennett, Daniel C.** (2003) **The New Replicators, Problems of Classification and Individuation, Is Cultural Evolution Darwinian?**
- **Dennett, Daniel C.** (2006a) **Breaking the Spell.** Viking.
- **Dennett, Daniel C.** (2006b) **There aren't enough minds to house the population explosion of memes.**
- **Dennett, Daniel C.** (2006c) **From Typo to Thinko: When Evolution Graduated to Semantic Norms** [earlier version from 2000].
- **Dennett, Daniel C.** (2006d) **Religion's Just a Survival Meme.**

- **Dennett, Daniel C. and McKay, Ryan** (2006e) **A continuum of mindfulness** Commentary on "Towards a unified science of cultural evolution".
- **Dennett, Daniel C.** (2006f) **The New Replicators** Appendix A of *Breaking the Spell*
- **Dennett, Daniel C.** (2007) **Ants, terrorism, and the awesome power of memes.** .
- **Dennett, Daniel C.** (2008a) **From Animal to Person: the role of culture in human evolution** .
- **Dennett, Daniel C.** (2008b) **From Animal to Person: the role of culture in human evolution** [podcast].
- **Dennett, Daniel C.** (2008c) **Dan Dennett on Darwin's legacy** Talk at Stanford University .
- **Dennett, Daniel C.** (2009a) **The Cultural Evolution of Words and Other Thinking Tools.**
- **Dennett, Daniel C.** (2009b) **The Evolution of Culture.** In Cosmos and Culture: Cultural Evolution in a Cosmic Context, edited by Steven Dick and Mark Lupisella.
- **Dennett, Daniel C.** (2009c) **How brains become minds - the role of Cultural software.**
- **Depew, D. & Weber, B.H. (eds).** (1986) **Evolution at a Crossroads: The New Biology and the New Philosophy of Science.** MIT Press.
- **Deutsch, David** (1978) **The Beginning of Infinity: Explanations That Transform the World** .
- **Diamond, J.** (1978) **The Tasmanians: the longest isolation, the simplest technology.** Nature 273:185'186.
- **Dibdin, Michael** (2006) **Why I've lost faith in Richard Dawkins.**
- **Dick , Steven J. and Lupisella, Mark** (2009) **Cosmos and Culture: Cultural Evolution in a Cosmic Context.**
- **Diettrich, Olaf** (1992) **Darwin, Lamarck and the Evolution of Science and Culture.** Evolution and Cognition, 1st Series, Vol.2, No. 3.
- **Dirlam, David K.** (2003) **Competing Memes Analysis.** Journal of Memetics - Evolutionary Models of Information Transmission, 7.
- **Dirlam, David K.** (2005) **Using Memetics to Grow Memetics.** Journal of Memetics - Evolutionary Models of Information Transmission, 9.
- **Distin, Kate** (1995) **Durkheim: Social Facts as Memes?.**
- **Distin, Kate** (1997) **Cultural evolution - the meme hypothesis.**
- **Distin, Kate** (2005) **The Selfish Meme: A Critical Reassessment.** Cambridge University Press.
- **Distin, Kate** (2011) **Cultural Evolution**
- **Donald, Merlin** (1991) **Origins of the Modern Mind: Three Stages in the Evolution of Culture and Cognition.** Harvard University Press.
- **Donald, Merlin** (1998) **Hominid enculturation and cognitive evolution.** In Cognition and material culture : the archaeology of symbolic storage.
- **Doran, Jim** (1997) **Simulating Collective Misbelief.**
- **Dosi, G., Pavitt, K., & Soete, L.** (1990) **The Economics of Technical Change and International Trade.** Harvester Wheatsheaf.
- **Dowd, S. B** (2002) **An Expansion and Critique of de Sousa's Framework for the Evolutionary Processes of Chess Openings.** Journal of Memetics - Evolutionary Models of Information Transmission, 7.
- **Downey , Greg** (2008) **We hate memes, pass it on...**
- **Downey , Greg** (2008) **Brain-culture, memes, and choosing examples.**
- **Drees, Willem** (2011) **The selfish gene? It's all in the mind. A review of Aping Mankind: Neuromania, Darwinitis and the Misrepresentation of Humanity.** Times Higher Education supplement.
- **Drexler, K. E.** (1987) **Hypertext publishing and the evolution of knowledge.** Social Intelligence, Vol. 1, No. 2, p. 87-120.
- **Driscoll, Catherine** (2011) **Why Sperber's Attractors do not Prevent Cumulative Cultural Evolution.**
- **Dugatkin, Lee Alan** (2000) **Animals imitate, too.** Scientific American, 283:4, 67.
- **Dugatkin, Lee Alan and Godin, J. G.** (1992) **Reversal of female mate choice by copying in the guppy (Poecilia reticulata).** Proc Biol Sci. 1992 Aug 22; 249(1325):179-84.
- **Dugatkin, Lee Alan** (2001) **The Imitation Factor: Evolution Beyond The Gene.** Scientific American, 283:4, 67.
- **Dunbar, Robin I. M.** (1992) **Neocortical size as a constraint on group size in primates.** Journal of Human Evolution. 22, 469-93.
- **Dunbar, Robin I. M.** (1998) **The social brain hypothesis.** Evolutionary Anthropology, 6, 178'190.
- **Dunbar, Robin I. M.** (2003) **The social brain.** Annual Review of Anthropology, 32, 163'181.
- **Dunbar, Robin** (2004) **Grooming, Gossip and the Evolution of Language.**
- **Dunbar, Robin I. M. & Barrett, L.** (2007) **Oxford Handbook of Evolutionary Psychology.** Oxford: Oxford University Press.
- **Durham, William H.** (1990) **Advances in Evolutionary Culture Theory.** Annual Review of

Anthropology, Vol. 19: 187-210 October.

- **Durham, William H.** (1991) **Coevolution: Genes, Culture, and Human Diversity.** Stanford University Press.
- **Durham, William H.** (1992) **Applications of Evolutionary Culture Theory.**
- **Durham, William H.** (1997) **Units of Culture.** In P. Weingart, S. D. Mitchell, P. J. Richerson, and S. Maasen (eds.), Human by Nature: Between Biology and the Social Sciences. Mahwah, NJ, USA: Lawrence Erlbaum Associates, Publishers. Pp. 300-313.
- **Duthie, A. Bradley** (2003) **A Letter on: The Fork and the Paperclip: A Memetic Perspective.** Journal of Memetics - Evolutionary Models of Information Transmission, 8.
- **Duthie, A. Bradley** (2002-2007) **Mixed Memes.**
E
- **Eades, Lucas Gwilym** (2011) **Place Memes: A Cree Ethnogeography.**
- **Earls, Mark** (2011) **Herd: How to Change Mass Behaviour by Harnessing Our True Nature.**
- **Edelman, Gerald M. and Mountcastle, Vernon B.** (1982) **The Mindful Brain: Cortical Organization and the Group-Selective Theory of Higher Brain Function.**
- **Edelman, Gerald M.** (1987) **Neural Darwinism: The theory of neuronal group selection.** New York: Basic Books.
- **Edelman, Gerald M.** (1992) **Bright Air, Brilliant Fire: On the Matter of the Mind.** Basic Books.
- **Edmonds, Bruce** (1996) **A Brief Overview and History of Memetics.** Journal of Memetics - Evolutionary Models of Information Transmission
- **Edmonds, Bruce** (1997) **Modelling Bounded Rationality using Evolutionary Techniques.** Lecture Notes in Computer Science, 1305, 31-42.
- **Edmonds, Bruce** (1998) **On Modelling in Memetics** Journal of Memetics - Evolutionary Models of Information Transmission. 2.
- **Edmonds, Bruce** (2002) **Three Challenges for the Survival of Memetics.** Journal of Memetics - Evolutionary Models of Information Transmission, 6.
- **Edmonds, Bruce** (2002) **Review of Selection Theory and Social Construction: the evolutionary naturalistic epistemology of Donald T. Campbell - edited by Cecilia eyes and David Hull.** Journal of Memetics - Evolutionary Models of Information Transmission, 6.
- **Edmonds, Bruce** (2005) **The revealed poverty of the gene-meme analogy - why memetics per se has failed to produce substantive results.** Journal of Memetics - Evolutionary Models of Information Transmission, 9.
- **Edwards A. W. F.** (2009) **Statistical methods for evolutionary trees.** Genetics 183: 5'12.
- **Eerkens, J. W., Bettinger, R. L. and McElreath, R.** (2005) **Cultural Cultural transmission, phylogenetics, and the archaeological record.** In Mapping our ancestors: Phylogenetic approaches in anthropology and prehistory, ed. C. P. Lipo, M. J. O'Brien.
- **Eerkens J. W. and Lipo, Carl P.** (2007) **Cultural Transmission Theory and the Archaeological Record: Providing Context to Understanding Variation and Temporal Changes in Material Culture.** J. Archaeol. Res. 15:239–274.
- **Egege, Sandra** (2008) **Culture and Language as Social Construction: A Case Against Cultural Difference.**
- **Ehrlich, Paul R.** (2000) **Human Natures: Genes, Cultures, and the Human Prospect.**
- **Ehrlich, Paul R. and Ehrlich, Anne H.** (2009) **The Dominant Animal: Human Evolution and the Environment.**
- **Ekstig, Börje** (2004) **The Evolution of Language and Science Studied by means of Biological Concepts.** Journal of Memetics - Evolutionary Models of Information Transmission, 8.
- **Eldredge, Niles** (2000) **Biological and material cultural evolution: Are there any true parallels?** Perspectives in Ethology 13: 113-153.
- **Eldredge, Niles** (2002) **An Overview of Piston-Valved Cornet History.** Historic Brass Sociey Journal 14: 337-390.
- **Eldredge, Niles and Barnet, Belinda** (2004) **Material Cultural Evolution: An Interview with Niles Eldredge.**
- **Enquist, Magnus, Eriksson, Kimmo and Ghirlanda Stefano** (2007) **Critical Social Learning: A Solution to Rogers's Paradox of Nonadaptive Culture** AMERICAN ANTHROPOLOGIST, Vol. 109, Issue 4, pp. 727–734.
- **Eriksson, Gunilla, Linderholma, Anna, Fornandera, Elin, Kanstrup, Marie, Schoultza, Pia, Olofssona, Hanna and Lidéna, Kerstin** (2008) **Same island, different diet: Cultural evolution of food practice on Öland, Sweden, from the Mesolithic to the Roman Period.** Journal of Anthropological Archaeology Volume 27, Issue 4, December, Pages 520-543.
- **Erwin, Greg** (1994) **This is the Holy Salvation Meme.**
- **Evers, John R.** (1998) **A justification of societal altruism according to the memetic application of**

Hamilton's Rule. Symposium on Memetics: Evolutionary Models of Information Transmission, 15th International Congress on Cybernetics, Namur (Belgium), August 24-28.

F

- **Failly, Denis** (2006) **Memetics: Why we copy each other** by Denis Failly - An interview with Susan Blackmore, author of 'The Meme Machine' by Denis Failly.
- **Feldman, M. W. and Cavelli-Sforza, L. L.** (1976) **Cultural and Biological Evolutionary Processes, Selection for a Trait under Complex Transmission.** Theoretical Population Biology 9.2: 238–259.
- **Feldman, M. W. and Aoki, Kenichi** (1991) **Assortative mating and grandparental transmission facilitate the persistence of a sign language.** Theoretical Population Biology, Volume 42, Issue 2, October 1992, Pages 107-116.
- **Feldman, M. W. and Cavelli-Sforza, L. L.** (1984) **Cultural and biological evolutionary processes: gene-culture disequilibrium.** Proc Natl Acad Sci U S A. March; 81(5): 1604–1607.
- **Feldman, M. W. and Zhivotovsky L. A.** (1992) **Gene-culture coevolution: toward a general theory of vertical transmission.** Proc Natl Acad Sci U S A. Dec 15;89(24):11935-8.
- **Feldman, M. W. and Laland K. N.** (1996) **Gene-culture coevolutionary -theory.** Trends in evology and evolution 11: 453-7.
- **Feldman, M. W., Aoki, Kenichi and Kumm, Jochen** (1996) **Individual versus social learning: Evolutionary analysis in a fluctuating environment.**
- **Felkins, Leon** (1995) **Strolling Through the Memetic Mine Field** *The Ethical Spectacle.*
- **Felkins, Leon** (1995) **The Memes of Love, Sex and Marriage.**
- **Fernando, Chrisantha, Karishma, K.K. and Szathmáry, Eörs** (2008) **Copying and Evolution of Neuronal Topology.** PLoS ONE 3 (11): 3775.
- **Fernando, Chrisantha and Szathmáry, Eörs** (2009) **Chemical, Neuronal, and Linguistic Replicators.**
- **Fernando, Chrisantha, Goldstein, R. and Szathmáry, Eörs** (2010) **The Neuronal Replicator Hypothesis.** Neural Computation 22 (11): 2809–2857.
- **Fernando, Chrisantha** (2010) **Neuronal replicators solve the stability-plasticity dilemma.** GECCO 2010: 153-154.
- **Fernando, Chrisantha, Vasas, Vera, Szathmáry, Eörs and Husbands, Philip** (2011) **Natural Selection of Paths in Networks.**
- **Findlay, C. S.** (1990) **Fundamental theorem of natural selection in biocultural populations.** Theor Popul Biol. Dec;38(3):367-84.
- **Findlay, C. S.** (1991) **Fundamental theorem of natural selection under gene-culture transmission.** Proc Natl Acad Sci U S A. Jun 1;88(11):4874-6.
- **Findlay, C. S.** (1992a) **Secondary theorem of natural selection in biocultural populations.** Theor Popul Biol. Feb;41(1):72-89.
- **Findlay, C. S.** (1992b) **Phenotypic evolution under gene-culture transmission in structured populations.** J Theor Biol. 1992 Jun 7;156(3):387-400.
- **Fiore, Frank** (1999) **Viral marketing: Spread A Cold, Catch A Customer.** *American City Business Journals*
- **Fisher, James, Hinde, Robert A.** (1949) **The opening of milk bottles by birds.** British Birds, vol. 42, no. 11, p. 347-357.
- **Fisher, James, Hinde, Robert A.** (1951) **Further observations on the opening of milk bottles by birds.** British Birds, vol. 44, no. 12, p. 393-396.
- **Fisher, R. A.** (1930) **The genetical theory of natural selection.** Clarendon Press, Oxford, U.K.
- **Fitch, W. Tecumseh** (2008) **Glossogeny and phylogeny: cultural evolution meets genetic evolution.** Trends in Genetics. Volume 24, Issue 8, August 2008, Pages 373-374
- **Finkelstein, Robert** (2008) **What is a meme? A functional definition.** Robotic Technology Inc. and University of Maryland University College.
- **Flegr, Jaroslav** (2008) **Frozen Evolution: Or, that's not the way it is, Mr. Darwin - Farewell to selfish gene.**
- **Flinn, Mark V. and Alexander, R. D.** (1982) **Culture theory: The developing synthesis from biology.** Human Ecology, Vol. 10, No. 3, Biology and Culture (Sep.), pp. 383-400.
- **Flinn, Mark V., Tedeschi, David, Quinlan, Robert, Decker, Seamus, Picha, Paul R., Sutter, Richard and Turner, Mark** (1994) **Review: Evolution and Culture Turf Wars: History, Mind, and/or Ecology?.** Journal of Anthropological Research Vol. 50, No. 3 (Autumn), pp. 327-333.
- **Flinn, Mark V.** (1997) **Culture and the evolution of social learning.** Evolution and Human Behavior (HBES) Volume 18, Issue 1, Pages 23-67 (January)
- **Fog, Agner** (1997) **Cultural R/K Selection.** Journal of Memetics - Evolutionary Models of Information Transmission, 1.
- **Fog, Agner** (1999) **Cultural Selection.**
- **Fog, Agner** (2003a) **Explaining unintended developments with cultural selection theory.**
- **Fog, Agner** (2003b) **The gap between cultural selection theory and sociology.** Paper presented at the

2003 meeting of the International Society for the History, Philosophy and Social Studies of Biology.
- **Fog, Agner** (2006) **An Evolutionary Theory of Cultural Differentiation.** Proceedings of the XV world congress of the International Union for Prehistoric and Protohistoric Sciences Lisbon.
- **Fog, Agner** (2009) **Towards a universal theory of competition and selection.**
- **Fog, Agner** (2011) **War, authoritarianism and behavioral plasticity.**
- **Forguson, Lynd** (2001) **Oxford and the "Epidemic" of Ordinary Language Philosophy** . In "The Epidemology of Ideas".
- **Formoso, Joe** (1993) **Memes, and Grinning Idiot Press: or, why I have been studying vampires since 1972.** *Grinning Idiot Press.*
- **Fracchia, Joseph and Lewontin, R. C.** (1999) **Does Culture Evolve?** History and Theory, Vol. 38, No. 4, Theme Issue 38: The Return of Science: Evolutionary Ideas and History, pp. 52-78.
- **Fracchia, Joseph and Lewontin, R. C.** (1999) **The price of metaphor.** History and theory (Weleyan University) 44 (44): 14–29.
- **Francis, Richard C.** (2011) **Epigenetics: The Ultimate Mystery of Inheritance**
- **Frank, Joshua** (1999) **Applying Memetics to Financial Markets: Do Markets Evolve towards Efficiency?** Journal of Memetics - Evolutionary Models of Information Transmission, 3.
- **Freeman C.** (1991) **Innovation, changes of techno-economic paradigm and biological anologies in economics.** Revue Economique No. 2, p. 211-232.
- **Fried, Michael S.** (1998) **The Evolution of legal concepts - The Memetic Perspective.**
G
- **Gabora, Liane M.** (1995a) **Meme and Variations: A Computational Model of Cultural Evolution.** Published in (L. Nadel and D. L. Stein, eds.) 1993 Lectures in Complex Systems, Addison Wesley, 1995.
- **Gabora, Liane M.** (1995b) **Meme and variations: A Computer Model of Cultural Evolution.** In D. Stein Ed. 1993 Lectures in Complex Systems. Addison-Wessley. 471-486. (different document to above).
- **Gabora, Liane M.** (1996) **A Day in the Life of a Meme.** *The Nature, Representation and Evolution of Concepts* - Philosophica, 57, 901-938. (Special issue on concepts, representations, and dynamical systems).
- **Gabora, Liane M.** (1997a) **The Origin and Evolution of Culture and Creativity.** Journal of Memetics: Evolutionary Models of Information Transmission, 1(1).
- **Gabora, Liane M.** (1997b) **Memes: The creative spark.** Wired 5.06, June.
- **Gabora, Liane M.** (1997c) **Memetics.** Volume 8 (2) of the Semiotic Review of Books.
- **Gabora, Liane M.** (1997d) **Taking Memes Seriously.**
- **Gabora, Liane M.** (1998) **Autocatalytic Closure in a Cognitive System: A Tentative Scenario for the Origin of Culture.** Psycoloquy.
- **Gabora, Liane M.** (1999a) **MemeStreams: Culture and Evolution of Our Conceptual Tapestry.**
- **Gabora, Liane M.** (1999b) **The Meme Machine** JASSS: A review of Blackmore's The Meme Machine. [also More on Memes]
- **Gabora, Liane M.** (2001) **Cognitive mechanisms underlying the origin and evolution of culture.** Dissertation.
- **Gabora, Liane M.** (2004) **Ideas are not replicators but minds are.** Biology & Philosophy, 19(1), 127-143.
- **Gabora, Liane M.** (2005a) **Creative thought as a non-Darwinian evolutionary process.** Journal of Creative Behavior, 39(4), 262-283.
- **Gabora, Liane M.** (2005b) **Application of a Contextual Perspective on Cultural Evolution to the Future of Humanity.** Cultural Evolution | Center for Human Evolution Proceedings of Workshop 4.
- **Gabora, Liane M. and Aerts, D.** (2005c) **Distilling the Essence of an Evolutionary Process and Implications for a Formal Description of Culture.** Cultural Evolution | Center for Human Evolution Proceedings of Workshop 4.
- **Gabora, Liane M.** (2007a) **Why the creative process is not Darwinian.** Commentary on 'The creative process in Picasso's Guernica sketches: Monotonic improvements versus nonmonotonic variants' by D. K. Simonton. Creativity Research Journal, 19(4), 361-365.
- **Gabora, Liane M.** (2007b) **Epigenetic and cultural evolution are not Darwinian.** Commentary on E. Jablonka & M. J. Lamb, Synopsis of 'Evolution in Four Dimensions'. Behavioral and Brain Sciences, 30(4), p. 371.
- **Gabora, Liane M.** (2007c) **Mind: What archaeology can tell us about the origins of human cognition.** In (R. A. Bentley, H. D. G. Maschner, & C. Chippendale, Eds.) Handbook of Theories and Methods in Archaeology, Altamira Press, Walnut Creek CA, (pp. 283-296).
- **Gabora, Liane M.** (2008) **The cultural evolution of socially situated cognition.** Cognitive Systems Research. Volume 9, Issues 1-2, March 2008, Pages 104-114.
- **Gabora, Liane M.** (2008) **Modeling Cultural Dynamics.** Proceedings of the Association for the Advancement of Artificial Intelligence AAAI Fall Symposium 1 Adaptive Agents in Cultural Contexts, 8. AAAI Press.[PDF]

- **Gabora, Liane M.** (2009) **Review of 'Epigenetic principles of evolution' by Nelson R. Cabej.** Quarterly Review of Biology, 84(2), p. 193.
- **Gabora, Liane M.** (2010a) **Why blind-variation and selective-retention is an inappropriate explanatory framework for creativity**
- **Gabora, Liane M.** (2010b) **Revenge of the 'neurds': Characterizing creative thought in terms of the structure and dynamics of human memory.** Creativity Research Journal, 22(1), 1-13.
- **Gabora, Liane M.** (2011a) **An analysis of the Blind Variation and Selective Retention (BVSR) theory of creativity.** Creativity Research Journal.
- **Gabora, Liane M.** (2011b) **Five clarifications about cultural evolution.** Journal of Cognition and Culture.
- **Gabora, Liane M., Leijnen, S. & Ghyczy, T.** (2011c) **The relationship bewteen creativity, imitation, and cultural diversity.** International Journal of Software and Informatics.
- **Gers, Matt,** (2008) **The Case for Memes.** Vol. 3, No. 4, Pages 305-315.
- **Gers, Matt,** (2009) **The long reach of philosophy of biology.** Biology & Philosophy.
- **Gardner, James** (1996) **Memetic Engineering.** Wired - Issue 4.05.
- **Gardner, Martin** (2000) **Kilroy was here. A review of** *The Meme Machine* **by Susan J. Blackmore.** Los Angeles Times, March 5.
- **Gatherer, Derek** (1997) **Macromemetics: Towards a Framework for the Re-unification of Philosophy.** Journal of Memetics - Evolutionary Models of Information Transmission, 1.
- **Gatherer, Derek G.** (1997) **The evolution of music - A comparison of Darwinian and dialectical methods.**
- **Gatherer, Derek G.** (1998) **Meme Pools, World 3, And Averroes's Vision Of Immortality.**
- **Gatherer, Derek G.** (1998) **Identifying cases of social contagion using memetic isolation.** Journal of Artificial Societies and Social Simulation vol. 5, no. 4.
- **Gatherer, Derek** (1998) **Why the 'Thought Contagion' Metaphor is Retarding the Progress of Memetics.** Journal of Memetics - Evolutionary Models of Information Transmission, 2.
- **Gatherer, Derek G.** (1999) **Reply to the commentaries on my paper: Why the 'Thought Contagion' Metaphor is Retarding the Progress of Memetics.** Journal of Memetics - Evolutionary Models of Information Transmission, 3.
- **Gatherer, Derek** (1999) **The Case for Commentary** Journal of Memetics - Evolutionary Models of Information Transmission, 3.
- **Gatherer, Derek** (1999) **A Plea for Methodological Darwinism - a commentary on Rose's paper: Controversies in Meme Theory.** Journal of Memetics - Evolutionary Models of Information Transmission, 3.
- **Gatherer, Derek** (2001) **Modelling the effects of memetic taboos on genetic homosexuality.** Journal of Memetics - Evolutionary Models of Information Transmission, 4.
- **Gatherer, Derek** (2002a) **Macromemetics.**
- **Gatherer, Derek G.** (2002b) **The Spread of Irrational Behaviours by Contagion: An Agent Micro-Simulation.** Journal of Memetics - Evolutionary Models of Information Transmission, 6.
- **Gatherer, Derek G.** (2002c) **Identifying cases of social contagion using memetic isolation: comparison of the dynamics of a multisociety simulation with an ethnographic data set.**
- **Gatherer, Derek G.** (2002d) **Report on the EPSRC Network on Evolvability in Biology and Software Systems Meeting.** Journal of Memetics - Evolutionary Models of Information Transmission, 6.
- **Gatherer, Derek G.** (2003) **Birth of a Meme: the Origin and Evolution of Collusive Voting Patterns in the Eurovision Song Contest.** Journal of Memetics - Evolutionary Models of Information Transmission, 8.
- **Gatherer, Derek G.** (2005) **Finding a Niche for Memetics in the 21st Century.** Journal of Memetics - Evolutionary Models of Information Transmission, 6.
- **Gatherer, Derek G.** (2004) **The Inherent Instability of Memetic Systems:Use of a Genetic Algorithm to Solve a Parameter Optimisation Problem in a Memetic Simulation.** Journal of Memetics - Evolutionary Models of Information Transmission, 8.
- **Gavrilets, S., Vose, A.** (2006) **The dynamics of Machiavellian intelligence.** Proc Natl Acad Sci U S A. 2006 Nov 7;103(45):16823-8. Oct 30.
- **Ghiselin, M. T.** (1982) **On mechanisms of cultural evolution, and the evolution of language and the common law.** The Behavioral and Brain Sciences, 5 , p. 11.
- **Ghiselin, M. T.** (1987) **Replicators and replicanda.** Bioeconomics and the metaphysics of selection. J. Soc. Biol. Structures 10: 361-369.
- **Ghiselin, M. T.** (1994) **Chapter 9 p143-p148** In Metaphysics and the origin of species. SUNY Press, Albany, NY.
- **Gick, Evelyn and Gick, Wolfgang** (2000) **Hayek's Theory of Cultural Evolution Revisited: Rules, Morality, and the Sensory Order.**

- Gil-White, Francisco J., (2001) **L'evolution culturelle a-t-elle des règles?** La rechérche Hors Série No. 5(Avril), 92-97.
- Gil-White, Francisco J., (2006) **Common misunderstandings of memes (and genes) The promise and the limits of the genetic analogy to cultural transmission processes.**
- Gil-White, Francisco J., (2006) **Let the Meme be (a Meme): Insisting too much on the Genetic Analogy will Turn it into a Straightjacket.**
- Gimenes, M. (2004) **A Memetic Approach to the Evolution of Rhythms in a Society of Society of Software Agents.**
- Gintis, Herbert (2006) **Towards a Unified Behavioral Science.**
- Gintis, Herbert, Henrich, Joseph, Bowles, Samuel, Boyd, Robert, Fehr, Ernst (2007a) **Strong reciprocity and the roots of human morality.** Social Justice Research.
- Gintis, Herbert (2007b) **A framework for the unification of the behavioral sciences.** BEHAVIORAL AND BRAIN SCIENCES (2007) 30, 1'61.
- Gintis, Herbert (2008) **Five principles for the unification of the behavioral sciences.**
- Gintis, Herbert (2010) **Gene-Culture Coevolution and the Nature of Human Sociality.**
- Gintis, Herbert and Bowles, Samuel (2011) **A Cooperative Species: Human Reciprocity and Its Evolution.**
- Giroux, Hélène, Taylor, James R. & Cooren, François (1998) **Memes and the persistence of organizational structures.** Symposium on Memetics: Evolutionary Models of Information Transmission, 15th International Congress on Cybernetics, Namur (Belgium), August 24-28.
- Given, John (2007) **Genes, memes memories and myths: The evolution of language and the 'storying of the world'.**
- Gleick, James (2011) **The Information: A History, a Theory, a Flood.**
- Gleick, James (2011) **What Defines a Meme.**
- Godfrey-Smith, Peter (2000) **The Replicator in Retrospect.** Biology and Philosophy 15 (3).
- Godfrey-Smith, Peter (2009) **Darwinian populations and natural selection.** Oxford: Oxford University Press.
- Godin, Seth (2000) **Unleashing the Ideavirus.**
- Godwin, Mike (2003) **Meme, Counter-meme** Wired.
- Goerner, S. J. (1994) **Chaos and the Evolving Ecological Universe.** Gordon and Breach.
- Goldman, Alvin I. (2001) **Social Routes to Belief and Knowledge.** In "The Epidemology of Ideas".
- Gontier, Nathalie (2006) **Evolutionary Epistemology.** The Internet Encyclopedia of Philosophy.
- Goodenough, Oliver R. and Dawkins, Richard (1994) **The St Jude mind virus.** Nature, vol. 372, no. 230.
- Goodman, Alan H. and Leatherman, Thomas Leland (1998) **Building a New Biocultural Synthesis: Political-Economic Perspectives on Human Biology (Linking Levels of Analysis).**
- Goody, J. (1977) **The domestication of the savage mind.** Cambridge: Cambridge University Press.
- Goppold, Andreas (1998) **The SEMsphere: The Peircean category of Thirdness as ontological place for the meme.** Symposium on Memetics: Evolutionary Models of Information Transmission, 15th International Congress on Cybernetics, Namur (Belgium), August 24-28.
- Gottsch, John D. (2001) **Mutation, Selection, And Vertical Transmission Of Theistic Memes in Religious Canons** Journal of Memetics - Evolutionary Models of Information Transmission, 5.
- Gould, Stephen Jay (1982) **Darwinism and the Expansion of Evolutionary Theory.** Science , 216, pp. 380-387.
- Gould, Stephen Jay (1994) **Evolution: The Pleasures of Pluralism.** Scientific American , 271, October, 4. pp. 84-91.
- Gould, Stephen Jay (1994) **The Evolution of Life on Earth.** Scientific American , 271, October, 4. pp. 84-91.
- Gould, Stephen Jay (1999) **Leonardo's Mountain of Clams and the Diet of Worms: Essays on Natural History.**
- Gould, Stephen Jay (1980) **A biological homage to Mickey Mouse.**
- Graber, Robert Bates (1995) **A Scientific Model of Social and Cultural Evolution.** Kirksville, Missouri: Thomas Jefferson University Press.
- Grant, Glenn (1990) **Memetic Lexicon.** In: Heylighen, F., Joslyn, C., Turchin, V., Eds.; Electronic document: Principia Cybernetica Web (Principia Cybernetica: Brussels).
- Grant, Glenn (1990) **Memes: Introduction** *Principia Cybernetica.*
- Gray, John (2008) **The atheist delusion**
- Gray, Russell D., Greenhill, Simon J., Ross, Robert M. (2007) **The Pleasures and Perils of Darwinizing Culture (with Phylogenies).** Biological Theory.
- Gray, Russell D. (2010) **The Pleasures and Perils of Darwinizing Culture (with Phylogenies).**
- Greenberg, Mark (2004) **Goals Versus Memes: Explanation in the Theory of Cultural Evolution.** In

Susan L. Hurley & Nick Chater (eds.), Perspectives on Imitation. MIT Press.
- **Greene, Penelope J.** (1978) **From genes to memes?** Contemporary Sociology 7, 06-709.
- **Greenhill, S. J., Currie, T. E., Gray., R. D.** (2009) **Does horizontal transmission invalidate cultural phylogenies?** Proceedings of the Royal Society B: Biological Sciences 276:1665, 2299-2306.
- **Greenhill, S. J., Currie, T. E., Mace., R.** (2010) **Is horizontal transmission really a problem for phylogenetic comparative methods? A simulation study using continuous cultural traits.** Philosophical Transactions of the Royal Society B: Biological Sciences 365:1559, 3903-3912.
- **Griesemer, James R.** (2000a) **Development, Culture, and the Units of Inheritance.** Philosophy of Science 67.
- **Griesemer, James R.** (2000b) **The units of evolutionary transition.** Ann NY Acad Sci 981 (1): 97–110.
- **Griesemer, James R.** (2002a) **What Is 'Epi' about Epigenetics?**
- **Griesemer, James R.** (2002b) **Limits of Reproduction.**
- **Griesemer, James R.** (2005) **The informational gene and the substantial body: on the generalization of evolutionary theory by abstraction.** In Idealization XII: Correcting the Model. Idealization and Abstraction in the Sciences, edited by M. R. Jones and N. Cartwright. Amsterdam: Rodopi Publishers: 59-115.
- **Greiner, Christine** (1998) **Memes and the creation of new patterns of movement in dance.** Symposium on Memetics: Evolutionary Models of Information Transmission, 15th International Congress on Cybernetics, Namur (Belgium), August 24-28.
- **Griffiths, Paul E. and Gray, Russell D.** (1997) **Replicator II – Judgement Day.**
- **Gross, Dave** (1993) **Epigenetic Solutions to the Adoption Problem in Evolutionary Psychology (or, the Adoption Meme).**
- **Gross, Dave** (1996) **The Blue Star Meme: Applying Natural Selection Thinking to Urban Legends.**
- **Gross, Dave** (1997) **Some Reflections on Creation Versus Evolution of Memes.**
- **Gruhl, Daniel, Liben-Nowell, David, Guha, R. and Tomkins, Andrew** (2004) **Information Diffusion Through Blogspace.** In Proceedings of the 13th International World Wide Web Conference (WWW'04), May, pp. 491–501.
- **Guilford, J. P.** (1979) **Some incubated thoughts on incubation.** Journal of Creative Behavior, 13, 1-8.
- **Gunders, John and Brown, Damon** (2010) **The Complete Idiot's Guide to Memes.**
H
- **Hahlweg, Kai and Hooker, C. A.** (1989) **Issues in Evolutionary Epistemology.**
- **Haldane, J. B. S.** (1957) **The Cost of Natural Selection.** J. Genet. 55:511-524.
- **Hale-Evans, Ron** (1995) **Memetics: A Systems Metabiology.**
- **Hales, David** (1995) **Modelling Meta-Memes.** Unpublished MSc Dissertation. Department Of Computer Science, University Of Essex, UK.
- **Hales, David** (1997) **Modelling Meta-Memes.** In Conte, R., Hegselmann, R. & Terna P. (Eds.) Simulating Social Phenomena. Berlin: Springer.
- **Hales, David** (1998a) **An Open Mind is not an Empty Mind: Experiments in the Meta-Noosphere** Journal of Artificial Societies and Social Simulation vol. 1, no. 4.
- **Hales, David** (1998b) **Artificial Societies, Theory Building and "Ceduction".** Unpublished paper, Presented at the CRESS workshop "The Potential of Computer Simulation in the Social Sciences", January 1988, University of Surrey, UK.
- **Hales, David** (1998c) **Selfish Memes and Selfless Agents: Altruism in the Swap Shop.** In The Proceedings of ICMAS 1998 (ICMAS'98). California: IEEE Computer Society.
- **Hales, David** (1998d) **Stereotyping, Groups and Cultural Evolution.** In Proceedings of the Multi-Agent Based Simulation Workshop 1998 (MABS'98) To be published by Springer in the LNAI series late 1998.
- **Hales, David** (1998e) **Artificial Societies, Theory Building and Memetics.** Symposium on Memetics: Evolutionary Models of Information Transmission, 15th International Congress on Cybernetics, Namur (Belgium), August 24-28.
- **Hales, David** (1999) **Belief Has Utility - An Intentional Stance.** a commentary on Gatherer's paper: Why the `Thought Contagion' Metaphor is Retarding the Progress of Memetics - Journal of Memetics - Evolutionary Models of Information Transmission, 3.
- **Hales, David** (2006) **Memetic Engineering and Cultural Evolution**
- **Hall, Spencer R., Becker, Claes and Caceres, Carla E.** (2007) **Parasitic castration: a perspective from a model of dynamic energy budgets.**
- **Hallpike, C. R.** (1986) **The principles of social evolution.** Clarendon Press, Oxford, U.K.
- **Hallpike, C. R.** (2004) **Memetics: a Darwinian pseudo-science.**
- **Hamilton, W.D.** (1964) **Genetical evolution of social behavior I, II.** Journal of theoretical Biology, 7, 1-52.
- **Hamilton, W.D.** (1975) **Innate social aptitudes of man: An approach from evolutionary genetics.** In Biosocial anthropology (ed. R.Fox), pp. 133-155. Malaby, London.

- **Hanann, M. T., & Freeman, J.** (1989) **Organizational Ecology.** Harvard University Press.
- **Hanush, H.** (1988) **Evolutionary Economics.** Cambridge. In Hays, D. G. (1993. The Evolution of Technology Through Four Cognitive Ranks. Connected Education.
- **Hardisty, Benjamin E.** (2010) **Memes and the Ecological Niche.** Biological Theory 5:2, 109-111.
- **Harris, Marvin** (1979) **Cultural Materialism: The Struggle for a Science of Culture.** AltaMira Press; Updated edition
- **Harrison, Xavier A., Tregenza, Tom, Inger, Richard, Colhoun, Kendrew, Dawson, Deborah A., Gudmundsson, Gudmundur A., Hodgson, David J., Horsburgh, Gavin J., Mcelwaine, Graham And Bearhop, Stuart** (2010) **Cultural inheritance drives site fidelity and migratory connectivity in a long-distance migrant.** Molecular Ecology 19, 5484–5496.
- **Hays, D. G.** (1993) **The Evolution of Expressive Culture.** Journal of Social and Evolutionary Systems 15(2): 187-215.
- **Hebb, D.** (1949) **The Organization of Behavior.** Wiley and Sons. Hofbauer, J. & Sigmund, K. (1988. The Theory of Evolution and Dynamical Systems. Cambridge University Press.
- **Heintz, Christophe** (2007) **Institutions as Mechanisms of Cultural Evolution: Prospects of the Epidemiological Approach.** Summer 2007, Vol. 2, No. 3, Pages 244-249.
- **Henrich, Joseph and Boyd, Robert** (1998) **The evolution of conformist transmission and the emergence of between-group differences.** Evolution and Human Behavior, 19: 215-241.
- **Henrich, Joseph** (2000) **Does culture matter in economic behavior? Ultimatum game bargaining among the Machiguenga.** American Economic Review, 90(4): 973-979.
- **Henrich, Joseph** (2001) **Cultural transmission and the diffusion of innovations: Adoption dynamics indicate that biased cultural transmission is the predominate force in behavioral change and much of sociocultural evolution.** American Anthropologist 103:992-1013.
- **Henrich, Joseph** (2001) **Why People Punish Defectors: Weak conformist transmission can stabilize costly enforcement of norms in cooperative dilemmas.** Journal of Theoretical Biology 208:79-89.
- **Henrich, Joseph and Gil-White F. J.** (2001) **The evolution of prestige: Freely conferred status as a mechanism for enhancing the benefits of cultural transmission.** Evolution and human behavior 22: 165-196.
- **Henrich, Joseph and Boyd, Robert** (2002) **On modeling cognition and culture: How formal models of social learning can inform our understanding of cultural evolution.** Journal of Cognition and Culture, 2, 87'112.
- **Henrich, Joseph and Boyd, Robert** (2002) **On modeling cognition and culture: Why replicators are not necessary for cultural evolution.** Journal of Cognition and Culture, 2, 87'112.
- **Henrich, Joseph and Boyd, Robert** (2002) **On modeling cognition and culture: Why replicators are not necessary for cultural evolution.** Journal of Cognition and Culture, 2, 87'112.
- **Henrich, Joseph and McElreath, Richard** (2003) **The evolution of cultural evolution.** Evolutionary Anthropology 12:123'135.
- **Henrich, Joseph** (2004a) **Cultural group selection, coevolutionary processes and large-scale cooperation.** Journal of Economic Behavior & Organization 53:3-35.
- **Henrich, Joseph** (2004b) **Demography and Cultural Evolution: Why adaptive cultural processes produced maladaptive losses in Tasmania.** American Antiquity 69(2):197-214.
- **Henrich, Joseph** (2006a) **Cooperation, Punishment, and the Evolution of Human Institutions.** Science 312:60-61.
- **Henrich, Joseph** (2006b) **Understanding Cultural Evolutionary Models: A Reply to Read's Critique.** American Antiquity 71(4).
- **Henrich, Joseph** (2006c) **Culture, Evolution and the Puzzle of Human Cooperation.** Cognitive Systems Research, 7 (221-245).
- **Henrich, Joseph and Gil-White F. J.** (2007) **Why societies vary in their rates of innovation. The evolution of innovation-enhancing institutions.**
- **Henrich, Joseph** (2008a) **A cultural species.** In Explaining Culture Scientifically. M. Brown, ed. Seattle: University of Washington Press.
- **Henrich, Joseph and McElreath, Richard** (2008b) **Dual Inheritance Theory: The Evolution of Human Cultural Capacities and Cultural Evolution.** In R. Dunbar & L. Barrett (Eds.), (pp. 555-570). Oxford Univ. Press.
- **Henrich, Joseph and Henrich N.** (2010) **The evolution of cultural adaptations: Fijian food taboos protect against dangerous marine toxins.** Proc Biol Sci. 2010 Dec 22;277(1701):3715-24. Jul 28. [PDF]
- **Henrich, Joseph and Broesch J.** (2011) **On the nature of cultural transmission networks: evidence from Fijian villages for adaptive learning biases.** Philos Trans R Soc Lond B Biol Sci.
- **Henrich, Joseph** (2011) **The Cultural Brain Hypothesis.** [presentation]
- **Henson, H. Keith.** (1985) **Memes, L5 and the Religion of the Space Colonies.** L-5 News, September, pp. 5'8.

- Henson, H. Keith (1986) **More on Memes - L5 NEWS**
- Henson, H. Keith (1987) **Memetics and the Modular-Mind** Analog August.
- Henson, H. Keith (1987) **Memetics: The Science of Information Viruses.** Whole Earth Review no. 57.
- Henson, H. Keith (1988) **Memes Meta-Memes and Politics.**
- Henson, H. Keith and Lucas, Arel (1989) **Memes, Evolution, and Creationism.** Journal of Ideas.
- Henson, H. Keith (1991) **The Guru Trap Or What Computer Viruses Can Tell Us About Saddam Hussein.**
- Henson, H. Keith and Lucas, Arel (1993) **Cryonics, religions and memetics - A Theoretical Understanding.**
- Henson, H. Keith (1997) **Memes, Mental Parasites, and the Evolution of Skepticism.**
- Henson, H. Keith (2002) **Sex, Drugs, and Cults. An evolutionary psychology perspective on why and how cult memes get a drug-like hold on people, and what might be done to mitigate the effects.** The Human Nature Review Volume 2: 343-355 (23 August)
- Henson, H. Keith (2002) **Evolutionary Psychology, Memes and the Origin of War.**
- Herre, E.A., Knowlton, N., Mueller, U.G., Rehner, S.A. (1999) **The evolution of mutualisms: Exploring the paths between conflict and cooperation.** Trends Ecol Evol 14: 49–53.
- Hewlett, B. S. and L. L. Cavalli-Sforza (1986) **Cultural transmission among Aka pygmies.** Am. Anthropol 88:922'934.
- Hewlett, B. S., De Silvestri, A. and Guglielmino, C. R. (2002) **Semes and genes in Africa.** Curr. Anthropol 43:313'321.
- Heyes, Cecilia M. and Plotkin, H. C. (1989) **Replicators and interactors in cultural evolution.** In (M. Ruse, ed.) What the philosophy of biology is: Essays dedicated to David Hull. Kluwer Academic Publishers. p. 139-162.
- Heyes, Cecilia M. (1993) **Imitation, culture and cognition.** Animal Behaviour.
- Heyes, Cecilia M. and Galef, Bennett G. Jr. (1996a) **Social Learning In Animals: The Roots of Culture.** San Diego: Academic Press.
- Heyes, Cecilia M. and Hull, David L. (2001b) **Selection Theory and Social Construction: The Evolutionary Naturalistic Epistemology of Donald T. Campbell.** State University of New York Press.
- Heylighen, Francis (1992) **Evolution, Selfishness and Cooperation.** Journal of Ideas, Vol 2, # 4, pp 70-76.
- Heylighen, Francis (1992) **Selfish Memes and the Evolution of Cooperation.** Journal of Ideas , Vol. 2, #4, pp 77-84.
- Heylighen, Francis (1993a) **Selection Criteria for the Evolution of Knowledge.** in: Proc. 13th Int. Congress on Cybernetics (Association Internat. de Cybernetique, Namur), p. 524-528.
- Heylighen, Francis (1993b) **Evolution of Cooperation.**
- Heylighen, Francis (1994a) **Structure Of Memes.**
- Heylighen, Francis (1994b) **Competition Between Memes And Genes.**
- Heylighen, Francis and Campbell, Donald T. (1995) **Selection of Organization at the Social Level: obstacles and facilitators of Metasystem Transitions.** In "World Futures: the journal of general evolution", Vol. 45:1-4, p. 181.
- Heylighen, Francis (1996) **Evolution of Memes on the Network: from chain-letters to the global brain** , in: Ars Electronica Festival 96. Memesis: the future of evolution, G. Stocker & C. Schepf (eds.) (Springer, Vienna/New York), p. 48-57.
- Heylighen, Francis (1997) **Objective, subjective and intersubjective selectors of knowledge.** Evolution and Cognition 3:1, p. 63-67.
- Heylighen, Francis (1997) **Memetic Scenarios for Evolving Cooperation.**
- Heylighen, Francis (1998) **What makes a meme successful?** , in: Proc. 16th Int. Congress on Cybernetics (Association Internat. de Cybern_(c)tique, Namur), p. 423-418.
- Heylighen, Francis (1998) **Editorial: the memetics community is coming of age** , Journal of Memetics - Evolutionary Models of Information Transmission, 2., p. 1-3.
- Heylighen, Francis (1999) **The necessity of theoretical constructs: a refutation of Gatherer's plea for a behaviorist memetics** , Journal of Memetics - Evolutionary Models of Information Transmission, 3:1.
- Heylighen, Francis and Chielens, Klaas (2005) **Operationalization of Meme Selection Criteria: procedures to empirically test memetic hypotheses** , Proceedings AISB 2005.
- Heylighen, Francis (2006) **Memetic Dynamics between Cognitive Agents**
- Heylighen, Francis and Chielens, Klaas (2008) **Evolution of Culture, Memetics.** In: Encyclopedia of Complexity and Systems Science, ed. B. Meyers (Springer).
- Higgs, P. G. (2000) **The mimetic transition: a simulation study of the evolution of learning by imitation.** Proc Biol Sci. 2000 Jul 7;267(1450):1355-61.

- **Hill, J.** (2004) **The origin of sociocultural evolution.**
- **Hill, J.** (2004) **Reproductive and sociocultural success in a dual evolutionary model.**
- **Hill, J.** (1989) **Concepts as units of cultural replication.** Journal of Social and Biological Structures, vol. 12, no. 4, p. 343-355.
- **Hinde, R. A. and L. A. Barden.** (1985) **The evolution of the teddy bear.** Anim. Behav 33:1371'1373.
- **Hirschleifer, J.** (1977) **Economics from a biological viewpoint.** Journal of Law and Economics, Vol:20, 1-52
- **Hodge, Karl** (2000) **It's all in the memes**
- **Hodgson, Geoffrey M.** (1991) **Economic Evolution: Intervention contra pangloss.** Journal of Economical Issues, Vol. XXV No. 2 June.
- **Hodgson, Geoffrey M.** (1992a) **Marx, Engels and economic evolution.** International Journal of Social Economics, Vol. 19 Nos 7/8/9, pp. 121-128. MCB University Press.
- **Hodgson, Geoffrey M.** (1992b) **The Reconstruction of Economics: Is there still a place for neoclassical theory?** Journal Of Economical Issues, Vol. XXVI No. 3, Sept.
- **Hodgson, Geoffrey M.** (1993a) **Theories of Economic Evolution: A Preliminary Taxonomy.** The Manchester School Vol LXI No. 2 June, 0025-2034, 125-134.
- **Hodgson, Geoffrey M.** (1993b) **The mecca of Alfred Marshall.** The Economic Journal, March, v. 103 p. 406-415.
- **Hodgson, Geoffrey M.** (1993c) **Why the problem of reductionism in biology has implications for economics.** World Futures, Vol. 37, p. 69-90.
- **Hodgson, Geoffrey M.** (1993d) **Economics and Evolution: Bringing Life Back into Economics.** Polity Press.
- **Hodgson, Geoffrey M.** (1996) **An Evolutionary Theory of Long-Term Economic Growth.** International Studies Quarterly, vol. 40, p. 391-410.
- **Hodgson, Geoffrey M.** (1998a) **On the Evolution of Thorstein Veblen's Evolutionary Economics.** Cambridge Journal of Economics, 22(3), July 1998, pp. 415-31.
- **Hodgson, Geoffrey M.** (1998b) **Evolutionary and Competence-Based Theories of the Firm.** Journal of Economic Studies, 25(1), 1998, pp. 25-56.
- **Hodgson, Geoffrey M.** (2002) **Darwinism in Economics: From Analogy to Ontology.** Journal of Evolutionary Economics, 12(2) , June 2002, pp. 259-81.
- **Hodgson, Geoffrey M.** (2003) **Darwinism and Institutional Economics.** Journal of Economic Issues 37, 1: 85-97.
- **Hodgson, Geoffrey M.** (2004a) **The Evolution of Institutional Economics: Agency, Structure and Darwinism in American Institutionalism.** London and New York: Routledge.
- **Hodgson, Geoffrey M.** (2004b) **Darwinism, Causality and the Social Sciences.** Journal of Economic Methodology 11, 2 (June): 175-94.
- **Hodgson, Geoffrey M.** (2004c) **Veblen and Darwinism.** International Review of Sociology 14, 3 (November): 339-57.
- **Hodgson, Geoffrey M.** (2005) **Generalizing Darwinism to Social Evolution: Some Early Attempts.** Journal of Economic Issues, 39(4), December, pp. 899-914.
- **Hodgson, Geoffrey M. and Knudsen, Thorbjørn** (2006a) **Why we need a generalized Darwinism, and why generalized Darwinism is not enough.**
- **Hodgson, Geoffrey M. and Knudsen, Thorbjørn** (2006b) **Dismantling Lamarckism: Why Descriptions of Socio-Economic Evolution as Lamarckian are Misleading'.** Journal of Evolutionary Economics, 16(4), October , pp. 343-66.
- **Hodgson, Geoffrey M. and Knudsen, Thorbjørn** (2006c) **Darwin's Conjecture: The Search for General Principles of Social and Economic Evolution.** Chapter 1 is online
- **Hodgson, Geoffrey M.** (2007) **Taxonomizing the Relationship between Biology and Economics: A Very Long Engagement.** Journal of Bioeconomics 9 (2007): 169-85.
- **Hodgson, Geoffrey M.** (2008) **How Veblen Generalized Darwinism.** JOURNAL OF ECONOMIC ISSUES Vol. XLII No. 2 June.
- **Hoenigswald, H. M. & Wiener, L. S.** (1987) **Biological Metaphor and Cladistics Classification.** Francis Pinter Publishers.
- **Hofstadter D. R.** (1985) **Metamagical themes: Questions for the essence of mind and pattern.** Basic Books.
- **Hogan, Bernie** (2008) **The Social Structures of (Memetic) Diffusion.**
- **Holdcroft, David and Lewis, Harry** (2000) **Memes, Minds and Evolution.** Philosophy, 75, pp 161-182.
- **Holland, J.H.** (1975) **Adaptation in Natural and Artificial Systems.** University of Michigan Press. Reprinted in by Bradford Books/MIT Press.
- **Holgate, P.** (1966) **A mathematical study of the founder principle of evolutionary genetic.** J. Appl. Probl., 3, 115-128.

- Holland, J.K. (1975) **Adaptation in Natural and Artificial Systems.** University of Michigan Press.
- Holland, J.H., Holyoak, K.J., Nisbett, R.E. & Thagard, P.R. (1986) **Induction.** MIT Press.
- Holmes, F. L. (1986) **Seymour Benzer and the definition of the gene.** In P.J. Beurton, R. Falk and H. Rheinberger. The Concept of the Gene in Development and Evolution: Historical and Epistemological Perspectives. Pp. 115-155. Cambridge University Press.
- Hopfield, J. J. (1982) **Neural networks and physical systems with emergent collective computational abilities.** Proceedings of the National Academy of Sciences (Biophysics). 79(8), 2554-2558.
- Howie, Luke (2006) **Thought Contagion Theory and Terrorism in the Media.**
- Howlett, Peter and Morgan, Mary (...) **MEMES - What Happens If You Say "Meme"?.** []
- Hull, C. L. (1943) **Principles of Behavior.** Appleton-Century-Crofts.
- Hull, David L. (1980) **Individuality and selection.** Ann. Rev. Ecol.Syst., 11, 311-332.
- Hull, David L. (1982) **The naked meme.** In (H.C. Plotkin, ed.) Learning, Development and Culture: Essays in Evolutionary Epistemology. John Wiley and Sons.
- Hull, David L. (1988a) **A mechanism and its metaphysics: an evolutionary account of the social and conceptual development of science.** Biology and Philosophy 3, 123-155.
- Hull, David L. (1988b) **Interactors versus vehicles.** In H.C. Plotkin, ed.: The Role of Behavior in Evolution. MIT Press.
- Hull, David L. (1988c) **Science as a Process: An Evolutionary Account of the Social and Conceptual Development of Science.** University of Chicago Press.
- Hull, David L. (2000) **Taking memetics seriously: Memetics will be what we make it.** In: Darwinizing culture: The status of memetics as a science, ed. R. Aunger, Oxford & New York: Oxford University Press.
- Hull, David L. (2001) **Science and selection.** Cambridge Univ. Press, Cambridge, U.K.
- Hull, David L., Langman, R. E., and Glenn, S. S. (2001) **A general account of selection: biology, immunology, and behavior.** Behav. Brain Sci. 24:511'573. CrossRef, PubMed, CSA.
- Hull, David L. (1999) **Strategies in Meme Theory - a commentary on Rose's paper: Controversies in Meme Theory.** Journal of Memetics - Evolutionary Models of Information Transmission, 3.
- Hull, David L., and Wilkins, John S. (2005-2009) **Replication.** Stanford Encyclopedia of Philosophy.
- Hurd, H., Warr, E. and Polwart, A. (2001) **A parasite that increases host lifespan.** Centre for Applied Entomology and Parasitology, School of Life.
- Hurley, Susan, and Chater, Nick (2005) **Perspectives on Imitation: From Neuroscience to Social Science - Volume 1: Mechanisms of Imitation and Imitation in Animals.**
- Hurley, Susan, and Chater, Nick (2005) **Perspectives on Imitation: From Neuroscience to Social Science - Volume 2: Imitation, Human Development, and Culture.**
- Hünneman, Ronald (2010) **On the Senselessness of Memes & How They Might Make Sense as Replicators**

I
- Ianneo, Francesco (1998) **The Symbiotic Mind. A Memetic Perspective on the Human Consciousness.** Symposium on Memetics: Evolutionary Models of Information Transmission, 15th International Congress on Cybernetics, Namur (Belgium), August 24-28.
- Iberall, D., Wilkinson, D. & White (1993) **Foundations for Social and Biological Evolution: Progress Toward a Physical Theory of Civilization and of Speciation.** Cri-de-Coeur Press.
- Irons, William (2009) **Genes and Cultures - Boyd and Richerson THE INTERTWINED ROLES OF GENES AND CULTURE IN HUMAN EVOLUTION.**

J
- Jablonka, Eva and Lamb, Marion J. (1995) **Epigenetic Inheritance and Evolution: The Lamarckian Dimension.** Oxford: Oxford University Press.
- Jablonka, Eva and Avital, Eytan (2000) **Animal Traditions: behavioural inheritance in evolution.**
- Jablonka, Eva, Lamb, Marion J. (2005) **Evolution in Four Dimensions.** Cambridge, MA: MIT Press.
- Jablonka, Eva, Lamb, Marion J. (2007) **Precis of Evolution in Four Dimensions.** Behav Brain Sci. Aug;30(4):353-65; discusssion 365-89.
- Jablonka, Eva, and Raz, Gal (2009) **Transgenerational epigenetic inheritance: prevalence mechanisms, and implications for the study of heredity and evolution.** Quarterly Review of Biology 84:131-176.
- Jackson, Peter (2007) **Some Thoughts on the Prospect of "Meme" in Religious Studies.**
- Jacobson, Rogan (1998) **Bridging the gap: Memetics as a methodological tool to close the ranks between social and traditional history.** Symposium on Memetics: Evolutionary Models of Information Transmission, 15th International Congress on Cybernetics, Namur (Belgium), August 24-28.
- James, William (1880) **Great Men, Great Thoughts, And The Environment**
- Jan, Steven (2000) **Replicating Sonorities: Towards A Memetics Of Music** Journal of Memetics - Evolutionary Models of Information Transmission, 4.
- Jan, Steven (2007) **The Memetics of Music.**

- Jerison, H. J. (1976) **Paleoneurology and the Evolution of Mind.** Scientific American, 234 (1), p. 90-101.
- Johansson, S. (2004) **The individual and the species in the cultural evolution of language.**
- Johnson, Steven (2010) **Where Good Ideas Come From: The Natural History of Innovation.**
- Jolink, A. (1991) **Liberte, egalite, rarete, the evolutionary economics of Leon Walras.** Thesis, Thinbergen Instructional Research Series: 3.

K
- Kamhi, A.G. (1988) **A meme's eye view of speech-language pathology.** Lang Speech Hear Serv Sch. 2004 Apr;35(2):105-11.
- Kanerva, P. (1988) **Sparse Distributed Memory.** MIT Press.
- Kaplan, N. L., Hudson, R. R., & Langley, C. H. (1989) **The "hitchhiking" effect revisited.** Genetics, 123, 887-899.
- Kary, K. (1982) **Can Darwinian inheritance be extended from biology to epistemology?** In P.D. Asquith & T. Nickles (eds.), PSA 1982, Volume 1. East Lansing, MI: Philosophy of Science Association Press, pp. 356-369.
- Kasher, Asa and Sadka, Ronen (2001) **Constitutive Rule Systems and Cultural Epidemiology.** In "The Epidemology of Ideas".
- Katz, Helena (1998) **Dance and Evolution: a non-stop combination of biology and culture.** Symposium on Memetics: Evolutionary Models of Information Transmission, 15th International Congress on Cybernetics, Namur (Belgium), August 24-28.
- Kawai, Masao (1965) **Newly acquired Pre cultural Behavior of the Natural Troop of Japanese Monkeys on Koshima Islet.** Primates, vol. 6, no. 1, p. 1.
- Keller, Albert Galloway (1916) **Societal Evolution.** New York: Macmillan.
- Kelly, Kevin (1984) **Information as a Communicable Disease.** CoEvolution Quarterly, Summer edition.
- Keil, F. C. (1979) **Semantic and Conceptual Development: An Ontological Perspective.** Harvard University Press.
- Keim, Brandon (2010) **Culture Evolves Slowly, Falls Apart Quickly.** Wired.
- Keller, Laurent and G. Ross, Kenneth (1993) **Phenotypic Plasticity and "Cultural Transmission" of Alternative Social Organizations in the Fire Ant Solenopsis invicta** Behavioral Ecology and Sociobiology Vol. 33, No. 2, pp. 121-129.
- Kelly, Jon and Sheerin, Jude (2010) **The strange virtual world of 4chan.**
- Kendal, Jeremy R. and Laland, K. (2000) **Mathematical Models For Memetics.** Journal of Memetics - Evolutionary Models of Information Transmission, 4.
- Kendal, Jeremy R. (2011) **Human niche construction in interdisciplinary focus.**
- Keirsey, David M. (2001) **Genes, Memes, Wemes, and Xemes.**
- Kennington, Alan U. (2011) **Richard Dawkins meme idea is nonsense.**
- Khan, Razib (2011) **We stand on the shoulders of cultural giants**
- Kidd, Benjamin (1894) **Social Evolution.** London: Macmillan.
- Kilpinen, Erkki (2006) **Memetics: A Critique** On the use of meaning concepts about nature and culture.
- Kilpinen, Erkki (2007) **Memes versus Signs** On the use of meaning concepts about nature and culture.
- Kimball, A. Samuel (2007) **The Infanticidal Logic of Evolution and Culture.**
- Kincaid, Harold (2006) **Evolutionary social science beyond culture.**
- King, Mike (2011) **Richard Dawkins and Memes - Can the Man Be Serious or Is He Pulling Our Leg?.**
- Kingwell, Mark (1999) **Viral Culture (why many people do the same thing at the same time)**
- Kirby, Justin and Marsden, Paul (2005) **Connected Marketing: The Viral, Buzz and Word of Mouth Revolution**
- Kirby, S., Cornish, H. and Smith, K. (2008) **Cumulative cultural evolution in the laboratory: an experimental approach to the origins of structure in human language.**
- Kirby, S. and Smith, K. (2008) **Cultural evolution: implications for understanding the human language faculty and its evolution.**
- Kirschen, Yaakov (2010) **Memetics and the Viral Spread of Antisemitism Through 'Coded Images' in Political Cartoons.**
- Kitcher, Philip (2001) **Infectious Ideas: Some Preliminary Explorations.** In "The Epidemology of Ideas".
- Klepper, Howard (2000) **Review of The Meme Machine by Susan Blackmore.**
- Kline , Michelle A. and Boyd, Robert (2010) **Population size predicts technological complexity in Oceania.**
- Koestler, A. (1964) **The Act of Creation.** Picador.
- Koneni, V. J. (2008) **A review of The Memetics of Music: A Neo-Darwinian View of Musical Structure and Culture.** Picador.

- Koestler, A. (1964) **The Act of Creation.** Picador.
- Kojima, K. & Schaeffer, H. E. (1967) **Survival processes of linked mutant genes.** Evolution, 21, p. 518-531.
- Kronfeldner, Maria E. (2007) **Darwinism, Memes, and Creativity: A Critique of Darwinian Analogical Reasoning from Nature to Culture.** University Regensburg.
- Kronfeldner, Maria E. (2007) **Is cultural evolution Lamarckian?**
- Kronfeldner, Maria E. (2009) **Darwinian 'Blind' Hypothesis Formation Revisited.**
- Kronfeldner, Maria E. (2011) **Darwinian Creativity and Memetics.** Acumen Research Edition.
- Krythia, Gillian and Crozier, Dawn (2011) **A critical examination of cultural evolution: natural selection in bird songs.** Acumen Research Edition.
- Kubo, Masao, Naruse, Keitaro, Sato, Hiroshi and Matubara Takashi (2007) **The possibility of an epidemic meme analogy for web community population analysis.** In Proceedings of the 8th international conference on Intelligent data engineering and automated learning (IDEAL'07), Hujun Yin, Peter Tino, Will Byrne, Xin Yao, and Emilio Corchado (Eds.). Springer-Verlag, Berlin, Heidelberg, 1073-1080.
- Kubose, S. K. & Umenoto, T. (1980) **Creativity and the Zen Koan.** Psychologia, 23(1), p. 1-9.
- Kuhn, T. S. (1970) **The Structure of Scientific Revolutions.** University of Chicago Press.
- Kull, Kalevi (2000) **Copy versus translate, meme versus sign: development of biological textuality.** European Journal for Semiotic Studies 12(1), 101–120.
- Kuper, A. (2000) **If memes are the answer, what is the question?** p. 175-188 in R. Aunger, ed. Darwinizing culture. Oxford Univ. Press, Oxford, U.K.
- Kuper, A. (2006) **Meme Wars Part 1**
- Kvasnicka, Vladimir and Pospichal, Jiri (2008) **Theory of Cooperative Coevolution of Genes and Memes.**

L

- Laiolo, P. (1990) **Erosion of animal cultures in fragmented landscapes.**
- Lake, Mark W., Renfrew, Colin, and Scarre, Christopher (1998) **Digging for memes: the role of material objects in cultural evolution.** In Cognition and material culture : the archaeology of symbolic storage.
- Laland, Kevin N. and Plotkin, H. (1990) **Social learning and social transmission of digging for buried food in Norway rats.**
- Laland, Kevin N., Kumm, Jochen and Feldman, Marcus W. (1995) **Gene-Culture Coevolutionary Theory: A Test Case.** Current Anthropology, vol. 36, no. 1, p. 131-156.
- Laland, Kevin N., Odling-Smee, J. and Feldman, M. W. (2000a) **Niche construction, biological evolution, and cultural change.** Behav. Brain Sci 23:131'175. CrossRef, PubMed, CSA.
- Laland, Kevin N. and Odling-Smee J. (2000b) **The evolution of the meme.** In: Darwinizing culture: The status of memetics as a science, ed. R. Aunger, Oxford & New York: Oxford University Press.
- Laland, Kevin N. and Odling-Smee J. and Feldman, M. W. (2000c) **Niche Construction Earns its Keep.** Behavioral and Brain Sciences 23 (1):164-172.
- Laland, Kevin N. (2001) **Gene-Culture Coevolution.**
- Laland, Kevin N. and Brown, Gillian R. (2002) **Sense and nonsense: evolutionary perspectives on human behaviour.** Oxford Univ. Press, Oxford, U.K.
- Laland, Kevin N. (2004) **Extending the Extended Phenotype.** Biology and Philosophy 19: 313–325.
- Laland, Kevin N. and Odling-Smee J. and Feldman, M. W. (2005) **On the Breadth and Significance of Niche Construction: A Reply to Griffiths, Okasha and Sterelny. Biology and Philosophy 20 (1).**
- Laland, Kevin N. (2007) **The niche construction perspective.**
- Laland, Kevin N. and Galef, Bennett G.. (2009) **The Question of Animal Culture.**
- Laland, Kevin N. and Odling-Smee J. and Myles, Sean (2010) **How culture shaped the human genome: bringing genetics and the human sciences together.** Nature Reviews Genetics 11, 137-148. The article's 5 boxes available online.
- Laland, Kevin N. and Odling-Smee J. and Feldman, M. W. (2011) **Conceptual Barriers to Progress Within Evolutionary Biology.** Foundations of Science.
- Langley, David J., Pals, J. Nico and Ortt, Roland (2005) **Adoption of behaviour: predicting success for major innovations.** European Journal of Innovation Management, Vol. 8 Iss: 1, pp.56 - 78.
- Langrish, John Z. (1999) **Different Types of Memes: Recipemes, Selectemes and Explanemes.** Journal of Memetics - Evolutionary Models of Information Transmission, 3.
- Langton, C.G. (1992) **Life at the edge of chaos.** In (C.G. Langton, C. Taylor, J.D. Farmer & S. Rasmussen, eds.) Artificial Life II. Addison-Wesley.
- Lanier, Jaron (2004) **Vaulting into a Rapturous techno-future with Jaron Lanier**
- Lanier, Jaron (1997) **The Value of Memes: A Powerful Paradigm or a Poor Metaphor?** The Edge.
- Lanier, Jaron and Dawkins, Richard (1997) **Evolution: The Dissent Of Darwin; A debate**

Psychology Today, Jan-Feb.

• **Lanier, Jaron** (1999) **Jaron Lanier on The Evolution of Culture by Daniel C. Dennett** The Edge.
• **Lass, Roger** (1996) **Of emes and memes: on the trail of the wild replicator.**
• **Lateiner, Joshua S.** (1992) **Of Man, Mind and Machine: Meme-Based Models of Mind and the Possibility for Consciousness in Alternate Media.**
• **Laurent, John** (1999) **A Note On The Origin Of 'Memes/Mnemes'** Journal of Memetics - Evolutionary Models of Information Transmission, 3.
• **Laurent, John and Nightingale, John** (2001) **Darwinism and evolutionary economics.**
• **Lefebvre, L.** (1995) **The opening of milk bottles by birds - evidence for accelerating learning rates, but against the wave?of?advance model of cultural transmission.** Behav. Processes 34, 43–53.
• **Lehmann, Laurent, Feldman, Marcus W. and Foster, Kevin R.** (2008a) **Cultural Transmission Can Inhibit the Evolution of Altruistic Helping.**
• **Lehmann, Laurent and Feldman, Marcus W.** (2008b) **The co-evolution of culturally inherited altruistic helping and cultural transmission under random group formation.** Theor Popul Biol. Jun;73(4):506-16.
• **Lehmann, Laurent, Foster, K.R., Borenstein, E. and Feldman, Marcus W.** (2008c) **Social and individual learning of helping in humans and other species.** Trends Ecol Evol. 2008 Dec;23(12):664-71. Epub 2008 Oct 23.
• **Lehmann, Laurent and Feldman, Marcus W.** (2009) **Coevolution of adaptive technology, maladaptive culture and population size in a producer-scrounger game.** Proc Biol Sci. Nov 7;276(1674):3853-62.
• **Lehmann, Laurent, Feldman, Marcus W. and Kaeuffer, R.** (2010) **Cumulative cultural dynamics and the coevolution of cultural innovation and transmission: an ESS model for panmictic and structured populations.** J Evol Biol. 2010 Nov;23(11):2356-69.
• **Lehmann, Laurent, Aoki, K and Feldman, Marcus W.** (2011) **On the number of independent cultural traits carried by individuals and populations.** Philos Trans R Soc Lond B Biol Sci. 2011 Feb 12;366(1563):424-35.
• **Leigh, Hoyle** (2010) **Genes, Memes, Culture, and Mental Illness: Toward an Integrative Model.**
• **Lende, D.** (2009) **Engaging & Dispatching Memetics.**
• **Lende, D.** (2010) **People, Not Memes, Are the Medium!**
• **Levinson, D. & Malone, M. J.** (1980) **Toward Explaining Human Culture: Critical Review of the Findings of Worldwide Cross-Cultural Research.** New Haven: HRAF Press.
• **Levinson, Stephen C. and Jaisson, Pierre** (2005) **Evolution and Culture: A Fyssen Foundation Symposium.**
• **Leskovec, Jure, Backstrom, Lars and Kleinberg, Jon** (2009) **Meme-tracking and the Dynamics of the News Cycle.**
• **Lester, D.** (2009) **Memes and suicide.** Psychol Rep. 2009 Aug;105(1):3-10.
• **Levi-Strauss, C.** (1966) **The Savage Mind.** University of Chicago Press.
• **Levi-Strauss, C.** (1969) **The Raw and the Cooked.** Harper and Row.
• **Levi-Strauss, C.** (1976) **Structural Anthropology, Vol. II.** Basic Books, pp. 146-197.
• **Lewis, Herbert S.** (2001) **Boas, Darwin and Science.**
• **Lewens, Tim** (2007) **Stanford Encyclopedia of Philosophy section of cultural evolution.**
• **Lewontin, R. C.** (1970) **The Units of Selection** Annual Review of Ecology and Systematics. Vol. 1: 1-18.
• **Lewontin, R. C.** (1981) **Review of "Cultural transmission and evolution: A quantitative approach".** [review]
• **Lewontin, R. C.** (1982) **Organism and environment.** In: Plotkin, E.C. (ed) Learning, Development and Culture. Wiley, pp. 151–170.
• **Lewontin, R. C.** (1983) **Gene, organism, and environment.** In: Bendall, D.S. (ed) Evolution from Molecules to Men. Cambridge University Press, pp. 273–285.
• **Lewontin, R. C.** (2000) **The Triple Helix: Gene, Organism and Environment.** Harvard University Press.
• **Lewontin, R. C.** (2003) **Does Culture Evolve?**
• **Linquist, Stefan** (1976) **The Evolution of Culture.** Volume 4, International Library of Essays on Evolutionary Thought.
• **Lissack, Michael R.** (2004) **The Redefinition of Memes: Ascribing Meaning to an Empty Cliche.** Journal of Memetics - Evolutionary Models of Information Transmission, 3.
• **Little A. C., Jones B. C., Debruine L. M., Caldwell C. A.** (2011) **Social learning and human mate preferences: a potential mechanism for generating and maintaining between-population diversity in attraction.** Philos Trans R Soc Lond B Biol Sci. 2011 Feb 12;366(1563):366-75.
• **Lopreato, Joseph and Crippen, Timothy** (2001) **Crisis in Sociology: The Need for Darwin.**
• **Lord, A. and Price, If** (2001) **Reconstruction of organisational phylogeny from memetic similarity**

analysis: **Proof of feasibility.** Journal of Memetics - Evolutionary Models of Information Transmission, 5.

- **Luchins, A. S.** (1942) **Mechanization in problem solving.** Psychological Monographs, 54, No. 248.
- **Lukaszewski, Aaron** (2004) **Perspectives on Memetics - Cultural Transmission as a Darwinian Selection Process.**
- **Lumsden, C. & Wilson, E. O.** (1981) **Genes, Mind, and Culture.** Harvard University Press.
- **Lumsden, C. & Wilson, E. O.** (1981) **Promethean Fire: Reflections on the Origin of Mind.** Harvard University Press.
- **Lumsden, C.** (1983) **Neuronal group selection and the evolution of hominid cranial capacity.**
- **Lumsden, C. & Wilson, E. O.** (1985) **The relation between biological and cultural evolution.** Journal of Social and Biological Systems. Volume 8, Issue 4, October 1985, Pages 343-359.
- **Lumsden, Charles, J.** (1989) **Psychological Development: Epigenetic Rules and Gene-Culture Coevolution.** In: MacDonald, Kevin B. (ed.): Sociobiological Perspectives on Human Development. New York: Springer.
- **Lumsden, Charles, J.** (1989) **Does Culture Need Genes?** Ethology and Sociobiology, vol. 10, no. 1-3, p. 11-28.
- **Lumsden, Charles, J. and Findlay, C. Scott** (1988) **Evolution of the creative mind.** Creativity Research Journal Volume 1, Issue 1.
- **Lyman, R. Lee and O'Brien, Michael J.** (2003) **Cultural Traits: Units of Analysis in Early Twentieth-Century Anthropology** Journal of Anthropological Research. Vol. 59, No. 2 (Summer, 2003), pp. 225-250.
- **Lycett S. J., Collard M., McGrew W. C.** (2007) **Phylogenetic analyses of behavior support existence of culture among wild chimpanzees.** Proc Natl Acad Sci U. S. A. 104: 17588'17592.
- **Lynch, Aaron** (1991) **Thought contagion as abstract evolution.** Journal of Ideas 2: 3-10.
- **Lynch, Aaron** (1996a) **Thought Contagion: How Belief Spreads Through Society, the New Science of Memes.** Basic Books.
- **Lynch, Aaron** (1997) **Thought contagion and mass belief.** Originally written for the Swiss journal gdi-impuls.
- **Lynch, Aaron** (1997) **Thought Contagion Theory and the Heaven's Gate Tragedy.**
- **Lynch, Aaron** (1998a) **Thought Contagion Theory and the Heaven's Gate Tragedy.** 1998 version - *very* different content.
- **Lynch, Aaron** (1998b) **Units, Events and Dynamics in Memetic Evolution** , Journal of Memetics - Evolutionary Models of Information Transmission, 2.
- **Lynch, Aaron** (1998c) **A response to Paul Marsden.**
- **Lynch, Aaron** (1998d) **Rationales for Mathematical Modeling and Points of Terminology** Journal of Memetics - Evolutionary Models of Information Transmission, 2.
- **Lynch, Aaron** (1998e) **The Millennium Contagion - Is Your Mental Software Year 2000 Compliant?**
- **Lynch, Aaron** (1998f) **Memes and Mass Delusion.** A Lecture Presented to the Philadelphia Association for Critical Thinking.
- **Lynch, Aaron** (1999) **Misleading Mix Of Religion And Science - a commentary on Gatherer's paper: Why the 'Thought Contagion' Metaphor is Retarding the Progress of Memetics** Journal of Memetics - Evolutionary Models of Information Transmission, 3.
- **Lynch, Aaron** (2000a) **Thought Contagions in the Stock Market.** Journal of Psychology and Financial Markets 1: 1, p. 10-23.
- **Lynch, Aaron** (2000b) **Thought contagion in the stock markets: A general framework and focus on the Internet bubble.**
- **Lynch, Aaron** (2001) **Thought Contagions in Deflating and Inflating Phases of the Bubble.**
- **Lynch, Aaron** (2002a) **Evolutionary Contagion in Mental Software.** In Sternberg, Robert, and Kaufman, James (eds.), The Evolution of Intelligence. Mahwah, NJ: Lawrence Erlbaum Associates.
- **Lynch, Aaron** (2002b) **Thought Contagion in the Dynamics of Mass Conflict.** Paper presented at the Swedish Defence Research Agency, Stockholm.
- **Lynch, Aaron** (2002c) **Thought Contagion in the AIDS Epidemic.** Presented at the Swedish Defence Research Agency, Stockholm.
- **Lynch, Aaron** (2003a) **Thought Contagions and Pathological Dieting** Based on a February, 2000 email and telephone interview with Megan McCafferty of Glamour Magazine, Revised January 23, 2003.
- **Lynch, Aaron** (2003b) **Units, Events, and Dynamics in the Evolutionary Epidemiology of Ideas.**
- **Lynch, Aaron** (2003c) **An Introduction to the Evolutionary Epidemiology of Ideas.**
- **Lynch, Alejandro and Baker, A. J.** (1986) **Congruence of morphometric and cultural evolution in Atlantic island chaffinch populations.** Canadian Journal of Zoology, 64:(7) 1576-1580, 10.1139/z86-236
- **Lynch, Alejandro, Plunkett, G. M., Baker, A. J., & Jenkins, P. F.** (1989) **A model of cultural evolution of chaffinch song derived with the meme concept.** The American Naturalist, Vol. 133, 634-

653.

- **Lynch, Alejandro & Baker, A. J.** (1993) **A population memetics approach to cultural evolution in chaffinch song: Meme divsersity within populations.** Am. Nat., Vol. 141, 597-620.
- **Lynch, Alejandro** (1996b) **The Population Memetics of Birdsong.** In Ecology and Evolution of Acoustic Communication in Birds, edited by D. E. Kroodsma and E. H. Miller, pp. 181'197. Ithaca.
- **Lynch, Gary and Granger, Richard** (2008) **Big Brain: The Origins and Future of Human Intelligence.**

M
- **Mace, Ruth and Pagel, Mark D.** (1994) **The comparative method in anthropology.** Curr. Anthropol 35:549'564.
- **Mace, Ruth, Holden, Claire J. and Shennan, Stephen** (2005) **The Evolution of Cultural Diversity: A Phylogenetic Approach.**
- **Mace, Ruth, Jordan, F. M.** (2011) **Macro-evolutionary studies of cultural diversity: a review of empirical studies of cultural transmission and cultural adaptation.** Philosophical Transactions of the Royal Society B: Biological Sciences 366:1563, 402-411
- **Machery, Edouard** (2005) **Review of The Origin and Evolution of Cultures. Boyd, Robert and Richerson, Peter J.**
- **Mackay, Craig** (2008) **Supergenes: What Really Makes Us Human.**
- **Magne, Sylvain** (2010) **Comments on "The evolution of the meme" by Kevin Laland and John Odling-Smee.**
- **Magne, Sylvain** (2010) **Comments on "An objection to the memetic approach of culture." by Dan Sperber.**
- **Magne, Sylvain** (2010) **Comments on Robert Boyd and Peter J. Richerson's article.**
- **Majoros, William** (2002) **Syntactic Structure in Birdsong: Memetic Evolution of Songs or Grammars?** Journal of Memetics - Evolutionary Models of Information Transmission, 6.
- **Malthus, T.** (1798) **An essay on the principle of population.** Republished in 1970 by Penguin, Harmondsworth, U.K.
- **Mandelbrot, B.B.** (1982) **The Fractal Nature of Geometry.** W.H. Freedman and Company.
- **Marks, Jonathan** (2000) **Can a holistic anthropology inform a reductive genetics?** Paper presented at the 99th Annual Meeting of the American Anthropological Association
- **Marks, Jonathan** (2002) **Review of: Darwinizing Culture: The Status of Memetics as a Science.** American Anthropologist
- **Marks, Jonathan** (2004) **What, if anything, is a Darwinian anthropology?**
- **Marks, Jonathan** (2005) **The meme shows. Review of Coevolution: Genes, culture, and human diversity.**
- **Marsden, Paul** (1997) **Crash contagion.** Unpublished Paper delivered at University of Sussex conference 'Death and Diana'
- **Marsden, Paul** (1998a) **Memetics and Social Contagion: Two Sides of the Same Coin?** Journal of Memetics - Evolutionary Models of Information Transmission, 2.
- **Marsden, Paul** (1998b) **Operationalising memetics - Suicide, the Werther effect, and the work of David P. Phillips.** Symposium on Memetics: Evolutionary Models of Information Transmission, 15th International Congress on Cybernetics, Namur (Belgium), August 24-28.
- **Marsden, Paul** (1998c) **Memetics: a new paradigm for understanding customer behaviour and influence.** Marketing Intelligence & Planning, Vol. 16 Iss: 6, pp.363 - 368.
- **Marsden, Paul** (1998d) **A Review of: Shifting the Patterns: Breaching the Memetic Codes of Corporate Peformance by If Price and Ray Shaw.** Journal of Memetics - Evolutionary Models of Information Transmission, 2.
- **Marsden, Paul** (1999a) **A Strategy for Memetics: Memes as Strategies** Journal of Memetics - Evolutionary Models of Information Transmission, 3.
- **Marsden, Paul** (1999b) **Review of Thought Contagion: How Belief Spreads Through Society** by Aaron Lynch, Journal of Artificial Societies and Social Simulation, 2.
- **Marsden, Paul** (1999c) **The selectionist paradigm: More implications for sociology.** Sociological Research Online.
- **Marsden, Paul** (2000) **Forefathers of Memetics: Gabriel Tarde and the Laws of Imitation.** Journal of Memetics - Evolutionary Models of Information Transmission, 4.
- **Marsden, Paul** (2001) **Copycat Terrorism: Fanning the Fire.** Journal of Memetics - Evolutionary Models of Information Transmission, 5.
- **Marsden, Paul** (2001) **Is Suicide Contagious? A Case Study In Applied Memetics.** Journal of Memetics - Evolutionary Models of Information Transmission, 5.
- **Marsden, Paul** (2005) **Seed to spread: how seeding trials ignite epidemics of demand.** In "Connected Marketing: The Buzz, Viral and Word of Mouth Revolution"

- **Marsden, Paul and Attia, Sharon** (2005) **A deadly contagion?**
- **Marsden, Paul** (2008) **Operationalising Memetics - Suicide, the Werther Effect, and the work of** David P. Phillips
- **Marshall, Garry** (1998) **The Internet And Memetics.** Symposium on Memetics: Evolutionary Models of Information Transmission, 15th International Congress on Cybernetics, Namur (Belgium), August 24-28.
- **Mason, Kelby** (1998) **Thoughts As Tools: The Meme In Daniel Dennett's Work.** Symposium on Memetics: Evolutionary Models of Information Transmission, 15th International Congress on Cybernetics, Namur (Belgium), August 24-28.
- **Masterman, M.** (1970) **The Nature of a Paradigm.** In (I. Lakatos, & A. Musgrave, eds.) Criticism and the Growth of Knowledge. Cambridge University Press.
- **May, R.M.** (1978) **The evolution of ecological systems.** Sci. Am. 239: 119-133.
- **Maynard-Smith, J. and Haigh, J.** (1974) **The hitchhiking effect of a favourable gene.** Genetic Research, 23, 23-35.
- **Maynard-Smith, J.** (1986) **Natural Selection of Culture? A review of Culture and the Evolutionary Process.** New York Review of Books. November 6.
- **Maynard-Smith, J.** (1988) **Did Darwin get it right : essays on games, sex, and evolution.**
- **Maynard-Smith, J. & Szathmáry, Eörs** (1995a) **The Major Transitions in Evolution.** Oxford: W. H. Freeman/Spektrum.
- **Maynard-Smith, John** (1995b) **Genes, Memes, & Minds.** November 30.
- **Maynard-Smith, John** (1999) **Evolution-Natural and Artificial**
- **Maynard-Smith, John and Szathmáry, Eörs** (1999) **The Origins of Life: From the. Birth of Life to the Origin of Language.** Oxford: Oxford University. Press.
- **Mayr, E.** (1976) **Evolution and the Diversity of Life.** Harvard University Press.
- **Mayr, E.** (1982) **The Growth of Biological Thought.** Harvard University Press.
- **McCulloch, W.S. & Pitts, W.** (1943) **A logical calculus of the ideas immanent in nervous activity.** Bulletin of Mathematical Biophysics, 5, p. 115-133.
- **McElreath, Richard, Boyd, Robert and Richerson, Peter J.** (2003) **Shared norms and the evolution of ethnic markers.** Current Anthropology, 44(1), 122-129.
- **McElreath, Richard, Lubell, M., Richerson, Peter J., Waring, T., Baum, W., & Edsten, E., et al.** (2005) **Applying evolutionary models to the laboratory study of social learning.** Evolution and Human Behavior, 26, 483-508.
- **McElreath, Richard and Boyd, Robert** (2007) **Mathematical Models of Social Evolution: A Guide for the Perplexed.** University Of Chicago Press
- **McElreath, Richard and Strimling, P.** (2008) **When natural selection favors learning from parents.** Current Anthropology, 49, 307-316.
- **McElreath, Richard and Henrich, Joseph** (2008) **Modeling Cultural Evolution.** In R. Dunbar & L. Barrett (Eds.), (pp. 571-585). Oxford Univ Press.
- **McElreath, Richard** (2009) **Linking the micro and macro in cultural evolution (Review of Shennan, Pattern and Process in Cultural Evolution).** Trends in Evolution and Ecology, 24, 588-589.
- **McElreath, Richard** (2010) **The coevolution of genes, innovation and culture in human evolution.** In J. Silk & P. Kappeler (Eds.), (pp. 451-474). Springer.
- **McElreath, Richard** (2011) **The Coevolution of Warfare, Punishment, and Culture in Homo sapiens.**
- **McFarland, D. J. & Sibly, R. M.** (1975) **The behavioural final common path.** Philosophical Transactions of the London Royal Society, 270B, p. 265-93.
- **McGrath, Alister** (2004) **Dawkins' God: Genes, Memes, and the Meaning of Life.**
- **McGrath, Alister** (2006) **The Spell of the Meme.**
- **McGrath, Alister and McGrath, Joanna Collicutt** (2007) **The Dawkins Delusion?: Atheist Fundamentalism and the Denial of the Divine.**
- **McGrath, Alister** (2011) **Darwinism and the Divine: Evolutionary Thought and Natural Theology.**
- **McGrew, W. C.** (1992) **Chimpanzee Material Culture: Implications for Human Evolution.** Cambridge University Press.
- **McMullin, Barry** (1995) **Replicators Don't.**
- **McNamara, Adam** (2011) **Can we measure memes?**
- **McShea, D.W.** (1991) **Complexity and evolution: What everybody knows.** Biology and Philosophy 6, p. 303-324.
- **Medawar, Sir Peter B.** (1959) **The Future Of Man.**
- **Medawar, Sir Peter B.** (1981) **Stretch Genes - A review of Genes, Mind, and Culture: The Coevolutionary Process by Charles J. Lumsden, by Edward O. Wilson.**
- **Meddin, J.** (1979) **Chimpanzees, Symbols, and the Reflective Self.**
- **Meneghetti, Antonio** (2003) **Ontopsychology and Memetics.** Psicologica Editrice.

- Merel, Peter (1999) **Why I am not a Memeticist.**
- Mery F, Varela SA, Danchin E, Blanchet S, Parejo D, Coolen I, Wagner RH. (2009) **Public versus personal information for mate copying in an invertebrate.** Curr Biol. 2009 May 12;19(9):730-4. Epub 2009 Apr 9.
- Mesoudi, Alex, Whiten, Andrew and Laland, Kevin N. (2004a) **Perspective: is human cultural evolution Darwinian? Evidence reviewed from the perspective of the Origin of Species.** PMID: 15058714.
- Mesoudi, Alex & Whiten, Andrew (2004b) **The hierarchical transformation of event knowledge in human cultural transmission.** Journal of Cognition and Culture, 4(1), 1-24.
- Mesoudi, Alex (2005a) **The transmission and evolution of human culture.** Ph.D. Thesis, University of St Andrews, UK.
- Mesoudi, Alex (2005b) **Book review of Richerson, P.J. and Boyd, Robert Not By Genes Alone: How Culture Transformed Human Evolution.** Quarterly Review of Biology 80(4), 506-507.
- Mesoudi, Alex, Whiten, Andrew and Laland, Kevin N. (2006a) **Towards a unified science of cultural evolution.** PMID: 17094820.
- Mesoudi, Alex, Whiten, Andrew, Laland, Kevin N. and Dunbar R. (2006b) **A bias for social information in human cultural transmission.** PMID: 16848951.
- Mesoudi, Alex, Whiten, Andrew and Laland, Kevin N. (2006c) **A science of culture: Clarifications and extensions**
- Mesoudi, Alex (2007a) **Biological and Cultural Evolution: Similar but Different.**
- Mesoudi, Alex (2007b) **A Darwinian Theory of Cultural Evolution Can Promote an Evolutionary Synthesis for the Social Sciences.**
- Mesoudi, Alex, Laland, Kevin N. (2007c) **Culturally transmitted paternity beliefs and the evolution of human mating behaviour.** PMID: 17360288.
- Mesoudi, Alex (2007d) **Using the methods of experimental social psychology to study cultural evolution.** Journal of Social, Evolutionary and Cultural Psychology 1(2), 35-58.
- Mesoudi, Alex (2007e) **Extended evolutionary theory makes human culture more amenable to evolutionary analysis** Commentary on Jablonka, E. & Lamb, M. J., Precis of Evolution in Four Dimensions. Behavioral and Brain Sciences 30(4), 374.
- Mesoudi, Alex (2007f) **Has mental time travel really affected human culture? Commentary on Suddendorf, T. & Corballis, M. C. The evolution of foresight: What is mental time travel and is it unique to humans?** Behavioral and Brain Sciences 30(3), 326-327.
- Mesoudi, Alex, Whiten, A. & Laland, K.N. (2007g) **Science, evolution and cultural anthropology. Anthropology Today 22, p.18. (A response to Ingold [2007] The trouble with "evolutionary biology").**
- Mesoudi, Alex & Laland, K.N. (2007h) **Extending the behavioral sciences framework: clarification of methods, predictions and concepts. Commentary on H. Gintis, A framework for the unification of the behavioral sciences,** Behavioral and Brain Sciences. 30(1), 36-37.
- Mesoudi, Alex, Whiten, A. & Laland, K.N. (2007i) **Book review of Levinson, S.C. and Jaisson, P. Evolution and Culture.** Quarterly Review of Biology 82(1), 45.
- Mesoudi, Alex, Whiten, Andrew (2008a) **The multiple roles of cultural transmission experiments in understanding human cultural evolution** PMID: 15058714. Philos Trans R Soc Lond B Biol Sci. 2008 Nov 12;363(1509):3489-501. Review.
- Mesoudi, Alex, Whiten, Andrew (2008b) **Review. Establishing an experimental science of culture: animal social diffusion experiments.** PMID: 18799418 .
- Mesoudi, Alex, Danielson P. (2008c) **Ethics, evolution and culture.** PMID: 18357481.
- Mesoudi, Alex (2008d) **The experimental study of cultural transmission and its potential for explaining archaeological data.** In Cultural Transmission and Archaeology: Issues and Case Studies, edited by M.J. O'Brien. Washington, D.C.: Society for American Archaeology Press.
- Mesoudi, Alex and O'Brien, M. J. (2008e) **The learning and transmission of hierarchical cultural recipes.** Biological Theory, 3(1), 63-72.
- Mesoudi, Alex, Danielson, P. & Stanev, R. (2008f) **N.E.R.D. and norms: Framework and experiments.** Philosophy of Science 75(5), 786-798.
- Mesoudi, Alex & O'Brien, M.J. (2008g) **The cultural transmission of Great Basin projectile point technology I: An experimental simulation** American Antiquity 73(1), 3-28.
- Mesoudi, Alex, Whiten A. & O'Brien, M.J. (2008h) **The cultural transmission of Great Basin projectile point technology II: An agent-based computer simulation.** American Antiquity, 73(4), 627-644.
- Mesoudi, Alex, Whiten A. (2008i) **An experimental simulation of the "copy-successful-individuals" cultural learning strategy: Adaptive landscapes, producer-scrounger dynamics and informational access costs.** Evolution and Human Behavior, 29(5), 350-363.

- **Mesoudi, Alex, Whiten A.** (2008j) **Foresight in cultural evolution.** Biology and Philosophy 23(2), 243-255.
- **Mesoudi, Alex** (2009a) **How cultural evolutionary theory can inform social psychology and vice versa.**
- **Mesoudi, Alex** (2009b) **The cultural dynamics of copycat suicide.** PLoS One. 2009 Sep 30;4(9) :e7252.
- **Mesoudi, Alex & Lycett, S. J.** (2009c) **Random copying, frequency-dependent copying and culture change.** Evolution and Human Behavior, 30(1), 41-48.
- **Mesoudi, Alex & O'Brien, M.J.** (2009d) **Placing archaeology within a unified science of cultural evolution.** In Pattern and Process in Cultural Evolution, edited by S.J. Shennan (pp. 21-32). Berkeley: University of California Press.
- **Mesoudi, Alex, O'Brien MJ, Lyman RL, VanPool TL.** (2010) **Cultural traits as units of analysis.** Philos Trans R Soc Lond B Biol Sci. 2010 Dec 12;365(1559):3797-806.
- **Mesoudi, Alex, Veldhuis, D. & Foley, R.A.** (2010) **Why aren't the social sciences Darwinian?** Journal of Evolutionary Psychology, 8(2), 93-104.
- **Mesoudi, Alex** (2010) **Evolutionary synthesis in the social sciences and humanities.** Cultural Science 3(1).
- **Mesoudi, Alex** (2010) **Studying cultural innovation in the psychology lab.** In Cultural Innovation: Contributions from Evolutionary Anthropology, edited by M.J. O'Brien and S.J. Shennan (pp.175-191). Cambridge, MA: MIT Press.
- **Mesoudi, Alex & Jensen, K.** (2010) **Culture and the evolution of human sociality.** In: The Oxford Handbook of Comparative Evolutionary Psychology, edited by J. Vonk & T. Shackelford. Oxford, UK: Oxford University Press.
- **Mesoudi, Alex** (2011) **Culture and the Darwinian Renaissance in the social sciences and humanities.** Journal of Evolutionary Psychology.
- **Mesoudi, Alex** (2011) **Cultural Evolution: How Darwinian theory can explain human culture and synthesize the social sciences.** Chicago, IL: University of Chicago Press.
- **Mesoudi, Alex** (2011) **Variable cultural acquisition costs constrain cumulative cultural evolution.** PLoS ONE 6, e18239.
- **Mesoudi, Alex** (2011) **An experimental comparison of human social learning strategies: Payoff-biased social learning is adaptive but under-used.** Evolution and Human Behavior.
- **Mesoudi, Alex, McElligott, A. & Adger, D.** (2011) **Integrating genetic and cultural evolutionary approaches to language.** Human Biology.
- **Mesoudi, Alex, Whiten, A. & Laland, K.N.** (20011) **Evolutionary psychology meets cultural psychology.** Book review of Schaller, Norenzayan, Heine, Yamagishi & Kameda: Evolution, Culture and the Human Mind. Journal of Evolutionary Psychology 9, 83-87.
- **Mesoudi, Alex** (20011) **An experimental comparison of human social learning strategies: payoff-biased social learning is adaptive but underused.** Evolution and Human Behavior 32 (2011) 334–342.
- **Michel, J .B., Shen, Y. K., Aiden, A. P., Veres, A., Gray, M. K.; Google Books Team, Pickett, J. P., Hoiberg, D., Clancy, D., Norvig, P., Orwant, J., Pinker, S., Nowak, M. A., Aiden, E. L.** (2011) **Quantitative analysis of culture using millions of digitized books.** Science. 2011 Jan 14;331(6014):176-82. Dec 16.
- **Midgley, Mary** (1979) **Gene-Juggling.** Philosophy 54 (210):439 - 458.
- **Midgley, Mary** (1999) **Of Memes and Witchcraft.**
- **Midgley, Mary** (2004) **The Myths We Live By.**
- **Miller, G. A.** (1956) **The magic number seven, plus or minus two: Some limits on our capacity for processing information.** Psychological Review, 63, p. 81-97.
- **Miller, Geoffrey F.** (2001) **The Mating Mind: How Sexual Choice Shaped the Evolution of Human Nature.**
- **Miller, Geoffrey F.** (2009) **Spent: Sex, Evolution, and Consumer Behavior.**
- **Miller, M. B.** (2007) **SUICIDE AND EVOLUTION.**
- **Miller, Tristan** (2010) **Meme skepticism.**
- **Millikan, Ruth Garrett** (2001) **Purposes and Cross-purposes: On the Evolution of Languages and Language.** In "The Epidemology of Ideas".
- **Minsky, M.** (1985) **The Society of Mind.** Simon and Schuster.
- **Miranker, W. L.** (2010) **Memes and their themata.** Am J Psychol. 2010 Fall;123(3) :307-17.
- **Modelski, George & Poznanski, K.** (1994) **Evolutionary paradigms in the social sciences.** Workshop Report, May 13-14, University of Washington, Seattle.
- **Modelski, George & Poznanski, K.** (1995) **Evolutionary paradigms in the social sciences II.** Workshop report, May 26-27, University of Washington, Seattle.
- **Modelski, George** (1990) **Is world politics evolutionary learning?** International Organization 44, 1, Winter issue.

- **Modelski, George** (1996) **Evolutionary Paradigm For Global Politics.**
- **Modelski, George** (1999) **An evolutionary theory of culture? - a commentary on Rose's paper: Controversies in Meme Theory.** Journal of Memetics - Evolutionary Models of Information Transmission, 3.
- **Moore, F. C. T.** (2001) **Scribes and Texts: A Test Case for Models of Cultural Transmission.** In "The Epidemology of Ideas".
- **Moravec, Hans** (1989) **Human Culture - A Genetic Takeover Underway.** in Artificial Life (Volume VI, Santa Fe Institute Studies in the Sciences of Complexity), Christopher G. Langton, editor, Addison Wesley, New York, pp. 167-200.
- **Moravec, Hans** (1988) **Mind Children: The Future of Robot and Human Intelligence.** Harvard University Press, Cambridge, Massachusetts.
- **Moravec, Hans** (2000) **Robot: Mere Machine to Transcendent Mind.**
- **Moritz, E.** (1990) **Memetic Science: I - General Introduction.** Journal of Ideas 1, p. 1-23.
- **Moritz, E.** (1995) **Metasystems, memes and cybernetic immortality.** In (F. Heylighen, C. Joslyn, & V. Turchin, eds.), The Quantum of Evolution: Toward a Theory of Metasystem Transitions. Gordon and Breach Science Publishers.
- **Moscato, P.** (1989) **On Evolution, Search, Optimization, Genetic Algorithms and Martial Arts: Towards Memetic Algorithms.** Caltech Concurrent Computation Program (report 826).
- **Moscovitch, Morris** (2008) **The Cognitive Neuroscience of Memory and its Relevance to Meme Research.** [presentation]
- **Mundinger, Paul C.** (1980) **Animal cultures and a general theory of cultural evolution.**
- **Murdock, G. P.** (1949) **Social Structure.** The Macmillan Company.
- **Myrskylä, Mikko, Kohler, Hans-Peter and Billari, Francesco C.** (2009) **Advances in development reverse fertility declines.** Nature 460, 741-743.

N
- **Naess, Halvor** (2005) **Evolution of culture in the light of the second law of thermodynamics.**
- **Nanay, Bence** (2011) **Replication Without Replicators.** Synthese 179 (455):477.
- **Nelson, Richard R. & Winter S.G. Jr.** (1982) **An Evolutionary Theory of Economic Change.** Belknap Press of Harvard University Press.
- **Nelson, Richard R.** (1987) **Understanding Technical Change as an Evolutionary Process.** North-Holland.
- **Nelson, Richard R.** (2005) **Evolutionary Theories of Cultural Change: An Empirical Perspective.**
- **Nersessian, N.** (1993) **In the theoretician's laboratory: Thought experimenting as mental modeling.** In PSA (1992, vol. 2, eds. D. Hull, M. Forbes, & K Okrulik. PSA.
- **Norenzayan, Ara** (2006) **Evolution and Transmitted Culture.**

O
- **O'Brien, Michael J. and Shennan, Stephen J.** (2009) **Innovation in Cultural Systems: Contributions from Evolutionary Anthropology (Vienna Series in Theoretical Biology)** The MIT Press.
- **Olney , T.J.** (1990) **An Approach To Gender And Consumer Behavior: Memetics.**
- **Odling-Smee, John F.** (1994) **Niche construction, evolution and culture.** In T. Ingold (ed.) Companion Encyclopedia of Anthropology. London: Routledge.
- **Odling-Smee, John F.** (2003) **Niche construction. The Neglected Process in Evolution.** Princeton, New Jesey: Princeton University Press.
- **Okasha, Samir** (2008) **Evolution and the Levels of Selection.** OUP Oxford.
- **Orr, H. Allen** (1996) **Dennett's Strange Idea - Natural Selection: Science of Everything, Universal Acid, Cure for the Common Cold... - a review of Darwin's Dangerous Idea.** Boston Review.
- **Orr, H. Allen** (1996) **Resonse to Dennett's response to my review of Darwin's Dangerous Idea.** Boston Review.
- **Orye, Lieve** (1992) **The poverty of selectionism: a critical assessment of Darwin's legacy for the study of religion.**

P
- **Pagel, Mark** (2006) **Darwinian Cultural Evolution Rivals Genetic Evolution.** Behavioral and Brain Sciences, 29: 360-360.
- **Pagel, Mark** (2009) **Human language as a culturally transmitted replicator.**
- **Palmer, M.W.** (1992) **The coexistence of species in fractal landscapes.** American Naturalist, 139, p. 375-397.
- **Pantzar, M.** (1991) **A replicative perspective on evolutionary dynamics, labour institute for economic research.** Tutkimuksia 37 Research Report.
- **Pattee, H.P.** (1977) **Dynamic and linguistic modes of complex systems.** Int. J. General Systems, Vol. 3, p. 259-266.
- **Paull, John.** (2009) **Meme Maps: A Tool for Configuring Memes in Time and Space.** European

Journal of Scientific Research Vol.31 No.1 (2009), pp. 11-18.
- **Peace, William J.** (2004) **Leslie White - Evolution and Revolution in Anthropology (Critical Studies in the History of Anthropology).**
- **Pech, Richard J.** (2003a) **Inhibiting Imitative Terrorism Through Memetic Engineering.**
- **Pech, Richard J.** (2003b) **Memetics and innovation: profit through balanced meme management.** European Journal of Innovation Management, Vol. 6 Iss: 2, pp.111 - 117.
- **Pech, Richard J.** (2003c) **"Memes and cognitive hardwiring: why are some memes more successful than others?.** European Journal of Innovation Management, Vol. 6 Iss: 3, pp.173 - 181.
- **Penrose, E.T.** (1952) **Biological anologies in the theory of the firm.** American Economic Review, Vol 42 (Dec), p. 804-819.
- **Penrose, E.T.** (1953) **Rejoinder.** American Economic Review, Vol 43 (Sept), p. 603-607.
- **Pepper, G.B.** (1960) **Leslie A. White's Theory of Cultural Evolution.**
- **Percival, R. S.** (1960) **Dawkins and incurable mind viruses? Memes, rationality and evolution.**
- **Perry, George and Mace, Ruth** (2010) **The lack of acceptance of evolutionary approaches to human behaviour.**
- **Phillippi, David** (2011) **By Any 'Memes' Necessary: Dennett's Distortion of Culture.**
- **Pierce, Christopher D.** (1999) **Toward a Unified Evolutionary Theory of Culture.**
- **Pigliucci, Massimo and Murren Courtney J.** (2003) **Perspective: Genetic assimilation and a possible evolutionary paradox: can macroevolution sometimes be so fast as to pass us by?** Evolution 57 (7): 1455–64. PMID 12940351.
- **Pigliucci, Massimo, Murren Courtney J. and Schlichting, Carl D.** (2006) **Phenotypic plasticity and evolution by genetic assimilation.**
- **Pigliucci, Massimo** (2007) **The trouble with memetics.** Skeptical Inquirer, Volume 32, No.2, March/April 2008, pp 65.[scanned PDF]
- **Pigliucci, Massimo** (2009) **Memes, Selfish Genes And Darwinian Paranoia.**
- **Pigliucci, Massimo and Müller, Gerd B.** (2010) **Evolution - the Extended Synthesis.**
- **Piironen, Henry M.** (2009) **Why Memetics?**
- **Pinker, S.** (1995) **Language acquisition.** Pp. 135-182 in L. R. Gleitman and M. Liberman, eds. Language: an invitation to cognitive science. Vol. 1. MIT Press, Cambridge, MA.
- **Pinker, Steven** (1994) **The Language Instinct.**
- **Pinker, Steven** (1997) **How the Mind Works.** W. W. Norton, New York.
- **Pinker, Steven** (1999) **Words and rules.** Basic Books, New York.
- **Pinker, Steven** (2009) **Objections to memetics.**
- **Pitt, Richard** (1998) **Memes and monotheism.** Symposium on Memetics: Evolutionary Models of Information Transmission, 15th International Congress on Cybernetics, Namur (Belgium), August 24-28.
- **Platnick N. I, Cameron H. D.** (1977) **Cladistic methods in textual, linguistic and phylogenetic analysis.** Syst Zool 26: 380'385.
- **Plotkin, Henry C. & Odling-Smee F.J.** (1979) **Learning, change and evolution.** Advances in the Study of Behavior, 10, p. 1-41.
- **Plotkin, H. C. and Odling-Smee, F. J.** (1981) **A multiple-level model of evolution and its implications for sociobiology.** Behav. Brain Sci 4:225'268. CSA.
- **Plotkin, Henry C.** (1982) **Learning, Development, and Culture: Essays in Evolutionary Epistemology.** John Wiley and Sons.
- **Plotkin, Henry C. & Odling-Smee, F.J.** (1982) **Learning in the context of a hierarchy of knowledge gaining processes.** In (H.C. Plotkin, ed.) Learning, Development and Culture: Essays in Evolutionary Epistemology. John Wiley & Sons.
- **Plotkin, Henry C.** (1988) **The Role of Behavior in Evolution.** MIT Press.
- **Plotkin, Henry C.** (1991) **The testing of evolutionary epistemology [review of Gerald M. Edelman, Neural Darwinism].** Biology and Philosophy, 6(4), 481-497.
- **Plotkin, Henry C.** (1994) **Darwin machines and the nature of knowledge.** Cambridge, MA: Harvard University Press.
- **Plotkin, Henry C.** (2000a) **People Do More Than Imitate.** Scientific American.
- **Plotkin, Henry C.** (2000b) **Culture and psychological mechanisms.** In: *Darwinizing culture*.
- **Plotkin, Henry C.** (2002) **The imagined world made real.** Penguin, London.
- **Plotkin, Henry C.** (2003) **We-Intentionality: An Essential Element in Understanding Human Culture?** Perspectives in Biology and Medicine 46 (2):283-296.
- **Plotkin, Henry C.** (2007) **Necessary knowledge.**
- **Plotkin, Henry C.** (2010) **Evolutionary Worlds without End** Oxford University Press, USA.
- **Pocklington, R., and M. L. Best.** (1997) **Cultural Evolution and Units of Selection in Replicating Text** Journal of Theoretical Biology 188: 79'87.
- **Pocklington, R.** (2006) **Memes and Cultural Viruses.** Encyclopedia of the Social and Behavioral

Sciences.

- **Polichak, James W.** (1998) **Memes-what Are They Good For?: a Critique of Memetic Approaches to Information Processing** Skeptic, Vol 6, No. 3.
- **Polichak, James W.** (2002) **Memes as Pseudoscience.** In Michael Shermer, Skeptic Encyclopedia of Pseudoscience. p.664
- **Popper, Karl R.** (1963) **The Logic of Scientific Discovery.** (translation of Logik der Forschung). Hutchinson, London, 1959
- **Popper, Karl R.** (1963) **The Poverty of Historicism (2nd. ed).** Routledge, London, 1961.
- **Popper, Karl R.** (1963) **Conjectures and Refutations: The Growth of Scientific Knowledge.** Routledge, London.
- **Popper, Karl R.** (1974a) **Autobiography of Karl Popper.** In: Schlipp [39], 14.
- **Popper, Karl R.** (1974b) **Evolution and World 3.** In: Schlipp [39], 1048-1080.
- **Popper, Karl R.** (1979) **Objective Knowledge: An Evolutionary Approach.** Clarendon Press, Oxford.
- **Popper, Karl R.** (1987) **Natural selection and the emergence of mind.** In Gerard Radnitzky & W. W. Bartley, III. (Eds.), Evolutionary epistemology, theory of rationality, and the sociology of knowledge (pp. 137-155). La Salle, IL: Open Court.
- **Potter, V. R.** (1987) **Society and Science. Can science aid in the search for sophistication in dealing with order and disorder in human affairs?** Science 20 November 1964: Vol. 146 no. 3647 pp. 1018-1022.
- **Potts, Jason** (2001) **The New Evolutionary Microeconomics: Complexity, Competence, and Adaptive Behaviour (New Horizons in Institutional and Evolutionary Economics).** Edward Elgar Publishing.
- **Poulshock, J.** (2002) **The Problem And Potential Of Memetics.** Journal of Psychology and Theology, Vol. 30, 2002.
- **Powell, G.** (2006) **Memes.** Encyclopedia of Language & Linguistics (Second Edition) Pages 6-8
- **Preti, Antonio and Miotto, Paola** (1997) **Creativity, Evolution, And Mental Illness.** Journal of Memetics - Evolutionary Models of Information Transmission, 1.
- **Price, Ilfryn and Evans, Lilly** (1993) **Punctuated Equilibrium: an organic model for the Learning Organisation.** FORUM the quarterly Journal of the European Foundation for Management Development , 93.1(1).
- **Price, Ilfryn** (1995) **Organizational Memetics?: Organizational Learning as a Selection Process.** Management Learning.
- **Price, Ilfryn and Shaw, R.** (1996) **Parrots Patterns and Performance - The Learning Organisation Meme: Emergence of a new Management Replicator.** Proceedings 3rd ECLO Conf.
- **Price, Ilfryn** (1997a) **Punctuating Organizational Equilibrium: Shifting the patterns that limit.** Critical Linkages Newsletter (1997).
- **Price, Ilfryn and Kennie, Tom** (1997b) **Punctuated Strategic Equilibrium and some Strategic Leadership Challenges for University 2000.** 2nd Int. Conf. on the Dynamics of Strategy.
- **Price, Ilfryn and Shaw, Ray** (1998) **Shifting the Patterns: Breaking the Memetic Codes of Corporate Performance.** Management Books 2000 Ltd (June 25, 1998)
- **Price, Ilfryn** (1999a) **Images or Reality? Metaphors, Memes and Management.** In M.R.. Lissack and H. P. Gunz Eds. Managing Complexity in Organisations: Westport,. Quorum Books pp 165-179.
- **Price, Ilfryn and Shaw, Ray** (1999b) **Organisational Memetics: Organisational Learning as a Selection Process.**
- **Price, Ilfryn and Shaw, Ray** (1999c) **Memetics and the Edge of Chaos - A response to Paul Marsden's review of Price's & Shaw's Shifting the Patterns.**
- **Price, Ilfryn** (1999d) **Steps toward the Memetic Self - a commentary on Rose's paper: Controversies in Meme Theory.** Journal of Memetics - Evolutionary Models of Information Transmission, 3.
- **Price, Ilfryn and Lord, Andrew** (2000) **Complexity, memetics and reality: A new science of organisations or not.** In Safi, S. and Button, W. (2000): Chaos, Complexity and Management, Routledge, London.
- **Pyper, Hugh S.** (1996) **The Selfish Text: The Bible And Memetics.**

Q
- **Quinn, Thomas** (1998) **Bacterial Models of Memetic Transmission: Conjugation, Transduction, and Transformation.** Symposium on Memetics: Evolutionary Models of Information Transmission, 15th International Congress on Cybernetics, Namur (Belgium), August 24-28.

R
- **Radnitzky, G. & Bartly, W.W. (eds).** (1987) **Evolutionary Epistemology, Rationality and the Sociology of Knowledge.** Open Court.
- **Rambo, A. Terry and Gillogly, Kathleen** (1991) **Profiles in Cultural Evolution: Papers from a Conference in Honor of Elman R. Service** Anthropological Papers (Univ of Michigan, Museum of Anthropology).

- **Rambo, A. Terry** (1991) **The Study of Cultural Evolution.** In Profiles in Cultural Evolution. A. T. Rambo and K. Gillogly (Eds.), Ann Arbor, MI, USA: Museum of Anthropology, University of Michigan. Pp. 23-109.
- **Rapport, D.J. & Turner, J.E.** (1977) **Economic models in ecology.** Science 195: p. 367-373.
- **Rapport, D.J.** (1991) **Myths in the foundations of economics and ecology.** Biological Journal of the Linnean Society, 44: 185-202. Ram, A. (1993. Creative conceptual change. Proceedings of the Fifteenth Annual Conference of the Cognitive Science Society, p. 17-26.
- **Read, Dwight** (2003) **From Behavior to Culture: An Assessment of Cultural Evolution and a New Synthesis** published in 'Complexity'.
- **Reader, Simon M., and Laland, Kevin N.** (1999) **Do Animals Have Memes?** Journal of Memetics - Evolutionary Models of Information Transmission, 3.
- **Reali F, Griffiths TL.** (2010) **Words as alleles: connecting language evolution with Bayesian learners to models of genetic drift.**
- **Rendell, L. and Whitehead, H.** (2001) **Culture in whales and dolphins.** Behavioral and Brain Sciences 24:309-382.
- **Rendell, L., Boyd, R., Cownden, D., Enquist, M., Eriksson, K., Feldman, M. W., Fogarty, L., Ghirlanda, S., Lillicrap, T. and Laland, K. N.** (2010) **Why Copy Others? Insights from the Social Learning Strategies Tournament.** Science, Vol. 328, No. 5975., pp. 208-213.
- **Rendell, L., Boyd, R., Enquist, M., Feldman, M. W., Fogarty, L., and Laland, K. N.** (2010) **How copying affects the amount, evenness and persistence of cultural knowledge: insights from the social learning strategies tournament.** Philos Trans R Soc Lond B Biol Sci. 2011 Apr 12;366(1567):1118-28.
- **Riede, Felix** (1999) **Why isn't archaeology (more) Darwinian? A historical perspective**
- **Reynolds, R., Whallon, R, and Goodhall, S.** (2001) **Transmission Of Cultural Traits By Emulation: An Agent-Based Model Of Group Foraging Behavior.** Journal of Memetics - Evolutionary Models of Information Transmission, 4.
- **Riedl, Rupert.** (1984a) **Biology of knowledge: The evolutionary basis of reason.** (Trans., P. Foulkes) New York: Wiley.
- **Richerson, Peter J.** (...) **Innateness and cumulative cultural evolution** [presentation]
- **Richerson, Peter J.** (...) **Cultural Evolution Lectures 11-14** [presentation]
- **Richerson, Peter J. and Boyd, Robert** (1983) **Why is culture adaptive?** Quarterly Review of Biology 58: (209-214.
- **Richerson, Peter J. and Boyd, Robert** (1984) **Natural Selection and Culture.** BioScience 34:430-434.
- **Richerson, Peter J. and Boyd, Robert** (1985) **Culture and the evolutionary process.** University of Chicago Press.
- **Richerson, Peter J. and Boyd, Robert** (1987) **Simple Models of Complex Phenomena: The Case of Cultural Evolution.** In The Latest on the Best: Essays on Evolution and Optimality, John Dupre (ed.), MIT Press, Cambridge MA, 27-52.
- **Richards, Robert J.** (1987) **Darwin and the emergence of evolutionary theories of mind and behavior.** Chicago: University of Chicago Press. [See esp. pp. 559-594.]
- **Richerson, Peter J. and Boyd, Robert,** (1988) **The evolution of reciprocity in sizable groups.** Journal of Theoretical Biology, 132, 337-56.
- **Richerson, Peter J. and Boyd, Robert,** (1989) **The role of evolved predispositions in cultural evolution: Or human sociobiology meets Pascal's Wager.** Ethology and Sociobiology 10: p195-p219.
- **Richerson, Peter J. and Boyd, Robert** (1992) **How Microevolutionary Processes Give Rise to History.** In History and Evolution, M.H. and D.V. Nitecki (eds.), SUNY Press, Albany, pp. 178-209.
- **Richerson, Peter J. and Boyd, Robert** (1992) **Cultural Inheritance and Evolutionary Ecology.** In *Evolutionary Ecology and Human Behavior*, E.A. Smith and B. Winterhalder (eds.), Aldine de Gruyter, New York, pp. 61-92.
- **Richerson, Peter J. and Boyd, Robert** (1993) **Rationality, Imitation, and Tradition.** In *Nonlinear Dynamics and Evolutionary Economics*, R. Day and P. Chen (eds.), Oxford University Press, New York, pp. 131-149.
- **Richerson, Peter J., Soltis, Joseph and Boyd, Robert** (1995) **Can Group-functional Behaviors Evolve by Cultural Group Selection? An Empirical Test** . Current Anthropology, 63: 473'494.
- **Richerson, Peter J. and Boyd, Robert** (1995) **Why Does Culture Increase Human Adaptability?** Ethology and Sociobiology. 16: 125'143.
- **Richerson, Peter J. and Boyd, Robert** (1996) **Why Culture is Common but Cultural Evolution is Rare.** Proceedings of the British Academy, 88: 73'93.
- **Richerson, Peter J. Bettinger, Robert and Boyd, Robert** (1996) **Style, Function, and Cultural Evolutionary Processes.** In: *Darwinian Archaeologies*, Herbert D.G. Maschner (ed.), New York, Plenum, pp. 133-164.

- **Richerson, Peter J. and Boyd, Robert** (1997) **Are Cultural Phylogenies Possible?** With M. Borgerhoff Mulder and W.H. Durham. In: P. Weingart, P. J. Richerson, S. D. Mitchell, and S. Maasen (eds.), Human by Nature, Between Biology and the Social Sciences. Lawrence Erlbaum Associates: Mahwah, NJ. Pp. 355'386.
- **Richerson, Peter J. and Boyd, Robert** (1998) **The Evolution of Human Ultra-sociality** , I. Eibl-Eibesfeldt and F. K. Salter (eds.), Indoctrinability, Ideology and Warfare. New York: Berghahn Books. Pp. 71-96.
- **Richerson, Peter J. and Boyd, Robert** (1998) **Homage to Malthus, Ricardo, and Boserup: Toward a General Theory of Population, Economic Growth, Environmental Deterioration, Wealth and Poverty.** Human Ecology Review, 4: 85-90,.
- **Richerson, Peter J. and Boyd, Robert** (1999) **Complex Societies: The Evolutionary Origins of a Crude Superorganism.** Human Nature, 10: 253-289.
- **Richerson, Peter J. and Boyd, Robert** (1999) **Built for Speed: Pleistocene Climate Variation and the Origin of Human Culture.** Perspectives in Ethology.
- **Richerson, Peter J. and Boyd, Robert** (2000a) **The Pleistocene and the Origins of Human Culture: Built for Speed, .** In Perspectives in Ethology, -Vol. 13:1-45, Francois Tonneau and Nicholas Thompson, editors.
- **Richerson, Peter J. and Boyd, Robert,** (2000b) **Memes: Universal Acid or Better Mouse Trap** , Boyd, Robert and Richerson PJ. In: Darwinizing Culture: The Status of Memetics as a Science, R. Aunger ed. pp.143'162, Oxford University Press, Oxford.
- **Richerson, Peter J. and Boyd, Robert** (2000c) **Climate, Culture, and the Evolution of Cognition.** In C.M. Heyes and L. Huber, Editors, The Evolution of Cognition, MIT Press.
- **Richerson, Peter J. and Boyd, Robert** (2000d) **Evolution: The Darwinian Theory of Social Change: An Homage to Donald T. Campbell.** In: Paradigms of Social Change, pp. 257-282, Waltrud Schelkle, Wolf-Hagen Krauth, Martin Kohli, and Georg Elwer (eds.), Frankfurt: Campus Verlag.
- **Richerson, Peter J. and Boyd, Robert** (2000e) **Meme theory oversimplifies how culture changes.** Scientific American, 283:4, 70-71.
- **Richerson, Peter J. and Boyd, Robert** (2001a) **Built For Speed, Not for Comfort: Darwinian Theory and Human Culture.** In History and Philosophy of the Life Sciences 23: 423-463.
- **Richerson, Peter J. and Boyd, Robert** (2001b) **The Evolution of Subjective Commitment to Groups: A Tribal Instincts Hypothesis.** In Randolph M. Nesse (ed.) The Evolution of Commitment. New York: Russell Sage Foundation. Pp. 186-220.
- **Richerson, Peter J. and Boyd, Robert** (2001c) **Was Agriculture Impossible During the Pleistocene But Mandatory During the Holocene? A Climate Change Hypothesis** with Robert L. Bettinger. American Antiquity, 66: 387-411.
- **Richerson, Peter J. and Boyd, Robert** (2001d) **Culture Is Part of Human Biology: Why the Superorganic Concept Serves the Human Sciences Badly.** In Science Studies: Probing the Dynamics of Scientific Knowledge, edited by S. Maasen and M. Winterhager, transcript Verlag, (2001. Also, to be published in Probing Human Origins, edited by Morris Goodman and Anne Simon Moffat, The American Academy of Arts & Sciences, Cambridge, MA.
- **Richerson, Peter J. and Boyd, Robert** (2001e) **Institutional Evolution in the Holocene: The Rise of Complex Societies.** In The Origin of Human Social Institutions, pp. (197-204, W.G. Runciman, editor. Proceedings of the British Academy, 110.
- **Richerson, Peter J. and Boyd, Robert** (2001f) **Norms and Bounded Rationality.** In: The Adaptive Tool Box, G. Gigerenzer and R. Selten, eds. pp 281'296, MIT Press, Cambridge MA, (2001.
- **Richerson, Peter J. and Vila, Bryan J.** (2001g) **Principles of Human Ecology**
- **Richerson, Peter J. and Boyd, Robert,** (2002a) **Meme Theory Oversimplifies Cultural Change.** Boyd, Robert and Richerson PJ.. October, Pp. 54-55. A full version of the whole Sue Blackmore article is here.
- **Richerson, Peter J. and Boyd, Robert** (2002b) **Group Beneficial Norms Can Spread Rapidly In a Structured Population.** (2002, Journal of Theoretical Biology
- **Richerson, Peter J. Paciotti, Brian, and Boyd, Robert** (2002c) **An Evolutionary Theory of Commons Management.** In Elinor Ostrom, Thomas Dietz, Nives Dolsak, Paul C. Stern, Susan Stonich, and Elke U. Weber (eds.) The Drama of the Commons. National Academy Press. Pp. 403-442.
- **Richerson, Peter J., Henrich, Joe and Boyd, Robert** (2003a) **Cultural Evolution of Human Cooperation.** In The Genetic and Cultural Evolution of Cooperation, Edited by Peter Hammerstein, MIT Press. Pp. 357-388.
- **Richerson, Peter J. and Boyd, Robert** (2003b) **The Evolution of Altruistic Punishment** , with Herbert Gintis and Samuel Bowles. Proceedings of the National Academy of Sciences (USA) 100: 3531'3535.
- **Richerson, Peter J. McElreath, Richard and Boyd, Robert** (2003c) **Shared Norms Can Lead to the Evolution of Ethnic Markers.** Current Anthropology 44: 122'130
- **Richerson, Peter J. and Boyd, Robert** (2004a) **Darwinian evolutionary ethics: Between patriotism and sympathy.** In Evolution and Ethics: Human Morality in Biological and Religious Perspective, Philip

Clayton and Jeffrey Schloss, editors, Pp. 50-77, .

- **Richerson, Peter J., Baum, William M., Efferson, Charles M. and Paciotti, Brian M.** (2004b) **Cultural Evolution in Laboratory Micro-Societies Including Traditions of Rule-Giving and Rule-Following** Evolution and Human Behavior 25: 305-326.
- **Richerson, Peter J. and Boyd, Robert** (2005a) **Not by Genes Alone: How Culture Transformed Human Evolution.** University of Chicago Press: Chicago, IL.
- **Richerson, Peter J. and Boyd, Robert** (2005b) **Evolution on a restless planet: Were environmental variability and environmental change major drivers of human evolution?** With Robert L. Bettinger and Robert Boyd. *Handbook of Evolution Vol. 2* edited by Franz M. Wuketits and Francisco J. Ayala, Pp 223-242.
- **Richerson, Peter J. and Boyd, Robert** (2005c) **Solving the puzzle of human cooperation.** In Evolution and Culture, edited by S. Levinson and P. Jaisson. MIT Press, Cambridge MA, pp. 105-132.
- **Richerson, Peter J. and Boyd, Robert** (2005d) **The Origin and Evolution of Culture.** Collected papers. Oxford University Press, USA; First Edition edition
- **Richerson, Peter J.** (2005e) **The Evolution of Cultural Maladaptations.** Cultural Evolution | Center for Human Evolution Proceedings of Workshop 4.
- **Richerson, Peter J. and Boyd, Robert** (2006) **Why possibly language evolved.** In press in Special Issue of *Biolinguistics* on *Explaining the (in)variance of human language: Divergent views and converging evidence.*
- **Richerson, Peter J., Whitehead, Hal** (2006) **Cultural Selection and Genetic Diversity in Humans.** Selection 3:115-125,
- **Richerson, Peter J. and Boyd, Robert** (2006) **Culture and the evolution of the human social instincts.** In: *Roots of Human Sociality: Culture, Cognition, and Interaction.* Edited by N.J. Enfield and Stephen C. Levinson. Berg. Pp. 453-477.
- **Richerson, Peter J., Paciotti, Brian and Boyd, Robert** (2006) **Cultural evolutionary theory: A synthetic theory for fragmented disciplines.** In The Benefits of Transdisciplinary Approaches, Paul Van Lange, Editor. Pp 365-70.
- **Richerson, Peter J. and Boyd, Robert** (2006) **Culture, adaptation, and innateness.** Pp23-38 in The Innate Mind: Volume 2 Culture and Cognition, P. Carruthers, S. Stich, & S. Laurence, eds., Oxford, Oxford University Press.
- **Richerson, Peter J., Efferson, Charles, McElreath, Richard, Lubell, Mark, Edsten, Ed, Waring, Timothy M., Paciotti, Brian and Baum, William** (2007) **Learning, productivity, and noise: an experimental study of cultural transmission on the Bolivian Altiplano.** *Evolution and Human Behavior* 28: 11-17.
- **Richerson, Peter J., Newson, Lesley, Postmes, Tom, Lea, S.E.G., Webley, Paul and McElreath Richard** (2007) **Influences on communication about reproduction: The cultural evolution of low fertility.** *Evolution and Human Behavior* 28: (199-210.
- **Richerson, Peter J., Newson, Lesley and Boyd, Robert** (2007) **Cultural evolution and the shaping of cultural diversity.** pp 454-476 in *Handbook of Culture Psychology,* Dov Cohen and Shinobu Kitayama, editors, New York, Guilford Press.
- **Richerson, Peter J.** (2007) **Large scale human cooperation and conflict.**
- **Richerson, Peter J., Boyd, Robert and Henrich, J,** (2008) **Five misunderstandings about cultural evolution** *Human Nature* 19: 119-137.
- **Richerson, Peter J. and Boyd, Robert** (2008) **The evolution of free enterprise values.** In Moral Markets: The Critical Role of Values in the Economy, edited by Paul Zak. Princeton University Press. Pp. 107-141.
- **Richerson, Peter J. and Boyd, Robert** (2008) **Cultural evolution: Accomplishments and future prospects.** In *Explaining Culture Scientifically,* edited by Melissa Brown. University of Washington Press. pp 75-99.
- **Richerson, Peter J., Cordes, Christian, McElreath, Richard and Strimling, Pontus** (2008) **A naturalistic approach to the firm: the role of cooperation and cultural evolution.** *Journal of Economic Behavior and Organization* 68: 125-139.
- **Richerson, Peter J. and Boyd, Robert** (2008) **Gene-culture coevolution and the evolution of social institutions.** In *Better than Consciousness? Decision Making, The Human Mind, and Implications for Institutions.* Edited by Christoph Engel and Wolf Singer. MIT Press. Pp. 305-323.
- **Richerson, Peter J., Newson, Lesley** (2008) **Is religion adaptive? Yes, no, neutral, but mostly we do't know** (short version). With In: The Evolution of Religion: Studies, Theories, & Critiques.. Collins Foundation Press. Pp. 73-78.
- **Richerson, Peter J. and Boyd, Robert** (2009a) **Culture and the evolution of human cooperation.** *Philosophical Transactions of the Royal Society* 364: 3281-3288.
- **Richerson, Peter J. and Boyd, Robert** (2009c) **Constraints on the development of agriculture.** With Robert Bettinger. Current Anthropology 50: 627-631.

- **Richerson, Peter J. and Boyd, Robert** (2009d) **Cultural innovations and demographic change** , with Robert L. Bettinger. *Human Biology* 81: 211-235.
- **Richerson, Peter J. and Henrich, Joseph** (2009e) **Tribal social instincts and the cultural evolution of institutions to solve collective action problems.** Discussion paper for Workshop on Context and the Evolutionary Mechanisms for Solving Collective Action Problems. Workshop on Political Theory and Policy Analysis, Indiana University, May.
- **Richerson, Peter J. and Lesley Newson** (2009f) **Why do people become modern? A darwinian mechanism.** *Population and Development Review* 35: 117-158.
- **Richerson, Peter J. and Newson, Lesley** (2009g) **Is religion adaptive? Yes, no, neutral, but mostly we don't know** (long version). *The Believing Primate: Scientific, Philosophical and Theological Perspectives on the Evolution of Religion* , Jeffrey Schloss and Michael Murray, editors. Oxford University Press, pp. 100-117.
- **Richerson, Peter J.** (2010a) **Rethinking paleoanthropology: A world queerer than we supposed.** In press in Evolution of Mind, Gary Hatfield, Editor. Penn Museum Conference Series.
- **Richerson, Peter J. and Boyd, Robert** (2010b) **The Darwinian theory of human cultural evolution and gene-culture coevolution.** Chapter 20 in Evolution Since Darwin: The First 150 Years. M.A. Bell, D.J. Futuyma, W.F. Eanes, and J.S. Levinton (eds.)
- **Richerson, Peter J. and Boyd, Robert** (2010c) **Gene-culture coevolution in the age of genomics.** With Joseph Henrich. *PNAS* 107 (suppl. 2): 8985-8992.
- **Richerson, Peter J. and Boyd, Robert** (2010d) **The Evolution of Ethnic Markers.** *Cultural Anthropology* 2: 65-79. 1987. Reprinted in *The Evolution of Culture*, Stefan Lindquist, editor. Ashgate Press.
- **Richerson, Peter J., Henrich, Joe and Boyd, Robert** (2010e) **Rapid cultural adaptation can facilitate the evolution of large-scale cooperation.**
- **Richerson, Peter J.** (2010f) **Culture Is an ACTIVE Part of Biology.** SYMPOSIUM ON THE QUESTION "HOW IS CULTURE BIOLOGICAL?" ~ Six Essays and Discussions: Essay # 4.
- **Richerson, Peter J., Henrich, Joe and Boyd, Robert** (2010g) **In the Light of Evolution V: Cooperation and Conflict Sackler Colloquium: The cultural niche: Why social learning is essential for human adaptation.** Proc Natl Acad Sci U S A. Jun 21.
- **Richerson, Peter J.** (2011) **Tribal Social Instincts and Human Cooperation** .
- **Ridley, Matt** (2011) **The Rational Optimist: How Prosperity Evolves.**
- **Ridley, Mark** (1993) **Evolution.**
- **Rindos, David** (1986) **The Evolution of the Capacity for Culture. - Sociobiology, Structuralism, and Cultural Selectionism/**
- **Ritt, Nikolaus** (1995) **Language Change As Evolution: Linguistic 'Genes'.**
- **Ritt, Nikolaus** (1996) **Darwinising historical linguistics: applications of a dangerous idea** In Vienna English Working Papers. 5/1&2: 27-47.
- **Ritt, Nikolaus** (1997) **Mutation, variation and selection in phonological evolution: a sketch based on the case of Late Middle English.** In: Fisiak, Jacek (ed.): Studies in Middle English Linguistics. Berlin: Mouton. 531-550.
- **Ritt, Nikolaus** (2004) **Selfish Sounds and Linguistic Evolution: A Darwinian approach to language change.** Cambridge: University Press.
- **Ritt, Nikolaus** (2008) **Putting memetic explanations to the test: the case of historical trends in English phonotactics.** Memory, Social Networks, and Language: Probing the Meme Hypothesis II
- **Robert, M.** (1990) **Observational learning in fish, birds, and mammals: A classified bibliography spanning over 100 years of research.** Psych Record 40, p. 289-311.
- **Rodgers, Alan R.** (1988) **Does Biology Constrain Culture?**
- **Rodgers, E.M.** (1993) **Diffusion of innovations, 3rd edition.** Macmillan, New York.
- **Rodgers, J. L. & Rowe, D. C.** (1993) **Social contagion and adolescent sexual behavior: A developmental EMOSA model.** Psych. Rev. Vol. 100, No. 3, 479-510.
- **Rose, Nick** (1998) **Controversies in Meme Theory.** Journal of Memetics - Evolutionary Models of Information Transmission, 2.
- **Rose, Nick** (1998) **Rationale for Commentary on Rose.** Journal of Memetics - Evolutionary Models of Information Transmission, 3.
- **Rose, Nick** (1999) **Okay, but exactly "who" would escape the Tyranny of the Replicators?** Journal of Memetics - Evolutionary Models of Information Transmission, 3.
- **Rosenfeldter, Mark** (2001) **The new pseudoscience of memes.** A review of Thought Contagion by Aaron Lynch.
- **Rothblatt, Martine** (2010) **On Genes, Memes, Bemes, and Conscious Things.**
- **Rowe, D. C. & Sherman, S. J.** (1992) **An epidemic model of adolescent cigarette smoking.** Journal of Applied Social Psychology, Vol. 22, No. 4, 261-285.
- **Rowe, D. C. & Rogers, J. L.** (1994) **A social contagion model of adolescent sexual behavior: Explaining race differences.** Social Biology, Vol. 41, 1-18.

- Runciman, W. G. (2005) **Culture Does Evolve.**
- Ruse, Michael (1989) **What the philosophy of biology is: Essays dedicated to David Hull.** Kluwer Academic Publishers.
- Ruse, Michael (1999) **Is Evolution a Secular Religion?**
- Ruse, Michael (1989) **The view from Somewhere - A critical defense of Evolutionary Epistemology.** In Issues in Evolutionary Epistemology.
- Ruse, Michael (2006) **Remarkable exchange between Michael Ruse and Daniel Dennett.**
- Ruse, Michael (2008) **Charles Darwin.**
- Ruse, Michael (...) **Meme**
- Ruse, Michael (...) **Culturgen**
- Runciman, W.G. (1999) **Darwinian Soup.** Vol. 21 No. 12. 10 June pages 25-26. Review of The Meme Machine by Susan Blackmore.
- Runciman, W.G. (2009) **The Theory of Cultural and Social Selection.** Cambridge University Press
- Ruse, Michael (1974) **Cultural Evolution.** Theory and Decision, vol. 5, p. 413.
- Rushkoff, Douglas (1994) **Media Virus!.** Ballantine Books.

S
- Sahlins, Marshall D. and Service, Elman R. (1988) **Evolution and Culture.**
- Salazar-Ciudad I. (2010) **A two level mutation-selection model of cultural evolution and diversity.** J Theor Biol. Nov 21;267(2):171-85.
- Salingaros, Nikos A. (2005) **Architectural memes in a universe of information.**
- Salingaros, Nikos, A. and Mikiten, Terry M. (2002) **Darwinian Processes and Memes in Architecture: A Memetic Theory of Modernism.** Journal of Memetics. Evolutionary Models of Information Transmission Vol. 6.
- Sakura, Osamu (1998) **History of Sciences as a Division of Memetics? Implications from Comparative Studies on the Reception of Sociobiology.** Symposium on Memetics: Evolutionary Models of Information Transmission, 15th International Congress on Cybernetics, Namur (Belgium), August 24-28.
- Sartika, Tiktik Dewi (2004) **Tracing Cultural Evolution Through Memetics.**
- Savage-Rumbaugh, S., McDonald, K., Sevcik, R.A., Hopkins, W.D., Rubert, E. (1986) **Spontaneous symbol acquisition and communicative use by pygmy chimpanzees (Pan paniscus).**
- Saviotti & Metcalf (1991) **Evolutionary Theories of Economic and Technological Change: Present Status and Future Prospects.**
- Scaglia, Beatriz (2011) **From Yuppies to Rickrolling: The Evolution of Cultural and Internet Memes and the Theory of Memetics.**
- Schaffner, Stephen F. (2008) **Evolutionary Adaptation and Positive Selection in Humans.**
- Schaller, Mark, Norenzayan, Ara, Heine, Steven J. and Yamagishi, Toshio (2009) **Evolution, Culture, and the Human Mind.**
- Schank, R. C. (1983) **Dynamic Memory.** Cambridge University Press.
- Schleicher A, Bikkers (1869) **Darwinism tested by the science of language.**
- Schmid, H.B. (1983) **Evolution by Imitation - Gabriel Tarde and the Limits of Memetics**
- Schultz, Emily (2009) **Resolving the Anti-Antievolutionism Dilemma: A Brief for Relational Evolutionary Thinking in Anthropology.**
- Schumann, Paul (2009) **Genes Memes and the Innovation Commons**
- Schuster, P. & Sigmund, K. (1983) **Replicator dynamics.** Journal of Theoretical Biology 100, p. 533-38.
- Sears, Greg and Baba, Vishwanath V. (2011) **Toward a Multistage, Multilevel Theory of Innovation.**
- Semon, R. (1921) **The mneme.** Allen and Unwin, London.
- Sereno, M.I. (1991) **Four analogies between biological and cultural/linguistic evolution.** Journal of Theoretical Biology 151:467-507.
- Shannon, C.E. & Weaver, W. (1963) **The Mathematical Theory of Communication.** University of Illinois Press.
- Shea, N (2009) **Imitation as an inheritance system.** Philos Trans R Soc Lond B Biol Sci. 2009 Aug 27;364(1528) :2429-43.
- Sheehan, Evan Louis (2005) **The Laughing Genes: A Scientific Perspective on Ethics and Morality.**
- Sheehan, Evan Louis (2006) **The Mocking Memes: A Basis for Automated Intelligence.**
- Shennan, Shennan (2002) **Pattern and Process in Cultural Evolution.**
- Shennan, Shennan (2009) **Genes, memes and human history.** Thames and Hudson, London.
- Shennan, Shennan (2010) **Descent with modification and the archaeological record.** Phil. Trans. R. Soc. B 12 April vol. 366 no. 1567 1070-1079.
- Shepherd, Jill and McKelvey, Bill (2009) **An empirical investigation of organizational memetic variation.**
- Shifman, Limor, Thelwall, Mike (2009) **Assessing global diffusion with Web memetics: The spread**

and evolution of a popular joke.

- Siegfried, André (1965) **Germs And Ideas - Routes of epidemics and ideologies.**
- Silby, Brent (2000) **What Is A Meme?**
- Silby, Brent (2000) **Memecosystems - Are Animal Minds Suitable Habitats For Memes?**
- Silby, Brent (2008) **Evolution Of Technology: Exposing Creative Design Myth**
- Signorelli, Mark Anthony (2010) **Taking Memes Seriously**
- Simitopoulou, K. E. and Xirotiris, N.I. (2004) **Memes of Ethics ' A Co-evolutionary Approach - The case of Religion's Memes.** Human Ecology Special Issue No. 12: 23-27.
- Simonton, Dean Keith (1995) **Foresight in insight? A Darwinian answer.** In R. J. Sternberg, ed. The nature of insight. MIT Press, Cambridge, MA. p. 465-494.
- Simonton, Dean Keith (1998) **Donald Campbell's model of the creative process: Creativity as blind variation and selective retention.** Journal of Creative Behavior, 32(3), 153–158.
- Simonton, Dean Keith (1999a) **Creativity as blind variation and selective retention: is the creative process Darwinian?** Psychological Inquiry. 10, 309?328.
- Simonton, Dean Keith (1999b) **Origins of genius: Darwinian perspectives on creativity.** New York: Oxford University Press.
- Simonton, Dean Keith (2003) **Scientific creativity as constrained stochastic behavior: The integration of product, person, and process perspectives.** Psychological Bulletin, 129, 475–494.
- Simonton, Dean Keith (2004) **Creativity in science: Chance, logic, genius, and zeitgeist.** New York: Cambridge University Press.
- Simonton, Dean Keith (2005) **Darwin as straw man: Dasgupta's (2004) evaluation of creativity as a Darwinian process.** Creativity Research Journal, 17, 299-208.
- Simonton, Dean Keith (2007a) **The creative process in Picasso's Guernica sketches: Monotonic improvements versus nonmonotonic variants.** Creativity Research Journal, 19(4), 329-344.
- Simonton, Dean Keith (2007b) **Rejoinder: Picasso's Guernica creativity as a Darwinian process: Definitions, clarifications, misconceptions, and applications.** Creativity Research Journal, 19(4), 381-394.
- Simonton, Dean Keith (2010) **Creative thought as blind-variation and selective-retention: Combinatorial models of exceptional creativity.** Physics of Life Reviews, 7(2), 156-179.
- Simonton, Dean Keith (2011) **Creativity and discovery as blind variation: Campbell's (1960) BVSR model after the half-century mark.** Review of General Psychology, Vol 15(2), Jun 2011, 158-174.
- Situngkir, Hokky (2004) **On Selfish Memes - Culture as complex adaptive system.** Journal of Social Complexity Vol.2 No.1, October, pp. 20-32.
- Situngkir, Hokky, Khanafiah, Deni (2004) **Innovation as Evolution: Case Study Phylomemetic of Cellphone Designs.**
- Situngkir, Hokky, Khanafiah, Deni (2006) **Innovation as Evolutionary Process.** Innovation in the Evolution of Technological Artifacts. Journal of Social Complexity, Vol.2, No.2, 2006, pp. 20-30.
- Situngkir, Hokky (2008) **Constructing the Phylomemetic Tree: Indonesian Tradition-Inspired Buildings.**
- Situngkir, Hokky (2008) **Conjectures to the Memes of Indonesian Songs.** Bandung Fe Institute; Indonesian Archipelago Cultural Initiatives (IACI). (BFI Working Paper Series WP-VI-2008).
- Situngkir, Hokky (2008) **Evolutionary Clustering in Indonesian Ethnic Textile Motifs.**
- Situngkir, Hokky (2009) **The Phylomemetics of Batik.**
- Skinner, B.F. (1953) **Science and Human Behavior.** New York, Macmillan. Spanos.
- Skinner, B.F. (1971) **Beyond Freedom and Dignity.**
- Skinner, B.F. (1981) **Selection by consequences.** Science 213:501'504. CrossRef, PubMed, CSA.
- Slater, P. J. B. & Ince, S. A. (1979) **Cultural evolution in chaffinch song.** Behavior, Vol. 71, 146-166.
- Smillie, David, van der Dennen, Johan M. and Wilson, Daniel R. (1999) **The Darwinian Heritage and Sociobiology.** Praeger.
- Smith, Kenneth (2003) **The Transmission of Language: models of biological and cultural evolution.**
- Smith, W. J. (1977) **The Behavior of Communicating.** Harvard University Press.
- Sober, E. and Wilson, D.S. (1998) **Unto Others: The Evolution and Psychology of Unselfish Behavior.** Cambridge MA: Harvard University Press.
- Spector, L. & Luke, S. (1996) **Culture enhances the evolvability of cognition.** In Proceedings of the 1996 Cognitive Science Society Meeting.
- Speel, Hans-Cees A.M. (1998) **Memes Are Also Interactors.**
- Speel, Hans-Cees A.M. (1995) **Memetics: On a conceptual framework for cultural evolution.** [PDF]In (F. Heylighen, & D. Aerts, eds.) The Evolution of Complexity. Kluwer.
- Speel, Hans-Cees A.M. & Antomarini, Brunella (1996) **Memetics And Montag - 5 Questions and Answers about Memetics.**
- Speel, Hans-Cees A.M. (1997) **A Memetic Analysis of Policy Making.** Journal of Memetics -

Evolutionary Models of Information Transmission, 1.
- **Speel, Hans-Cees A.M.** (1999) **On Memetics And Memes As Brain-Entities.** Journal of Memetics - Evolutionary Models of Information Transmission, 3.
- **Speel, Hans-Cees A.M.** (1997) **A Short Comment from a Biologist.** On William Benzon's essay 'Culture as an Evolutionary Arena'. Journal of Social and Evolutionary Systems 20 (3): 309-322.
- **Speel, Hans-Cees A.M., H.C., Vromen, J. and Wilkins, J.** (2000) **Why Memetic Evolution is not Lamarckian.**
- **Spencer, Herbert** (1864) **Illustrations of universal progress; a series of discussions.** New York: D. Appleton and Company.
- **Spencer, Herbert** (1867) **The Principles of Biology** . New York and London.
- **Spencer, M., Davidson, E. A., Barbrook, A. C., Howe, C. J.** (2004) **Phylogenetics of artificial manuscripts.** J Theoret Biol 227: 503'511.
- **Sperber, Dan** (1985) **Anthropology and psychology: towards an epidemiology of representations.** Man (N.S.) 20, 73-89.
- **Sperber, Dan** (1990) **The epidemiology of beliefs.** in: Fraser, Colin; Gaskell, George (eds.): The Social Psychological Study of Widespread Beliefs. Oxford: Clarendon, p. 25.
- **Sperber, Dan and Wilson, Deirdre** (1995) **Relevance: Communication and cognition, Second Edition.** Oxford: Blackwell.
- **Sperber, Dan** (1996) **Explaining culture: a naturalistic approach.** Oxford, UK; Cambridge, Mass.: Blackwell.
- **Sperber, Dan** (1998) **Are Folk Taxonomies 'Memes'?** Behavioral and Brain Sciences 21 (4):589-590.
- **Sperber, Dan** (2000) **Why memes won't do. An objection to the memetic approach to culture.** In: Darwinizing culture: The status of memetics as a science, ed. R. Aunger, Oxford & New York: Oxford University Press, p. 163'174.
- **Sperber, Dan** (2011) **Cultural Attractors.**
- **Sperry, Roger W.** (1966) **Mind, brain, and humanist values.** Bulletin of the Atomic Scientists - Vol. 22, No. 7.
- **Sperry, Roger W.** (1983) **Science and Moral Priority: Merging Mind, Brain and Human Values.** Blackwell.
- **Stanovich, Keith E.** (2005) **The Robot's Rebellion: Finding Meaning in the Age of Darwin.**
- **Stanovich, Keith E.** (2006) **Memetics and money.**
- **Stanovich, Keith E.** (2007) **Rationality, Evolution, and the Meme Concept.** University of Toronto.
- **Steele, J., Jordan, P., Cochrane, E.** (2010) **Evolutionary approaches to cultural and linguistic diversity.** Philos Trans R Soc Lond B Biol Sci 365: 3781'3785.
- **Stefik, Mark** (1986) **The Next Knowledge Medium.** The AI Magazine, Spring , Vol.7, #1.
- **Stein, Edward., & Lipton, Peter.** (1989) **Where guesses come from: Evolutionary epistemology and the anomaly of guided variation.** Biology & Philosophy, 4(1), 33-56.
- **Steele J, Jordan P, Cochrane E.** (2010) **Evolutionary approaches to cultural and linguistic diversity.**
- **Sterelny, Kim, Smith, Kelly and Dickison, Michael** (1996) **The extended replicator.**
- **Sterelny, Kim, and Griffiths, P.** (1999) **Sex and Death: An Introduction to the Philosophy of Biology.** Chicago: University of Chicago Press.
- **Sterelny, Kim** (2001) **Niche Construction, Developmental Systems and the Extended Replicator.** in Cycles of Contingency, R. Gray, P. Griffiths and S. Oyama (eds.), Cambridge: MIT Press. pp. 329'349.
- **Sterelny, Kim** (2003) **Thought in a Hostile World.** Oxford: Blackwell.
- **Sterelny, Kim** (2006a) **The Evolution and Evolvability of Culture.**
- **Sterelny, Kim** (2006b) **Memes Revisited.** British Journal for the Philosophy of Science 57. 145'165.
- **Sterelny, Kim** (2007) **Snafus: An Evolutionary Perspective.** Biological Theory.
- **Sternberg, R. J.** (1998) **Cognitive mechanisms in human creativity: Is variation blind or sighted?** Journal of Creative Behavior.
- **Steward, J. H.** (1955) **Theory of Culture Change: The Methodology of Multilinear Evolution.** Urbana: University of Illinois Press.
- **Stone, Linda, Lurquin, Paul F. and Cavalli-Sforza, L. Luca** (2006) **Genes, Culture, and Human Evolution: A Synthesis.**
- **Stove, David C.** (1996) **Darwinian Fairytales.** Ashgate Publishing.
- **Stove, David C.** (1996) **Genetic Calvinism, or Demons and Dawkins.**
- **Strickberger, Monroe** (1996) **Evolution.**
- **Stryker, Coyle** (2011) **How Memes Work (A Review of The Complete Idiot's Guide to Memes)**
- **Stoneking, Mark** (2010) **Does Culture Prevent or Drive Human Evolution?**
- **Stuart-Fox, M.** (1986) **The Unit of Replication in Sociocultural Evolution.** Journal of Social and Biological Structures, 9, 67-89.
- **Sugorakova, Daria** (2009) **The Dragon: Memes, Culture and Evolution.**

- Sullivan, Anne (2005) **The "Promiscuous" Meme: A Look at Cultural Evolution in Dennett's Terms.**
- Sullivan, Damien (1977) **Review of Memes: the New Replicators.**
- Swanson, Carl P. (1983) **Ever-Expanding Horizons: The Dual Informational Sources of Human Evolution.** Univ of Massachusetts.
- Szamado, Szabolcs (1998) **Basic Questions in Memetics: Life-cycle, reproduction and Resources** Symposium on Memetics: Evolutionary Models of Information Transmission, 15th International Congress on Cybernetics, Namur (Belgium), August 24-28.
- Szathmáry, Eörs (1999) **Chemes, Genes, Memes: A revised classification of replicators.** Lectures on Mathematics in the Life Sciences. 26, 1-10.
- Szathmáry, Eörs (2000) **The evolution of replicators.** Phil. Trans. R. Soc. Lond. B 29 November 2000 vol. 355 no. 1403 1669-1676.
- Szathmáry, Eörs (2006) **Cultural Processes: The Latest Major Transition in Evolution.**

T

- Tallis, Raymond (2011) **Aping Mankind: Neuromania, Darwinitis and the Misrepresentation of Humanity.**
- Tamariz, Mónica (2006) **Evolutionary dynamics in language form and language meaning** In A Cangelosi, ADM Smith & K. Smith (eds.) The Evolution of Language: Proceedings of the 6th International Conference on the Evolution of Language. World Scientific Press.
- Tamariz, Mónica (2008) **Why the transition to cumulative symbolic culture is rare** Proceedings of the 7th Conference on the Evolution of Language.
- Tamariz, Mónica (2009) **The role of arbitrary imitation and pattern completion in the origin and evolution of human communication.** Proceedings of the 31st International Conference of the Cognitive Science Society.
- Tamariz, Mónica (2009) **Evolutionary transitions and co-evolutionary dynamics in biology and in culture.** In H. Muscio and G. Lopez (eds.), Proceedings of the XVth Congress of the Union for Prehistoric and Protohistoric Sciences, Workshop WS22: Theoretical and Methodological Issues in Evolutionary Archaeology: Towards a Unified Darwinian Paradigm, pp. 103-110, (pdf).
- Tamariz, Mónica, Brown, J.E. & Murray, K.M. (2011) **The role of practice and literacy in the evolution of linguistic structure.** In A.D.M. Smith, K. Smith and M. Schwoustra, Eds. The Evolution of Language. Proceedings of the 10th International Conference on the Evolution of Language, pp. 313-320.
- Tamariz, Mónica (2011) **Identifying selective pressures in language evolution: Polya urns and the Price equation.** In A.D.M. Smith, K. Smith and M. Schwoustra, Eds. The Evolution of Language. Proceedings of the 10th International Conference on the Evolution of Language, pp. 501-502.
- Tamariz, Mónica (2011) **What are the analogues of genotype and phenotype in language evolution?** In A.D.M. Smith, K. Smith and M. Schwoustra, Eds. The Evolution of Language. Proceedings of the 10th International Conference on the Evolution of Language, pp. 503-504.
- Tarde, G. (1884) **Darwinisme naturel et Darwinisme social.** Revue Philosophique XVII; 607.
- Tarde, G. (1903) **The Laws of Imitation.** Mass: Peter Smith.
- Taylor, M. A. (1903) **Fiction as artificial life: exploring the ideosphere.** Cybernetics and Systems '96, Robert Trappl (ed.), (Austrian Society for Cybernetic Studies, Vienna, 1996), p. 893-896.
- Ilya Temkin (2004) **The evolution of the Baltic psaltery: A case for phyloorganology.** The Galpin Society Journal 57:219–30.
- Ilya Temkin and Niles Eldredge (2007) **Phylogenetics and Material Cultural Evolution.** Current Anthropology, 48(1), 146-153.
- Tennie, C., Call, J., Tomasello, M. (2009) **Ratcheting up the ratchet: on the evolution of cumulative culture.** Philos Trans R Soc Lond B Biol Sci. Aug 27;364(1528):2405-15.
- Thagard, P. (1980) **Against evolutionary epistomology.** PSA - ed. P.D. Asquith & R.N. Giere 187-96.
- Thorpe, W. H. (1963) **Ethology and the coding problem in germ cell and brain.**
- Tomasello, Michael, Kruger, A. C., & Ratner, H. H. (1993) **Cultural learning.** Behavioral and Brain Sciences, 16, 495-552.
- Tomasello, Michael (1994) **The question of chimpanzee culture.** In R. Wrangham, W. McGrew, F.de Waal, & P. Heltne (eds.) Chimpanzee cultures. Cambridge, MA: Harvard University Press.
- Tomasello, Michael (1996) **Do Apes Ape?** In C. M. Heyes and B. G. Galef, Jr. (eds.) Social Learning in Animals: The Roots of Culture. San Diego: Academic Press. Pp.319'346.
- Tomasello, Michael (2001) **The Cultural Origins of Human Cognition.**
- Tooby, J., Cosmides L. (1989) **Evolutionary psychology and the generation of culture, Part I: theoretical considerations.** Ethology and sociobiology 10: 29-49.
- Tooby, J. and Cosmides, L. (1989) **Evolutionary Psychology and the Generation of Culture, Part II-case study: a Computational Theory of Social Exchange.** In: Ethology and Sociobiology 10:50-79.
- Tooby, J., Cosmides L. (1992) **The psychological foundations of culture.** In: The adapted mind:

Evolutionary psychology and the generation of culture. eds. J. H. Barkow, L. Cosmides and J. Tooby, New York and Oxford: Oxford University Press.
- **Tool, M. C.** (1988) **Evolutionary Economics.**
- **Toulmin, Stephen and Mead, Margaret** (1959) **Continuities in Cultural Evolution.**
- **Trigger, Bruce G.** (1998) **Sociocultural Evolution: Calculation and Contingency.**
- **Trivers, R.L.** (1971) **The evolution of reciprocal altruism.** Quarterly Review of Biology, 46, 35-57.
- **Trivers, R.L.** (1985) **Social Evolution.** Benjamin-Cummings Pub Co.
- **Turchin, Peter** (2010) **The Rise of Complex Human Societies as a Major Evolutionary Transition.**
- **Turchin, V.** (1977) **The Phenomenon of Science: A Cybernetic Theory of Human Evolution.** Columbia University Press.
- **Turner, J. Scott** (2000) **The Extended Organism: The Physiology of Animal-Built Structures.**
- **Turner, J. Scott** (2004) **Extended Phenotypes and Extended Organisms.** Biology and Philosophy 19: 327–352.
U
V
- **Vajk, J. Peter** (1989) **Memetics: The Nascent Science of Ideas and Their Transmission.**
- **Van Driem, George** (2007) **Symbiosis and the Leiden Definition of the Meme** Imitation, Memory, and Cultural Changes: Probing the Meme Hypothesis.
- **Van Wyhe, J.** (2005) **The descent of words: evolutionary thinking 1780-1880.**
- **Vaneechoutte, Mario** (1997) **Vaneechoutte, M., 1997; Bird song as a possible cultural mechanism for speciation.** Journal of Memetics - Evolutionary Models of Information Transmission, 1.
- **Vaneechoutte, Mario and Skoyles, J.R.** (1998) **The memetic origin of language: modern humans as musical primates.** Journal of Memetics - Evolutionary Models of Information Transmission, 2.
- **Vaneechoutte, Mario** (1998) **The Replicator: A Misnomer.** Symposium on Memetics: Evolutionary Models of Information Transmission, 15th International Congress on Cybernetics, Namur (Belgium), August 24-28.
- **Vaneechoutte, Mario** (1993) **The memetic basis of religion.** Nature 365: 290.
- **Vaneechoutte, Mario** (2002) **A Review of: De Jong, M., Lalenis, K. and Mamadouh, K. (eds.) (2002) The theory and practice of institutional transplantation. Experiences with transfer of policy institutions.** Journal of Memetics - Evolutionary Models of Information Transmission, 7.
- **Veblen, Thorstein B.** (1898) **Why Is Economics Not an Evolutionary Science?** Quarterly Journal of Economics 12, 3 (July): 373-97.
- **Viciana, Hugo, Bourrat, Pierrick** (2010) **Is God an Adaptation?** Philosophia.
- **Vincenti, Walter G.** (1990) **What engineers know and how they know it: Analytical studies from aeronautical history.** Baltimore: The Johns Hopkins University Press. [See chap. 8, "A variation-selection model for the growth of engineering knowledge."].
- **Vogt, Paul** (2006) **Cumulative cultural evolution: Can we ever learn more?**
- **Von Neumann, J.** (1966) **Theory of Self-reproducing Automata.** University of Illinois Press.
- **Vos, Ed and Kelleher, Ben.** (2001) **Mergers and Takeovers: A Memetic Approach.** Journal of Memetics - Evolutionary Models of Information Transmission, 5.
- **Vromen, Jack J.** (1994) **Evolution and Efficiency: An Inquiry into the Foundations of 'New Institutional Economics'.** Eburon Delft.
- **Vromen, Jack J.** (2001) **A Review of : Jason Potts (2000) The New Evolutionary Microeconomics: Complexity, Competence and Adaptive Behaviour.** Journal of Memetics - Evolutionary Models of Information Transmission, 5.
- **Vygotsky, L. S.** (1962) **Thought and Language.** MIT Press.
W
- **Waddington, C.H.** (1959) **Evolutionary systems: Animal and human.** Nature, Vol 183, no 4676, June 13.
- **Wade, Nicholas** (2010) **Human Culture, an Evolutionary Force.** New York Times.
- **Waldschmidt, Geoffrey B.** (2004) **Preliminary Remarks On The Meme And The Text - Their Relationship Within the Discipline of Language and Literature.**
- **Wallas, G.** (1926) **The Art of Thought.** Harcourt, Brace & World.
- **Walter, Alex** (1997) **The trouble with memes: deconstructing Dawkins's monster An Essay Review of The Selfish Meme: A Critical Reappraisal by Kate Distin and Not by Genes Alone: How Culture Transformed Human Evolution by Peter J. Richerson and Robert Boyd.** Biology and social life: book review
- **Waltz , Robert B.** (1997) **Memes and Motifs: Living Memories.**
- **Waring, Timothy M.** (2008) **New evolutionary foundations: Theoretical requirements for a science of sustainability.** Ecological Economics. Volume 69, Issue 4, 15 February 2010, Pages 718-730.
- **Watts, Duncan J., Peretti, Jonah and Frumin, Michael** (2007) **Viral Marketing for the Real World.**

- Watts, Duncan J., Peretti, Jonah (2007) **Viral Marketing for the Real World.**
- Weeks, A.R., Turelli, M., Harcombe, W.R., Reynolds, K.T., Hoffmann, A.A. (2007) **From parasite to mutualist: Rapid evolution of Wolbachia in natural populations of Drosophila.** PLoS Biol 5(5): e114
- Weick, K.E. (1969) **The Social Psychology of Organizing.** Addison-Wesley.
- Weiner, J. (1995) **Evolution Made Visible.** Science, 267, pp. 30-33.
- Weingart, Peter, Mitchell, Sandra D., Richerson, Peter J. and Maasen, Sabine (1997) **Human By Nature: Between Biology and the Social Sciences.**
- Wellman, Barry (2008) **Social Networks Theory: Networked Lives and Meme Fields.**
- Weisberg, R. W. (1986) **Creativity: Genius and Other Myths.** Freeman. Wenegrat, B. (1990. The Divine Archetype: The Sociobiology and Psychology of Religion. Lexington Books.
- Westoby, Adam (1994) **The Ecology of intentions: How to make memes and influence people: Culturology.**
- Wheeler, M., J. Ziman, and M. A. Boden (2002) **The evolution of cultural entities.** Proc. Brit. Acad. Oxford Univ. Press, Oxford, U.K.
- White, Leslie A. (1959) **The concept of culture.** American Anthropologist, 61, 227-251.
- White, Leslie A. (2005) **The Science of Culture: A Study of Man and Civilization (Foundations of Anthropology).**
- Whiten, A., D. M. Custance, J. C. Gomez, P. Teixidor, and K. A. Bard. (1996) **Imitative learning of artificial fruit processing in children (Homo sapiens) and chimpanzees (Pan troglodytes).** J. Comp. Psychol 110:3'14. CrossRef, PubMed.
- Whiten, A., J. Goodall, McGrew, W. C., Nishida, T., Reynolds, V., Sugiyama, Y., Tutin, C. E G., Wrangham R. W., and Boesch, C. (1999) **Cultures in chimpanzees.** Nature 399:682'685. CrossRef, PubMed, CSA.
- Whiten, A., J. Goodall, McGrew, W. C., Nishida, T., Reynolds, V., Sugiyama, Y., Tutin, C. E G., Wrangham R. W., and Boesch, C. (2001) **Charting cultural variation in chimpanzees.** Behaviour 138:1481'1516. CrossRef, CSA.
- Whiten, A., Caldwell C.A. (2002) **Evolutionary perspectives on imitation: is a comparative psychology of social learning possible?** Anim Cogn. 2002 Dec;5(4):193-208. Oct 12.
- Whiten, A. (2005a) **The second inheritance system of chimpanzees and humans.** Nature, 437, 52' 55.
- Whiten, A., Horner, Victoria and de Waal, Frans B. M. (2005b) **Conformity to cultural norms of tool use in chimpanzees.** Nature 437, 737-740.
- Whiten, A. (2007) **Pan African culture: memes and genes in wild chimpanzees.** Proc Natl Acad Sci U S A. 2007 Nov 6;104(45):17559-60. Epub Oct 29.
- Whiten, A., Marshall-Pescini S. (2008) **Chimpanzees (Pan troglodytes) and the question of cumulative culture: an experimental approach.** Anim Cogn. 2008 Jul;11(3):449-56. Jan 19.
- Whiten, A., Hinde, R.A., Laland, K.N., Stringer, C.B. (2011a) **Culture evolves.** Philos Trans R Soc Lond B Biol Sci. Apr 12;366(1567) :938-48.
- Whiten, A., McGuigan N., Makinson J. (2011b) **From over-imitation to super-copying: Adults imitate causally irrelevant aspects of tool use with higher fidelity than young children.** Br J Psychol. 2010 Mar 19. [Epub ahead of print]
- Whitfield, John. (2006) **Literary darwinism: Textual selection** Nature 439, 388-389 (26 January)
- Whitling, Lloyd (2002) **The Complete Universe of Memes: Branches of Reality on The Reality Tree**
- Wiklanski, David (2008) **Understanding Suicide Terrorism from a Cultural and Memetic Perspective.**
- Wilder, R. L. (1968) **Evolution of mathematical concepts.** Open Univ. Press, Milton Keynes, U.K.
- Wilkins, John S. (1995) **Evolutionary models of scientific change.**
- Wilkins, John S. (1998a) **The evolutionary structure of scientific theories.** Biology and Philosophy, 13: 479-504. [PDF].
- Wilkins, John S. (1998b) **What's in a meme? Reflections from the perspective of the history and philosophy of evolutionary biology.** Journal of memetics - Evolutionary models of information transmission 2 [PDF] [also here].
- Wilkins, John S. (1999a) **On choosing to evolve: strategies without a strategist.** Journal of Memetics - Evolutionary Models of Information Transmission 3.
- Wilkins, John S. (1999b) **Memes ain't (just) in the Head.** Journal of Memetics - Evolutionary Models of Information Transmission, 3. [also here].
- Wilkins, John S. (1999c) **From Modules to Memes.** .
- Wilkins, John S., Stanyon, Clem, Musgrove, Ian (2000) **Selection without replicators: The origin of genes, and the replicator/interactor distinction in etiobiology.**
- Wilkins, John S. (2000) **Jacob's Ladder and Darwin's Tree.**
- Wilkins, John S. (2001a) **The appearance of Lamarckism in the evolution of culture.** In Darwinism

and evolutionary economics, edited by J. Laurent and J. Nightingale. Cheltenham UK: Edward Elgar: 160-183.

- **Wilkins, John S.** (2001b) **Defining evolution.** Reports of the National Centre for Science Education. 21(1-2): p. 29-37.
- **Wilkins, John S.** (2002) **Darwinian Metaphor and Analogy: The Things That Evolve in Life and Language.** Selection: Molecules, Genes, Memes. 3 (1): 57-74.
- **Wilkins, John S.** (2005) **Is 'meme' the new 'idea'? Reflections on Aunger.** Biology and Philosophy (20 (2-3): 585-598.
- **Wilkins, John S.** (2008) **The adaptive landscape of science.** Biology and Philosophy.
- **Williams, G. C.** (1966) **Adaptation and Natural Selection.** Princeton University Press.
- **Williams, G. C.** (1992) **Natural Selection: Domains, Levels, and Challenges.**
- **Williams, Russell** (2000) **The business of memes: memetic possibilities for marketing and management.** Management Decision, Vol. 38 Iss: 4, pp.272 - 279.
- **Williams, Russell** (2004) **Management fashions and fads: Understanding the role of consultants and managers in the evolution of ideas.** Management Decision, Vol. 42 Iss: 6, pp.769 - 780.
- **Wilner, Eduardo.** (2001) **The Evolution of Science.** Biology and Philosophy Volume 16, Number 2, 261-271, DOI: 10.1023/A:1006782520572.
- **Wilson, Edward O.** (1975) **Sociobiology: The New Synthesis.** Balknap Press.
- **Wilson, Edward O.** (1998) **Consilience: The Unity of Knowledge.**
- **Wilson, Edward, Unruh, Wes and Carney, Ray** (2010) **The Art of Memetics.**
- **Wilson, Michael** (1993) **Memetic Engineering PsyOps and Viruses for the Wetware.**
- **Wilson, Michael** (1993) **Application of Memetics.**
- **Wimsatt, William C** (1981) **Units of Selection and the Structure of the Multi-Level Genome.** In P. D. Asquith and R. N. Giere (eds), Proceedings of the Biennial Meeting of the Philosophy of Science Association, 2, Bloomsburg, PA: Philosophy of Science Association, pp. 122–83.
- **Wimsatt, William C** (1981) **Developmental Reductionistic Research Strategies and Their Biases in the Units of Selection Controversy.** In T. Nickles (ed.), Scientific Discovery.Vol. II, Case Studies, Boston Studies in the Philosophy of Science, 60, Boston: Reidel, pp. 213–59.
- **Wimsatt, William C** (1986) **Developmental Constraints, Generative Entrenchment, and the Innate-Acquired Distinction.** In P. Betchel (ed.), Integrating Scientific Disciplines, Dordrecht: Martinus Nijhoff, pp. 185–208.
- **Wimsatt, William C** (1999) **Genes, Memes, and Cultural Inheritance, invited contribution for April 1999 Biology and Philosophy special issue on influence of R. C. Lewontin.** 279-310. Contains "In the Laboratory of a Natural Philosopher (Richard Lewontin)", 303-310.
- **Wimsatt, William C.** (2002) **False Models as means to Truer Theories: Blending Inheritance in Biological vs. Cultural Evolution.** Philosophy of Science 69 (3): S12-S24.
- **Wimsatt, William C.** (2006a) **Generative Entrenchment and an Evolutionary Developmental Biology for Culture, invited commentary on Mesoudi, Whiten and Laland, Towards a Unified Science of Cultural Evolution.** Brain and Behavioral Sciences, 29: 364-366.
- **Wimsatt, William C.** (2006b) **Reproducing Generative entrenchment and an evolutionary developmental biology for culture.**
- **Wimsatt, William C.** (2006c) **Re-Engineering the Darwinian Sciences in Social Context. Invited commentary on Levins and Lewontin, Biological Theory: Integrating Development, Evolution, and Cognition**
- **Wimsatt, William C., and James R. Griesemer.** (2007) **Reproducing Entrenchments to Scaffold Culture: The Central Role of Development in Cultural Evolution.** In Integrating Evolution and Development: From Theory to Practice, edited by R. Sansom and R. Brandon. Cambridge: MIT Press: 227-323.
- **Wimsatt, William C.** (2010) **Memetics does not provide a useful way of understanding cultural evolution: A developmental perspective.** In Contemporary Debates in Philosophy of Biology, Ed. Francisco Ayala and Robert Arp, Chichester, Wiley-Blackwell, 255-72.
- **Winter, S. G. Jr.** (1964) **Economic 'natural selection' and the theory of the firm.** Yale Economic Essays, p. 224-272.
- **Witt, Ulrich (ed).** (1992) **Explaining Process and Change: Approaches to evolutionary economics.** University of Michigan Press.
- **Witt, Ulrich** (2006) **Evolutionary Concepts in Economics and Biology.** Journal of Evolutionary Economics 16, 5 (December): 473-76.
- **Wrangham, Richard W., McGrew, W. C., De Waal, Frans B. M. and Heltne, Paul** (1996) **Chimpanzee Cultures** Harvard University Press
- **Wright, Robert** (1999) **You Can Copy Off Me** A review of The Meme Machine.
- **Wright, Robert** (2001) **Nonzero: The Logic of Human Destiny** Vintage Chapter 1 is online

- **Wright, Robert** (2001) **A Few Kind Memes About Memes.** An excerpt from "NONZERO".
- **Wright, Robert** (2010) **The Evolution of God.** Back Bay Books
- **Wuketits, Franz M.** (1984) **Evolutionary epistemology: A challenge to science and philosophy.** In F. M. Wuketits (Ed.), Concepts and approaches in evolutionary epistemology (pp. 1-29). Dordrecht & Boston: Reidel.

X

Y

- **Yoon, Susan** (2008) **Using memes and memetic processes to explain social and conceptual influences on student understanding about complex socio-scientific issues.**
- **Yudkowsky, Eliezer** (2005) **World's Most Important Math Problem.** Future Salon.
- **Yudkowsky, Eliezer** (2007) **No Evolutions for Corporations or Nanodevices.** Less Wrong.

Z

- **Zachar, István and Szathmáry, Eörs** (2010) **A New Replicator: A theoretical framework for analysing replication.**
- **Zarella, Dan** (2009) **The Science of Blogging.**
- **Zarella, Dan** (2009) **The Science of Retweets.**
- **Zarella, Dan** (2009) **Big Seed Viral Marketing.**
- **Zarella, Dan and Driscoll, Alison** (2009) **The Anatomy of a Facebook Meme.**
- **Zarella, Dan** (2009) **The Social Media Marketing Book.**
- **Zarella, Dan** (2011) **The Science of Social Media: Engineering Contagious Ideas.**
- **Zarella, Dan** (2011) **Meshed 3 social media conference.**
- **Zarella, Alison, and Zarella, Dan** (2010) **The Facebook Marketing Book.**
- **Zeanah, David** (2011) **The Rejection of Cultural Evolution (How Evolution Came to be a Dirty Word in Cultural Anthropology and Archaeology)**
- **Zentall, T.** (2001) **Imitation in animals: Evidence, function, and mechanisms.** Cybernetics and Systems, 32:53–96.
- **Zuk, Marlene** (2007) **Riddled with Life: Friendly Worms, Ladybug Sex, and the Parasites That Make Us Who We Are.**

33 Alphabetical index

CPSIA information can be obtained at www.ICGtesting.com
Printed in the USA
LVOW01s1230150915

454106LV00032BA/2302/P